# Concepts in Economics

## Fifth Edition

## Debbie A. Meyer
*Brookdale Community College*

McGraw-Hill, Inc.
**College Custom Series**

*New York  St. Louis  San Francisco  Auckland  Bogotá*
*Caracas  Lisbon  London  Madrid  Mexico  Milan  Montreal*
*New Delhi  Paris  San Juan  Singapore  Sydney  Tokyo  Toronto*

McGraw Hill's **College Custom Series** consists of products that are produced from camera-ready copy. Peer review, class testing, and accuracy are primarily the responsibility of the author.

## CONCEPTS IN ECONOMICS

1 2 3 4 5 6 7 8 9 0 MAL MAL 9 0 9 8 7 6 5 4 3

**ISBN 0-07-041786-5**

*Editor: Constance Ditzel*

*Cover Design: Christopher J. Siwinski*

*Printer/Binder: Malloy Lithographing, Inc.*

To my inner circle--my family

# CONTENTS

# MICROECONOMICS

## UNIT I

## UNIT II:

## Unit III

# ACKNOWLEDGMENTS

Grateful acknowledgment is made to the following for permission to reprint material copyrighted or controlled by them:

| PAGE NO. | SOURCE |
| --- | --- |
| xiii | Reprinted from the February 2, 1987 issue of Business Week by special permission, copyright (c) 1987 by McGraw-Hill, Inc. |
| 5 | Reprinted by permission of the Federal Reserve Bank of Cleveland, Economic Trends, May 1993. Sources: U.S. Department of Commerce, Bureau of Economic Analysis, and Board of Governors of the Federal Reserve System. |
| 6-8 | Reprinted from Contemporary Macroeconomics, Fifth Edition, by Milton Spencer, reproduced by permission of Worth Publishers, the copyright holder. |
| 22-23 | Reprinted by permission The Associated Press, February 1, 1990, copyright (c) 1990 by The Associated Press. |
| 27-28 | Reprinted by permission of the Asbury Park Press, June 4, 1992, copyright (c) 1992 by Asbury Park Press, Inc. |
| 39-42 | Reprinted by permission of The Wall Street Journal, copyright (c) 1986 Dow Jones & Company, Inc. All rights reserved worldwide. |
| 53-54 | Reprinted by permission of The Wall Street Journal, copyright (c) 1984 Dow Jones & Company, Inc. All rights reserved worldwide. |
| 65-67 | Reprinted by permission of The Wall Street Journal, copyright (c) 1986 Dow Jones & Company, Inc. All rights reserved worldwide. |
| 79-80 | Reprinted by permission of the Asbury Park Press, March, 1993, copyright (c) 1993 by Asbury Park Press, Inc. |
| 82 | Reprinted from Study Guide to Contemporary Macroeconomics, Fifth Edition, by Milton Spencer, reproduced by permission of Worth Publishers, the copyright holder. |
| 83-85 | Reprinted from Contemporary Macroeconomics, Fifth Edition, by Milton Spencer, reproduced by permission of Worth Publishers, the copyright holder. |
| 91-92 | Reprinted by permission of The Wall Street Journal, copyright (c) 1993 Dow Jones & Company, Inc. All rights reserved worldwide. |
| 101-102 | Reprinted by permission of The Wall Street Journal, copyright (c) 1988 Dow Jones & Company, Inc. All rights reserved worldwide. |

## To The Student

Concepts in Economics is split between Macroeconomics and Microeconomics. Within each area there are three units which correspond to your course syllabus.

Each unit is composed of several chapters. Each chapter is broken down into:

- Chapter Orientation - to acquaint you with the purpose and focus of the chapter.

- Learning Objectives - are brief statements of expected learning which require you to define, compare, explain, contrast, list, and evaluate each chapter.

- Chapter Highlights - a detailed outline of the chapter's most important content.
- Key Terms - lists the important concepts which you should be able to define.

- Real World Example - relates the theory presented to the real world, which gives you a better understanding of the concept.

- Problems - a "hands on approach" to learning the material.

- Self-Test - provides additional opportunities to assess your mastery of the material. Be sure to check your answers with the "Answer Key" provided.

This student manual is designed to be used in conjunction with Economics, by Campbell R. McConnell and Stanley L. Brue. However, this manual may be used to stand alone or accompany another introductory economics textbook. If you attend the class lectures, read the text carefully and complete the exercises in this concepts book, you should achieve mastery of the economic principles and their applications.

Below is the suggested format for studying:

1. Read the "Chapter Orientation", "Learning Objectives", "Chapter Highlights", "Key Terms", and "Real World Example" sections in this workbook prior to reading the chapter in the text (this gives you an idea of what will be covered in the chapter).

2. Then read the chapter in the text, highlighting important points.

3. After reading the chapter, take notes (use the "Chapter Highlights" in this workbook as a guide).

4. Attend the classroom lecture of the chapter and take notes.

5. Reread the "Chapter Highlights", "Key Terms", and your lecture notes. If there is any concept that seems unclear to you, go to the text and reread the topic.

6. Tackle the problems in this workbook and any additional problems that have been assigned.

7. Answer the questions under the "Self-Test" section. Be sure to check your answers.

8. Finally, go back to the "Learning Objectives" and see if you can answer each item.

## Acknowledgements

I would like to thank everyone who helped with the production of this workbook -- my family, friends and colleagues. A special note of gratitude goes to Valerie Hamilton, who spent countless hours on the production of this workbook. Her patience and many suggestions were extremely helpful and her contribution is greatly acknowledged. Also, a special thanks to Daren Eilert, our computer consultant.

Also, I am grateful to the students at Brookdale Community College -- for without their support and encouragement this Concepts Book would never have come into existence.

# Why We Can't Live Without Economists

## By Gary S. Becker

Jokes about the shortcomings of economists are endless. The reason is simple. Both business and government need guidance that only economists can provide, especially forecasts of inflation, aggregate employment and output, and of the effects of tax reform, the federal deficits, and other events that affect the future of the economy. Yet-and this is the source of the jokes and criticism-such predictions are often unreliable. The fact is economists are poor at forecasting short-term changes in the economy.

The recent annual meeting of the American Economic Assn. in New Orleans spotlighted the current state of thinking about the profession's limitations, as well as its achievements. The 6,000 members in attendance could choose from over 100 sessions on many subjects. The meetings on macroeconomics, which deals with inflation and changes in aggregate output and employment in an economy, were the most popular, whether the speakers holding forth were Keynesians, monetarists, rational expectationists, or supply siders.

The extent of the disagreements at these sessions testifies to the conflicting views within macroeconomics. In one panel, four excellent economists analyzed the effects of federal deficits on the economy. Their conclusions ranged from predictions that there would be rather little effect to moderately adverse effects to sizable adverse effects. Sadly, the available evidence is too weak to permit a choice among these views. My own opinion, and I am not a specialist in macroeconomics, is that even large deficits do not damage an economy if they last for only a few years.

**UNSUNG SPECIALTY.** My field is microeconomics. This discipline studies how consumers, workers, and other participants in economic activities decide such economic issues as what to buy, how much to save, where to work, and how many hours to work at any given wage. Although microeconomics stirs its share of controversy, economists generally agree-and they have substantial evidence to support their view-about its basic assumption: that economic participants make rational choices. Microeconomics attracts less attention from the media than does macroeconomics, yet it has had stunning practical successes during the past decade.

Although these successes include the industry deregulation movement and several other issues, I will concentrate on two subjects popular at the recent AEA meeting: finance and law.

A revolution in thinking initiated during the 1950s replaced ad hoc precepts about financial issues with models of rational choice. One model, for example, explains how investors determine the type of securities to hold in their portfolios by analyzing the trade-offs between expected return and risk. Related models are used to analyze the effect of company debt on prices of common stock and to guide the use of options and arbitrage.

As a result of such applications, the intellectual foundations of finance have been recast into a microeconomic framework. This approach now dominates the teaching of finance. It also permeates mutual fund management and the behavior of commercial and investment banks and other financial intermediaries.

**LEGAL INFLUENCE.** The law and economics movement began with the academic economists and lawyers who believed that economic analysis could greatly improve antitrust policy. It has spread to all other legal fields and has also infiltrated legal practice. Microeconomic analysis in legal decisions has grown rapidly partly because scholars of the law and economics, such as Robert H. Bork, Frank H. Easterbrook, and Richard A. Posner, moved from academia to the bench.

Microeconomics has also achieved great success in altering thinking about criminal law. Claims that criminals cannot be deterred by punishment because they are mentally sick or alienated from society dominated thinking about criminal justice in the 1950s and 1960s. The microeconomic approach assumes that, on the contrary, most criminals make rational choices given their circumstances. This view has had an enormous influence on public policy and judicial decision-making during the past decade. Hostile reaction to judges and legislators considered soft on crime and the revival of capital punishment are part of the evidence that the microeconomic interpretation of criminal behavior has won many followers.

This discussion explains why economists are prominent in public policy debate and in analysis of business decisions. My attention to the important practical and theoretical achievements of microeconomics should not suggest that macroeconomics remains stagnant. The large disagreements among macroeconomists today is far healthier than the agreement in the 1940s and 1950s on an unrealistic model of the economy.

Despite economics' accomplishments, the public demands more from it, especially from macroeconomics, than it can deliver at present. This conflict between what the public wants and what economists can deliver explains why economists continue to face ridicule at the same time they are courted by government, business, and the media.

# Nobel Memorial Prize in Economic Science

| YEAR | NAME(S) | NATIONALITY | RESEARCH |
|---|---|---|---|
| 1969 | Ragnar Frish & Jan Tinbergen | Norwegian, Dutch | Development of econometrics |
| 1970 | Paul A. Samuelson | American | Application of a new scientific analysis to economic theories |
| 1971 | Simon Kuznets | American | Introduction of the concept of the gross national product |
| 1972 | Kenneth J. Arrow and John R. Hicks | American British | Contributions to equilibrium and welfare theories |
| 1973 | Wassily Leontief | American | Analysis showing how changes in one economic variable affect other sectors |
| 1974 | Gunnar Myrdal & Friedrich A. von Hayer | Swedish Austrian | Contributions in the theory of money and economic fluctuations |
| 1975 | Leonid V. Kantorvich & Tjalling C. Koopmans | Russian American | Applying statistical methods to resource allocation |
| 1976 | Milton Friedman | American | Development of monetary theory |
| 1977 | Bertil Ohlin & James Edward Meade | Swedish British | Contributions to the theory of international trade |
| 1978 | Herbert A. Simon | American | Pioneering work on the decision-making processes in complex economic organizations |
| 1979 | Theodore W. Schultz & Sir Arthur Lewis | American | Work in economic development research with special regard to the problems of developing countries |
| 1980 | Lawrence R. Klein | American | Pioneering econometric models to forecast economic trends |
| 1981 | James Tobin | American | Analysis of financial markets and their relations to spending decisions, employment, production and prices |
| 1982 | George J. Stigler | American | Pioneering studies of industrial production |
| 1983 | Gerard Debreu | American | Research on equilibrium in a market economy |
| 1984 | Sir Richard Stone | British | Developing accounting systems that help governments allocate their financial resources |
| 1985 | Franco Modigliani | American | Analysis of savings and financial markets |
| 1986 | James McGill Buchanan | American | Contributions to the theory of economic and political decision-making |
| 1987 | Robert M. Solow | American | Showing the impact of Technology on economic growth |
| 1988 | Maurice Allans | French | Pioneering development of theories to better understand market behavior and efficient use of resources |
| 1989 | Tryare Haavelmo | Norwegian | Pioneering work in methods for testing economic theories that help pave the way for modern economic forecasting |
| 1990 | Merton H. Miller | American | Work on the cost of finance and capital structure of corporations |
| 1991 | Ronald Coase | American | Explanations of how market economies are shaped by contracts, laws and property rights |
| 1992 | Gary S. Becker | American | Extended the domain of economic theory to aspects of human behavior, which had been previously dealt with, if at all, by other social science disciplines. |

# MACROECONOMICS

## UNIT 1

# CHAPTER 1       "The Nature and Method of Economics"

## Chapter Orientation

Chapter 1 sets the stage for your study of economics. After studying these concepts, you will have a foundation with which to build. This chapter acquaints you with several reasons for studying economics; how economic policy is derived; a review of graphing techniques and several important terms. Your study of economics will be more meaningful/enjoyable if you grasp the general framework of the economic concepts outlined in this chapter.

## Learning Objectives

After studying this chapter in the text and completing the following exercises in this concepts book, you should be able to:

1. Define economics and give several reasons for studying the economy.
2. List the steps, using positive economics, in deriving economic policy.
3. Cite several potential pitfalls in economic models.
4. Construct graphs from data presented, calculate slopes, and define their relationship.
5. List the seven economic goals in our society.
6. Understand the role of economic models, theory, and assumptions in the study of economics.
7. List the difficulties that economics students often face in studying economics.

## Chapter Highlights

I. The Importance of Studying Economics
    A. Economics
        1. Definition of Economics
        2. Macro vs. Micro Economics defined
        3. Ceteris paribus defined
        4. Comparative advantage defined
    B. Reasons for study
        1. Informed citizens (voters)
        2. Knowledge of social environment and behavior
        3. Information for business executives
II. Deriving Economic Policy
    A. The Scientific Method (positive economics)
        1. Gathering of relevant facts (descriptive economics)
        2. Deriving principles from facts (economic theory), also called "laws", "theories", and "models"
            a. Generalizations, assumptions, and abstractions
            b. Forms of economic models: verbal statements, numerical tables, graphs, and mathematical equations
        3. Test (inductive vs. deductive methods)
        4. Economic policy (to solve a social problem)
            a. Predictions and implications for the real world
            b. Steps
               1. Establish a clear statement of goals
               2. Knowledge of alternative policies

        3.  Monitor and re-evaluate effectiveness
  B.  Potential "pitfalls" in economic models
     1.  Use of statistics
     2.  Oversimplification
     3.  Value judgments (normative economics)

III. Economic Goals
  A.  Eight economic goals in our society (some are complementary; others are mutually exclusive):
     1.  Economic growth
     2.  Full employment
     3.  Economic efficiency
     4.  Price level stability
     5.  Economic freedom
     6.  Equitable distribution of income
     7.  Economic security
     8.  Balance of trade

IV. Difficulties in Studying Economics
  A.  Economics students beware of:
     1.  Preconceived ideas or bias
     2.  Discipline terminology
     3.  Changes in the business cycle
     4.  The fallacy of composition
     5.  The post hoc fallacy (or fallacy of false cause)
     6.  The fallacy of division

V.  Last Word:   Fast-Food Lines:  An Economic Perspective

VI. The Economic Perspective
  A.  Decision making
     1.  Rational behavior
     2.  Cost-benefit perspective

VII. Appendix: Graphs and their meaning
  A.  To express economic principles or models
  B.  Tools
     1.  Plotting points from a schedule of data
     2.  Calculating the slope of a straight line and a nonlinear curve
     3.  Determining direct or inverse relationships

<u>Key Terms</u>

| | |
|---|---|
| economics | direct/inverse relationship |
| scientific method | slope of a line |
| descriptive method | positive/normative economics |
| economic theory | economic goals |
| generalization | complementary goals |
| abstraction | mutually exclusive goals |
| ceteris paribus assumption | fallacy of division |
| economic models | post hoc fallacy |
| inductive/deductive | correlation |
| economic policy | causation |
| graphing techniques | macro/micro economics |

Real World Example

• • • • • • • •

# *Personal Income and Spending*

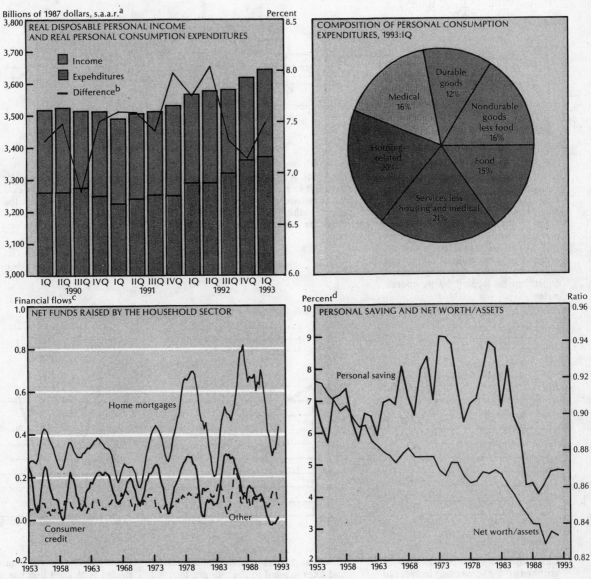

Billions of 1987 dollars, s.a.a.r.[a]                                                                         Percent

**REAL DISPOSABLE PERSONAL INCOME AND REAL PERSONAL CONSUMPTION EXPENDITURES**

- Income
- Expenditures
- Difference[b]

IQ IIQ IIIQ IVQ IQ IIQ IIIQ IVQ IQ IIQ IIIQ IVQ IQ
1990        1991        1992      1993

**COMPOSITION OF PERSONAL CONSUMPTION EXPENDITURES, 1993:IQ**

- Durable goods 12%
- Nondurable goods less food 16%
- Food 15%
- Services less housing and medical 21%
- Housing-related 20%
- Medical 16%

Financial flows[c]                                                                                            Ratio

**NET FUNDS RAISED BY THE HOUSEHOLD SECTOR**

Home mortgages

Other

Consumer credit

1953 1958 1963 1968 1973 1978 1983 1988 1993

Percent[d]                                                                                                   Ratio

**PERSONAL SAVING AND NET WORTH/ASSETS**

Personal saving

Net worth/assets

1953 1958 1963 1968 1973 1978 1983 1988 1993

a. Seasonally adjusted annual rate.
b. Difference between real disposable personal income and real personal consumption expenditures as a percent of income.
c. As a percent of real disposable personal income; four-quarter moving average.
d. Personal saving as a percent of real disposable personal income; annual average of quarterly data.
SOURCES: U.S. Department of Commerce, Bureau of Economic Analysis; and Board of Governors of the Federal Reserve System.

## WORKING WITH GRAPHS

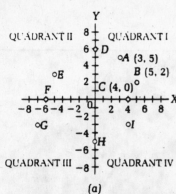

*(a)*

| x | -3 | -2 | -1 | 0 | 1 | 2 | 3 | 4 |
|---|----|----|----|---|---|---|---|---|
| y | -2 | -1 | 0 | 1 | 2 | 3 | 4 | 5 |

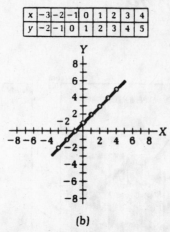

*(b)*

| x | -3 | -2 | -1 | 0 | 1 | 2 | 3 | 4 |
|---|----|----|----|---|---|---|---|---|
| y | 5 | 4 | 3 | 2 | 1 | 0 | -1 | -2 |

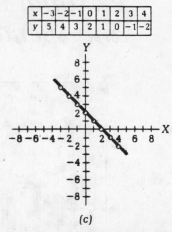

*(c)*

**Chart (a).** The two intersecting straight lines divide the chart into four quadrants numbered counter-clockwise. Positive values are measured to the right along the X axis and upward along the Y axis. Negative values are measured to the left along the X axis and downward along the Y axis. Any point on the chart can be located by its coordinates.

**Chart (b).** *A line that slopes upward from left to right exhibits a direct relation between the two variables. As one variable increases, so does the other; as one decreases, so does the other.*

**Chart (c).** *A line that slopes downward from left to right exhibits an inverse relation between the two variables. As one variable increases, the other decreases; as one decreases, the other increases.*

| x | 2 | 3 | 4 | 5 | 6 |
|---|---|---|---|---|---|
| y | 3 | | | 4 | |
| y | 7 | 6 | | | |

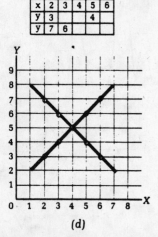

*(d)*

| t | 0 | 4 | 8 | 12 | 16 |
|---|---|---|---|----|----|
| P | | | | | |

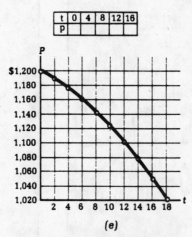

*(e)*

| Q | | 2 | | 4 | | 6 | |
|---|---|---|---|---|---|---|---|
| C | 90 | | 30 | | 30 | | 90 |

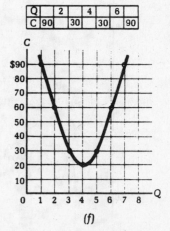

*(f)*

**Chart (d).** *Two or more lines may be graphed on the same chart in order to study their interrelationships. Can you complete the table from the graph?*

**Chart (e).** *Scales should be chosen and axes labeled in the manner that best suits a particular problem. Can you use the graph to estimate the missing numbers in the table?*

**Chart (f).** *The points should be connected with care because the resulting curve may be quite pronounced. Can you fill in the table from the graph?*

## MACRO PROBLEMS

Please use graph paper.

For problems 1-6, sketch the graphs of the following relationships and calculate the slopes for problems 1-4 only.

1.

| X | Y |
|---|---|
| 1 | 1 |
| 2 | 2 |
| 3 | 3 |
| 4 | 4 |
| 5 | 5 |
| 6 | 6 |
| 7 | 7 |
| 8 | 8 |

2.

| X | Y |
|---|---|
| 1 | 7 |
| 2 | 6 |
| 3 | 5 |
| 4 | 4 |
| 5 | 3 |
| 6 | 2 |
| 7 | 1 |

3.

| X | Y |
|---|---|
| -2 | -8 |
| 0 | -4 |
| 2 | 0 |
| 4 | 4 |

4. Sketch the following data on the same graph. Estimate the coordinates of the point of intersection of the two lines. Calculate the slope of each line.

| X | Y |
|---|---|
| 1 | 2 |
| 2 | 3 |
| 3 | 4 |
| 4 | 5 |

| X | Y |
|---|---|
| 1 | 5 |
| 2 | 4 |
| 3 | 3 |
| 4 | 2 |

5. Sketch the graph of prices as a function of time:

| X time (t) | Y prices (P) |
|---|---|
| 0 | 8 |
| 1 | 33 |
| 2 | 40 |
| 3 | 35 |
| 4 | 24 |
| 5 | 13 |
| 6 | 8 |
| 7 | 15 |
| 8 | 40 |

## MACRO PROBLEMS (continued)

6. You are given the following relationship between A and B:

| A | B |
|---|---|
| 2 | 9 |
| 3 | 7 |
| 4 | 6 |
| 5 | 8 |
| 6 | 9 |

a. Graph the relationship, putting A on the X axis and B on the Y axis.

b. The relationship between A and B is inverse when A is between _____ and _____ and direct when A is between _____ and _____.

c. The coordinates of the point at which B is a minimum are _____, _____.

7.

TABLE I

| X | Y |
|---|---|
| Income | Savings |
| $2,500 | $-500 |
| 5,000 | -0- |
| 10,000 | 1,000 |
| 15,000 | 2,000 |

a. Graph Table I above.
b. Calculate the slope.
c. Do you have a direct or inverse relationship?

8.

TABLE II

| X | Y |
|---|---|
| Billions of Dollars | Rate of Interest |
| $0 | 10% |
| 5 | 8 |
| 10 | 6 |
| 15 | 4 |
| 20 | 2 |

a. Graph Table II above.
b. Calculate the slope.
c. Do you have a direct or inverse relationship?

## MICRO PROBLEMS

Please use graph paper.
For exercises 1-3
(a) Sketch the graphs of the following relationships.
(b) Calculate the slopes.
(c) State whether there is a direct or inverse relationship.

| 1. | X<br>Qty of<br>ties | Y<br>Price per<br>tie | | 2. | X<br>Qty of<br>wallets | Y<br>Price per<br>wallet |
|---|---|---|---|---|---|---|
| | 20 | $10 | | | 300 | $100 |
| | 30 | 9 | | | 250 | 80 |
| | 40 | 8 | | | 200 | 60 |
| | 50 | 7 | | | 150 | 40 |
| | 60 | 6 | | | 100 | 20 |

| 3. | X | Y |
|---|---|---|
| | -6 | -2 |
| | -4 | 0 |
| | -2 | 2 |
| | 0 | 4 |
| | 2 | 6 |
| | 4 | 8 |

4. (a) Sketch the following curves on the same graph.
   (b) Calculate the slope for each.
   (c) What are the coordinates of the point of intersection?

| X | Y | | X | Y |
|---|---|---|---|---|
| 4 | $9.00 | | 16 | $9.00 |
| 6 | 8.50 | | 14 | 8.50 |
| 8 | 8.00 | | 12 | 8.00 |
| 10 | 7.50 | | 10 | 7.50 |
| 12 | 7.00 | | 8 | 7.00 |
| 14 | 6.50 | | 6 | 6.50 |

5. Plot the graph from the following data:

| X<br>Years | Y<br>Profits (in billions) |
|---|---|
| 1980 | $50 |
| 1981 | 45 |
| 1982 | 43 |
| 1983 | 48 |
| 1984 | 55 |
| 1985 | 64 |
| 1986 | 62 |

<u>Self-Test</u>

1. Macroeconomics is primarily concerned with:
    a.    a company                    b.    the aggregate levels of income, employment, and output
    c.    a union                       d.    individual government sectors

2. Economics may be defined as:
    a.    various amounts of a commodity that consumers are willing and able to purchase at alternative prices
    b.    a social science dealing with the production of goods and services, with scarce resources, for production now and in the future
    c.    what is good for the whole will also be good for the part
    d.    the ability of firms to maximize profit or minimize loss in the short-run

3. Which of the following represents the steps involving the scientific method in economics?
    a.    theory, verification, hypothesis, empirical testing
    b.    theory, hypothesis, empirical testing, verification
    c.    empirical testing, theory, hypothesis, verification
    d.    hypothesis, empirical testing, theory, verification

4. Which of the following is not a reason for studying economics?
    a.    inform citizens (voters)          b.    knowledge of the social environment
    c.    information for business executives    d.    all of the above are valid reasons

5. Which of the following depicts the "fallacy of composition"?
    a.    All economics texts are long and dull, therefore this economics book should also be long and dull.
    b.    Tourism for the summer season is down; the ocean is polluted, therefore, tourism is down due to the pollution.
    c.    At the end of a concert, one person could drive out of a parking lot easily, but if everyone tried to leave at once, everyone would be delayed.
    d.    None of the above depict the "fallacy of composition".

6. If two variables are <u>directly</u> related, then:
    a.    when one variable is increasing, the other is decreasing.
    b.    when one variable is increasing, the other is increasing.
    c.    when one variable is decreasing, the other is increasing.
    d.    when one variable is decreasing, the other can either increase or decrease.

7. The term "ceteris paribus" is defined as:
    a.    the value of the best alternative.
    b.    other things being equal.
    c.    unlimited wants with limited resources.
    d.    taking facts of a generalization or principle.

8. Which of the following is not one of the seven economics goals of our society:
    a.    full employment       b.    price stability    c.    equality       d.    growth

9. Calculate the slope of the following straight line:
    (5,25), (10,50), (15,75)
    a.    5           b.    -5           c.    .2           d.    -.2

10. Microeconomics is primarily concerned with:
    a.    establishing economic policy
    b.    calculating national statistics, such as GDP
    c.    studying the workings of specific units, which make up our economic system
    d.    none of the above

$$\frac{Y}{X} = \frac{VC}{HC} \quad \frac{25}{5} = 5$$

# CHAPTER 2          "The Economizing Problem"

## Chapter Orientation

The objective of this chapter is to explain the need to economize. There are always trade-offs -- society cannot have all that it wants. We have unlimited wants with limited resources, (the Law of Scarcity) hence, the need to choose among alternatives. The Production- Possibilities Curve depicts the various combinations of two goods which a nation can produce under full-employment. A point inside the curve represents less than full-employment; a point outside the curve is unattainable with the present technology. The trade-off of producing one good over another, yields greater and greater sacrifices (Law of Increasing Costs) due to the differing suitabilities of resources. In addition, this trade-off decreases your efficiency, hence the "Law of Diminishing Returns". An excellent illustration of the PPC and how it applies to Japan and the United States is found in this chapter.

Economic systems differ in answering the five great (fundamental) economics questions -- How much? What? How? Who? Accommodate change? Under a command economy (communism) decisions are centralized (at the top); under pure or laissez-faire capitalism (pure capitalism) decisions are decentralized (in the market); under a mixed system, (socialism; capitalism; or real world economies), decisions lie somewhere in between.

## Learning Objectives

After studying this chapter in the text, and completing the following exercises in this concepts book, you should be able to:

1. Define the law of scarcity.
2. List and define the four factors of production (resource categories).
3. Define economics including scarcity and efficiency.
4. Calculate the trade-offs (sacrifices) when producing one good over another.
5. Construct a production possibilities curve from a schedule.
6. Illustrate economic growth, under-employment, and the law of increasing costs using a production possibilities curve.
7. List and explain the five fundamental questions in economics.
8. Distinguish between pure capitalism and a command economy.

## Chapter Highlights

I. The Law of Scarcity
   A. Definition of the law of scarcity
   B. Factors of production or resource categories and (money payments)
      1. Land (rent)
      2. Labor (wages)
      3. Capital (interest)
      4. Entrepreneurial ability (profits)
   C. Definition of economic efficiency
      1. Production (technical)
      2. Consumption (allocative)
   D. Production possibilities curve
      1. Assumptions (4):
         a. Efficiency - economy is operating at full employment and full production

      b.  Fixed resources - supplies are fixed in quantity and quality and may be shifted
      c.  Fixed technology - technology is constant at a point in time
      d.  Two products - only two goods are produced.  For example, capital goods and consumer goods
  2.  Law of increasing opportunity costs (concave curve vs. straight line)
  3.  Optimum product mix
  4.  Expansion and contraction of the curve
  5.  Opportunity cost
  6.  Law of Diminishing Returns
  7.  Real world applications
      a.  Microeconomic budgeting
      b.  Going to War
      c.  Discrimination
      d.  Productivity slow down
      e.  Growth:  Japan vs. United States
      f.  International Trade aspects

II. Economic Systems (to make these decisions)
  A.  Types of systems:
    1.  Command economy (communism) - centralized decision making at the top.
    2.  Pure or laissez-faire capitalism (pure capitalism) - decentralized decision making in the market.
    3.  Mixed system (socialism, capitalism) - real world economies lie in between pure capitalism and the command economy.
    4.  Traditional (or customary) economies are found in some underdeveloped countries.  The system of distribution is based on custom.

III.Last Word:  Operation Desert Storm and Iraq's Production Possibilities

## Key Terms

| | |
|---|---|
| law of scarcity | economic contraction |
| economics | optimum product mix |
| land, labor, capital and | opportunity cost |
|    entrepreneurial ability | efficiency |
| production possibilities curve | pure (laissez-faire) capitalism |
| law of increasing opportunity costs | command economy (communism) |
| consumer goods | traditional (customary) economies |
| full-employment | economic expansion |

## Real World Example

    It is about an hour before class is scheduled to begin.  You start thinking of all the things you could be doing with your time instead of attending class-- working, watching television, going out to dinner, going to the health spa, etc.  You have to make a decision -- you can't possibly accomplish all of these activities at once -- you will have to make a sacrifice and decide which it will be.

    You decide that you'd better attend class (a wise decision if you wish to pass the course) and postpone the other choices for another time. . .  (This is similar to the Production Possibilities Model-- you are given the choices based upon resources and someone - the President, Congress, Prime Minister, etc. - has to make a decision as to which will be taken).

| Characteristics | PURE CAPITALISM | COMMUNISM | SOCIALISM |
|---|---|---|---|
| 1. Ownership of Production | Private Property | State owns almost all production facilities. | Many owned privately, state converts basic industries - steel, utilities, transportation, health care. |
| 2. Relationship of Government to Business | Laissez-faire, (Adam Smith, popular 18th Century) functions of Government limited. | Government owns and operates all economic units according to plan ("5-Year" or "1-Year" Plan). | State develops a master plan to which most economic activity is geared. |
| 3. Capital | Private Investment (credit reliability). | Comes from state-levied taxes on all goods that are sold. | Citizen investment in bonds - prices paid for goods. |
| 4. Risk and Losses: Price System | Rewards = Profits<br>Losses = Penalties<br>Everything exchanged has its price -- Supply and Demand | Risk assumed by State; losses are made up by a lowered standard of living. | Assumed by people - made up by taxes. |
| 5. Competition | Basic right to determine prices in free market. | Prohibited - Government sets quotas and prices. | Basic production according national economic plan for use rather than profit. |
| 6. Incentives | Wages earned; profits made, self-interest - Adam Smith 1776. Economic Man (satisfaction/cost) | Norms plus bonuses and fear of police action. Farms. | Wages according to "from each according to his ability to each according to need." |
| 7. Labor | Freedom of Choice (place and type of work) - education. | Based on testing (ability) by state (only employer). | Freedom of Choice (education). |
| 8. Management | Selected on ability (acceptance). | Party Membership required of key managers. (Authority backed by police action. | Based on ability. Non-monetary incentives. |

**CAPITALISM** - Most American businessmen agreed with Adam Smith, including John Hancock (used in designing the shape of the United States). By the 1890's the Government began to play a role in supervising and regulating business, to smooth out recessions and depressions.

**COMMUNISM** - Latin word communis "belonging to all". Philosophy: From each according to his capacity, to each according to his work. New ideology called "glasnost" (openness) and "perestroika" (restructuring).

## PROBLEMS

1. You are given the "production-possibilities schedule" below:

| Alternative | X<br>Capital Goods | Y<br>Consumer Goods | Sacrifice of Consumer<br>Goods for Capital Goods |
|---|---|---|---|
| A | 0 | 15 | |
| B | 1 | 14 | _____ |
| C | 2 | 11 | _____ |
| D | 3 | 6 | _____ |
| E | 4 | 0 | _____ |

a. Fill in the last column of the table.
b. Graph the production-possibilities curve from the data above.
c. Plot a point "U" which represents underutilization on your graph.
d. Show economic growth on the same graph.
e. What law is represented given the table above?  Why?
f. Redraw the diagram from part b (above).  Show what would happen if there was a technological break-through in capital goods only.  Label this new curve "T".
g. Redraw the diagram from part b (above).  Illustrate what would happen if a natural resource used in production of consumer goods only were restricted. Label this new curve "R".

The following graph applies to questions 2-5.

2. At point D, the economy's resources:
   a.   are fully employed
   b.   are efficiently utilized
   c.   are underemployed
   d.   unable to determine
3. The shifting of the curve from AB to EG represents:
   a.   economic contraction
   b.   inefficient utilization
   c.   recession
   d.   economic expansion
4. To reach point H the society must:
   a.   improve technology
   b.   show economic growth
   c.   operate at technical efficiency
   d.   all of the above
5. The production possibilities curve is:
   a.   concave
   b.   convex
   c.   linear
   d.   positive

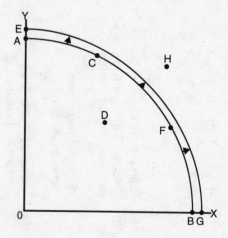

<u>Self-Test</u>

1. Assume that an economy is operating at an output level which leaves some of its productive resources unemployed. Given that the curve below is the production-possibility curve of that economy, which of the following output combinations would the economy most likely be producing?
   a. (13, 16)
   b. (10, 13)
   c. (7, 9)
   d. (18, 2)

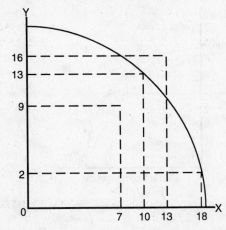

2. The United States and the United Kingdom are able to produce the same commodities, machine tools and automobiles. The U.S., for its part, is producing more of both outputs, but the United Kingdom is relatively more efficient (higher productivity) in the production of machine tools than the United States. Select the diagram which has production possibility curves most appropriate for this situation.

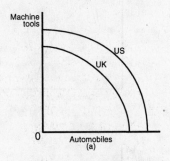

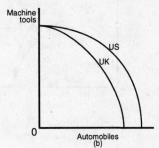

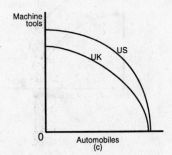

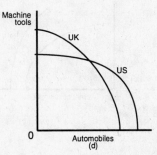

<u>Self-Test</u> (continued)

3. In the year 1993, country A and country B were both producing on the same production possibility curve for current consumption vs. new capital formation.  Country A was at A1 and country B was at B1 on the curve; otherwise the countries were identical.

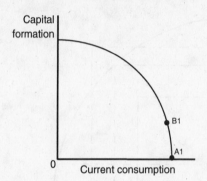

In 1998, country A was still producing at A1, but country B was at B2.  Which figure most likely reflects the production possibility frontiers for each in 1998?

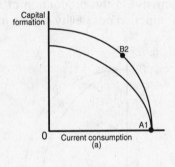

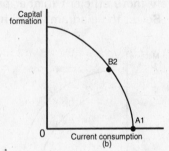

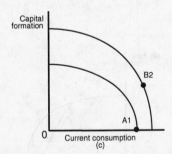

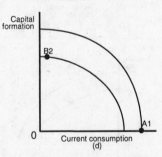

<u>Self-Test</u> (continued)

4. Assume that in 1817 the United States was producing at full employment of all resources. By 1825 the completion of the Erie Canal had speeded up transportation and lowered costs to the extent that the price of grain was reduced by two-thirds. This greatly lowered the real costs of producing both bread and whiskey. Select the diagram which best shows the change in this two-commodity production possibility curve, all other things unchanged.

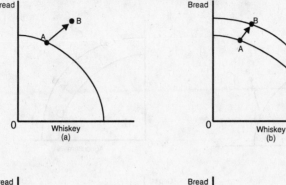

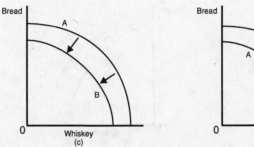

5. Consider a society which is producing at full employment of all resources. Assume that this economy produces only 2 goods: apples and butter. Suppose a new fertilizer is invented which greatly increases the productivity of apple trees. From the figures below, choose the one which best shows the change in production possibilities caused by this increased productivity, all other things unchanged.

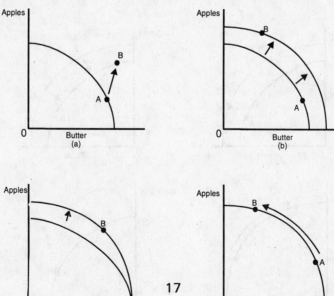

17

6. Consider a society which is producing at full employment of all resources.  Suppose that the percentage of the population in the labor force increases because of the baby boom twenty years earlier.  Given the following figures, choose the one which best shows the change in production possibilities caused by the change in the labor force, all other things unchanged.

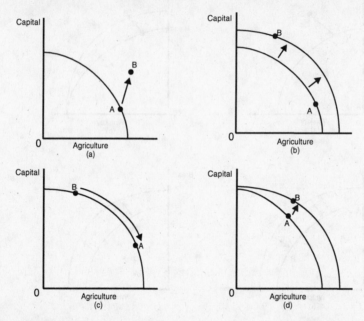

7. Consider a society which is producing at full employment of all resources.  suppose that the discovery of new oil wells increases the country's supply of oil for lubricants and for paints.  Given the following diagrams, choose the one which best shows the change in production possibilities caused by the increase in the supply of oil, all other things unchanged.

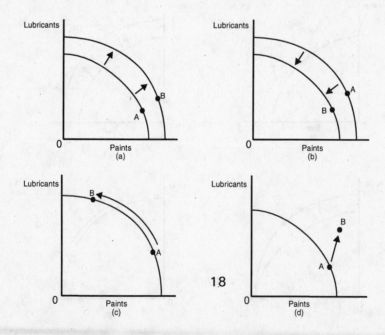

18

<u>Self-Test</u> (continued)

8. Consider a society which is producing at full employment of all resources. Suppose that an epidemic suddenly reduces its labor force greatly. From the following figures, choose the one which best shows the change in production possibilities caused by reduction of the labor force, all other things remaining unchanged.

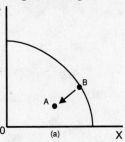

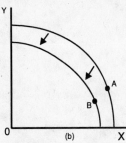

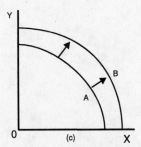

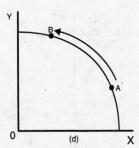

Consider the following production possibility curves. Assuming that in 1993, Japan and the United States are both producing at full employment, the combinations of food and luxuries most probably produced by each of the two nations. Place the letter of the point in front of the appropriate nation. Japan was at point "A" and the U.S. was producing at point "B". In the future, which curve is likely to represent Japan? the U.S.?

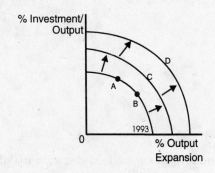

_____    9. Japan
_____    10. United States

19

Self-Test (continued)

11. In 1993 a country was producing at point "P" on its production possibility curve for current consumption vs. new capital formation. At which of the following points is the country most likely to be producing by 1998, all other things unchanged?

    a.   X
    b.   Y
    c.   Z
    d.   P

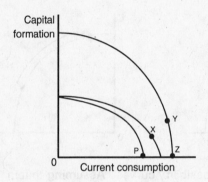

12.    "Perestroika" is defined as:
    a.   Openness to communicate more fully
    b.   Restructuring from a command economy to centralized decision making
    c.   Restructuring from a command economy toward a market economy
    d.   Restructuring from a pure market economy to a mixed economy

# CHAPTER 3          "Pure Capitalism and the Circular Flow"

## Chapter Orientation

Chapter 3 opens with the six foundations of pure capitalism - private property, freedom of enterprise and choice, the role of self-interest, competition, markets and prices, and a limited role for government. By examining the characteristics of a pure economic system, you can better understand our current economic systems. Three areas, common to all advanced economic systems are: (1) extensive use of capital goods, (2) specialization, and (3) the use of money. In addition, Chapter 3 also includes a new section on the PPC to illustrate comparative advantage.

Lastly, the chapter wraps up with a diagram of the circular flow model illustrating the flow of money and the flow of goods/services in and economy.

## Learning Objectives

After studying this chapter in the text, and completing the following exercises in this concepts book, you should be able to:

1. Identify and define the six foundations of pure capitalism.
2. List the three characteristics common to all economic systems.
3. Apply the PPC to comparative advantage.
4. Draw the simple circular flow diagram and trace the money and goods/services flows.
5. Label the sectors and the markets on the circular flow diagram in #3.

## Chapter Highlights

I. Pure Capitalism (not Mixed Capitalism)
   A. Foundations (See chart in Chapter 2)
      1. Private property
      2. Freedom of enterprise and choice
      3. Self-interest (vs. selfishness)
      4. Competition
      5. Markets and prices
      6. Limited role for government
   B. Common characteristics of modern economic systems
      1. Extensive use of capital goods and advanced technology
      2. Specialization and efficiency
         a. Division of labor
         b. Geographic specialization
         c. Specialization and comparative advantage
         d. Advantages and Disadvantages
      3. Use of money for trade and specialization
II. The Circular Flow Model
   A. Circular flow diagram
      1. Definition of the circular flow
      2. Two flows:
         a. goods and services
         b. money

      3.  Sectors and markets:
         a.  household and business
         b.  product and resource
      4.  Demand-side and supply-side
      5.  Limitations of the simple model
         a.  Overview (no specifics)
         b.  No mention of the role of government
         c.  Assumes all money is spent and invested
         d.  No explanation of how resource and product prices are determined
III.Last Word: Back to Barter

## Key Terms

| | |
|---|---|
| private property | money |
| free enterprise | capital goods |
| freedom of choice | circular flow model |
| self-interest | resource market |
| competition | product market |
| roundabout production | household |
| specialization | barter |
| business | Adam Smith |
| division of labor | David Ricardo |

## Real World Example

### Soviets Get First Taste of Fast Food

MOSCOW - American fast food got off to a fast start in Moscow yesterday, with thousands of people lining up beneath the golden arches and hammer and sickle for their first taste of a McDonald's "gamburger."

They also eagerly tried "chizburgers" and "Filay-o-feesh" sandwiches. The queue-hardened consumers seemed unfazed by the long line that snaked out the door. They moved briskly, thanks to the 27 cash registers at the world's largest McDonald's, the first of 20 planned in the Soviet Union.

"I only waited an hour and I think they served thousands before me," said a happy middle-aged woman from the aluminum plant on Dmitrovskoye Highway.

"And it was only 10 rubles for all this," she said, pointing to a bag packed with unfamiliar treats like cheeseburgers and fish sandwiches. "I'm taking it back for the girls at the factory to try."

Unlike nearly all other Western companies opening in Moscow, McDonald's is selling for rubles, which are worthless outside the Soviet Union and won't even buy much in their homeland, with its chronic shortages. It took McDonald's of Canada 14 years, but thousands of Soviets finally got a first-hand look at such alien concepts as efficiency and fast, friendly service.

Normally dour citizens broke into grins as they caught the infectious cheerful mood from youthful soviet staffers hired for their ability to smile and work hard. Accordions played folk songs and women in traditional costumes danced with cartoon characters, including Mickey Mouse and Baba Yaga, a witch of Russian fairy tales.

One Muscovite, accustomed to clerks who snarl if they say anything at all, asked for a straw and was startled when a smiling young Soviet woman found him one and popped it straight into his drink.

For most customers, it was their first experience with a hamburger.  Sandwiches were served in the familiar bag marked with the golden arches, but were packed in wrappers bearing Cyrillic letters, approximating "gamburger."

They tried them one-handed.  They picked their sandwiches apart to examine the contents.  One young woman finally squashed her "Beeg Mak" to fit her lips around it.

"It tasted great!" a 14-year-old boy said.

"It's a lot different from a stolovaya," he continued with a smile, referring to the run-down, dirty cafeterias that slop rice and fat or boiled sausage in the Soviet Union's closest approximation of fast food.

Under the sign of the golden arches, accented by the Soviet hammer-and-sickle flag, hundreds of people lined up for the long-awaited grand opening at 10 a.m. on Pushkin Square, reaching out excitedly for McDonald's flags and pins as the hamburger chain's army fulfilled the Soviet penchant for souvenirs with Western logos.

Publicity-conscious managers had the staff shout "Good morning, America!" in English and Russian, for an American TV network.

McDonald's of Canada Chairman George Cohon, the man behind the deal, said many people were buying multiple orders and the restaurant serve 15,000 to 20,000 people in just the first five hours of operation.  No official figures on the first day's sales would be available until today.

The enthusiasm was so great that store managers decided to stay open an extra two hours.

The restaurant, a joint venture of McDonald's of Canada and the city of Moscow, limited purchases to 10 Big Macs per customer in hopes of preventing an enterprising citizen from setting up an unauthorized subsidiary selling burgers without the wait for an inflated price.

Three American students said they flew 1,200 miles from Yerevan to Moscow just for the opening.

"Well, my wife makes better food," said Victor Kunyasev of Moscow.  "But it was nice, a good place to take a break and grab a bite to eat."

Big Macs were priced at 3.75 rubles and double cheeseburgers at 3 rubles - about two hours' pay for a starting McDonald's staffer or the average Soviet.

Reprinted by permission The Associated Press, February 1, 1990, copyright (c) 1990 by The Associated Press.

## PROBLEMS

1. Draw the simple circular flow diagram.  Label the two complete flows, the two markets, and the two sectors.  Briefly describe what is happening in the model.

2. What are the advantages of specialization and what are the drawbacks?

3. Explain why the institution of private property forms a basis for pure capitalism.  How does this relate to Adam Smith's "invisible hand"?

4. Compare and contrast pure capitalism, socialism, and communism.

5. Discuss the reallocation of resources implicit in the Russian reforms.

Self-Test
1. Which of the following is not a characteristic of pure capitalism?
   a.   private property           c.     government management of capital goods
   b.   self-interest              d.     the price system
2. Which of the following is not common to all modern economic systems?
   a.   specialization            c.     money
   b.   quality                 d.     capital goods
3. The two markets in the circular flow diagram are:
   a.   households and business     c.     wages and resources
   b.   product and resource        d.     receipts and expenditures
4. Bartering in the United States
   a.   is illegal
   b.   is inefficient due to transactions costs
   c.   is efficient because there are no taxes involved
   d.   no longer exists
5. Which of the following is not a limitation of the simple circular flow model?
   a.   overview with no specifics
   b.   no mention of the role of government
   c.   assumes all money is spent and invested
   d.   represents the flows of money and goods/services
6. Which of the following statements represents Adam Smith's "invisible hand" concept?
   a.   the government robs the private sector with its invisible hand
   b.   the government and the private sector work together, guided by an invisible hand
   c.   the government guides the economy with an invisible hand
   d.   individuals acting in their own self-interest will guide the market through an invisible hand that
       will benefit both the buyer and the seller.
7. Which of the following represents a drawback to specialization?
   a.   jobs tend to become routine and boring
   b.   jobs tend to be more interdependent
   c.   workers specialize in various production tasks
   d.   both a and b are correct
8. The concept of comparative advantage illustrated that:
   a.   specialization enhances efficiency even if a nation can produce both goods at a lower cost
   b.   specialization can be inefficient if a country has absolute advantage
   c.   countries should be self-sufficient
   d.   none of the above
9. In the simple circular flow model of economic activity:
   a.   businesses are on the Demand-side in the Product Market
   b.   businesses are on the Demand-side and Supply-side of the Product Market
   c.   households are on the Demand-side and Supply-side of the Resource Market
   d.   households are on the Supply-side of the Resource Market.
10. "Roundabout production" is defined as:
   a.   diversifying your production of goods and services
   b.   the construction and use of capital to produce consumer goods
   c.   specializing in one product to enhance efficiency
   d.   none of the above

# CHAPTER 4    "Understanding Individual Markets:  Demand and Supply "

## Chapter Orientation

This chapter presents the most basic and important tools of economics -- supply and demand.  A complete understanding of these concepts will provide insights into how price and output are determined.  Supply and demand provide answers to many economic questions.  The chapter illustrates the concepts of supply and demand by applying them to the foreign exchange market.

When studying demand, put yourself in the role of the consumer or "buyer" to figure out the relationship between price and quantity.  How do people react to a sale? (Certainly at a lower price people will want a higher quantity of the product).  How do people react to prices going up?  (Many people will not be able to, or want to, afford the product, which causes a decrease in the quantity being purchased).  As you can see, when there is a price change, people purchase higher or lower quantities, which is called a "change in quantity demanded" (movement along the original demand curve), due to a change in price. This represents an inverse relationship between price and quantity demanded.  Other than price, what non-price factors would cause people to demand more or demand less of a product? (income, taste, expectation, number of buyers, and related goods).  These factors would cause a change in demand -- an all new demand curve shifting to the right (an increase) or to the left (a decrease).  Note:  the word "quantity" is omitted.

When studying supply, put yourself in the role of the seller or "producer" to determine the relationship between price and quantity.  What happens when there is a price war?  (Think of the airlines, many companies cannot afford to compete and drop out of the market which causes a decrease in the quantity of seats available).  When price increases, more sellers are interested in making the product available for sale (higher quantity).  This is called a "change in quantity supplied" (movement along the original supply curve) due to a change in price. This represents a direct relationship between price and quantity supplied.  Other than price, what non-price factors would lure businesses into the market or steer them away?  (resource prices, technology, prices of related goods, number of sellers, expectations, and taxes and subsidies).

Market forces act to maintain an equilibrium market (quantity demanded equals quantity supplied).  A surplus results when the selling price is above the equilibrium; a shortage results when the selling price is below the equilibrium.

The government may legally set prices above the equilibrium price (price floor or price supports) or may set prices below the equilibrium price (price ceilings or price caps) to reduce fluctuations in the economy. The artificially setting of price is currently under debate. (Example: increasing the minimum wage).

## Learning Objectives

After studying this chapter in the text, and completing the following exercises in this concepts book, you should be able to:

1. Define a market and give two examples.
2. Define demand and supply.
3. Graph the supply and demand curves and explain the relationship between price and quantity (demanded or supplied) for each curve.

4. Distinguish between a "change in quantity demanded" and a "change in demand".
5. Distinguish between a "change in quantity supplied" and a "change in supply".
6. List the reasons behind a "change in demand" and a "change in supply".
7. Give two examples of complementary and substitute goods.
8. Distinguish between normal and inferior goods.
9. Label the equilibrium price and quantity on a supply and demand graph.
10. Explain how equilibrium is achieved in a competitive market.
11. Explain the effects of changes in supply and demand on equilibrium price and equilibrium quantity.
12. Present the rationale for the government's legally setting prices.

Chapter Highlights

I.   Market
     A.   Definition of a market
     B.   Examples
II.  Demand
     A.   Definition of demand
     B.   Law of demand
          1.  Inverse relationship between price and quantity
          2.  Diminishing marginal utility
          3.  Income and substitution effects
     C.   Demand schedule
     D.   Demand curve (individual and market)
     E.   "Change in quantity demanded"
          1.  Price change (movement along the curve)
     F.   "Change in demand" (new curve) -- non-price determinants:
          1.  Income (superior, normal or inferior and independent goods)
          2.  Tastes
          3.  Expectations
          4.  Number of buyers
          5.  Prices of related goods (complements and substitutes)
III. Supply
     A.   Definition of supply
     B.   Law of supply
          1.  Direct relationship between price and quantity
     C.   Supply schedule
     D.   Supply curve (individual and market)
     E.   "Change in quantity supplied"
          1.  Price change (movement along the curve)
     F.   "Change in supply" (new curve) -- non-price determinants:
          1.  Resource prices
          2.  Taxes and subsidies
          3.  Prices of other goods
          4.  Expectations
          5.  Number of sellers
          6.  Technology

IV. Market Equilibrium
   A.  Equilibrium price and quantity
      1.  Rationing function of prices (eliminates surpluses and shortages)
      2.  Effects of changes in demand and supply
   B.  Government's setting price in the market
      1.  Price floor or support price
      2.  Price ceiling or price cap
V.  Application of Supply and Demand
   A.  The Foreign Exchange Market
      1.  Depreciation and Appreciation of Currency
      2.  Economic Consequences
VI.  Last Word:  The High Price of Marijuana

## Key Terms

| | |
|---|---|
| market | supply |
| demand | law of supply |
| law of demand | direct relationship |
| inverse relationship | quantity supplied |
| diminishing marginal utility | individual supply |
| quantity demanded | market supply |
| individual demand | non-price determinants of supply |
| market demand | increase (or decrease) in supply |
| non-price determinants of demand | equilibrium price and quantity |
| increase (or decrease) in demand | rationing function of prices |
| normal and inferior goods | price floor (support) |
| complementary and substitute goods | price ceiling (cap) |
| depreciation | foreign exchange market |
| appreciation | |

## Real World Example

### Demand Soars as Air Fares Fall

### By John T. Ward

   To some airlines and many travel agents, they're nothing short of insane, but the discount air fares offered in the past week have been a bonanza for consumers, say Shore residents who've snapped them up and the agents who've sold them.
   Carol Frankel of the Forked River section of Lacey Township paid $145 yesterday for a round trip between Newark and nashville, Tenn., tickets that two weeks ago would have cost between $400 and $500, she said.  John Kane of Dover Township had the price of a round-trip ticket to Wisconsin cut in half, to $130.  And the ticket agent for Joseph Soldano of Freehold Township exchanged a $238 roundtrip ticket to Albuquerque, N.M., for one at $190 as soon as the discounting started more than a week ago.
   "This is amazing to me," said Kane a dean at Ocean County College in Dover Township.  "I know people who are picking up the phone and saying, 'I'm flying right now.'"
   It's now or never, said some industry observers.  Though some travel agents expect the offers to

be extended, the discount sales are slated to end tomorrow.  To qualify for the discounts, the airlines require that tickets be paid for by the deadline.

With the expiration of the offers no doubt in mind, bargainhunters have been scrambling for tickets to domestic destinations in the 48 states affected by the sales.  Those who tried to contact the airlines directly have found themselves spending hours trying to get past the busy telephone signals or waiting on hold.  Agents, who link up to reservations systems via computer also have encountered significant delays, the said.

"It takes us an hour and a half of sitting at the computer terminal to make a simple reservation," said Gerhard Angersbach, owner of Worldwide Travel in Manasquan.

"For the most part the seats are available, but you can't get to them because of the system overload," he said.  "Basically, the airlines are throwing this into our laps and saying, 'Here, deal with this.'"

As always, the cheap seats to the most popular destinations, including California, Florida and Las Vegas, went the fastest, agents said.

But the lower fares to those places may still be available to travelers who are flexible about departure days and times, and willing to make stopovers, they said.

"We've made available a good number of seats" priced at discount levels, said Richard Danforth, spokesman for Continental Airlines, the dominant carrier at Newark International Airport.  "But, quite naturally, with demand as it is, there will be instances in which there simply are not (discount) fares available for a particular flight."

Less popular destinations are easier to book, of course.  Frankel, who works in purchasing at Ocean County College, called a travel agent yesterday morning and had her reservation by afternoon, she said.

"I gave her the prospective dates I wanted to go, and she got me my first choice," Frankel said.

The discounting has renewed talk about the likely demise of ailing carriers, the one that can't keep pace with the price cutting and meet operating expenses.

Danforth said the latest fare wars, launched by Northwest Airlines, will lead to an additional $390 million in industry losses this year -- on top of an already-expected deficit of $665 million.

Critics say the thinning of the carrier ranks will eventually lead to higher prices.

"We're going to remain competitive, but that doesn't change the fact that the prices are irrational," Danforth said.

But agents and others say the short-term gains for the industry, economy and consumers are clear.

"It's incredible," said Jay Truppo, owner of Empress Travel in Seaview Square Mall, Ocean Township.  "This is the most business in five days I've seen in 20 years in the industry."

The economic benefits are beginning to accrue down the line, as travelers book hotels, rental cars and restaurants -- none of which are being sold at deep discounts, Truppo said.

Angersbach said the lower fares have "created a tremendous amount of interest, which is good, because now people are thinking travel," he said.

For that reason and others, Angersbach said he expects the airlines to continue discounting programs.

"Obviously, the airlines are doing a tremendous amount of business," he said.  "The consumers are responding because they see a good deal."

Tim Neal, spokesman for the carrier trade group Air Transport Association, said airlines probably won't announce extensions, if there are to be any, "until right at the end" of the current offerings.

## MACRO PROBLEMS

| # of Bushels Demanded | Price per Bushel | # of Bushels Supplied | Amount of Surplus or Shortage |
|---|---|---|---|
| 2,000 | $5 | 12,000 | + 10,000 |
| 4,000 | 4 | 10,000 | + 6,000 |
| 7,000 | 3 | 7,000 | 0 Equilibrium |
| 11,000 | 2 | 4,000 | − 7,000 |
| 16,000 | 1 | 1,000 | −15,000 |

*This problem on test*

1. Fill in the "Amount of Surplus or Shortage" column above and answer the following questions.
   a. What will be the equilibrium price and quantity?
   b. Where does a surplus occur?  A shortage? *Surplus z above Equilibrium shortage below Equilibrium*
   c. "Surpluses drive prices up; shortages drive them down."  Do you agree? *No*
   d. Graph the demand and supply curves, using the schedules above.  Label.
   e. Using the graph from part d, what would happen to the demand for a normal good if the buyers' incomes increased.  Label the new curve D1.  Also, show what would happen to the supply of a good if more competitors entered the market.  Label the new curve S1.  Label new equilibrium point (E').  List two reasons that might have been behind these changes.
   f. Now suppose the government establishes a ceiling price -- show graphically.  What might prompt the government to establish a ceiling price? (two reasons)
   g. Now assume the government establishes a floor (supported) price -- show graphically.  What rationale might prompt the government into this action?  (two reasons)

2. The demand schedules for three people (Erin, Kristen, and Erica), for ice cream cones, are shown in table 4-1 below.
   a. Assuming they are the only buyers of ice cream cones, calculate the total (market) demand for ice cream cones.
   b. Graph the market demand curve from table 4-1 below.

### TABLE 4-1
Quantity demanded for ice cream cones

| Price | Erin | Kristen | Erica | Total |
|---|---|---|---|---|
| $1.50 | 1 | 1 | 0 | ____ |
| 1.25 | 2 | 2 | 1 | ____ |
| 1.00 | 4 | 3 | 2 | ____ |
| .75 | 6 | 4 | 3 | ____ |
| .50 | 10 | 6 | 4 | ____ |

   c. What happens to the demand for ice cream cones when we have a long and hot summer?  Show the change on your graph from part (b).

### MACRO PROBLEMS (continued)

3a. Label the supply and demand curves below (D, D1, S, S1).  The broken line represents a new curve.

b.  Label the axes for each graph.

c.  For each graph, state what has happened to demand and what has happened to supply (increase, decrease, or change in quantity).

d.  Label the old (E) and the new (E1) equilibrium points on each graph.

e.  Label the new equilibrium price (Pe) and equilibrium quantity (Qe) for each graph.

f.  In each graph, state what has happened to the new equilibrium price and quantity.

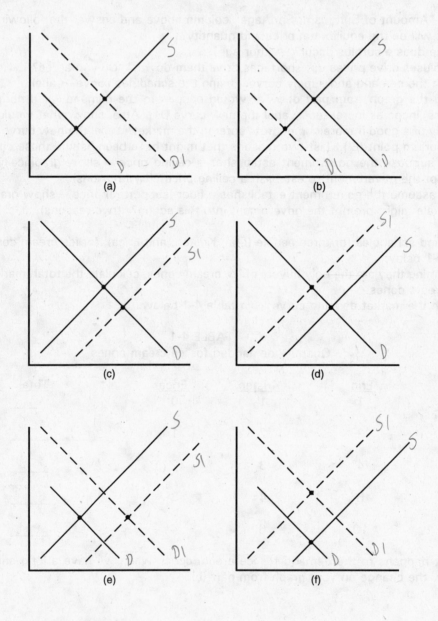

# CHAPTER 4          "Understanding Individual Markets:  Demand and Supply "

## MICRO PROBLEMS

| # of Videos Demanded | Price per Video | # of Videos Supplied | Amount of Surplus (+) or Shortage (-) |
|---|---|---|---|
| 200 | $15 | 100 *150* | *−100* |
| 175 | 18 | 125 *175* | *− 50* |
| 140 | 21 | 140 *190* | *Equilibrium* |
| 130 | 24 | 155 *205* | *+25* |
| 100 | 27 | 175 *225* | *+75* |
| 75 | 30 | 200 *250* | *+125* |

1. Fill in the "Amount of Surplus or Shortage" column above and answer the following questions:

   a. What is the equilibrium price and quantity?

   *This problem on Test*

   b. Where does a surplus occur?  Where does a shortage occur?

   c. "Surpluses drive prices up:  shortages drive them down."  Do you agree?

   d. Graph the demand and supply curves, using the table above--be sure to label the curves.  Label the equilibrium point (E).

   e. Using the graph from part d, show an <u>increase</u> in demand and an <u>increase</u> in supply.  Label the new equilibrium point (E').  List the two <u>reasons</u> that might have been behind these changes.

   f. Now suppose the government establishes a ceiling price--show this graphically in relation to the equilibrium points.  List two reasons why the government might establish a ceiling price.

   g. Now assume the government establishes a floor (supported) price--show this geographically in relation to the equilibrium points.  List two reasons why the government might take this action.

   h. At a price floor (support) of $27, what happens in the market?

   i. If the quantity supplied increased by 50 videos at every price, what would be the new equilibrium price and quantity?

2. Below are the individual demand schedules for three people (Pat, Denise, and Joe) for plants. Assuming they are the only buyers in the market,

   (a) Calculate the total market demand at each price.

   (b) Draw the demand curve below.

   (c) What is the relationship between price and quantity?

|  |  | Quantity Demanded of Plants | | |
|---|---|---|---|---|
| Price | Pat | Denise | Joe | Total Market |
| $25 | 0 | 1 | 1 | _____ |
| 20 | 1 | 2 | 2 | _____ |
| 15 | 2 | 4 | 5 | _____ |
| 10 | 4 | 6 | 7 | _____ |
| 5 | 5 | 8 | 10 | _____ |

   (d) Suppose that Pat learns that she is allergic to plants, and therefore, purchases 0, regardless of the price.

   1. Recalculate the total market demand

   2. Graph the new curve on the graph above.

   3. What has happened to demand?

31

<u>Self-Test</u> (Macro)

1. A decrease in the price of pretzels occurs.  What happens to the demand for beer?
   a. demand increases
   b. demand decreases
   c. a change in quantity demanded
   d. unable to determine

2. In question number one (above) what happens to the demand for pretzels?
   a. increase in demand
   b. decrease in demand
   c. increase in quantity demanded
   d. decrease in quantity demanded

3. New information is disclosed that Vitamin E helps to keep you healthy.  What happens to the demand for Vitamin E?
   a. increase in quantity demanded
   b. decrease in quantity demanded
   c. increase in demand
   d. decrease in demand

4. What happens to the demand for single family houses when the mortgage rates increase?
   a. increase in demand
   b. decrease in demand
   c. a change in the quantity demanded
   d. unable to determine

5. The H.O.T. company sells bows for women's hair.  Last month the company sold 1,000 bows @ $3/each.  This month the company sold 1,000 bows @ $4/each.  Obviously, the company has experienced:
   a. a change in quantity demanded
   b. an increase in demand
   c. a decrease in demand
   d. unable to determine

6. What would cause the quantity demanded for orange juice to rise or fall?
   a. a freeze in Florida
   b. a change in price
   c. a bumper crop of oranges
   d. unable to determine

Self-Test (Macro - continued)

Fill in questions 7-13 based upon Graph 4-1 below:

GRAPH 4-1

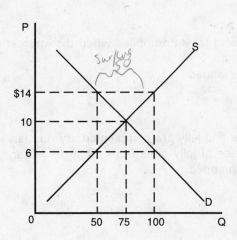

7.  The equilibrium price is __$10__ and quantity is __75__.
8.  At $14, there is a __Surplus__ of __50__, in the market.
9.  At $6, there is a __Shortage__ of __50__, in the market.
10. $ __6__ is the highest price the buyer will pay for 100 items.
11. $ __6__ is the lowest price the producer will sell 50 items.

12. Which of the following prices represents a price ceiling?
    a.   $14                    c.   $6
    b.   $10                    d.   Unable to determine

13. Which of the following represents a price floor?
    a.   $14                    c.   $6
    b.   $10                    d.   Unable to determine

14. Rent control is an example of a price __Ceiling__.

# CHAPTER 4    "Understanding Individual Markets:  Demand and Supply "

Self-Test (Micro)

1. If the price of wine goes from $10/bottle to $7/bottle, what will happen to the demand for cheese--its complement?
   a. increase in demand
   b. decrease in demand
   c. change in quantity demanded
   d. unable to determine

2. What happens to the demand for automobiles when the interest rates drop?
   a. decrease in demand
   b. change in quantity demanded
   c. increase in demand
   d. unable to determine

3. Assume that peanut butter and jelly are complementary goods.  What happens to the demand for peanut butter when the price of jelly goes from $3/jar to $4/jar.
   a. change in quantity demanded
   b. increase in demand
   c. decrease in demand
   d. unable to determine

4. Price ceilings:
   a. benefit the consumer
   b. keep prices artificially low
   c. are utilized for wage and price controls
   d. al of the above

5. When the price of product "B" increases, the demand for "C" decreases.  Obviously, "B" and "C" are:
   a. complementary goods
   b. substitute goods
   c. inferior goods
   d. independent goods

6. When the demand for a product increases as consumer income increases, that product is said to be:
   a. complementary
   b. competitive
   c. normal
   d. inferior

<u>Self-Test</u> (Micro - continued)

Answer the following questions based upon Graph 4-1 below:

Graph 4-1

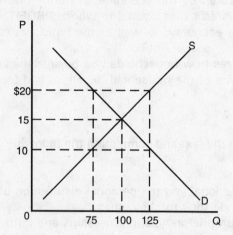

7.  The equilibrium price is ____$15____ and quantity is ___100___.
8.  At $10, there is a __Shortage__ of ___50___, in the market.
9.  At $20, there is a __Surplus__ of ___50___, in the market.
10. $___20___ is the highest price the buyer will pay for 75 items.
11. $___20___ is the highest price the producer will sell 125 items.
12. Which of the following represents a price ceiling?
    a.  $20
    b.  $15
    c.  $10
    d.  Unable to determine

13. Which of the following represents a price floor?
    a.  $20
    b.  $15
    c.  $10
    d.  Unable to determine

14. Wage and Price Controls are examples of a price __Ceiling__.

# CHAPTER 5     "The Private Sectors and the Market System"

## Chapter Orientation

This chapter synthesizes the elements you have studied in Chapters 2, 3 and 4, to explain how the price system operates. The price system directs the (free) market by determining WHAT, HOW, HOW MUCH, FOR WHOM, and ACCOMMODATING CHANGE. What goods and services will be produced? Who receives the output? How does the system accommodate change? These five fundamental (great) questions must be answered by the economic system. Under pure capitalism, for example, these questions would be answered based upon one word: **PROFIT!** Chapter 5 examines the price system and what it does for our economy, as well as the criticisms of the price system.

In addition, Chapter 5 explores how households and businesses are the primary decionmakers in our economy. The characteristics of the household, business and foreign components are analyzed.

## Learning Objectives

After studying this chapter in the text and completing the following exercises in this concepts book, you should be able to:

1. Distinguish between the functional and the personal distribution of income.
2. Identify how households divide their total incomes.
3. Compare and contrast sole proprietorships, partnerships and corporations.
4. List the advantages and disadvantages of the major legal forms of business enterprises.
5. Explain to what degree big business prevails in our economy.
6. Discuss the impacts of global trade and finance on the U.S. economy.
7. Distinguish between normal profit and economic profit.
8. Explain how the competitive price system determines what will be produced.
9. Explain how profits and losses are industry "signals".
10. Explain how the competitive price system organizes production.
11. Define the least-cost approach to production.
12. Explain how the competitive price system allocates output.
13. List several ways the competitive price system adjust for change.
14. Explain how resources are allocated or distributed among the population.
15. Contrast the major points for and against the competitive price system.

## Chapter Highlights
I. Households as Income Receivers
   A. The Functional Distribution of Income
      1. Definition
   B. The Personal Distribution of Income
      1. Definition
II. Households as Spenders
   A. Personal taxes
      1. Definition
   B. Personal saving
      1. Definition of saving and reasons for saving
   C. Personal Consumption Expenditures
      1. Definition of durable, nondurable and services

# CHAPTER 5      "The Private Sectors and the Market System"

III. The Business Population
- A. Terms:
  1. Definition of a plant; firm; conglomerates and an industry;
  2. Definition of horizontal and vertical combinations

IV. Legal Forms of Business Enterprises
- A. Sole Proprietorship
  1. Definition
  2. Advantages and Disadvantages
- B. Partnership
  1. Definition
  2. Advantages and Disadvantages
- C. Corporation
  1. Definition
  2. Advantages and Disadvantages
  3. Decision whether or not to incorporate

V. Industrial Distribution and Business
- A. Types of Industries
- B. Degree big business prevails in our economy

VI. The Foreign Sector
- A. Volume, Pattern and Linkages of U.S. trade with the rest of the world
- B. Economic implications of global trade on U.S.
  1. Specialization and living standards
  2. Competition
  3. Finance and banking
  4. Instability and Policy

VII. The Competitive Market System
- A. Definition

VIII. The Five Fundamental Questions
- A. "<u>What</u> is to be produced?"
  1. Calculation of profit
     a. Economic cost
     b. Total revenue
     c. Normal profit
     d. Economic (pure) profit
  2. Profits and losses are industry "signals"
     a. Expanding industry
     b. Declining industry
  3. Consumer sovereignty (dollar votes)
  4. Derived demand
- B. "<u>How</u> is production organized?"
  1. Profitability insures resources
  2. Economic efficiency
  3. Least-cost production
- C. "<u>Who</u> receives the output?"
  1. Resource prices determine money income for households
  2. Prices for goods and services are set in the market
  3. Ability (income) to pay for these goods and services

D.   "How much should be produced?"
E.   "Adapt to (accommodating) change?"
     1.   Directing or guiding function of prices
     2.   Technological advance
     3.   Capital accumulation
     4.   Invisible hand
IX. The Case for the Market System
    A.   Merits of the Market System
         1.   Efficiently allocates scarce resources
         2.   Emphasizes personal freedom
X. Last Word:  The Financing of Corporate Activity

## Key Terms

| | |
|---|---|
| functional distribution of income | personal distribution of income |
| durable and nondurable goods | services |
| plant | vertical and horizontal combinations |
| firm | conglomerates |
| industry | sole proprietorship |
| partnership | corporation |
| limited liability | double taxation |
| economic profit | dollar votes |
| normal profit | derived demand |
| economic cost | least-cost production |
| expanding industry | guiding function of prices |
| declining industry | invisible hand |
| consumer sovereignty | market failure |

## PROBLEMS

TABLE 5-1 Production Costs for 100 Units of Product X

| Inputs | Input Unit Price | Production Technique A | Production Technique B |
|---|---|---|---|
| Labor | $10 | 5 | 4 |
| Capital | 8 | 4 | 5 |

1a.   Calculate from Table 5-1 (above), the total cost of Technique A and Technique B.
 b.   Which technique represents the least-cost combination?
 c.   Why will virtually all firms opt for the least-cost technique?
 d.   If Product X sells for $85 each unit, what will be the total profit or loss?

2. List the advantages and disadvantages of the major legal forms of business enterprises. Which form is the most prevalent in our economy?

3. Currently, the U.S. has a trade deficit. How large is it and how is it financed? What impact does it have on our economy?

Real World Example

### Growing Gap
#### U.S. Rich and Poor Increase in Numbers; Middle Loses Ground

### Many Families Are Well Off Due to a Working Wife; Single Mothers in Trouble

### Business and Politics Affected

#### By David Wessel

Ellen and Richard Bellicchi will earn about $150,000 this year from their chain of women's health clubs. They live with their two children in an ocean-front house in Connecticut with seven bathrooms, vacation in Hilton Head and Nassau and own three boats and four cars. "We live like kings," she says.

Marcia Myshrall and here three children get by on the $14,000 that she earns as an account analyst at a hospital near Boston and on sporadic child-support payments from her estranged husband. The closest she comes to a vacation is a day at the beach with the kids - if her seven-year-old car is working. "I'm barely surviving," she says.

America, like all nations, has always had its rich and its poor. Today, it has more of both classes than it did a decade ago. At the top is a growing overclass of well-educated, two-income families. At the bottom is a growing underclass of single mothers, baby-boomers stuck in low-paying jobs and children who inherited poverty from their parents. Between them is a middle class that has stopped growing by nearly all measures.

**A Sharp Change**

These trends mark a sharp change. For about 25 years after World War II, income in the United States was divided a bit more evenly every year. The rich got richer, but the middle class got richer, too, and it grew. Poverty didn't disappear, but it dwindled. However, sometime between the late 1960s and mid-1970s - well before Ronald Reagan moved into the White House - the trends changed. Although the economy has grown in the past 15 years, the gains haven't been dived as evenly.

"The middle class still cuts itself a large slice of the American pie," says David Bloom, a Harvard University economist, "but the country has moved in the direction of becoming a nation of haves and have-nots, with less in between."

If this gradual polarization continues, it is bound to affect business and society deeply. Already, some retailers shun the once-popular mass market in favor of narrower pockets of wealthier or poorer consumers. The Democratic Party struggles to define an economic platform that appeals both to its traditional lower-class backers and to the growing upper class.

**No Statistical Fluke**

Economists of varying persuasions are surprisingly united on what is happening. "If there were just one number pointing toward more inequality, it could be ignored as statistical fluke," says Lester Thurow, a Massachusetts Institute of Technology economist. "Given the wide variety of data, all of which point in the same direction, there can be little doubt."

Last year, the top fifth of American families - those earning more than $48,000 - got 43% of all family income, a post-war high. The bottom fifth - earning less than $13,200 -got 4.7%, the least in 25 years. Families earning $15,000 to $35,000 a year, adjusted for inflation, fell to 39% of the total last year from 46% in 1970.

However, economists disagree on the cause of this new inequality and on whether such trends will continue. Mr. Thurow and some other liberals say the economy isn't producing as many middle-wage jobs as it once did. They see increasing inequality ahead. Other economists play down the job trends and, instead, blame changes in the family and effects of the baby boom. They don't expect recent trends to continue. Some even see growth of the middle class resuming.

Clearly, several social and economic factors are increasing inequality in the distribution of income.

Among married couples, the working woman is lifting millions of families out of the middle class. If a husband and wife each earned $24,000 last year, their total income put them among the top 20% of all families; if only one spouse earned that much, they were smack in the middle.

"I spend a lot of time fighting the myth that there's a huge increase in couples with an M.B.A. married to a doctor out there," says Barbara Casey, a market researcher for John Hancock Mutual Life Insurance Co. Far more common is the family with two decent jobs at a combined income of $50,000 to $60,000 - and their growing ranks produce a surge at the top of the income distribution.

Although households with incomes above $50,000 are relatively few, they get attention because they have so much money. They get a third of all personal income and an even greater share of the money available for luxuries, the Conference Board estimates. "By the year 2000," predicts Fabian Linden, an economist for the business-research group, "40% to 50% of all personal income will be at the disposal of those with (inflation-adjusted) household incomes of $50,000 or more."

## Living Well

Kate Evans-Correia, 26, and her husband, Richard Evans, 27, earn about $52,000 a year, only because both work. He fixes machinery at a Boston hotel; she is a computer-magazine editor. "We're maybe doing better than some, but we're not rich," she says.

They own a videocassette recorder, a microwave oven, an antique bedroom set and two cars, a 1986 Pontiac and a 1971 Volkswagen. Her main complaint: "We can't afford a house in this area, and that's pretty discouraging." She adds: "We're not willing to think about having a child yet because we don't want to give up that second income. Without one or the other salary, it would be real tough."

Ellen and Richard Bellicchi have become far more affluent from their health club business, which they founded with a $5,000 loan shortly after graduating from college. Today, they have $3 million in assets. They send their three-year-old daughter to a nursery school and eight-year-old son to an expensive private school. Almost the only thing they lack is time. They haven't, for instance, had much chance to use their 37-foot sailboat.

Economists expect a steady increase in families with two highly paid wage-earners because the number of women professionals and managers is skyrocketing. Women account for a fifth of all doctors, for instance, double the proportion in 1970, and a third of all medical students. Moreover, Harvard's Mr. Bloom says, high-income men and women increasingly tend to marry each other, a trend that widens the gap between rich and poor.

At the same time, divorce and unwed motherhood are creating more households headed by women - and half of the 7.2 million poor families in America are headed by women with no husband present. Congressional Research Service economists say that of all factors increasing inequality, the rising divorce rate has "the strongest erosive effect on the middle class."

## Scraping By

Marcia Myshrall, for example, lived a modest but comfortable middle-class life on Cape Cod when she and her husband, a plumber, were together. After they broke up, however, she reluctantly went on welfare for about a year and a half.

And though she has been working full time for five months, money is tight. She shops at discount clothing outlets, can afford day care for her three-year-old only because of state subsidies and can't recall the last time she hired a babysitter for an evening out. But she is luckier than many single parents: She pays only $300 a month to rent a house from relatives. "If it wasn't for that, I don't know what I'd do," she says.

The trend toward single-parent families, which shows no sign of abating, puts more and more children in poverty. Last year, 20% of all children were living below the poverty line, up from 15% in 1970. Sen. Daniel Patrick Moynihan says that by the turn of the century, about half of all American children "will have lived some parts of their lives in poverty. This will not be good for them." The New York Democrat adds that it also won't be good for adults whose "economic well-being in retirement" largely depends on the productivity of younger generations.

Besides families headed by women, baby boomers, too, are swelling the lower class. "Everyone looks at the success of the young urban professionals and doesn't realize there are so many more young urban failures," says Stephen Rose, a budget analyst for the Washington State Senate. The first baby boomers turn 40 this year, but far more are 22 to 32 years old, and younger workers generally earn less than middle-aged.

## Divergent Views

Optimists expect the baby boomers to earn more as they age. "The middle ranks of the earnings distribution are likely to burgeon considerably as the baby-boom generation matures," says Robert Lawrence, a Brookings Institution economist. But others argue that competition among baby boomers for jobs probably will keep their incomes from climbing as rapidly as those of earlier generations. Mr. Thurow warns: "There is no reason to believe that having more older people will generate more middle-class jobs."

The early evidence is that baby boomers' incomes are rising as they grow older, but not as quickly as in previous, smaller generations, Mr. Bloom says.

The level of economic activity also has been increasing inequality. Compared with earlier postwar years, the unemployment rate in the past 15 years has been steep, rising higher in recessions and failing to fall as far during recoveries. Unemployment tends to push families out of the middle class. A decade of high inflation widened the gap between the affluent and the poor, and now the persistent trade deficit, Mr. Thurow says, takes "a large chunk out of the middle of earnings distribution" by destroying high-paying factory jobs.

Some economists contend that the economy is generating more high-paid jobs and more low-paid jobs and fewer in the middle. Compared with manufacturing, the growing service sector employs a smaller share of workers at annual wages of $15,000 to $35,000 and a greater share above and below the range, says Lyn Browne, a Federal Reserve Bank of Boston economist. "What appears to be missing from service industries are the high-wage blue-collar jobs," she says. Also missing are unions, which tend to pay rates.

## Reagan Policies

The Reagan administration's policies haven't narrowed the gap between rich and poor. The tax cuts in the first five years of Mr. Reagan's presidency favored one wealthy: Reducing capital-gains taxes benefited those with capital. Government programs aimed exclusively at the poor were trimmed, but others that help a broader group - Social Security and veterans' benefits, for instance - weren't.

The pending tax-revision bill eliminates taxes for about six million poor people and, to that extent, should tend to reduce inequality. But it won't substantially alter the distribution of taxes between high-income and middle-income taxpayers. And it eliminates the steeply progressive rates long symbolizing the goal of distributing income more equally, even though loopholes and tax shelters eroded their effectiveness.

Even small shifts in income can have big effects:  If the upper fifth of American households gets an additional 1% of total income, its purchasing power rises about $20 billion.  And although the poverty rate last year was only one percentage point higher than in 1980, 3.8 million more people were living in poverty.

Businesses already are reacting to the increased inequality.  Scores of companies are focusing not on the once-popular mass market but on niches at the top or bottom of the economic ladder.

For 80 years, Oshkosh B'Gosh Inc., for example, was a small manufacturer of overalls for farmers, denim jackets for railroad engineers and uniforms for delivery-truck drivers.  Ten years ago, Oshkosh began making clothing for children - not for those of working people but for those whose parents can afford $35 for red corduroy overalls and a matching shirt.  Now, Oshkosh's sales have grown tenfold, and 86% of its volume is in high-priced children's clothing.

In retailing, the most successful companies are no longer those aiming at the middle.  Sears, Roebuck & Co. - which says its customers' median income is about $27,850, right smack in the middle - remains America's biggest retailer, but it has been losing market share.  Gimbels and Ohrbach's, which once prospered by selling to middle-class New Yorkers, are closing.

"Retailers have either got to go upscale or go to the lower end," says Carl Steidtmann, an economist at Management Horizons, a market-research arm of Price Waterhouse & Co.  Thus, the best-performing retailer by almost any yardstick is Wal-Mart Inc., which targets lower-income consumers.  At the same time, posh stores such as Bloomingdale's prosper.

On the grocery shelf, the growth is not in staples but in the fancy stuff.  Sales of frozen vegetables stagnate, but sales of costlier, deluxe varieties - tiny peas, sweet corn - are up to 20%.  High-priced frozen dinners now account for 44% of all frozen dinners.  A spokesman for Campbell Soup Co. says, "We are using a rule of thumb that on the average, 20% of the market in any product line" will buy premium products.  "We've seen this market driven by groups such as the dual wage-earner family."

Among appliance makers, a two-pronged strategy is evolving.  Whirlpool Corp. recently bought Kitchenaid Corp. and plans to market two distinct lines of washers, dryers, refrigerators and other appliances:  the standard Whirlpool line and a pricier Kitchenaid line.  Hank Bowman, the vice president for sales, says Whirlpool is reacting to projections of "higher disposable income at the high end," with middle-income householders rising to the top of falling to the bottom.

## Political Impact

Income shifts affect politics, too.

Some analysts say the Democratic Party's prospects are hurt by its inability to bridge the gap between the growing numbers of low income and high income voters.  A crucial problem, says Thomas Edsall, the author of a book on politics and inequality, is the party's inability "to develop a political strategy that serves the party's historical roots - a core allegiance to those...struggling to move up the economic ladder - while developing policies appropriate to contemporary economic complexities and the interests of those already above the median income."

Or, as Eddie Mahe, a Republican political consultant, puts it:  "The Democrats are trying to hold together the bottom and the top without the middle as glue."

The same could be said of America, suggests Rep. David Obey, a Wisconsin Democrat and the chairman of the Joint Economic Committee.  "The worst thing that can happen to a democracy," he says, "is for the public to gain the impression that the system is being run...for a small number of top-siders."

42

Self-Test
1. The price system
   a.   helps to determine what will be produced.
   b.   aids business executives in deciding what resources to use in production.
   c.   influences which goods and services people receive.
   d.   all of the above.
2. Which of the following is not one of the Five Fundamental Questions?
   a.   What goods and services should be produced?      c.      Which firms will produce?
   b.   How is production organized?                      d.      Who receives the output?
3. If the profits in the stereo industry started to decline, you would expect
   a.   resources to flow out of the industry.
   b.   more firms to enter the industry and drive the inefficient one out.
   c.   increase resource allocation to lower costs.
   d.   none of the above.
4. Economic profits are:
   a.   the same as "Gross Profit" in accounting.
   b.   a normal rate of return according to economists.
   c.   a cost because they are paid to the owner.
   d.   not a cost because they are "surplus profits" and were an unexpected pleasure.
5. Which of the following is not a criticism of the price system?
   a.   causes a decline in competition over time.
   b.   causes inefficient production.
   c.   limits personal freedom by imposing government regulations.
   d.   does not account for spillovers.
6. When a competitive industry is in equilibrium,
   a.   every firm is enjoying economic profits.      c.      economic profits will be equal to zero.
   b.   normal profits will not be realized.           d.      the government will impose a price
                                                               support.
7. The functional distribution of income refers to the:
   a.   division of income between personal taxes, consumption expenditures, and saving.
   b.   division of income on the basis of industry sources, e.g., agriculture, transportation, mining, etc.
   c.   distribution of income according to basic resource classes, i.e., wages, rents, interest, and
        profits.
   d.   manner in which income is distributed among specific households or spending units.
8. Listed in descending order of relative size, total consumption spending is comprised of:
   a.   nondurable goods, durable goods, and services.
   b.   services, nondurable goods, and durable goods.
   c.   services, durable goods, & nondurable goods.
   d.   durable goods, nondurable goods, and services.
9. Which of the following is numerically the dominant type of business in the United States?
   a.   corporations                                    c.      partnerships
   b.   proprietorships                                 d.      cooperatives
10. United States merchandise exports and imports have:
   a.   grown absolutely, but remained a constant proportion of the national output.
   b.   grown absolutely, but declined as a proportion of the national output.
   c.   grown both absolutely and as a percentage of the national output.
   d.   declined both absolutely and as a percentage of the national output.

## Chapter 1 - "The Nature and Method of Economics"
I.   The Importance of Studying Economics
   A.   Definition of economics, macro, micro, ceteris paribus and comparative advantage
   B.   Reasons for study
II.  Deriving Economic Policy
   A.   The Scientific Method (positive economics)
      1.   Descriptive economics
      2.   Economic theory
         a.   Generalizations, assumptions, and abstractions
         b.   Forms of economic models
      3.   Test (inductive vs. deductive methods)
      4.   Economic policy
         a.   Predictions and implications for the real world
         b.   Steps
   B.   Potential "pitfalls" in economic models
III. Economic Goals
   A.   List of eight economic goals in our society
      1.   Some are complementary; others are mutually exclusive
IV. Difficulties in Studying Economics
   A.   List of areas to beware of in economics
V.  Economic Perspective
   A.   Decision making
      1.   Rational behavior
      2.   Cost-benefit perspective
VI. Graphs and their Meanings
   A.   Definition
   B.   Tools
      1.   Plotting points
      2.   Calculating the slope of a straight line and a nonlinear curve
      3.   Direct or inverse relationship determination

## Chapter 2 - "The Economizing Problem"
I.   The Law of Scarcity
   A.   Definition of the "Law of Scarcity"
   B.   Factors of production and their money payments
   C.   Definition of economic efficiency
   D.   Production possibilities curve
      1.   Assumptions
      2.   Law of increasing opportunity costs (concave curve)
      3.   Optimum product mix
      4.   Expansion and contraction of the curve
      5.   Opportunity cost
      6.   Law of Diminishing Returns
      7.   Real world applications (6)
II.  Economic Systems
   A.   Types of systems
      1.   Command economy (communism) -- centralized
      2.   Pure or laissez-faire capitalism -- decentralized

    3.  Mixed system - real world -- economies

    4.  Traditional (or customary) economies of underdeveloped countries

## Chapter 3 - "Pure Capitalism and the Circular Flow"

I.  Pure Capitalism (not American Capitalism)

    A.  Six foundations

    B.  Three common characteristics of all modern economic systems

II. The Circular Flow Model

    A.  The circular flow diagram

        1.  Definition

        2.  Flows

        3.  Sectors and markets

        4.  Demand-side and supply-side

        5.  Limitations

## Chapter 4 - "Understanding Individual Markets:"

I.  Market

    A.  Definition of a market

    B.  Examples

II. Demand

    A.  Definition of demand

    B.  Law of demand

        1.  Inverse relationship

        2.  Diminishing marginal utility

        3.  Income and substitution effects

    C.  Demand schedule and curve (individual and market)

    D.  "Change in quantity demanded" vs. "change in demand"

    E.  Non-price determinants of demand

III.Supply

    A.  Definition of supply

    B.  Law of supply

        1.  Direct relationship

    C.  Supply schedule and curve (individual and market)

    D.  "Change in quantity supplied" vs. "change in supply"

    E.  Non-price determinants of supply

IV.Market Equilibrium

    A.  Equilibrium price and quantity

        1.  Rationing function

        2.  Effects of changes in demand and supply

    B.  Government's setting price in the market

        1.  Price floor (support)

        2.  Price ceiling (cap)

    C.  Word Problems

V. Application of Supply and Demand

    A.  The foreign exchange market

        1.  Depreciation and appreciation of currency

        2.  Economic consequences

**Chapter 5 - "The Private Sectors and the Market System"**
I.  Households as Income Receivers
    A.  Functional vs. Personal Distribution of Income
II.  Households as Spenders
    A.  Personal taxes
    B.  Personal saving
    C.  Personal Consumption Expenditures
III. The Business Population
    A.  Terms: plant; firm; conglomerates; industry; horizontal and vertical combinations
IV. Legal Forms of Business Enterprises
    A.  Sole Proprietorship
        1.  Definition
        2.  Advantages and Disadvantages
    B.  Partnership
        1.  Definition
        2.  Advantages and Disadvantages
    C.  Corporation
        1.  Definition
        2.  Advantages and Disadvantages
        3.  Decision to incorporate
V.  Industrial Distribution and Business
    A.  Types of Industries
    B.  Degree big business prevails in our economy
VI. The Foreign Sector
    A.  Volume, Pattern and Linkages of U.S. trade
    B.  Economic implications
VII. The Competitive Market System
    A.  Definition
VIII. The Five Fundamental Questions
    A.  "What is to be produced?"
        1.  Calculation of profit
        2.  Profits and losses are industry "signals"
            a.  Expanding industry
            b.  Declining industry
        3.  Consumer sovereignty (dollar votes)
        4.  Derived demand
    B.  "How is production organized?"
        1.  Profitability insures resources
        2.  Economic efficiency
        3.  Least-cost production
    C.  "Who receives the output?"
        1.  Resource prices determine money income
        2.  Prices for goods and services are set in the market
        3.  Ability (income) to pay for these goods and services
    D.  "How Much" should be produced?
    E.  "Adapt to change?"
        1.  Guiding function of prices

2. Invisible hand
3. Technological advance
4. Capital accumulation

IX. The Case for the Market System
   A. Merits of the Market System
      1. Efficiently allocates scarce resources
      2. Emphasizes personal freedom

## UNIT I FORMULAS

$$\text{Slope} = \frac{\blacktriangle Y}{\blacktriangle X} = \frac{\text{rise}}{\text{run}} = \frac{Y_2 - Y_1}{X_2 - X_1}$$

# MACROECONOMICS

## UNIT II

## Chapter Orientation

National income accounting gives us a method to measure our nation's (as well as other nation's) overall economic health.  Calculation of the "bottom line" figures (GDP, NDP, NI, PI, and DPI) allows us to see how well off we are (standard of living) as compared to other years.  In addition, by looking at several years, we can plot the trend and predict the future cycle of the economy.  In 1992, the United States switched from using Gross National Product (GNP) to Gross Domestic Product (GDP), both terms will be defined and contrasted.

To simplify the process of calculating national income accounting, "NIA sheets" are provided in this concepts book (they will also be given to you at the time of the test).  The more practice, the better you will get, so six countries' data is given to you.  More important than just memorizing the accounts to tally, is the knowledge of what the account means, as well as the figures.

National income accounting can be analyzed in two ways:  the expenditures approach (monies spent) and the incomes approach (monies received).  An elaborate circular flow diagram in your text (pg. 118) shows both approaches.  Economists avoid double accounting by including only the final (final use) goods, using a value added approach.  In addition, only productive activities are included; nonproductive are excluded.  To accurately compare years, GDP must be adjusted for inflation (using a GDP deflator) called "Real GDP" since money is not a stable measuring rod.

Lastly, since GDP measures the total overall production, is it a good measure of social welfare (for individuals)?  The answer to this question will be discussed in the chapter.

## Learning Objectives

After studying this chapter in the text and completing the following exercises in this concepts book, you should be able to:

1. Define GNP and GDP explain the differences.
2. Distinguish between the expenditures approach and the income approach to measuring GDP.
3. Calculate GDP, NDP, NI, PI, and DPI (using the NIA sheets provided) given the necessary data.
4. Define NDP, NI, PI and DPI and their components.
5. Compute Real GDP by adjusting money GDP using the GDP deflator.
6. Calculate the price index in a given year.
7. Discuss GDP as a measure of social welfare.

## Chapter Highlights

I. The Importance of Studying National Income Accounting
   A. Reasons for study
      1. Measure the nation's economic health
      2. Mode of comparison
      3. Explain its size and the reason for changes
      4. Aids in the creation of economic polices

II. Gross Domestic Product
   A.   Definition of Gross National Product (GNP) -- the total market value of all final goods and services produced by Americans, whether in the U.S. or abroad, during a certain time period (usually one year)
   B.   Definition of Gross Domestic Product (GDP) -- the total market value of all final goods and services produced with the boundaries of the U.S., whether by American or foreign-supplied resources.
   C.   Avoiding double counting
      1.   Final goods vs. intermediate goods
      2.   Value added approach
   D.   Define "per capita GDP"
   E.   Calculation (use the NIA sheets provided)
      1.   Incomes approach (wages + rents + interest + profits + nonincome charges minus GNP -GDP adjustment).
      2.   Expenditures approach (C + I + G + Xn)
      3.   Include productive activities:
         a.   Rent of owner occupied homes
         b.   Farm consumption of home grown food
      4.   Exclude nonproductive activities:
         a.   Transfer payments
         b.   Securities transactions
         c.   Used goods sales
         d.   Gross national disproduct
         e.   Leisure
         f.   Quality changes
III. Other National Income Accounts
   A.   Define NDP, NI, PI, and DPI
   B.   Calculation of NDP, NI, PI, and DPI (using the NIA sheets provided)
   C.   Relationship between the major social accounts
      1.   The circular flow diagram (revisited)
IV. Measuring the Price Level
   A.   Money is not a stable measuring rod
   B.   Definition of Real GDP vs. Nominal GDP
      1.   The adjustment process
         a.   Inflating and deflating using a price index
   C.   Calculation of Real GDP using a GDP deflator (or price index) and money GDP

real GDP        =        $\dfrac{\text{money GDP}}{\text{GDP deflator}}$   x   100

real GDP        =        $\dfrac{\text{nominal GDP}}{\text{price index (as a decimal)}}$

price index     =        $\dfrac{\text{price in any given year}}{\text{price in the base year}}$  x  100        = $\dfrac{\text{Each year's price}}{\text{Base year's price}}$

V. GDP as a Measure of Social Welfare
  A. GDP is <u>not</u> an index of social welfare because it fails to include:
    1. Nonmarket transactions
    2. Leisure
    3. Improved product quality
    4. Composition and distribution of output
    5. Per capita output
    6. Disproduct (costs of pollution to the environment)
    7. The underground economy
    8. Impact on the economy: tax revenue, GDP statistic, unemployment statistic, etc.
VI. Last Word: The Consumer Price Index

<u>Key Terms</u>

| | |
|---|---|
| GDP | personal consumption expenditures |
| NDP | capital consumption allowance |
| NI | (depreciation) |
| PI | indirect business taxes |
| DPI | corporation profit before taxes |
| real GDP | dividends |
| GDP deflator | undistributed corporate profits |
| base year | disproduct |
| double counting | nonmarket transactions |
| value added | proprietor's income |
| nonproductive | rental income |
| incomes approach | net interest |
| expenditures approach | social contributions |
| final goods | transfer payments |
| nominal dollars | personal income taxes |
| net exports | personal savings |
| gross private investment | underground economy |
| government expenditures for goods | |
|    and services | |

<u>Real World Example</u>

<u>Briton Wins Nobel Economic Prize For Work on National Income Accounts</u>

By Lindley H. Clark, Jr. and George Anders

Sir Richard Stone of Cambridge University won the 1984 Nobel Memorial Prize in Economics for his pioneering work in developing national income accounts, the system that measures a country's economic activities.

The economics prize, sponsored by the Riksbank, Sweden's central bank, has been awarded each year since 1965. This was only the fourth time the award wasn't won or shared by a U.S. economist. Even this year the award had an American angle, since Sir Richard to some extent had built on the earlier national-income work of Simon Kuznets, an American who won the prize in 1971.

For the second consecutive year, the Royal Swedish Academy's Nobel Selection Committee chose an economist uninvolved in policy controversy and little-known to the general public. Last year's prize went to economist Gerard Debreu of the University of California at Berkeley, who developed a mathematical foundation for supply and demand theory.

In its citation, the committee said Sir Richard's work "greatly improved the basis for empirical economic analysis. Systems for national accounts have had a unique international impact and are indispensable ..."

Sir Richard, 71 years old, is soft-spoken, modest and shuns the limelight. In the latest edition of Who's Who, he listed his chief recreation as "staying at home." When the award was announced and reporters tried to reach him, however, he wasn't there.

The retired economist's selection was hailed by academics in Britain, who credit him in the 1940s with standardizing such calculations as national output, consumption and personal income.

"In those days, people just made guesses," said Prof. Alan Prest at the London School of Economics, who once studied under Sir Richard. "He played a big part in developing a U.K. system of national accounts, and then developing international standards."

American economists expressed mild surprise at Sir Richard's selection, but generally seemed to feel the group had chosen well. Allan H. Meltzer, professor of economics at Carnegie-Mellon University, said, "Sir Richard's work, though rather specialized, is highly regarded by the profession."

Since the Nobel economics prize was begun in 1969, the selection committee has been hesitant to cite work in fast-moving fields, preferring to honor research from several decades ago.

"There's a queue of older economists who made their great achievements in the 1940s and 1950s," said Assar Lindbeck, head of the Swedish selection panel. "We're trying to cut down the queue as fast as we can."

Mr. Lindbeck said Sir Richard's ideas are used by all major international organizations and by more than 100 countries. The widespread use of national income accounting has made it easier to assess the strength or weakness of a country's economy, and to compare it with other countries.

## PROBLEMS

1. Below are the National Product and Income Data (in billions of dollars) for six countries for a given year. A dash (-) opposite any account means that the number is not given to you - do not assume zero. Calculate GDP, NDP, NI, PI, and DPI for each country using the NIA sheets provided.

| Account | \_Countries\_ | | | | | |
|---|---|---|---|---|---|---|
| | 1 | 2 | 3 | 4 | 5 | 6 |
| 1. Personal consumption expenditures | 100 | 180 | --- | --- | 400 | 267 |
| 2. Corporation profits (before taxes) | --- | --- | 50 | --- | --- | 70 |
| 3. Corporate taxes | 15 | 15 | 10 | --- | 36 | 28 |
| 4. Depreciation | 10 | 25 | 10 | 52 | 43 | 14 |
| 5. Government expenditures for goods and services | 50 | --- | 60 | 84 | 128 | 69 |
| 6. Transfer payments | 10 | 30 | 15 | --- | 10 | 16 |
| 7. Gross private investment | --- | --- | 50 | 46 | 88 | --- |
| 8. Proprietors income | --- | --- | 20 | --- | 52 | 25 |
| 9. Indirect business taxes | 20 | 30 | 40 | 22 | 50 | 15 |
| 10. Net interest | --- | --- | 10 | --- | 15 | 12 |
| 11. Net private investment | 50 | --- | --- | --- | --- | 47 |
| 12. Personal income taxes | 15 | 24 | 20 | 38 | 15 | 38 |
| 13. Personal savings | --- | 40 | 30 | 10 | --- | --- |
| 14. Rental income | --- | --- | 20 | --- | 12 | 18 |
| 15. Social contributions | 0 | 12 | 5 | 23 | 5 | 8 |
| 16. Undistributed corporate profits | 10 | 9 | 10 | --- | 22 | 19 |
| 17. Wages and salary earnings | --- | --- | 250 | --- | 369 | 240 |
| 18. Net exports | 0 | 0 | 0 | --- | --- | --- |
| 19. Exports | --- | --- | --- | 9 | 10 | 14 |
| 20. Dividends | --- | --- | --- | 13 | 24 | 23 |
| 21. Imports | --- | --- | --- | 12 | 3 | 17 |

GDP:_____

NDP:_____

NI:_____

PI:_____

DPI:_____190_____

# NATIONAL INCOME ACCOUNTING

**FORMULAS:**

$$GDP - CCA = NDP \text{ or Dep}$$

$$NDP - IBT = NI$$

NI ± the following = PI (incomes)

$$PI - PIT = DPI$$

**GROSS DOMESTIC PRODUCT**

- Gross Private Investment
- Government Expenditures for Goods and Services
- Personal Consumption Expenditures
- Net Exports: Exports – Imports

**NET DOMESTIC PRODUCT**

- Capital Consumption Allowance or Depreciation
- Net Private Investment
- Government Expenditures for Goods and Services
- Personal Consumption Expenditures
- Net Exports: Exports – Imports

**NATIONAL INCOME**

- Indirect Business Taxes
- Wages and Salaries
- Corporation Profit BT = + Corporate Taxes + Dividends + Undistributed Corporate Profits
- Proprietors Income
- Rental Income
- Net Interest

**PERSONAL INCOME**

- – Social Contributions
- – Corporate Taxes
- – Undistributed Corporate Profits
- + Transfer Payments

**DISPOSABLE PERSONAL INCOME**

- Personal Income Taxes
- Personal Consumption Expenditures
- Personal Savings

## PROBLEMS (continued)

2a. Complete the table below, which shows actual data for the U.S. economy.
 b. This economy has been characterized by _____.

| Year | Money GDP (Billions) | GDP Deflator (1987 = 100) | Real GDP (Billions) |
|------|------|------|------|
| 1960 | $513.4 | 26.0 | _____ |
| 1970 | 1010.7 | 35.1 | _____ |
| 1980 | 2708.0 | 71.7 | _____ |
| 1987 | 4539.9 | 100.0 | _____ |
| 1989 | 5244.0 | 108.4 | _____ |
| 1991 | 5671.8 | 117.0 | _____ |

3a. Complete the table below using year 2 as the base year (hypothetical data).
 b. This economy has been characterized by _____.

| Year | Qty. | Price | Price Index | Nominal/or Current $ | Real/or Constant $ |
|------|------|------|------|------|------|
| 1 | 3 | $2 | _____ | _____ | _____ |
| 2 | 5 | 4 | _____ | _____ | _____ |
| 3 | 6 | 5 | _____ | _____ | _____ |
| 4 | 8 | 6 | _____ | _____ | _____ |
| 5 | 9 | 8 | _____ | _____ | _____ |

## FORMULAS:

Real GDP = $\dfrac{\text{Money GDP}}{\text{GDP deflator}}$ x 100 = $\dfrac{\text{nominal GDP}}{\text{Price Index (as a decimal)}}$

Current $ = Price x Qty.

Constant $ = $\dfrac{\text{Current \$}}{\text{Price Index}}$

Price Index = $\dfrac{\text{Each year's price}}{\text{Base year's price}}$ = $\dfrac{\text{Price in any given year}}{\text{Price in the base year}}$ x 100

Self-Test

Below are the National Product and Income Data in billions of dollars. Use the NIA sheets provided to compute the following accounts to answer questions 1 - 6.

| | |
|---|---|
| Corporate Taxes | 30 |
| Depreciation | 25 |
| Government Expenditures for goods and services | 95 |
| Indirect Business Taxes | 47 |
| Net Private Investment | 60 |
| Personal Income Taxes | 57 |
| Undistributed Corporate Profits | 26 |
| Exports | 75 |
| Imports | 60 |
| National Income | 343 |
| Disposable Income | 277 |

1. GDP is:
   a.   $415            c.      $435
   b.   $400            d.      unable to determine

2. NDP is:
   a.   $375            c.      $390
   b.   $400            d.      unable to determine

3. PI is:
   a.   $56             c.      $278
   b.   $334            d.      unable to determine

4. Personal consumption expenditures are:
   a.   $57             c.      $220
   b.   $205            d.      unable to determine

5. Personal savings is:
   a.   $57             c.      $220
   b.   $334            d.      unable to determine

6. Gross private investment is:
   a.   $35             c.      $60
   b.   $85             d.      unable to determine

7. GDP is not a good measure of social welfare; which of the following is not a reason why?
   a.   fails to include nonmarket transactions
   b.   fails to include changes in quality
   c.   fails to include productive activities such as home grown food
   d.   fails to include the underground economy

Self-Test  (Continued)

TABLE I

| Year (1) | Money GDP (2) | GDP Deflator (3) | Real GDP (4) |
|---|---|---|---|
| 1 | $550 | 140 | _____ |
| 2 | 560 | 135 | _____ |
| 3 | 576 | 120 | _____ |
| 4 | 586 | 117 | _____ |
| 5 | 604 | 108 | _____ |

8. In Table I, "Real GDP" in year 1 is_____.
9. In Table I, "Real GDP" in year 3 is_____.
10. In Table I, "Real GDP" in year 5 is_____.
11. In Table I, this economy is experiencing inflation or deflation?_____

12. Which of the following is not considered a nonproductive activity?
    a.   used goods
    b.   securities transactions
    c.   rent of an owner occupied home
    d.   leisure
13. Gross National Product is defined as:
    a.   the monetary value of all goods and services produced by Americans in U.S. or abroad.
    b.   the monetary value of all final goods and services produced by Americans in U.S. or abroad.
    c.   the monetary value of all intermediate gods and services produced by Americans in U.S. or abroad.
    d.   the monetary value of all economic resources produced by Americans in U.S. or abroad.
14. Net exports is a negative figure when:
    a.   exports exceed imports
    b.   the country's imports exceed exports
    c.   the country's equity is declining
    d.   net private investment exceeds gross private investment
15. Real GDP and money GDP differ because real GDP:
    a.   excludes depreciation or capital consumption allowance
    b.   has been adjusted for changes in the price level
    c.   does not include nonproductive activities
    d.   includes the international sector
16. The GDP may be defined as:
    a.   the monetary value of all goods and services produced with the U.S.
    b.   the national income minus all nonincome charges against output.
    c.   the monetary value of all economic resources used in the production of a year's output.
    d.   the monetary value of all goods and services, final and intermediate, produced in a given year, within the U.S.

59

# CHAPTER 10          "Classical and Keynesian Theories of Employment"

## Chapter Orientation

The next two chapters (Chapters 10 and 11) will focus on determining how our economy operates as a whole (aggregate).  We will explore how aggregate demand (all planned expenditures for the entire economy added together) and aggregate supply (all planned production for the entire economy added together) determine the equilibrium real national output and the equilibrium price level of the economy.  Chapter 10 begins with just the private sector of AD which is consumption and investment.  Remember, these are two components of the equation AD = C + I + G + Xn.

The Keynesian viewpoint of what determines the demand for the real national output (real NDP), as well as the equilibrium level of output, will be covered in detail.  In addition, the Classical School and Supply-side Economics will be presented.  In this Concepts book, a page has been devoted to comparing these three economic schools of thought.

Three areas to keep in mind while studying these theories are (1) What was the time period? (2) What event caused the theory to lose credibility?   (3) What was the role of the government (Laissez-faire or to fine-tune)?

Since we know that business cycles (fluctuations) are recurrent, and that history repeats itself, (Supply-side economics is an outgrowth of the Classical School), it is imperative that we study the past to help predict the future. . .

## Learning Objectives

After studying this chapter in the text, and completing the exercises in this concepts book, you should be able to:
1. List the assumptions of our model to determine the equilibrium national output level (NDP).
2. Contrast the Classical School, Keynesian Economics and Supply-side Economics.
3. Define "Say's Law" and the implications for the Classical School.
4. Discuss how the flexibility of wages and prices would eliminate problems in the economy.
5. Present the Classical viewpoint and Keynesian viewpoint concerning the interest rate and savings and investment.
6. List two reasons why the price-wage flexibility, according to the Keynesians, will not guarantee full employment.
7. Explain how consumption (C) and savings (S) are related to disposable income (DI).
8. Calculate APC, APS, MPC, and MPS when given the necessary data.
9. List and explain five nonincome determinants of consumption and savings.
10. Distinguish between a change in consumption (savings) and a change in quantity consumed (saved).
11. List the two basic determinants of investment and explain why a firm will or will not invest their money.
12. Calculate the economy's investment-demand schedule and explain the inverse relationship between investment spending and the real interest rate.
13. List and explain five noninterest determinants of investment expenditures.
14. Distinguish between a change in investment-demand and a change in quantity of investment-demand.
15. Explain the variables found in the investment schedule and their relationship.
16. List what factors contribute to the instability of investment spending.

# CHAPTER 10     "Classical and Keynesian Theories of Employment"

## Chapter Highlights

I. Model to Determine Equilibrium
   A. Assumptions:
      1. Classical economy (domestic or closed economy)
      2. Laissez-faire role for government
      3. Savings will be personal savings
      4. Depreciation and net American income earned abroad are zero.

II. The Classical School (Supply-side)
   A. Foundations:
      1. Say's Law
      2. Savings
      3. Investment
      4. Interest rate
      5. Price-wage flexibility
      6. Laissez-faire role of government
      7. Adam Smith, Father of Economics
         a. Wealth of Nations (1776)

III. Keynesian Economics (Demand-side)
   A. Foundations:
      1. Consumption
      2. Savings
      3. Investment
      4. Interest rate
      5. Money balances by householders and banks
      6. Discrediting of Price-wage flexibility
   B. John Maynard Keynes, Father of Modern Economics
      1. General Theory of Employment, Interest and Money, (1936)
   C. Reasons against the price-wage flexibility
      1. Market imperfections:
         a. Union and business monopolies
         b. Minimum-wage legislation
         c. Wage cuts would dampen motivation and morale
         d. Price-wage cuts will lower income and therefore demand (for goods/services and labor)
   D. Defenders of Classical Economics
      1. Argue against government interference
         a. Crowding-out

IV. Comparison of Classical and Keynesian Economics
  A.  Aggregate Demand and Aggregate Supply Models:
    1.  According to Classical theory, the aggregate supply curve is vertical at the economy's full employment level; a decrease in aggregate demand (demand shifts to the left) will cause a lower equilibrium price at real output (at full employment) will not change (automatic tendency).  See Exhibit 10-1 below:

Exhibit 10-1 Classical View

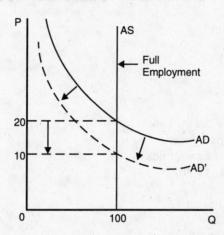

    2.  According to Keynesian theory, the aggregate supply curve is horizontal, at the current price (prices are inflexible); a decrease in aggregate demand will lower real output (and lower employment) and the price will not change.  See Exhibit 10-2 below:

Exhibit 10-2 Keynesian View

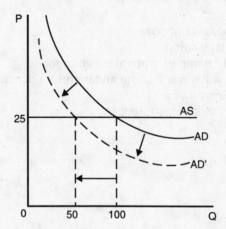

    3. In both models, the aggregate demand curve (AD) is downward sloping.
       a. The Classical model shows AD is influenced by falling prices which will increase purchasing power.
       b. The Keynesian model shows that total output and employment are directly related to total (aggregate) expenditures, which include consumption, investment, government purchases, and net exports. Each of these four components will be discussed in detail.

V. Tools of Keynesian Theory
  A. Consumption and Saving
    1. Consumption is the largest component of aggregate demand (aggregate expenditures).
    2. It is assumed that any disposable income not spent will be saved. Hence, DI = C + S.
    3. The consumption schedule shows the amount of consumption at various levels of disposable income, during a certain time period. The relationship between consumption and disposable income is called the "consumption function". There is a direct relationship between C and DI. "Break-even income" is when households spend their entire disposable income.
    4. The savings schedule shows the amount of savings at various levels of disposable income, during a certain time period the relationship between savings and disposable income is called the "savings function". There is a direct relationship between S and DI.
    5. The Average Propensity to Consume (APC) is the ratio of consumption to disposable income:
$$APC = \frac{C}{DI}$$
    6. The Average Propensity to Save (APS) is the ratio of savings to disposable income:
$$APS = \frac{S}{DI}$$
    7. The Marginal Propensity to Consume (MPC) measures the change in consumption resulting from a change in income. The MPC is the slope of the consumption function.
$$MPC = \frac{\blacktriangle C}{\blacktriangle DI}$$
    8. The Marginal Propensity to Save (MPS) measures the change in savings resulting from a change in income. The MPS is the slope of the savings function.
$$MPS = \frac{\blacktriangle S}{\blacktriangle DI}$$
    9. Since disposable income is either consumed or saved:
       APC + APS = 1.0
       MPC + MPS = 1.0
  10. In addition to income, there are five nonincome determinants of consumption and savings which cause a change (shift) in consumption (new curve):
       a.    Wealth
       b.    Price level
       c.    Expectation
       d.    Consumer indebtedness
       e.    Taxation
  11. We can derive the average and marginal propensities from the consumption and savings schedules.
  12. Movement along the consumption (or savings) curve from one point to another, is called a change in <u>quantity</u> (amount) consumed (saved) due to a change in disposable income.

13. Shifts in consumption and saving curves move in opposite directions. Example: A decrease in consumption (consumption curve shifts to the left) will cause an increase in savings (savings curve shifts to the right); however the schedules are relatively stable.

14. Consumption and savings schedules are generally stable.

VI. Investment
  A. Definition - expenditures on new plant, capital equipment, machinery, etc.
  B. Determinants of net investment spending
     1. Expected rate of net profit = $\dfrac{\text{Net Revenue}}{\text{outlay cost}}$
     2. Real rate of interest is the price paid for the use of money adjusted for inflation
     3. Comparison of the expected rate of net profit and the real rate of interest must be made to determine if the firm will go ahead with the investment.
     4. Therefore, the lower the real rate of interest, the higher will be the level of Investment spending and vice versa.
  C. The Investment-Demand Curve
     1. Definition - shows the inverse relationship between the real rate of interest and the level of spending (investing) for capital goods. See Exhibit 10-3 below:

Exhibit 10-3  Investment - Demand Curve

**Investment - Demand Curve**

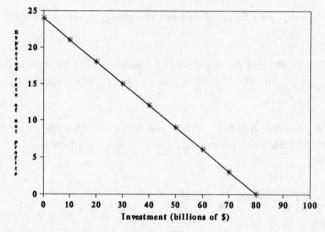

2. Movement along the Investment-Demand curve, from one point to another, is called a change in quantity (amount) of investment-demanded, due to a change in the interest rate.

3. In addition to the interest rate, there are five noninterest determinants of investment-demand which cause a change (shift) in the investment-demand (new curve):
   a. Acquisition, maintenance, and operating costs
   b. Business taxes
   c. Technological change
   d. Stock of capital goods on hand
   e. Expectations

4. Because these five noninterest determinants of investment-demand may change suddenly, investment spending tends to be unstable.

     D.  Investment Spending and Income
         1.  We will assume that business investment is projected for long-term hence, it is independent of income (autonomous).  However, in reality, business investment may be caused (induced) by changes in household and company incomes.
     E.  Instability of Investment
         1.  The investment schedule is unstable as compared to the consumption schedule.   The factors which explain the variability are:
             a.  Durability
             b.  Irregularity of innovation
             c.  Variability of profits
             d.  Variability of expectations
VII.Last Word:  The Share Economy -- Making Wages Flexible

## Key Terms

| | |
|---|---|
| aggregate demand (expenditures) | John Maynard Keynes |
| aggregate supply | nonincome determinants of C and S |
| closed economy | change in quantity (amount) consumed or saved |
| laissez-faire | change in consumption (savings) |
| classical school | expected rate of net profits |
| Say's Law | real rate of interest |
| Adam Smith | investment-demand schedule |
| full employment equilibrium | autonomous investment |
| price-wage flexibility | induced investment |
| Keynesian economics | noninterest determinants of investment |
| consumption schedule | market imperfections |
| consumption function | crowding out |
| savings schedule | change in quantity (amount) of |
| savings function | investment-demand |
| slope | change in investment-demand |
| break-even income level | fine-tune |
| dissavings | APC, APS, MPC, MPS |

## Real World Example

### KEYNES:  A DEFUNCT ECONOMIST AND HIS SLAVES

By Lindley H. Clark, Jr.

SAN FRANCISCO-Late last month 16 economists assembled here - not to praise John Maynard Keynes but to try to understand him a little better.  Lord Keynes has been dead for 40 years, but many of his ideas live exuberantly on.

No one would have been less surprised by this immortality than Lord Keynes himself.  It isn't merely that the man had a considerable ego.  It's also that he knew, or thought he knew, the way the world works.

In "The General Theory of Employment, Interest and Money," his major work he wrote:

"The ideas of economists and political philosophers, both when they are right and when they are wrong, are more powerful than is commonly understood.  Indeed the world is ruled by little else.

Practical men, who believe themselves to the quite exempt from any intellectual influences, are usually the slaves of some defunct economist."

None of the 16 economists here really considered himself a Keynes slave. Robert Lucas, a University of Chicago economist, once said that he knew of no economist under the age of 40 who even considered himself a Keynesian.

Yet everyone had to admit the man's lasting influence. Milton Friedman, after running down a list of Keynes' alleged errors, commented: "Now don't misunderstand me. Keynes was a great economist."

The immediate occasion for the meeting here was a book, "Keynes' Monetary Theory: A Different Interpretation," now being completed by Allan H. Meltzer of Carnegie-Mellon University. Mr. Meltzer is a monetarist, a firm believer in the virtues of the free market. Lord Keynes, by contrast, came to believe that the free market, if left to its own devices, would cause the economy to flounder along at a level well short of full employment. The 16 economists, whose views of Lord Keynes varied greatly, were invited here by the Cato Institute, a Washington-based think tank, and the Liberty Fund, an Indianapolis foundation interested in promoting economic education.

Mr. Meltzer focused mainly on Lord Keynes' views in the 1920s and 1930s, but that was enough of a chore. The man was famous for changing his mind, sometimes in the middle of a book. When he was chided by a friend for this habit, he looked the friend in the eye and said, "When I find I'm wrong, I change my mind. What do you do?"

Still, there were elements in Lord Keynes' work that didn't change. He was a businessman, a capitalist, a man who thought he could outsmart the stock market (and occasionally did). He believed that government should play a role in investment, but he rejected the sort of socialism that some of his later followers embraced.

As several economists here remarked, Lord Keynes was an aristocrat, an elitist. He wanted a government carefully chosen from Britain's best and brighter (among whom, of course, he included himself). This government would work with private companies to make sure that investment was large enough and wise enough to push the economy to full employment.

Mr. Meltzer noted that Lord Keynes in the 1920s believed the great economics evils "'are the fruits of risk, uncertainty and ignorance.'" These cause unemployment, disappointment of expectations, and reduce economic efficiency.

"Keynes gives three examples of collective action to reduce risk, uncertainty and ignorance. First is a central institution to control credit and to collect and make public all business facts which it is useful to know.' Second is the regulation of saving and investment... 'I do not think these matters should be left entirely to the chances of private judgment and private profits, as they are now.'" He also wanted population control, but he was never too clear about ho meant to achieve it.

His other ideas, however, were thoroughly mapped out. He continued to believe in controls on investment, foreign lending and money, and in many cases his ideas were implemented by governments.

Lord Keynes always stressed the importance of investment and capital accumulation. Even when the depression deepened in the 1930s, he thought government's role was to stimulate investment, not consumption. Instability and uncertainty in the economy, Mr. Meltzer writes, increased risk and raised the required real (inflation-adjusted) returns on investment. A primary source of instability, in the Keynesian view, was price fluctuations.

How to reduce price fluctuations? Lord Keynes didn't regard the gold standard as ideal, but neither was he in favor of complete discretion for policy makers. He wanted rules that would prevent both inflation and deflation. His stress on the importance of price stability continued throughout his life.

Some people won't thank him for it, but more than anyone else Lord Keynes created macroeconomics, the branch of economics that deals with all of the forces at work in an economy. His interest was international, with a special concentration on the U.S. Some of his prescriptions were and still are controversial, but at least he saw the patient whole.

It was difficult, though. He continually pressed governments to improve the quantity and quality of their economic statistics. Economics numbers even now aren't as good as they should be, and in the 1920s and 1930s they were far worse. At present, economists and politicians complain about the quality of our gross national product statistics. In the 1920s and 1930s, such statistics didn't exist.

Even with inadequate statistics, Lord Keynes sometimes analyzed developments much better than did his contemporaries. In the late-1920s, for instance, he predicted that the boom in stock prices in the U.S. would be followed by deflation. He wrote to Fed officials, arguing that it was a mistake to interpret the stock-price as inflationary. He said the rise instead reflected an increase in the inflation-adjusted return on investment.

The Fed, because of its fear of inflation, was curbing member-bank borrowing. The reduction of bank borrowing, Lord Keynes wrote, "would mean that the demand deposits of the member banks would have to fall...to a figure which certainly would not finance the present income of the United States or anything like it."

All of this reconsideration of Lord Keynes left me with one overriding impression: He was the original fine-tuner. He did much to legitimize the notion that government should intervene in the economy whenever anything was felt to be going wrong. He believed that he would always know exactly what to do. Even if that were true, he never seemed to see that others, following his lead, would not always be so omniscient.

In that sense many economists still are Keynesians. The Bretton Woods agreement, designed by Lord Keynes, broke down, but a number of economists are eager to return to something like it. National planning, a Keynes' idea, still has quite a few supporters. And hardly anyone argues anymore for anything other than a reduction in the degree of intervention in the economy.

We may not be slaves but we're certainly still under the influence of that defunct economist.

# ECONOMIC SCHOOLS OF THOUGHT

## Classical School

### Introduction
1. Time period-mid 18th C. to the 1930's.
2. Lost credibility due to the Great Depression (10 yrs.).

### Foundation
3. Say's Law: supply creates its own demand.
4. Automatic tendency toward full-employment equilibrium.
- Invisble hand concept
- Self-interest concept
5. Emphasis on long-run adjustments in the market.
6. Aggregate Expenditure equals Aggregate Income (or output).
7. All savings are invested at full-employment because of interest rates, which are flexible.
8. Price-wage flexibility.
9. Real output remains stable while prices fluctuate to changing market conditions. (Classical view).
10. Government should be laissez-faire or else it will do more harm than good.

Adam Smith - The Wealth of Nations (1776); David Ricardo, Jean Baptiste Say

## Keynesian Economics

### Introduction
1. Time period - 1930's to the mid 1970's.
2. Lost credibility due to "stagflation".

### Foundation
3. Demand creates its own supply.
4. The economy could remain at less than a full-employment level indefinitely.
- Keynesian cross (AE = NP)
- Leakages-Injection approach
5. Emphasis on short-run adjustments or "fine-tuning", by the Government (fiscal policy).
6. Aggregate Expenditure may not equal full-employment and aggregate income.
7. Savers and investors have different goals, therefore, interest rates may fail to bring about equality.
8. Most wages and prices are not flexible. (Example: Unions and minimum-wage).
9. The price level remains stable while real output fluctuates to changing market conditions. (Keynesian view).
10. Government needed to adjust Aggregate Expenditure.

John Maynard Keynes -The General Theory of Employment, Interest and Money. (1936)

## Supply-side Economics

### Introduction
1. Time period - mid 1970's to the present.
2. Losing credibility due to high budget deficits.

### Foundation
3. Rebirth of classical economics -- policies to stimulate production.
4. Use of incentives:
- Cut personal income tax rates
- Cut corporate income tax rates
- Accelerated depreciation allowance
- Investment tax credits
- Incentives for saving
- Deregulation of industries and markets
5. Tight monetary control to curb inflation. Tax reduction to increase spending and output.
6. Advocate permanent low tax rates and low Government spending.
7. Increase productivity which will increase output.
8. Laffer Curve.
9. "Trickle-down" economics.
10. Government macroeconomics policies shape the business environment and sets the stage for growth in Aggregate Supply. Massive fiscal policy will dampen AS.

Arthur Laffer, Ronald Reagan (Reaganomics)

## PROBLEMS

1. Complete the following table.

| Disposable Income | C Consumption | S Savings | APC | APS | MPC | MPS |
|---|---|---|---|---|---|---|
| (1) | (2) | (3) | (4) | (5) | (6) | (7) |
| $3,000 | $3,400 | -400 | ___ | ___ | | |
| 4,000 | 4,200 | ___ | ___ | ___ | ___ | ___ |
| 5,000 | 5,000 | ___ | ___ | ___ | ___ | ___ |
| 6,000 | 5,800 | ___ | ___ | ___ | ___ | ___ |
| 7,000 | 6,600 | ___ | ___ | ___ | ___ | ___ |
| 8,000 | 7,400 | ___ | ___ | ___ | ___ | ___ |

Formulas:  DI      =   C + S

$$APC = \frac{C}{DI} \qquad MPC = \frac{\blacktriangle C}{\blacktriangle DI}$$

$$APS = \frac{S}{DI} \qquad MPS = \frac{\blacktriangle S}{\blacktriangle DI}$$

a. Graph the consumption and savings curves from the table above.

b. Label the break-even points on the graphs.

c. Draw a 45 degree reference line on the consumption graph.

d. Label and shade the area of dissavings on both graphs.

e. Label and shade the area of savings on both graphs.

f. What is the break-even level of income? _____

g. What is the slope of the consumption function? _____

h. What is the slope of the savings function? _____

PROBLEMS (continued)

2. Answer the following questions based upon the consumption and savings curves below:

A Family's  Consumption and Savings Curves

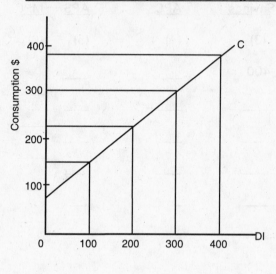

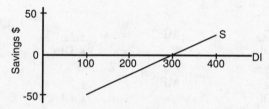

a. Draw a 45 degree reference line on the consumption graph.
b. Where is the break-even income level?_____
c. At what levels of disposable income does savings take place?_____
d. At what levels of disposable income does dissavings take place?_____
e. What is the amount of autonomous (independent) consumption?_____
f. Where does induced (caused) consumption begin? _____
g. At $400 of Disposable Income, what is APC? _____ APS? _____
h. What is the MPC when income goes from $100 to $200? _____
i. What is the MPS when income goes from $200 to $300? _____
j. What is the slope of the consumption curve when income goes from $300 to $400?_____
k. Shade and label the areas of savings and dissavings.
l. Label the break-even points.

3. Compare and contrast the Classical School, Keynesian Economics, and Supply-side Economics.

Self-Test

1. Which of the following is <u>not</u> a foundation of the Classical School?
   a.  demand creates its own supply
   b.  there is an automatic tendency toward full-employment equilibrium
   c.  all savings are invested at full-employment
   d.  prices and wages are flexible

2. Which of the following is <u>not</u> a foundation of Keynesian economics?
   a.  emphasis on short-run adjustments of "fine-tuning" by the government
   b.  savers and investors are brought together by the interest rate, which is flexible
   c.  the economy can remain at less than full-employment indefinitely
   d.  most wages and prices are not flexible

3. According to Keynesian theory, the aggregate supply curve is:
   a.  upward sloping, positive slope
   b.  downward sloping, negative slope
   c.  horizontal, zero slope
   d.  vertical, undefined slope

Exhibit 10-5
Consumption and Savings Curves

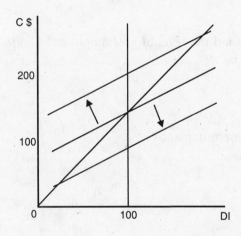 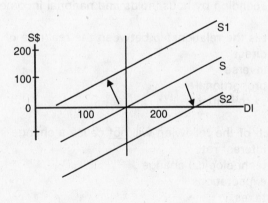

4. In Exhibit 10-5, when consumption shifts from C to C1, you would expect savings to:
   a.  shift from S to S1
   b.  shift from S to S2
   c.  savings would remain at S
   d.  movement along the S curve

5. In Exhibit 10-5, when savings shifts from S to S1, you would expect consumption to:
   a.  shift from C to C2
   b.  shift from C to C1
   c.  consumption would remain at C
   d.  movement along the consumption curve

6. In Exhibit 10-5, a change in the disposable income would cause consumption to:
   a.  shift from C to C1
   b.  shift from C to C2
   c.  move along the consumption curve
   d.  unable to determine

7. Which of the following would not cause a shifting of the consumption or savings curves?
   a.  wealth
   b.  price level
   c.  expectation
   d.  income

8. What are the two determinants of net investment spending?
   a.  consumption and investment
   b.  the real interest rate and the level of investment spending
   c.  the real interest rate and the level of savings
   d.  spending by households and national income

9. What is the relationship between the real rate of interest and the level of investment spending?
   a.  direct
   b.  inverse
   c.  proportional
   d.  exponential

10.Which of the following will not cause a change in investment-demand?
   a.  interest rate
   b.  technological change
   c.  expectations
   d.  taxes

Self-Test (continued)

Answer the next three questions based upon the following consumption schedule:

| DI | C | S | APC | APS | MPC | MPS |
|------|------|---|-----|-----|-----|-----|
| $100 | $140 | | | | | |
| 200 | 210 | | | | | |
| 300 | 300 | | | | | |
| 400 | 340 | | | | | |
| 500 | 400 | | | | | |

11. The marginal propensity to consumer when DI goes from $200 to $300 is?
    a.   .7
    b.   .9
    c.   .4
    d.   .1

12. At a disposable income level of $500,
    a.   savings equals $100
    b.   APC is .8
    c.   APS is .2
    d.   all of the above

13. The break-even income level is:
    a.   $400
    b.   $500
    c.   $300
    d.   unable to determine

14. Dissavings occurs when:
    a.   income exceeds consumption
    b.   savings exceeds consumption
    c.   savings exceeds income
    d.   consumption exceeds income

15. Which of the following equations is not correct?
    a.   MPC + MPS = 1.0
    b.   APC + APS = 1.0
    c.   1 - MPC = MPS
    d.   APC + MPC = 1.0

# CHAPTER 11    "Equilibrium Domestic Output in the Keynesian Model"

Chapter Orientation

Chapter 11 builds on what you have learned in Chapter 10. Using the Consumption (C), Savings (S), and Investment (I) schedules, we will build a model to determine the equilibrium levels of income, employment, and output for an economy. Two techniques are used to calculate the equilibrium level: The Keynesian Cross ("Aggregate Expenditures - Domestic Output") and the Leakages-Injections Approach ("Bathtub Theorem").

Initially we start off with a schedule of data (table) from the private sector; from this schedule we can then calculate the equilibrium level and graph the two techniques. Upon completion, we will see that either technique will us the same equilibrium. Then the foreign sector is brought into the model to show how exports and imports affect the equilibrium level of output, income, and employment. This equilibrium level will tell us where we currently are; the next chapter will focus on where we want to be (target level) and what vehicles are available to reach our target level.

Whenever changes in aggregate demand occur, there is a magnified increase or decrease in the economy (NI). This "snowball effect" is calculated by using the Simple Multiplier (M). Today, the complex multiplier is equal to approximately 2.

If you save money are you better off in the future? If everyone saves, will everyone be better off in the future? These questions, and their economic impact, will be addressed by the "Paradox of Thrift".

The difference between the "potential GDP" and the "actual GDP" is called the "GDP gap". There are two types of gaps: recessionary (too little spending) and inflationary (too much spending). Under Keynesian Economics, the government will want to "fine tune" the economy to try to close these gaps.

Lastly, we will compare the Keynesian model with a constant price level, to a model with varying prices. We will see that any price level increase will weaken the multiplier because part of the multiplier's effect is lost to higher prices (inflation), and only part is left to increase real income.

Learning Objectives

After studying this chapter in the text and completing the following exercises in this concepts book, you should be able to:

1. Locate the equilibrium output (GDP) level using two techniques, when given the necessary data.
2. Explain the tendency of employment, output, and incomes toward equilibrium.
3. Understand how the foreign sector affects the equilibrium.
4. Distinguish between planned investment and actual investment.
5. Explain why savings and actual investment are always equal.
6. Calculate the new equilibrium when C, S, or I have changed.
7. Calculate the simple multiplier when given the data.
8. Define the "Paradox of Thrift" and draw the graph.
9. Explain what is meant by the GDP gaps?
10. Define an "inflationary gap" and a "recessionary gap".
11. Locate the inflationary and recessionary gaps on a graph.

12. Explain the changes in aggregate demand (AD) on the price level and the equilibrium (GDP), in the three ranges along the aggregate supply (AS) curve.
13. Explain how changes in price effect the multiplier which in turn, effects national income (NI).

Chapter Highlights

I.  Determining the Equilibrium NI (=GDP) Level:
    A.  The Keynesian Cross (aggregate expenditure -- domestic output approach), where Aggregate Demand (=AE) = Aggregate Supply (=GDP).
        1.  Aggregate Demand in the private sector only is equal to consumption (C) by households at investment (I) by business. As a result, in equilibrium, planned savings equals planned investment. AD = C + I
        2.  Aggregate Demand is both the private _and_ public sectors is equal to:
            (C)    consumption by households
          + (I)    investment by business
          + (G)    government spending
          + (Xn) net exports (exports - imports)

            AD =      C + I + G + (Xn)
        3.  Aggregate Supply is a 45 degree reference line, where every dollar of output generates a dollar of income.
        4.  The intersection of AD and AS will determine the equilibrium level of output, employment, and income.

                      Keynesian Cross
        (Aggregate Expenditures - Domestic Output Approach)

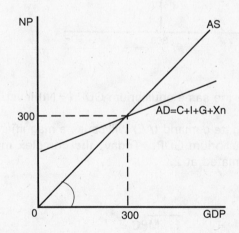

        5.  When AD is greater than, or less than AS, there will be a tendency for output, employment, and income to increase or decrease (business reaction to an increase (or decrease) in spending.
                        AD > AS        ↑0, E, $
                        AD < AS        ↓0, E, $
    B.  The Leakages-Injections Approach (The Bathtub Theorem) where total leakages equal planned

75

injections.

1. Total leakages in the economy are savings (S), taxes (T), and imports (M), which represent withdrawals from the economy.
2. Planned injections in the economy are investment (I), government spending (G), and exports (X), which represent a supplement to the economy.
3. S + T + M = I + G + X
4. The intersection of total leakages and planned injections will determine the equilibrium level of output, employment, and income.
5. Planned savings always equals actual investment because actual investment includes both planned and unplanned investment.

### Leakages-Injections Approach
### The Bathtub Theorem

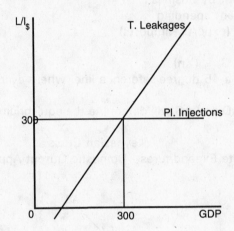

C. Either technique will give you the same equilibrium GDP ( =NI) level.
II. The Simple Multiplier Effect (M)
   A. Definition - a change in aggregate demand (AE) will cause a magnified change in the economy which in turn effects the equilibrium GDP. Today, the complex multiplier, which takes all leakages into account, is estimated at 2.
   B. Techniques to calculate (M)
      1. Numerical table
      2. Graph
      3. Formula:   $M = \dfrac{1}{MPS} = \dfrac{1}{1 - MPC}$
   C. The multiplier is significant because it implies a small change in leakages or injections will trigger a much larger change in the economy ("snowball effect").
III. The Paradox of Thrift
   A. Definition - the apparent contradiction that as households try to save more, they may find that they are only savings the same amount out of a smaller total income (autonomous investment) or even saving less than they were originally (induced investment).
   B. The "fallacy of composition" is illustrated by the "Paradox of Thrift". If I save, I am better off

76

in the future, therefore, If everyone saves, everyone is better off in the future. (But are they?) Obviously, if everyone is busy saving, they are not, spending, hence AD falls. When AD falls below AS, the tendency in the market is to start slowing down production, laying off workers, etc. As a result, the tendency is to decrease O, E, and $ and the new GDP equilibrium level is lower.

C. Explanation - a decrease in consumption causes income to fall by the amount of the decrease in consumption times the multiplier. A new GDP equilibrium level will be reached when income has fallen to a level where savings is equal to investment.

Inflationary and Recessionary Gaps

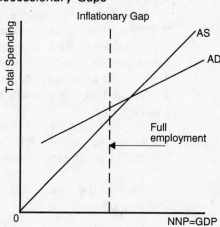

IV.    The GDP Gaps:
   A.  Definition - the difference between
       "potential GDP" and "Actual GDP" at
       a full employment GDP.
   B.  Types:
       1.  Recessionary gap - falls short
           (too little spending)
       2.  Inflationary gap - exceeds
           (too much spending)

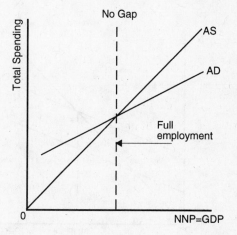

V. International Trade and Equilibrium Output
   A.  Net Exports and Aggregate Expenditures
       1.  Net Exports (Xn) = X - M
   B.  The Net Export Schedule
       1.  When exports are greater
           than imports, the economy
           experiences a trade surplus
           (or a positive net exports figure).
       2.  When Imports are greater than
           exports, the economy experiences
           a trade deficit, (or a negative
           net exports figure).
   C.  Net Exports and Equilibrium GDP
       1.  Positive Net Exports, elevate
           the aggregate expenditure schedule
           and increase domestic GDP
           ("expansionary effect").

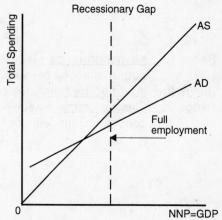

77

      2.  Negative Net Exports, decrease the aggregate expenditures schedule and reduce domestic GDP ("contractionary effect").

    D.  International Economic Linkages

      1.  Policies abroad affect our domestic GDP.

        a.  Prosperity of our trading partners influences their ability to buy more imports.

        b.  High tariffs on American goods reduces our exports.

        c.  Value of the dollar relative to other currencies affects trade.

VI.Reconciling the Keynesian Expenditures -- Output Model and the AD - AS Model

    A.  Aggregate Supply (AS)

      1.  Viewed as a 45 degree reference line (comparing production and income)

      2.  Viewed as a curve with three ranges (comparing how the Keynesian and Classical economists view the relationship between price and production)

    B.  Aggregate Demand (AD = AE)

      1.  Viewed as an upward sloping curve (comparing production and income)

      2.  Viewed as a downward sloping curve (when comparing price and production)

    C.  Equilibrium

      1.  The intersection of AS and AD

      2.  When AD shifts (for reasons other than price) the two models will show the same multiplied change in real GDP.  (See below).

Reconciling the two models:  Shifts in AD (=AE) results in the same equilibrium GDP level (holding price constant).

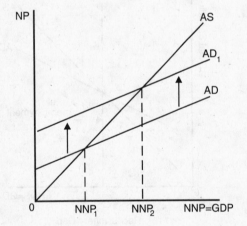

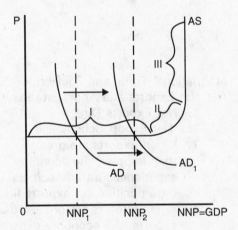

Range I:    Keynesian range - (equilibrium at less than full employment) Price level remains constant; output changes because there are unemployed resources, prices do not have to change.

Range II:   Intermediate range   Price level and output change.

Range III   Classical range - (equilibrium at full employment) Price level changes; output remains constant. Since we are fully utilizing our resources, only price will change with AD.

VII. Different-Sized Multipliers
   A.   Effect -- the larger the multiplier, the greater the impact on the economy.
   B.   Size -- is effected by changes in the price level.
        1.   Price level increases weaken the multiplier because part of the effect is lost to inflation and only part is left to increase real income.
VIII. Last Word: Squaring The Economic Circle

## Key Terms

| | |
|---|---|
| Keynesian Cross | paradox of thrift |
| aggregate expenditure | potential GDP |
| aggregate output | actual GDP |
| "bathtub Theorem" | inflationary gap |
| leakages | recessionary gap |
| injections | snowball effect |
| planned investment | complex multiplier |
| actual investment | 45 degree line |
| equilibrium GDP | private sector |
| unplanned investment | public sector |
| multiplier effect | GDP gap |
| autonomous investment | Keynesian range |
| induced investment | Intermediate range |
| simple multiplier | Classical range |
| net exports | |

## Real World Example

### Pemberton Wants Help Coping with Fort Dix Cutbacks

#### By Kirk Moore

PEMBERTON TOWNSHIP - School and municipal officials are demanding federal help to ease the blow of planned cutbacks at Fort Dix, where the possibility of major Army transfers has chilled the business climate and threatens to leave homeowners holding the bag for a $20 million school expansion.

An environmental impact study by the Army focuses on the economic effect of closing down training programs at Fort Dix, now the Army's second biggest training center. At a public hearing last night, township Mayor Clarence "Dave" Davis told Army officials his community is already suffering.

"You do not have to wait for a report to see what's happening," Davis said. "People have refused to move into Pemberton. People are moving out."

But Rep. H. James Saxton, R-N.J., warned against overstating the economic effects of present plans, saying the Army is likely to find a new mission for the post where, he said over $200 million has been spent on renovations in the past decade.

"Perception plays a very important part in what's happening here in Pemberton," Saxton said at the hearing in the township high school. Since the cutbacks were first proposed in December 1988, there has been "confusion, chaos and genuine fear" among the base's civilian work force and neighbors, he said.

The school system is being expanded with a $20 million high school addition. But about 42 percent of the district's children come from families dependent on the base, and school officials said they stand to lose state and federal aid if the student population shrinks.

A special federal commission that audited military bases called for transferring basic and advanced training programs from Fort Dix to installations in South Carolina, Kentucky, Virginia and Missouri.

Such "realignment" would disperse the bunks for an average 6,700 soldiers who go through training cycles at Fort Dix (up to 35,000 recruits are trained there each year). Also proposed for transfer is an anti-aircraft defense school that trains Air Force personnel.

The plan would take away 2,590 full-time, permanent military positions, eliminating 25 percent of the positions, said Richard Muller, project manager for the Army Corps of Engineers impact study.

Civilian employment, 1,922 staff as of last Jan. 1, would be reduced by 1,250 jobs, half transferred with the Army programs and the other half eliminated totally, Muller said.

About 200 buildings, with 3 million square feet of space, would be "mothballed" for possible future use, he said. Pentagon planners say Fort Dix will remain important for Army Reserve training and could be built up again to support American forces during an overseas crisis.

The impact study forecasts "adverse socio-economic effects" on nearby communities when the post and its $349 million annual budget are scaled back.

"Over the long run, however, the regional economy is expected to recover and resume its growth," Muller said.

The new school addition will cost local taxpayers $2 million a year for 20 years, and if it stands half-empty because of Army transfers, the federal government should pay, said Board of Education member Washington Georgia.

Pemberton residents just yesterday learned their new $44 million school budget will cost an average annual property tax increase of more than $400, Mayor Davis said outside the meeting.

To ease that burden, Davis and other officials said they want school aid, the use of a modern trash incinerator at the base, and an invitation to private industry to lease mothballed Fort Dix buildings to help create new jobs.

"We can do things ourselves," Davis said. "But we need something to help us through this transition."

Department of Defense officials have said they will try to use Fort Dix housing for dependent families associated with other military bases in the region, to "mitigate" the effect of Pemberton schools, Saxton said.

## Problems

### Determining the Equilibrium GDP in the Private Sector

#### TABLE 11-1 (billions of dollars)

| (1) Employment (millions) | (2) AS and GDP=NI =DI | (3) Planned C | (4) Planned S | (5) Planned I | (6) AD and AE | (7) Unplanned Inventory Changes | (8) Direction of NI |
|---|---|---|---|---|---|---|---|
| 5 | 1,000 | 1,100 | ___ | 100 | ___ | ___ | ___ |
| 10 | 1,200 | 1,250 | ___ | 100 | ___ | ___ | ___ |
| 15 | 1,400 | 1,350 | ___ | 100 | ___ | ___ | ___ |
| 20 | 1,600 | 1,500 | ___ | 100 | ___ | ___ | ___ |
| 25 | 1,800 | 1,650 | ___ | 100 | ___ | ___ | ___ |
| 30 | 2,000 | 1,800 | ___ | 100 | ___ | ___ | ___ |
| 35 | 2,200 | 1,900 | ___ | 100 | ___ | ___ | ___ |

1a. Fill in Table 11-1 above (hint: column 8 should read, "increase", "decrease", or "equilibrium".

b. What is the equilibrium GDP level?

c. At the equilibrium GDP level, what is the relationship between Planned Savings and Planned Investment?

d. What is the equilibrium employment level?

e. Graph the Planned Consumption Curve, the Aggregate Expenditure Curve, and a 45 degree reference line, all on one graph.

f. Label the equilibrium point (E) on the graph in part "e" (above).

2. Fill in the tables given below, find the simpler multiplier from the data.

| MPC | M |
|---|---|
| .9 | ___ |
| .8 | ___ |
| .75 | ___ |
| .5 | ___ |
| .6 | ___ |
| .95 | ___ |

| MPS | M |
|---|---|
| .2 | ___ |
| .5 | ___ |
| .4 | ___ |
| .1 | ___ |
| .05 | ___ |

Formulas:

$$M = \frac{1}{MPS} = \frac{1}{1 - MPC}$$

## PROBLEMS

### 3. Technique #1:  Keynesian Cross
a. Fill in the table below.
b. Graph AS and AD and label equilibrium NI (on graph paper - top half).

| (1)<br>GDP<br>(AS) = NI | (2)<br>C | (3)<br>I | (4)<br>G | (5)<br>(Xn) | (6)<br>AD ( = AE) |
|---|---|---|---|---|---|
| 100 | 140 | 20 | 10 | 10 | _____ |
| 200 | 220 | | | | _____ |
| 300 | 300 | | | | _____ |
| 400 | 380 | | | | _____ |
| 500 | 460 | | | | _____ |
| 600 | 540 | | | | _____ |
| 700 | 620 | | | | _____ |
| 800 | 700 | | | | _____ |
| 900 | 780 | | | | _____ |

AD = C + I + G + (Xn)

### 4. Technique #2:  Leakages - Injections Approach
a. Fill in the table below.
b. Graph total leakages and planned injections (bottom half).
c. Label the equilibrium NI level.
d. Compare the equilibrium NI with technique #1.

| (1)<br>NI | (2)<br>DI | (3)<br>C | (4)<br>S | (5)<br>T | (6)<br>(M) | (7)<br>Total<br>Leakages | (8)<br>I | (9)<br>G | (10)<br>X | (11)<br>Planned<br>Injections |
|---|---|---|---|---|---|---|---|---|---|---|
| 100 | ____ | 140 | ____ | 0 | 5 | _____ | 20 | 10 | 15 | _____ |
| 200 | ____ | 220 | ____ | | | _____ | | | | _____ |
| 300 | ____ | 300 | ____ | | | _____ | | | | _____ |
| 400 | ____ | 380 | ____ | | | _____ | | | | _____ |
| 500 | ____ | 460 | ____ | | | _____ | | | | _____ |
| 600 | ____ | 540 | ____ | | | _____ | | | | _____ |
| 700 | ____ | 620 | ____ | | | _____ | | | | _____ |
| 800 | ____ | 700 | ____ | | | _____ | | | | _____ |
| 900 | ____ | 780 | ____ | | | _____ | | | | _____ |

Formulas:

Total Leakages = S + T + M       NI - T = DI
Planned Injections = I + G + X    DI = C + S

# CHAPTER 11     "Equilibrium Domestic Output in the Keynesian Model"

## REVIEW PROBLEMS

1a. Fill in the table below and graph the consumption and savings curves separately.
b. Determine the break-even point (label on the graph).

| DI | C | S | APC | APS | MPC | MPS |
|----|----|----|----|----|----|----|
| 100 | 120 | ____ | ____ | ____ | | |
| 120 | 130 | ____ | ____ | ____ | ____ | ____ |
| 140 | 140 | ____ | ____ | ____ | ____ | ____ |
| 160 | 150 | ____ | ____ | ____ | ____ | ____ |
| 180 | 160 | ____ | ____ | ____ | ____ | ____ |

2. Determine the Equilibrium NI Level (2 techniques)
   Technique #1 -- Keynesian Cross

| (AS) = NI | C | I | G | (Xn) | AD |
|----|----|----|----|----|----|
| 1800 | 1400 | 200 | 200 | 100 | ____ |
| 2000 | 1550 | | | | ____ |
| 2200 | 1700 | | | | ____ |
| 2400 | 1850 | | | | ____ |
| 2600 | 2000 | | | | ____ |

Technique #2 -- Leakages -Injections Approach

| NI | DI | C | S | T | (M) | Total Leakages | I | G | X | Planned Injections |
|----|----|----|----|----|----|----|----|----|----|----|
| 1800 | ____ | 1400 | ____ | 200 | 25 | ____ | 200 | 200 | 125 | ____ |
| 2000 | ____ | 1550 | ____ | | | ____ | | | | ____ |
| 2200 | ____ | 1700 | ____ | | | ____ | | | | ____ |
| 2400 | ____ | 1850 | ____ | | | ____ | | | | ____ |
| 2600 | ____ | 2000 | ____ | | | ____ | | | | ____ |

a. Fill in the tables above.
b. Determine the Equilibrium NI level using both techniques.
c. Prepare two graphs--one for each technique (AS = AD and Total Leakages = Planned Injections).
d. Compare the equilibrium NI using the two techniques.

Formulas:
$$Xn = X - M$$
$$AD = C + I + G + (Xn)$$
AS = 45 degree reference line
$$DI = NI - T$$

Total Leakages = S + T + M
Planned Injections = I + G + X
DI = C + S

<u>Self-Test</u>
1. According to Keynes, Investment and Saving are:
   a. the same thing
   b. done by different people for different reasons
   c. both done primarily by households
   d. both done primarily by the government
2. Which of the following is <u>not</u> a leakage?
   a. imports
   b. government spending
   c. savings
   d. taxes
3. If MPC is 1/5, and investment spending increases by $4 billion, the level of GDP (=NI) will increase by:
   a. $5 billion
   b. $8 billion
   c. $20 billion
   d. $40 billion
4. Which of the following is <u>not</u> an injection?
   a. exports
   b. government spending
   c. investment
   d. taxes
5. The multiplier effect tends to:
   a. smooth out the peaks and troughs of the business cycle.
   b. promotes price stability.
   c. magnifies small changes in spending into much larger changes in output, employment, and income.
   d. reduce MPS.
6. For an economy without a public sector, when savings exceeds investment (S > I):
   a. actual income is less than equilibrium income
   b. actual income is greater than equilibrium income
   c. income will decrease
   d. both b and c
7. Households propensity to save is influenced by their desire to:
   a. provide for retirement security
   b. meet unforeseen emergencies
   c. earn interest income
   d. all of the above
8. If MPC is 80%, a one dollar change in income changes consumption by:
   a. 80¢
   b. 25¢
   c. 50¢
   d. $1.00

Self-Test (continued)

9. If income rises from $650 to $800 billion, and as a result consumption rises from $500 billion to $635 billion, the MPC is:
   a.   .35                                    c.      .90
   b.   .75                                    d.      .10
10. If MPC is .6, the simple multiplier is:
   a.   1.67
   b.   .06
   c.   .4
   d.   2.5
11. If the full employment-noninflationary GDP is $400 billion, and equilibrium occurs to the right of that point there exists:
   a.   a recessionary gap
   b.   an inflationary gap
   c.   the economy is now at the new full employment-noninflationary level
   d.   a deflationary gap
12. Planned Savings:
   a.   always equals actual investment
   b.   always equals potential investment
   c.   always equals investment
   d.   is an injection into the economy
13. The Keynesian Cross technique for determining the equilibrium GDP or NI level is also called the:
   a.   Bathtub Theorem
   b.   Aggregate expenditure - domestic output approach
   c.   Leakages-Injections approach
   d.   Paradox of Thrift
14. The private sector consists of:
   a.   households
   b.   households and business
   c.   households, business, and the government
   d.   the government
15. In the Keynesian Cross model, price and output
   a.   can vary
   b.   are constant
   c.   do not influence aggregate demand
   d.   price is constant and output can vary
16. Price level increases:
   a.   strengthen the multiplier
   b.   weaken the multiplier
   c.   have no effect on the multiplier
   d.   cause deflationary pressures

Self-Test (continued)

17. As households attempt to save more at each level of GDP (= NI), they may find that they tried to save more, but ended by saving less!  This is known as:
  a.   Keynes Law
  b.   Say's Law
  c.   The Paradox of Thrift
  d.   the complex multiplier

Exhibit 11-1

| Disposable Income<br>GDP = NI = DI | Consumption |
|------------------------------------|-------------|
| $400                               | $460        |
| 500                                | 530         |
| 600                                | 600         |
| 700                                | 670         |
| 800                                | 740         |

18. In Exhibit 11-1, the simple multiplier is approximately:
  a.   1
  b.   3.3
  c.   5.2
  d.   6

19. In Exhibit 11-1, an increase of investment of $2 billion will cause GDP (= NI) to increase by approximately:
  a.   $2 billion
  b.   $6.6 billion
  c.   $12 billion
  d.   $14 billion

20. If an economy saves 20% of an increase in income, then an increase in investment of $5 billion will cause GDP (= NI) to increase by approximately:
  a.   $5 billion
  b.   $10 billion
  c.   $25 billion
  d.   $50 billion

# CHAPTER 12          "Fiscal Policy"

## Chapter Orientation

Chapter 12 analyzes the role of government (the public sector) in our equilibrium national output, and national income model.

Remember that according to Keynesian Economics, the government's role is to "fine-tune" the economy. As problems in employment, price levels, etc. arise the government should be there to "prime the pump" and therefore, stimulate the economy through its ability to spend (G) and/or tax (T). The government spending and taxing greatly influences aggregate expenditures, income, and employment -- by a magnified amount (the multiplier). Government purchases of goods and services is included in aggregate demand; and changes in taxes either increases or decreases disposable income, which influences consumption and savings.

Discretionary fiscal policy requires that Congress, use its discretion or good judgment, to vote on appropriate changes in government spending and taxing. (Example: the tax reform of 1986). Nondiscretionary or "built-in stabilizers are already in place in our system and are automatically triggered when appropriate -- no action on the part of Congress is necessary.

There are many concerns and problems in using fiscal policy: timing and political problems, government debt raising the interest rates and "crowding out" the private sector, and lastly, the government may have only small changes in output and employment at the expense of inflation.

The Supply-side economists (supply-siders) advocate that a reduction in taxes will not only increase aggregate demand, but will also expand aggregate supply (which the Keynesians do not consider).

## Learning Objectives

After reading this chapter in the text, and completing the following exercises in this concepts book, you should be able to:
1. List and explain the legislative changes, following the Great Depression, that resulted from Keynesian employment theory.
2. Define fiscal policy.
3. Discuss "Discretionary Fiscal Policy" and the assumptions invoked.
4. Find the equilibrium real GDP in an economy in which the government purchases goods and services and imposes taxes when given the necessary data.
5. Draw the new aggregate expenditures curve (AE) which will now include the government.
6. Show the proof of the balanced budget multiplier.
7. Explain the courses of action for the government to follow during expansionary fiscal policy and fiscal policy.
8. List the ways the government can finance a debt and distribute surplus.
9. Describe how automatic (or built-in) stabilizers reduce pressures in the economy.
10. Discuss the limitations of nondiscretionary fiscal policy.
11. Distinguish between a cyclical deficit and structural deficit.
12. Define the "crowding out effect" and its impact on real output and employment including graphically.
13. Discuss how Keynesian Economists look solely on the demand-side and that Supply-side Economists argue that Keynesian fiscal policy impacts on aggregate supply.

# CHAPTER 12 "Fiscal Policy"

## Chapter Highlights

I. Introduction: Keynesians vs. Supply-siders
   A. Keynesians
      1. The government should fine-tune the economy using fiscal tools (government spending and taxing).
      2. Government should "prime the pump" to stimulate employment, savings, and investment.
   B. Supply-siders
      1. Low tax rates and low government spending to stimulate employment, savings, and investment.
      2. Government should not compete with the private sector (crowding out).

II. Legislative Fiscal Actions
   A. Introduction: After the Great Depression, Keynesian economics was gaining widespread acceptance. As a result, a stronger role for Government was emerging. Keynesian employment theory played a major role in influencing legislative action.
   B. Employment Act of 1946
      1. Definition - passed as a result of economic conditions in the United States after World War II. The act authorizes the federal government to favorably influences aggregate economic performance. The goal of high employment is specified and the goal of price stability is implied.
         a. The act created a Council of Economic Advisors (CEA) to assist and advise the President on matters relating to economic policy making.
         b. The act created a Joint Economic Committee (JEC) of the Congress, which investigates economic problems of national interest.

III. Discretionary Fiscal Policy
   A. Definition - requires that Congress use its discretion or good judgment to vote on appropriate changes in government spending and taxing.
   B. Six assumptions are made to simplify explanation of the effects, but will be examined when we discuss the shortcomings of fiscal policy in the real world.
   C. Adding the government sector to our model will shift the aggregate expenditures curve upward (increase) or downward (decrease) which in turn will have a magnified (multiplied) effect on GDP.
   D. Taxation influences consumption in the Keynesian Cross (aggregate expenditure - domestic output approach) which will have a magnified effect on GDP. Using the Leakages-Injections approach or (bathtub theorem) are we find that taxes influence DI, which in turn effects saving (a leakage), as well as taxes (which is also a leakage). Either technique will give you the same equilibrium GDP level.
   E. Multipliers:
      1. <u>Government purchases or investment</u>, use the simple multiplier (M):
$$M = \frac{1}{MPS} = \frac{1}{1 - MPC}$$
      2. <u>Taxes only</u>, use the tax multiplier (Mt) $= \dfrac{MPC}{MPS} = M - 1$
      3. <u>Government purchases and taxes</u> (by the same amount, in the same direction), use the balanced budget multiplier (BBM) = 1

  F.   Fiscal policy over the cycle
       1.  Expansionary fiscal policy -- used during a recession:
           a.  Increased government spending
           b.  Lower taxes
           c.  Combination of G and T
       2.  Contractionary fiscal policy -- used during a demand-pull inflation:
           a.  Decreased government spending
           b.  Higher taxes
           c.  Combination of G and T
IV.    Changes in Equilibrium GDP ( = NI) Level
  A.   Steps:
       1.  Determine the equilibrium GDP ( = NI) level (using the Keynesian Cross or the Leakages-Injections approach).  This will tell you <u>where the economy is</u> at the present time.
       2.  Determine the target level (check to see if you need to close an inflationary or recessionary gap).  This will tell you <u>where you want to be</u>.
       3.  Determine the method to be used to reach your target (and be sure to use the appropriate multiplier) this tells you <u>what policy will be implemented</u> to achieve the target.
V.  How the Government Finances Debt or Retires Surplus:
  A.   Financing the deficit:
       1.  Borrowing money in the money market
           a.  Competes with private sector for funds, which causes the interest rates to rise.
           b.  High interest rates will discourage investment (crowding-out)
       2.  Money creation is the issuing of new money by the government.
           a.  Avoids the crowding-out of private investment.  In an accounting sense, the Treasury "borrows" the money from the Federal Reserve, which actually creates new money.
           b.  The creation of new money is more expansionary than borrowing.
       3.  Taxation -- changes in the rate structure of taxes can affect both government revenues and the level of economic activity.
       4.  Sale of existing assets -- sale of government assets, such as land ,is another way to raise revenues.
       5.  Regulation or confiscation channels the allocation of resources (eminent domain).
  B.   Retiring the surplus
       1.  Apply surplus to the national debt (over $4 trillion today).
           a.     Transfer of surplus tax revenues back into the money market, causing interest rates to fall.
           b.     Lower interest rates stimulate investment.
       2.  Impounding the surplus funds --  the government is withholding purchasing power from the economy by keeping the surplus funds idle.
           a.     Idle funds will not cause inflationary pressures.
           b.     Impounding a budget surplus is more than using the surplus to reduce the national debt.
VI.Nondiscretionary Fiscal Policy: Built-in Stabilizers
  A.   Definition -- changes are automatically triggered in the economy without legislative action.
  B.   Examples of built-in stabilizers
       1.  Tax receipts
       2.  Unemployment benefits
       3.  Corporate dividend policy

89

   4. Welfare payments

   5. Subsidies to farmers

  C. Effects of fiscal stabilizers:

   1. Increases the deficit (or reduces surplus) during a recession.

   2. Increases surplus (or reduces the deficit) during inflation.

  D. Limitations of built-in stabilizers

   1. Reduces, but cannot eliminate cyclical fluctuations.

   2. Creates a "fiscal drag" problem (tendency of a high-employment economy to be held back from its full growth potential because of incurring budgetary surpluses which trigger a contractionary impact.

   3. Requires that the full employment budget be utilized to determine the federal budget's surplus or deficit throughout the year, as opposed to the actual budget surplus or deficit.

  E. Full Employment Budget

   1. Definition

   2. Structural deficit vs. cyclical deficit

VII.Applications of Fiscal Policy

  A. Timing problems:

   1. Recognition lag -- the time it takes to identify a cyclical turning point.

   2. Administrative lag -- the time from when a need is recognized and the time of action by Congress.

   3. Operation lag -- the time it takes for the action to effect output, employment, income, or prices.

  B. Political problems:

   1. Other goals -- full employment is not the single goal of government.

   2. Expansionary bias -- it is politically popular to spend (budget deficits) rather than cut or raise taxes (budget surplus).

   3. Public choice problems:  political business cycles -- legislators seeking reelection will often adopt policies designed to achieve favorable short-term results regardless of what the unfavorable long-term consequences will be (James McGill Buchanan won the 1986 Nobel Memorial Prize in Economic Science, for his contributions to the theory of economics and political decision-making).

  C. Restrictive effects: crowding-out

   1. Crowding-out can occur when the federal government pursues expansionary fiscal policy and borrows heavily to finance the debt.  This causes interest rates to rise and impacts upon investment spending.  As a result, the negative multipliers will reduce the positive multipliers arising from fiscal policy.

   2. The crowding-out effect may not be as large as many economists perceive.  The money supply may be increased which would offset any increases in the interest rate (the crowding-out effect would be zero).

  D. Offsetting Saving

   1. Some prominent economists believe people save more due to expected tax increases due to the deficit.

  E. Fiscal Policy Open Economy

   1. Aggregate Demand Shocks (from abroad)

   2. Net Export Effect

F.   Aggregate Supply and Inflation
1.   When a realistic aggregate supply (AS) curve is imposed, and the economy is close to full employment, a portion of the impact of fiscal policy will be reflected in price level increases (inflation) rather than increases in GDP.
2.   An expansionary fiscal policy which lowers taxes (according to the Supply-side economists) will increase aggregate supply which in turn will expand income, employment, and output.

VIII. Last Word:  The Leading Indicators

## Key Terms

| | |
|---|---|
| Keynesian economics | target level |
| Supply-side economics | financing the deficit |
| Employment Act of 1946 | returning the surplus |
| Council of Economic Advisors (CEA) | impounding |
| Joint Economic Committee (JEC) | nondiscretionary fiscal policy |
| Humphrey-Hawkins Act of 1978 | built-in stabilizers |
| discretionary fiscal policy | fiscal drag |
| lump sum tax | actual budget |
| Keynesian Cross | full-employment budget |
| Leakages-Injections approach | recognition lag |
| simple multiplier (M) | administrative lag |
| tax multiplier (Mt) | operational lag |
| balanced-budget multiplier (BBM) | public choice problems |
| expansionary fiscal policy | political business cycle |
| contractionary fiscal policy | James McGill Buchanan |
| crowding-out | aggregate supply effects |
| structural deficit | cyclical deficit |
| net export effect | |

## Real World Example

### The Tax and Revenue Equation

#### By W. Kurt Hauser

"Answer: 19.5%"
Question:  What percentage of Gross Domestic Product (GDP) is collected in taxes, regardless of tax rates?

The historical record is quite simple, if surprising.  No matter what the tax rates have been, in postwar America, tax revenues have remained at about 19.5% of GDP.

Over the past 44 years there have been 25 substantive changes in federal tax codes, with the top marginal personal income tax rate ranging as high as 92% and as low as 28%.  During the period illustrated on the chart, the quarterly data of federal receipts as a percentage of GDP have temporarily strayed as high as 21.5% and as low as 16.9%.  On an annual basis, revenues have been as high as 21.1% (1981) of GDP and as low as 17.9% (1964 and 1965).  Variations around the mean of 19.5% have occurred when there were no changes in the tax code, as well as during periods of change.

Raising taxes encourages taxpayers to shift, hide and under-report income.  The creative rich will avoid paying higher taxes while the less creative rich will pay more taxes, one offsetting the other. Tax shelters flourish during periods of high taxation.  Higher taxes reduce the incentives to work, produce, invest, save, thereby dampening overall economic activity and job creation.  Higher taxes reduce demand.

There is not economic theory, be it classical, neoclassical, Keynesian, supply-side, or Marxist, that promotes higher taxes as a stimulus to economic activity.  Indeed, both the Keynesian and supply-side models agree that lowering taxes stimulates economic activity, while raising taxes hampers economic activity.  Thus, under a tax increase, revenues will rise less than the forecast, while GDP will also advance less than the forecast - but the percentage collected will be the same.

Conversely, lower taxes causes taxpayers to report more and hide less of current income.  Lower tax rates also act as a stimulus to economic activity by increasing incentives and demand.  Thus under a tax reduction, revenues will rise to a greater degree than would otherwise be the case.

If the bogeyman is the deficit, then its cause has to be addressed.  While taxes as a percentage of GDP have narrowly fluctuated around the average of 19.5% over the past four decades, federal spending as a percentage of GDP has risen from 19% in the early 1960s to a range of 22% to 25% over the past 10 years.  The deficit is the result not of a shortfall of revenues but of an excess of spending.  Therefore, if reducing the deficit, or even balancing the budget, is the principal policy goal, it can be achieved only through spending reductions.

Legislators have initiated the debate on President Clinton's budget proposals, including an increase in the top marginal personal tax rate to 36% from 31%, a 10% surtax on income above $250,000, an increase in the alternative minimum tax to 28% from 24%, an increase in inheritance taxes to 55% from 50%, an increase in employee and employer Medical taxes (called a spending reduction), an increase in the corporate tax rate from 34% to 36% , and an increase in energy taxes.

Both the administration and Congress should review their history texts.  Changes in the rate of taxation do not alter revenues relative to GDP.  Lower taxes, however, do provide a greater stimulus to economic activity and job formation than higher taxes.  Improved economic activity raises GDP and total employment.  More employment means more tax receipts and an increase in absolute revenues to the government.  19.5% of a larger GDP is preferable to 19.5% of a smaller GDP."

## PROBLEMS

Fiscal Policy to Action
TABLE 12-1

| (1)<br>GDP = AS<br>(=NI) | (2)<br>Employ-<br>ment | (3)<br>C | (4)<br>I | (5)<br>G | (6)<br>(Xn) | (7)<br>AD (=AE) |
|---|---|---|---|---|---|---|
| 800 | 100 | 625 | 100 | 125 | 50 | _____ |
| 900 | 200 | 700 | 100 | 125 | 50 | _____ |
| 1000 | 300 | 775 | 100 | 125 | 50 | _____ |
| 1100 | 400 | 850 | 100 | 125 | 50 | _____ |
| 1200 | 500 | 925 | 100 | 125 | 50 | _____ |
| 1300 | 600 | 1000 | 100 | 125 | 50 | _____ |
| 1400 | 700 | 1075 | 100 | 125 | 50 | _____ |

1a.    Fill in the aggregate demand (AD) column.
b.     Graph AS and AD on graph paper (top half).
c.     Determine the equilibrium GDP and label.

| (1)<br>GDP = AS<br>(=NI) | (2)<br>DI | (3)<br>C | (4)<br>S | (5)<br>T | (6)<br>M | (7)<br>Total<br>Leakages | (8)<br>I | (9)<br>G | (10)<br>X | (11)<br>Planned<br>Injections |
|---|---|---|---|---|---|---|---|---|---|---|
| 800 | ___ | 625 | ___ | 100 | 25 | _____ | 100 | 125 | 75 | _____ |
| 900 | ___ | 700 | ___ | 100 | 25 | _____ | 100 | 125 | 75 | _____ |
| 1000 | ___ | 775 | ___ | 100 | 25 | _____ | 100 | 125 | 75 | _____ |
| 1100 | ___ | 850 | ___ | 100 | 25 | _____ | 100 | 125 | 75 | _____ |
| 1200 | ___ | 925 | ___ | 100 | 25 | _____ | 100 | 125 | 75 | _____ |
| 1300 | ___ | 1000 | ___ | 100 | 25 | _____ | 100 | 125 | 75 | _____ |
| 1400 | ___ | 1075 | ___ | 100 | 25 | _____ | 100 | 125 | 75 | _____ |

2a.    Fill in the table above
b.     Graph Total Leakages and Planned Injections on graph paper (bottom half).
c.     Determine the equilibrium GDP and label.
d.     Compare the equilibrium (=NI) using the two methods.

---

Formulas:
   AD = C + I + G + (Xn)          NI - Taxes = DI
   Planned Injections = I + G + X     DI = C + S
   Total Leakages = S + T + M

---

3. If the marginal propensity to save is .4, the value of the simple multiplier (M) is:
   a.   1.66                 c.   4
   b.   2.5                  d.   6
4. If the marginal propensity to save is .2, the value of the tax multiplier (Mt) is:
   a.   5                    c.   4
   b.   20%                  d.   1

5. If the marginal propensity to consume is .75, the value of the balanced-budget multiplier (BBM) is:
   a.   4                              c.      1.3
   b.   3                              d.      1

6. If the multiplier is 2, an increase of $6 billion in income would require an increase in investment of:
   a.   $6 billion                    c.      $1 billion
   b.   $2 billion                    d.      $3 billion
   e.   None of these

7. If an economy saves 20% of an increase in income, then an increase in investment of $2 billion can produce an increase in income of as much as:
   a.   $0.4 billion                  c.      $2.0 billion
   b.   $1.6 billion                  d.      $10 billion
   e.   Infinity

8. According to the balanced-budget multiplier model, a simultaneous increase in both G and T of $10 billion will:
   a.   increase GDP by $10 billion   c.      increase GDP by $50 billion
   b.   cause no change in GDP        d.      decrease GDP by $50 billion
   e.   decrease GDP by $10 billion

9. According to the balanced-budget multiplier model, a simultaneous increase in both G and T of $20 billion will:
   a.   decrease GDP by $20 billion   c.      increase GDP by $60 billion
   b.   increase GDP by $20 billion   d.      decrease GDP by $6.67 billion
   e.   decrease GDP by $10 billion

10. If the marginal propensity to consume is .9, a $100 increase in government purchases combined with a $100 increase in net taxes would result in what in change in equilibrium nominal national income?
   a.   a $100 increase               c.      no change
   b.   a $100 decrease               d.      none of the above

11. Suppose that in a two-sector economy consisting of households and businesses (1) the MPS is 1/5, (2) consumption equals income at $100 billion, and (3) the level of investment is $50 billion. The new equilibrium level of GDP is:
   a.   $180 billion                  c.      $300 billion
   b.   $220 billion                  d.      $350 billion
   e.   more than $350 billion

12. If the equilibrium level of nominal GDP is $4,000.00, the target level is $3,600, the marginal propensity to consume is .75, and there is no income tax, what change in government purchases would be necessary to reach the target?
   a.   a $100 increase               c.      a $400 increase
   b.   a $100 decrease               d.      a $400 decrease

13. If the target level of nominal GDP exceeds the equilibrium level by $1,000 and the marginal propensity to consume is .8, which of the following changes in lump sum taxes would permit the target to be reached?
   a.   a $200 increase               c.      a $250 increase
   b.   a $200 decrease               d.      a $250 decrease

14. If the equilibrium level of GDP is $2,500, the target level is $3,300, and the marginal propensity to consume is .80, what changes in imports would permit the target to be reached?
   a.   $200 increase                 c.      $160 increase
   b.   $200 decrease                 d.      $160 decrease

# CHAPTER 12     "Fiscal Policy"

Self-Test

1. If the marginal propensity to save is .25, the value of the simple multiplier (M) is:
   a.  1.3
   b.  1
   c.  4
   d.  3

2. If the marginal propensity to consume is .9, the value of the tax multiplier (Mt) is:
   a.  10
   b.  9
   c.  8
   d.  7

3. If the marginal propensity to consume is .6, the value of the balanced-budget multiplier (BBM) is:
   a.  1.67
   b.  2.5
   c.  1.5
   d.  1.0

4. If an economy saves 50% of any increase in income, then an increase in investment of $10 billion can produce an increase in income of as much as:
   a.  $5 billion
   b.  $10 billion
   c.  $15 billion
   d.  $20 billion
   e.  infinity

## Exhibit I

| DI | S |
|----|----|
| $100 | 25 |
| 200 | 50 |
| 300 | 75 |
| 400 | 100 |
| 500 | 125 |

5. In Exhibit I, the value of MPS is:
   a.  .25
   b.  .75
   c.  1.00
   d.  unable to determine

6. In Exhibit I, the simple multiplier (M) is:
   a.  1.0
   b.  3.0
   c.  4.0
   d.  1.3

7. In Exhibit I, the marginal propensity to consume (MPC) is:
   a.  .25
   b.  .75
   c.  1.00
   d.  unable to determine

8. If the marginal propensity to consume is 0.9, a $100 increase in planned investment expenditure, other things being equal, will cause an increase in equilibrium GDP level of:
   a.  $90
   b.  $100
   c.  $900
   d.  $1000

9. If the marginal propensity to save is 0.4, the value of the simple multiplier (M) will be:
   a.  1.66
   b.  2.5
   c.  4
   d.  6

10. According to the balanced-budget multiplier model, if MPS is .2, a $500 increase in government spending combined with a $300 decrease in taxes, would result in what effect on GDP?
    a.  $3,700 increase
    b.  $3,700 decrease
    c.  $1,300 increase
    d.  $200 increase

11. If the equilibrium level of GDP is $10,000, the target level is $5,000, and the MPS is .4, what change in government purchases would be necessary to reach the target?
    a.  $2,000 increase
    b.  $2,000 decrease
    c.  $2,994 approximately, increase
    d.  $2,944 approximately, decrease

12. If the equilibrium level of GDP is $1,000 and the target level is $1,400, MPS is .5, what changes in lump sum taxes would be necessary to reach the target?
    a.   $400 increase                    c.     $200 increase
    b.   $400 decrease                    d.     $200 decrease

13. Suppose that in a two-sector economy consisting of households and businesses, (1) the MPC is .8, (2) consumption equals income at $240 billion, and (3) the level of investment is $50 billion. The new equilibrium level of GDP is:
    a.   $250 billion                     c.     $290 billion
    b.   $240 billion                     d.     $490 billion

14. Suppose you have recessionary gap of $600 million, MPC is .75, what change in exports would be necessary to reach the target?
    a.   $150 increase                    c.     $450 increase
    b.   $150 decrease                    d.     $600 increase

15. If the MPS is equal to 1/3, a $750 decrease in taxes combined with $750 decrease in government purchases will have what effect on GDP?
    a.   $3,795 decrease                  c.     $750 increase
    b.   $3,795 increase                  d.     $750 decrease

16. A full-employment budget means that:
    a.   every person in the economy, over age 16, will be employed.
    b.   there is an automatic tendency toward full-employment GDP.
    c.   the size of the federal budget's surplus or deficit when the economy is operating at full employment.
    d.   discretionary fiscal policy will cause inflation and, therefore, lower interest rates and tax revenues.

17. The restrictive effects of fiscal policy:
    a.   may cause crowding-out
    b.   can occur when the federal government pursues expansionary fiscal policy
    c.   can cause the level of investment to decline
    d.   negative multiplier will reduce the positive multiplier
    e.   all of the above

18. A $1 increase in government spending (injection) will have a greater impact on GDP than will a $1 decline in taxes (leakage) because:
    a.   a portion of the tax cut may be saved
    b.   government spending and taxing have different multipliers
    c.   part of the reduction in taxes may leak out of the economy
    d.   all of the above

19. Which of the following is not a source of financing the deficit?
    a.   money creation
    b.   borrowing money
    c.   taxation
    d.   impounding

20. Which of the following is not a timing problem for fiscal policy?
    a.   recognition
    b.   administrative
    c.   fiscal policy
    d.   operational

# CHAPTER 18    "Budget Deficits and the Public Debt"

## Chapter Orientation

Currently our nation's federal debt is over 4 trillion dollars. What impact does that amount have on the economy -- interest rates, employment, inflation, income, etc.? Is the federal debt a serious problem? What impact does the deficit financing have on our future generations? If we buy now, who pays later? What should our budget philosophy reflect? Why has the public debt risen so drastically since the early 1980's? What has been the foreign reaction to our debt? These questions will be examined in this chapter.

## Learning Objectives

After reading this chapter in the text, and completing the following exercises in this concepts book, you should be able to:

1. Define budget deficit (and surplus).
2. List and explain the three budget philosophies.
3. State the dollar amount of the debt, the percentage of the debt to GDP, the annual dollar amount of the interest payments, the principle causes of the debt, and the impact of accounting and inflation on the debt.
4. Contrast the effects of internal debt with external debt.
5. State two "myths" surrounding the public debt and explain their implications.
6. Explain the effects of the public debt on income distribution and investment.
7. Compare the crowding-out effect of borrowing to finance the budget deficits, on future generations, as compared to raising taxes to finance the debt.
8. Discuss the implications of a large deficit, which have increased interest rates, and increased the demand for American Securities, which has increased the value of the dollar, making our exports more expensive (cause and effect chain).
9. Define four remedies to reduce or eliminate budget deficits.
10. Explain why the debt plays a positive role in a growing and expanding economy.

## Chapter Highlights

I. Budgets
   A. Definition of budget deficit (or budget surplus) expenditures exceed revenues (or revenues exceed expenditures).
   B. Definition of public debt (national debt) -- the total accumulation of the Federal governments deficits and surpluses over time.
   C. Budget philosophies:
      1. Annually balanced budget -- revenues equal expenditures every year
         a. Limits the government's ability to employ fiscal policy
         b. It is procyclical (not counter cyclical); it intensifies the business cycle.
         c. Limits expansion in the public sector (will not crowd-out the private sector)
      2. Cyclically balanced budget -- the budget is balanced over the business cycle.
         a. Deficit spend during recessions
         b. Pay back the deficits with the surplus during prosperity
         c. Problem: Upswings may not match the downswings of the business cycle

3. Functional finance
   a. Goals of full-employment, without inflation should be achieved
   b. Government expenditures will stimulate GDP
   c. Arguments: taxes will increase as GDP expands, the government's ability to finance debt is unlimited, and the debt is less of a burden than most people think.
4. Full employment balanced budget -- balanced at the full employment level.

II. Facts and Figures Concerning the Debt
   A. Causes of the debt
      1. Wars -- deficit financing of wars has added tremendously to our debt. (Examples: World War I and World War II)
      2. Recessions -- built-in stability of an economy generates budget deficits automatically. (Examples -- the oil crisis of 1974-1975, and 1980-1982.)
      3. Tax cuts -- part of the Economic Recovery Act of 1981, were not offset by reductions in government spending.
   B. Quantitative Aspects
      1. Currently the public debt is in excess of $4 trillion (1993).
      2. Public debt, as a percentage of GDP, is actually slightly smaller than between 1946-1955.
      3. Since the early 1970's, the interest payments on the debt have increased tremendously (because of the increases in size of the debt and the interest rates); as a percentage of GDP it has been a dramatic increase.
      4. The public debt is held by:
         a. 33% government agencies and the Fed.
         b. 67% others (private individuals, banks, insurance companies, corporations, etc.).
         c. Approximately, 12% is held by foreigners (external debt).
      5. Governmental accounting procedures
         a. Do not include the government's assets
         b. Rising price levels reduce the real value or purchasing power of the dollars paid back. By taking this "inflationary tax" into account, a nominal deficit can convert to a surplus.

III. Economic Implications of the Public Debt
   A. Government bankruptcy
      1. Debt cannot bankrupt the government because the government simply refinances the debt ("borrow from Peter to pay Paul").
      2. The government can always print or create new money.
      3. The government can always levy and collect taxes.
   B. Burden on future generations?
      1. If the debt was incurred to cushion a period of unemployment, to the extent that resources would have remained idle are thereby put to work, there is no added burden -- society has benefited from the increased production, and some of the output has added to the nation's capital stock (inherited by our future generations).
      2. In the case of financing war, those people who lived during the war had to do without many civilian goods for military goods (the production-possibilities curve). Spending on a war lessens the amount of capital goods which is not replaced as quickly as they are used up. However, this burden is independent of debt financing.
      3. In 1960, about 5% of our public debt was held by foreigners (external debt). In 1970, the figure was less than 10%. Today, about 12% of our public debt is held by foreigners. Today, the foreign debt is growing and that may impose a burden on our future generations

when we make interest payments, without having that money being spent in our country.

IV. Economic Implications:  Substantive Issues

A.  Income distribution-payment of interest on the debt probably increases income inequality (bondholders are from the wealthier class).

B.  Raising taxes, to finance the interest payments, may not motivate people to take risks, to innovate, to invest, and to work (dampens economic growth).

C.  External debt may impose a burden, if the payment of interest to foreigners, results in the money not being spent in the United States.

D.  An increase in government spending may or may not impose a burden on future generations:

1.  If the government crowds-out investment, then this will indeed lower the capital stock and be a burden to our future generations.

2.  If government spending is primarily investment-type outlays (bridges, harbors, etc.) or human-capital investments (education, research and development, etc.) these expenditures will increase the future productive capacity.

3.  If government spending occurs at less than full-employment of resources, then the economy can move to full-employment without sacrificing capital accumulation.

V.  Deficits of the 1980s

A.  Recent Concerns Over the Deficits and Public Debt

1.  Size -- the public debt nearly tripled during the 1980s.

2.  Interest payments -- have increased more than tenfold since 1970.($188 billion in 1991).

3.  Large deficits have taken place in a peacetime economy operating at close to full-employment.

4.  Large deficits promote imports and stifle exports, as well as giving the U.S. the "world's leading debtor nation" and the so called "selling of America" to foreign investors.

B.  Large deficits have produced a cause-and-effect chain of events:

1.  The large deficit has increased interest rates, which has crowded-out domestic investment, but increased foreign demand for U.S. securities (increased external debt) which has increased the value of the dollar, which has decreased exports and increased imports which has had a contractionary effect on employment, income, and output in the United States economy.

C.  Contrary View:  Ricardian Equivalence Theorem

1.  As discussed in Chapter 12, because people anticipate taxes increasing due to the large deficit, they spend less today which does not cause interest rates to change.

VI. Policy Responses (to control deficit spending)

A.  Constitutional amendment to balance the budget every year.

1.  Pros

a.  Force Congress to live within its means

b.  Reduces inflation

c.  Desirable balance between private and public sectors

2.  Cons

a.  Congress now has the power to balance the budget

b.  Legislators elected to make decisions about economic priorities

c.  The built-in stability would be undermined by the amendment, making the budget procyclical

d.  Government deficits are not necessarily inflationary

B. Gramm-Rudman-Hollings Deficit Reduction Act of 1985
   1. The law sets up specific processes to enable agreement between Congress and the administration on a deficit-reduction package.
   2. If Congress and the President are unable to reach or agreement, there are automatic selective spending cuts -- half are from defense and the other half from domestic social programs (several large components are exempt from any cuts).
   3. Critics contend that reducing the deficit too rapidly could lead the economy into a recession, putting further pressure on deficit, with more spending cuts, etc.
   4. Within hours of Gramm-Rudman became law, it was challenged in the courts. In February of 1986, a federal district court ruled that the automatic spending cut process was an unconstitutional delegation of executive power.
   5. In 1987, this act was reversed to allow a more gradual reduction in the budget deficits and a balanced budget by 1993.
C. Budget Legislation of 1990
   1. Budget Reconciliation Act of 1990
      a. A package of tax increases and spending cuts designed to reduce the budget deficits by $500 billion between 1991 and 1996.
   2. Budget Enforcement Act of 1990
      a. Established a "pay-as-you-go" test for new spending or tax decreases. Between 1991 and 1996, new legislation that increases government spending must be offset by corresponding decrease in existing spending or an increase in taxes.
D. Tax increases
   1. Value-added tax (national sales tax)
   2. Special tax on imported oil
   3. Repeal the tax cuts of the Economic Recovery Act of 1981
E. Privatization -- the government's divesting itself of certain assets and programs through their sale to private firms.
   1. "Grass-roots" approach
   2. Provides revenue to offset the deficit
F. Line-item veto
   1. Would permit the President to veto individual spending items in appropriation bills.
VII.A Positive Role for Public and Private Debt
A. Benefits of debt
   1. Absorbs the saving done in a growing economy at full-employment.
   2. Sustains the aggregate expenditures of consumers, businesses, and governments at the full-employment level.
   3. Debt is increased when households and businesses do not borrow sufficient amounts to maintain full-employment.
VIII. Last Word: PUBLIC DEBT: International Comparisons

## Key Terms

| | |
|---|---|
| budget deficit | internal debt |
| budget surplus | external debt |
| public debt | inflationary tax |
| national debt | human-capital investments |
| annually balanced budget | Gramm-Rudman-Hollings Act of 1985 |
| cyclically balanced budget | value-added tax |
| functional finance | privatization |
| procyclical | grass-roots approach |
| crowding-out | line-item veto |
| Ricardian equivalance theorem | Budget Reconciliation Act of 1990 |
| | Budget Enforcement Act of 1990 |

## Real World Example

### Gramm-Rudman Fails to Shrink Deficit Much, Causing Pressure to Use Gimmicks to Meet Targets
### By David Wessel

The targets set by the Gramm-Rudman deficit-reduction law, the primary restraint on federal profligacy these days, look comforting: If Congress and President-elect George Bush simply obey the law, the deficit will steadily diminish until it vanishes in 1993.

But don't count on it.

For all the bluster and all the constraints imposed by the three-year-old law, the deficit hasn't shrunk much lately. It was $150.4 billion in fiscal 1987, $155.1 billion in fiscal 1988 and, by the most optimistic estimates, will exceed $146 billion this fiscal year, which began Oct. 1.

Even this limited progress reflects bookkeeping tricks encouraged by the intricate Gramm-Rudman mechanism and a good measure of luck. With Washington facing a tough $100 billion deficit target for fiscal 1990, the pressure to resort to gimmickry is growing and attacks on the law mounting.

The savings-and-loan crisis illustrates the problem. Some of the best minds in Washington are looking for a way to protect the savings of Americans who deposited money in thrifts that made billions of dollars in bad loans.

Because of Gramm-Rudman, a lot of intellectual energy goes into evading the deficit targets rather than solving the thrift crisis. The mission is to seek ways to cram costs into the current fiscal year so they don't count against next year's deficit target and to hide the rest of the cost from Gramm-Rudman scorekeepers by borrowing money through some off-budget entity. The latter maneuver - which hasn't any justification besides Gramm-Rudman - will cost taxpayers $200 million in extra interest every year for the next 30 years, estimates Robert Litan of the Brookings Institution.

The Gramm-Rudman law was enacted in 1985 and revised two years later to fix constitutional problems and to make the targets easier to meet. The law imposes across-the-board spending cuts if the White House budget office projects that the government will overshoot preset deficit targets. But two weeks after a fiscal year begins - On Oct. 15 -the threat is lifted. It is as if the chairman of General Motors Corp. were judged on his projections of company profits rather than on his actual track record.

The law probably has helped restrain federal spending. And it may prove to be the lever that forces President-elect Bush and congressional Democrats to the bargaining table in 1989. "It encourages presidential-congressional negotiations to avoid a sequester (spending cuts)," says Allen Schick, a professor of public policy at the University of Maryland.

Yet there is increasing concern that Gramm-Rudman may be outliving its usefulness. Former President Gerald Ford has called it "a parliamentary robot in substitution of wisdom and will power." And in a new book, former Congressional Budget Office director Rudolph Penner urges repeal of the law "in the interest of simplicity and honesty."

Critics of Gramm-Rudman say the law is so complicated that few even in Washington understand it. M. Danny Wall, chairman of the Federal Home Loan Bank Board, rushed to sell some troubled thrifts before Oct. 1 because he believed - incorrectly - he was facing a Gramm-Rudman deadline of some sort.

Mr. Penner complains that the law makes the federal budgeting process "as complex as our tax laws with about the same number loopholes." This erodes public confidence in government, Mr. Schick adds. "You cook up the numbers in the first place and then move them around. It costs you alot of credibility," he says.

What's more, much of the limited progress already made in reducing the deficit reflects economic conditions and a growing Social Security surplus rather than some new congressional discipline. "Artificial mechanisms that decree rigid, long-run budget targets independent of prevailing conditions simply do not work well," Mr. Penner says.

The Gramm-Rudman deficit targets are fixed in law. Yet the stronger the economy, the easier the targets are to meet. That's because tax receipts are greater and spending on programs such as unemployment compensation is lower. Sometimes luck of sorts also contributes. In fiscal 1988, the drought drove up farm prices, reducing farm subsidies enough to help avoid Gramm-Rudman spending cuts.

Those unanticipated and uncontrollable forces - and the fact that Congress set relatively easy targets for fiscal 1988 and 1989 - give the illusion of progress in bringing down the deficit.

Social Security contributes to this illusion. Each year, Social Security collects more than it spends in benefits. The notion was to save now for the retirement of baby boomers so that younger generations wouldn't be saddled with an unmanageable burden later on. Instead, the government spends the surplus on other programs.

Take away the Social Security surplus and the federal deficit actually has been growing from $174 billion in fiscal 1987 to $194 billion in fiscal 1988 to a projected $200 billion in the current fiscal year, according to the Congressional Budget Office.

## PROBLEMS

1. Compare and contrast the for budget philosophies: (a) annually balanced budget, (b) cyclically balanced budget, (c) functional finance, and (d) full-employment balanced budget.

2. Explain the difference between external and internal debt. In the case of financing a war, why is the burden (cost) not passed on to future generations? What are the implications on the economy's capital stock?

3. Could the government go bankrupt financing the debt? Why or why not?

4. Name three causes of the public debt and explain each.

5. Approximately how much of the national debt is held by foreigners? Is this amount a cause for concern?

6. Do you feel the public and private debt is a burden on our future generations? Why or why not?

7. What are four remedies to control deficit spending? Explain each.

8. What are the benefits (positive role) of public and private debt?

9. What is meant by a "cause-and-effect chain of events" produced by large deficits? Trace from beginning to end.

10. When should the fiscal tool of government spending be utilized?

11. In 1986, James McGill Buchanan, an American, received the Nobel Memorial Prize in Economic Science for his contributions to the theory of economic and political decision making. Discuss the political impact of cutting the budget deficits and getting reelected.

12. Explain the basis of the Gramm-Rudman-Hollings Act of 1985. Do you favor this approach to trimming the budget deficit? Why or why not?

13. Recent polls show that the American public is not concerned about deficit spending by the government. Should they be?

14. Recently, President Clinton unveiled his $1.51 trillion budget which increased ways to achieve his goal of close to $500 billion in deficit reduction over five years. Do you think he will reach his goal? Why? Why not?

15. Explain the view of some prominent econnomists that embrace the Ricardian equivalence theorem.

Self-Test
1. Government borrowing:
   a.   increases total spending in the economy          b.      leads to the accumulation of federal debt
   c.   may cause interest rates to increase and crowd-out private investment
   d.   all of the above
2. Our current debt is approximately:
   a.   $1.6 trillion     b.      $4 trillion      c.      $139.8 trillion          d.      $6.6 billion
3. The philosophy of functional finance states that:
   a.   the federal budget should be balanced over a business cycle
   b.   the federal budget should reflect only nondiscretionary fiscal policy
   c.   the primary function of the federal budget is to stabilize the economy and not worry that revenues equal expenditures
   d.   the primary function of the federal budget is to strive for full employment and trim the budget each year until 1991
4. The "crowding-out effect" suggests that:
   a.   most employees would rather work for the federal government in civil service which causes shortages in labor for the private sector
   b.   when net exports is a negative number, the U.S. economy starts to contract
   c.   when the government borrows money to finance the debt, interest rates increase and causes a decrease in investment
   d.   the fiscal tools -- spending and taxing cancel each other out or weaken the multiplier
5. The Federal Government budget is in surplus whenever:
   a.   it spends more than it receives in taxes          b.      it spends less than it receives in taxes
   c.   it spends the same amount it receives in taxes
   d.   it pays out alot of money in welfare benefits
6. If a government adopted an annually balanced budget, then during a recession, the government would undertake the following fiscal policy:
   a.   both taxes and spending would decrease
   b.   lower taxes and/or increase spending
   c.   both taxes and spending would increase
   d.   raise taxes and/or reduce spending
7. If a government adopted a cyclically balanced budget, then during a recession it would:
   a.   raise taxes and/or reduce spending
   b.   lower taxes and/or increase spending
   c.   both taxes and spending would increase
   d.   both taxes and spending would decrease
8. The largest portion of the public debt is held by:
   a.   governmental agencies     b.      federal reserve          c.      American public
   d.   foreign investors
9. Which of the following is not a problem of the public debt?
   a.   income inequality          c.      dampens economic growth
   b.   external debt               d.      absorbs the saving done in a growing economy at full employment
10. Which of the following is not a recent concern over the deficits and the   public debt?
   a.   magnitude of the debt          b.      increasing interest payments
   c.   deficits have produced a cause-and-effect chain of events
   d.   if the spending is primarily real or human-capital investments

# UNIT II REVIEW SHEET  MACROECONOMICS

**Chapter 7**      **"Measuring Domestic Output, National Income, and Price Level"**
I.  The Importance of Studying National Income Accounting
   A.  Reasons for study (4)
II. Gross Domestic Product
   A.  Definition of GDP, GNP, and "per capita GDP"
   B.  Avoid double counting
      1.     Final goods
      2.     Value added approach
   C.  Calculation (NIA Sheet)
      1.     Incomes approach
      2.     Expenditures approach
      3.     Include productive activities
      4.     Exclude nonproductive activities
III. Other Domestic Income Accounts
   A.  Define NDP, NI, PI, and DPI
   B.  Calculate NDP, NI, PI and DPI
   C.  Relationship between the major social accounts
      1.     The circular flow diagram
IV. Measuring the Price Level
   A.  Money not a stable measuring rod
   B.  Definition of real GDP vs. nominal GDP
      1.     The adjustment process
          a.     Inflating and deflating using a price index
   C.  Calculation of real GDP using a GDP deflator or (price index) and money GNP
      1.     Formulas
V.  GDP as an Index of Social Welfare
   A.  Reasons why GDP is not a measure of social welfare (7)
**Chapter 10** **"Classical and Keynesian Theories of Employment"**
I.  Model to Determine Equilibrium
   A.  Assumptions
      1.     Closed economy (domestic economy)
      2.     Laissez-faire (role for government)
      3.     Savings will be personal savings
      4.     Depreciation and net American income earned abroad
II. The Classical School (Supply-side)
   A.  Foundations: (Refer to "Economic Schools of Thought" in this concepts book)
      1.     Say's Law
      2.     Savings
      3.     Investment
      4.     Interest rate
      5.     Price-wage flexibility
      6.     Laissez faire role of Government
      7.     Adam Smith (Wealth of Nations -- 1776)
III. Keynesian Economics (Demand-side)
   A.  Foundations
      1.     Consumption
      2.     Savings

        3.      Investment
        4.      Interest rate
        5.      Money balances by households and banks
        6.      Discrediting of price-wage flexibility
  B.  John Maynard Keynes (<u>General Theory of Employment, Interest, and Money</u> -1936).
  C.  Reasons against the price-wage flexibility
        1.      Market imperfections (4)
  D.  Defenders of Classical Economics
        1.      Argue against government interference
IV. Comparison of Classical and Keynesian Economics
  A.  Aggregate Demand and Aggregate Supply Models:
        1.      Classical view (theory and graph)
        2.      Keynesian view (theory and graph)
V. Tools of Keynesian Theory
  A.  Consumption and savings
        1.      Consumption is the largest component of aggregate demand (aggregate expenditures)
        2.      DI = C + S
        3.      Consumption schedule and function
        4.      Break-even income level
        5.      Savings schedule and function
        6.      Definition and calculation of: APC, APS, MPC, and MPS
        7.      Change in quantity (amount) consumed versus change in consumption
        8.      Change in quantity (amount) saved versus change in savings
        9.      Five nonincome determinants of consumption and savings which cause new curves
        10.    Shifts in consumption and savings move in opposite directions and are relatively stable
VI.Investment
  A.  Definition
  B.  Two determinants of net investment spending
  C.  The Investment-Demand Curve
        1.      Definition
        2.      Change in quantity (amount) of investment-demand versus change in investment-demand
        3.      Five noninterest determinants of investment-demand which cause new curves
        4.      Investment spending tends to be unstable
  D.  Investment spending and income
        1.      Independent of income (autonomous) is assumed
        2.      Caused (induced) by income changes in reality
  E.  Instability of Investing
        1.      Reasons (4)
**Chapter 11**  **"Equilibrium Domestic Output in the Keynesian Model"**
I. Determining the Equilibrium NI ( =GDP) Level:
  A.  The Keynesian Cross (aggregate expenditure -- domestic output approach), where Aggregate Expenditure ( =AD) = National Output (GDP) = Aggregate Supply (AS)
        1.      AE = C + I + G + Xn = AD
                GDP = 45 degree reference line = AS
        2.      Intersection of AD and AS is the equilibrium NNP level.
        3.      AD > AS; AD < AS causes an increase or decrease of output, employment and

income.
  B.  The Leakages-Injections Approach (The Bathtub Theorem) where Total Leakages equal Planned Injections.
      1.  Total Leakages = S + T + M
          Planned injections = I + G + X
      2.  Intersection of total leakages and planned injections is the equilibrium NNP level
      3.  Planned savings always equals actual investment because actual investment includes both planned and unplanned investment.
  C.  Either technique will give you the same equilibrium GDP ( =NI) level.
II. The Simple Multiplier (M)
  A.  Definition
  B.  Techniques to calculate (M)
  C.  Significance of the multiplier (M)
III. The Paradox of Thrift
  A.  Definition
  B.  Explanation of the concept
IV. The GDP Gaps:
  A.  Definition
  B.  Types:
      1.  Recessionary gap
      2.  Inflationary gap
  C.  Graphs
V.  International Trade and Equilibrium Output
  A.  Effect of net Exports on Aggregate Expenditures
  B.  Calculating a trade surplus or deficit
  C.  Effect of Net Exports on the equilibrium GDP
  D.  International Economic Linkages
VI. The Keynesian Cross (expenditures -- output model) and the AD - AS Model
  A.  Keynesian Cross -- hold the price level constant
  B.  AD - AS -- variable price level
  C.  Compatibility
  D.  Three ranges of the AS curve
VII. Different-Sized Multipliers
  A.  Effect
  B.  Size

## Chapter 12  "Fiscal Policy"
I.  Introduction: Keynesians vs. Supply-siders
  A.  Keynesians
      1.  Government should fine-tune the economy using fiscal tools
      2.  Government should "prime the pump" to stimulate NNP
  B.  Supply-siders
      1.  Low tax rates and low government spending to stimulate NNP
      2.  Government should not compete with the private sector (crowding-out).
II. Legislative Fiscal Actions
  A.  Influence of Keynesian economics on the U.S. after the Great Depression
      1.  Employment Act of 1946
          a.  Definition

        b.      Council of Economic Advisors (CEA)

        c.      Joint Economic Committee (JEC)

III.Discretionary Fiscal Policy
- A. Definition
- B. Six assumptions
- C. AE = C + I + G + (Xn) = AD = GDP
- D. Influences of taxation
- E. Multipliers:
  1. Government purchases or investment, use the Simple multiplier (M):

  $$M = \frac{1}{1 - MPC} = \frac{1}{MPS}$$

  2. Taxes only, use the Tax multiplier (Mt):

  $$Mt = \frac{MPC}{MPS} = M - 1$$

  3. Government purchases <u>and</u> taxes by the same amount, in the same direction, use the Balanced budget multiplier (BBM):  BBM = 1
- F. Fiscal policy over the business cycle
  1. Expansionary fiscal policy
     - a. Tools to utilize during a recession
  2. Contractionary fiscal policy
     - a. Tools to utilize during demand-pull inflation

IV.Changes in Equilibrium GDP ( = NI) Level
- A. Steps:
  1. Determine the equilibrium GDP ( = NI) level
  2. Determine the target level (check gaps).
  3. Determine the method to be used to reach your target and use the appropriate multipliers.

V.How the Government Finances Debt or Retires Surplus:
- A. Financing the deficit:
  1. Borrowing money
  2. Money creation
  3. Taxation
  4. Sale of existing assets
  5. Regulation or confiscation
- B. Retiring the surplus
  1. Apply surplus to the national debt
  2. Impounding the surplus

VI.Nondiscretionary Fiscal Policy: Built-in Stabilizers
- A. Definition
- B. Examples of built-in stabilizers
- C. Effects of fiscal stabilizers:
- D. Limitations of built-in stabilizers (3)
- E. Full-employment budget
  1. Definition
  2. Structural vs. cyclical deficit

VII.Applications of Fiscal Policy
- A. Timing problems:

      1.      Recognition lag
      2.      Administrative lag
      3.      Operational lag

B.  Political problems:
      1.      Other goals
      2.      Expansionary bias
      3.      Public choice problems

C.  Restrictive effects: crowding-out
      1.      Definition
      2.      Impact on the interest rates
      3.      Offset by an increased money supply

D.  Offsetting saving

E.  Fiscal Policy in the Open Economy
      1.      Aggregate Demand Shocks (from abroad)
          a.      Net Export Effect

F.  Supply-side Fiscal Policy
      1.      Impact of fiscal policy on inflation.
      2.      Lower tax rates will increase AS, which in turn will expand GDP (=NI).

## Chapter 18 - "Budget Deficits and the Public Debt"

I. Budgets
  A.  Definition of budget deficit (or budget surplus)
  B.  Definition of public debt (or national debt)
  C.  Budget philosophies:
      1.      Annually balanced budget
      2.      Cyclically balanced budget
      3.      Functional finance
      4.      Full-employment balanced budget

II. Quantitative Aspects
  A.  Causes of the debt
      1.      Wars
      2.      Recessions
      3.      Tax cuts
  B.  Facts and figures
      1.      Currently the public debt is in excess of $4 trillion.
      2.      Public debt, as a percentage of GDP
      3.      Interest payments, total dollar amount and as a percentage of GNP
      4.      How the public debt is held
      5.      Governmental accounting procedures

III. Economic Implications of the Public Debt
  A.  Bankrupt the government?
      1.      Refinancing
      2.      Print or create new money
      3.      Tax
  B.  Burden on future generations?
      1.      Used to cushion a period of unemployment
      2.      Incurred to finance a war
      3.      External debt (held by foreigners)

IV. Economic Implications:  Substantive Issues
   A. Income distribution
      1. Payment of interest on the debt may increase income inequality
   B. Raising taxes
      1. May dampen incentives to take risks, invest, work, etc.
   C. External debt (held by foreigners)
      1. May be burdensome if money flows out of the country.
   D. Increasing government spending may or may not impose a burden:
      1. May crowd-out investment.
      2. Investment in real or human-capital will increase the future productive capacity.
      3. At less than full-employment, government spending can move the economy to full-employment, without sacrificing capital accumulation.

V. Deficits of the 1980s
   A. Recent Concerns Over the Deficits and Public Debt
      1. Size
      2. Increase of interest payments
      3. Large deficits during peacetime
      4. Large deficits have produced a cause-and-effect chain of events
      5. World's largest debtor nation (U.S.)
      6. Ricardian Equivalence Theorem

VI. Courses of Action (Remedies) to Control Deficit Spending:
   A. Constitutional amendment to balance the budget every year.
      1. Pros
      2. Cons
   B. Gramm-Rudman-Hollings Deficit Reduction Act of 1985
      1. Description
      2. Unconstitutionality
      3. Critics
      4. 1987 Revision
   C. Budget Legislation of 1990
      1. Budget Reconciliation Act of 1990
      2. Budget Enforcement Act of 1990
   D. Tax increases
      1. Value-added tax
      2. Special tax on imported oil
      3. Repeal the tax cuts of the Economic Recovery Act of 1981
   E. Privatization
      1. Definition
      2. "Grass-roots" approach
      3. Provides revenue to offset the deficit
   F. Line-item veto

VII. A Positive Role for Public and Private Debt
   A. Benefits of debt
      1. Absorbs the saving done in a growing economy at full-employment.
      2. Sustains the aggregate expenditures (AE).
      3. Debt is increased when the private sector borrows insufficient amounts to maintain full-employment.

## FORMULA SHEET

### I.  Inflation

$$\text{Real GDP} = \frac{\text{Money GDP}}{\text{GDP Deflator}} \times 100 \quad \text{or} \quad \frac{\text{Nominal GDP}}{\text{Price Index (as a decimal)}}$$

$$\text{Price Index} = \frac{\text{Price in any given year}}{\text{Price in the base year}} \times 100$$

### II.  Consumption and Savings

$$\text{DI} = \text{NI} - \text{Taxes} \qquad\qquad \text{DI} = \text{C} + \text{S}$$

$$\text{APC} = \frac{\text{C}}{\text{DI}} \qquad\qquad \text{MPC} = \frac{\blacktriangle\text{C}}{\blacktriangle\text{DI}} \qquad\qquad \text{APC} + \text{APS} = 1.0$$

$$\text{MPC} + \text{MPS} = 1.0$$

$$\text{APS} = \frac{\text{S}}{\text{DI}} \qquad\qquad \text{MPS} = \frac{\blacktriangle\text{S}}{\blacktriangle\text{DI}}$$

### III.  Techniques for determining the equilibrium National Income (NI) level:
1.  Keynesian Cross - where Aggregate Demand (AD) = Aggregate Supply (AS)
    C + I + G + (Xn) = 45 degree line
2.  The Leakages-Injections Approach (or "Bathtub Theorem")
    Total Leakages = Planned Injections
    S + T + M       = I + G + X

### IV.  Multipliers:

$$\text{Simple Multiplier (M)} = \frac{1}{\text{MPS}} = \frac{1}{1 - \text{MPC}}$$

$$\text{Tax Multiplier (Mt)} = \frac{\text{MPC}}{\text{MPS}} = \frac{1}{\text{MPC} \times \text{MPS}} = \text{M} - 1$$

Balanced Budget Multiplier (BBM) = 1

### V.  Techniques for Changing Aggregate Demand (AD)

| | | | | | |
|---|---|---|---|---|---|
| ▲ I | x | Simple Multiplier | = | ▲ NI = | ▲ GDP |
| ▲ G | x | Simple Multiplier | = | ▲ NI = | ▲ GDP |
| ▲ M | x | Simple Multiplier | = | ▲ NI = | ▲ GDP |
| ▲ X | x | Simple Multiplier | = | ▲ NI = | ▲ GDP |
| ▲ T | x | Tax Multiplier | = | ▲ NI = | ▲ GDP |
| ▲ G and ▲ T x | | Balanced Budget Multiplier = | | ▲ NI = | ▲ GDP |

# MACROECONOMICS

## UNIT III

## Chapter Orientation

Nothing ever seems to stay the same . . . whether we look at business or economic activity, we see fluctuations in income, output, employment, and prices.  When we look back at the history of these business fluctuations, we see irregular cycles that are recurrent.

Two of the most important aspects of the business cycle are changes in unemployment (unemployment rate) and changes in prices (inflation rate) which will be covered in detail in Chapter 8.

On a micro level, predicting or forecasting the business cycle would enable you to plan your investment strategy accordingly (buy/sell securities, take out loans, etc.) in the hope of higher profits.

On a macro level, the ability to predict the start of a recession or an expansion in the economy, affords policymakers the lead time needed to make adjustments in the economy to avoid severe fluctuations.

## Learning Objectives

After reading this chapter in the text, and completing the following exercises in this concepts book, you should be able to:

1. Define the business cycle and explain the four phases of an idealized business cycle.
2. Identify the two noncyclical fluctuations.
3. List the two facts which explain industry vulnerability to the business cycle.
4. Explain the types of unemployment: frictional (transitional), cyclical, and structural.
5. Describe how the Bureau of Labor Statistics measures the unemployment rate.
6. Explain how the unemployment statistic is overstated and understated.
7. Define full-employment and the full-employment unemployment rate (natural rate).
8. Describe the economic and social costs of unemployment.
9. Define inflation (and deflation)and the "rule of 70".
10. Explain the three indexes used to measure inflation: (a) Consumer Price Index -- CPI, (b) Producer Price Index -- PPI, and (c) the GDP deflator.
11. Contrast the types of demand-side inflation:  demand-pull with supply-side inflation: cost-push, structural, and expectational.
12. Explain the effect of increasing output on the price level and employment levels in ranges 1, 2, and 3.
13. Discuss the costs and benefits of inflation -- who it hurts and who it helps.
14. Explain three output effects of inflation.

## Chapter Highlights

I. Overview of the Business Cycles
   A.   The historical record - our long term economic growth has not been steady.
   B.   Definition -- fluctuations (ups and downs) in general economic activity.  The fluctuations are recurrent but nonperiodic (irregular).
   C.   Phases -- there are four phases of an idealized business cycle:
        1.      Peak -- full-employment with near-capacity production

      2.      Recession -- decline in output and employment with "sticky" prices

      3.      Trough -- a "bottoming out" of output and employment

      4.      Recovery -- output and employment expand toward full-employment

D.  Causation:  A First Glance

      1.      Major innovations

      2.      Political and random events

      3.      Monetary impact

      4.      Aggregate expenditure

E.  Noncyclical variations

      1.      Seasonal fluctuations (Example:  upswing in retail sales during the pre-Christmas period)

      2.      Secular trends (Example: long-run growth or decline)

F.  Cyclical impact:  Durables and Nondurables

      1.      Durable goods (hard goods) do not have to be replaced at a particular time (postponability) -- they can be repaired to last longer

      2.      In a recession or depression, "hard goods" industries experience wide declines in output and employment, but small changes in price.  The reverse holds true for nondurable, or "soft goods" industries.

      3.      During recovery and prosperity, "hard goods" industries or experience wide increases in output and employment but, small changes in price.  The reverse holds true for "soft goods" industries.

      4.      The degree of competition in an industry is often influenced by the number of sellers, which in turn impacts on production and price.

            a.      Durable-goods industries tend to be characterized by a few sellers (a highly concentrated industry), who maintain price stability to avoid touching off a price war.  As a result, during hard economic times, they try to maintain profit margins by cutting costs (cutting production and employment).

            b.      Nondurable industries have many sellers (each with a small market share) competing in the same market.  Consequently, when aggregate demand declines, these firms drop their prices while holding output and employment relatively constant.

G.  NBER indicators

      1.      Leading -- move ahead of economic activity (Example: new orders for plants and equipment).

      2.      Coincident--move in phase with economic activity (Example: GDP).

      3.      Lagging -- trails behind economic activity (Example:  manufacturing inventories).

II. Unemployment

A.  Types of unemployment

      1.      Frictional (transitional) -- is the loss of work that occurs when workers change jobs or locations.  It is usually temporary.  It consists of search unemployment and wait unemployment.

      2.      Structural -- usually results from a major industrial change in a region, causing many people to lose their jobs, or when people's skills become outdated or obsolete.

      3.      Cyclical -- is the relationship between unemployment and the business cycle: the more prosperous the economy, the lower the unemployment rate.  This type of unemployment is severe because it reflects the entire nation.  It is also called "deficient-demand unemployment."

4.    Seasonal -- results from a decrease in demand for labor due to the changing seasons; usually found in such fields as agriculture and construction.

B.    Definition of "full employment"

1.    The "full-employment unemployment rate" or the "natural rate of unemployment" is equal to the total of frictional and structural unemployment.  Today it is between 5-6 percent.

C.    Definition of unemployment -- the percentage of people in the labor force who are not working.

1.    The labor force is defined as all people 16 years of age or older who are employed, plus those unemployed who are <u>actively</u> seeking work.

2.    The total labor force includes those in the armed services, as well as those in the civilian labor force.

D.    Measurement of unemployment

1.    The Bureau of Labor Statistics (BLS) conducts a random survey of 60,000 households each month.

2.    The unemployment rate equals

$\dfrac{\text{\# of unemployed}}{\text{labor force}} \times 100$

3.    Reliability of the unemployment rate

a.    The statistic can be <u>overstated</u> because those workers in the underground economy are not counted and because of false information.

b.    The statistic can be <u>understated</u> because "discouraged workers" (given up looking for a job) are not counted in the labor force and part-time workers, who want more hours (full-time) are counted as fully-employed.

E.    Economic costs of unemployment

1.    Economic costs -- lost production of potential goods and services (GDP gap).

a.    Okun's Law -- for every 1% increase in the unemployment rate over the natural rate, a 2.5% GDP gap is generated.

b.    Unequal burdens -- unemployment is not equally divided among all demographic groups (occupation, age, race, gender and duration).

2.    Noneconomic (social costs) -- unemployment causes people to experience social trauma -- depression, suicide, etc.

a.    Our responsibility to try to "head-off" severe unemployment in our society (Employment Act of 1946).

3.    International Comparisons

a.    Unemployment varies from country-to-country because of differing natural rates of unemployment as well as on different phases of the business cycle.

b.    The U.S., historically has had higher unemployment rates than most industrially advanced nations.  This pattern has begun to change in the 1980s.

III. Inflation:  Defined and Measured

A.    Definition -- inflation is a rising general level of prices, resulting in a loss of the purchasing power of money (inverse relationship).

B.    Measuring Inflation

1.    Rate of Inflation = $\dfrac{P2 - P1}{P1}$        x        100

2.    Rule of 70 -- number of years required for a doubling of the price level.

$\dfrac{\text{Approximate \# of years}}{\text{required to double}} = \dfrac{70}{\text{\% annual rate of increase}}$

    C.   Indexes for measuring inflation:

        1.      Consumer Price Index (CPI) -- measures the change in prices of a fixed market basket of goods and services (600 items in 100 areas).  Payments made to half of our population is tied to CPI.

        2.      Producer Price Index (PPI) -- has replaced the Wholesale Price Index (WPI), as the most important monthly measure of prices at the wholesale level.  The PPI is really three price indexes: finished goods, intermediate products, and crude commodities.

        3.      GDP deflator (covered in Chapter 9) -- adjusts for GDP for inflation -- "Real GDP".

    D.   The Facts of Inflation

        1.      The U.S. inflation rate has been in the middle range of rates for other advanced nations, and far below the rates experienced by some nations.

    E.   Causes: Theories of Inflation

        1.      Demand-Pull inflation (See Figure 8-9, Text page 142)

            a.     Definition -- consumers "bid-up" prices as the economy nears full-employment

            b.     Three Ranges of Graph

                (1)   Range I - (constant prices) output and employment expand, while prices remain constant.

                (2)   Range II - (premature or creeping inflation) relatively low rates of inflation which occurs before the economy reaches full-employment.

                (3)   Range III - (hyperinflation) output and employment are constant at the full-employment level, however, prices are rising.

        2.      Cost Push or Supply-side inflation

            a.     Cost-push or "sellers' inflation" occurs when prices increase because businesses's <u>costs have risen</u> (Example:  wage increase without productivity increases).

            b.     Wage-Push variant -- Unions may push up wages for both union and nonunion workers which are excessive relative to other factors.

            c.     Supply-Shock variant -- Production costs increase due to the costs of new materials such as oil.

    F.   Redistributive Effects of Inflation

        1.      Real-income costs -- changes in our standard of living.

        2.      Fixed income -- people on fixed incomes without indexing for inflation, lose purchasing power.

        3.      Savers -- people who do not consumer their entire income may lose purchasing power if the rate of return on their investment does not at least keep up with inflation.

        4.      Debtors (borrowers) and creditors (lenders) are effected by inflation.  The debtors benefit in that they are paying back their loan with cheaper dollars.

        5.      Anticipated inflation -- cost-of-living adjustments (COLA) automatically adjust workers' incomes to inflation.

        6.      The government has borrowed heaving to finance budget deficits hence, wealth has shifted from households to the government.

        7.      Our progressive tax structure permitted inflation to push us into higher tax brackets or "bracket creep", (indexed tax rates to inflation began in 1985).

        8.      Inflation can benefit and cost a family to some degree -- these effects must be balanced.

   G.   Output effect of inflation
        1.     Mild demand-pull inflation usually increase output employment with creeping inflation.
        2.     Cost-push inflation may cause output and employment to contract.
        3.     Hyperinflation may lead to the demise of the economy.
IV. Last Word:  The Stock Market and Macroeconomic Instability

<u>Key Terms</u>

| | |
|---|---|
| business cycle | GDP gap |
| contraction/recession | Okun's Law |
| expansion/recovery | inflation |
| trough/depression | deflation |
| peak/prosperity | Rule of 70 |
| nonperiodic | consumer price index (CPI) |
| seasonal variations | producer price index (PPI) |
| secular trends | GDP deflator |
| durable goods | demand-side inflation |
| nondurable goods | demand-pull inflation |
| NBER indicators | creeping inflation |
| labor force | hyperinflation |
| unemployment | supply-side inflation |
| unemployment rate | cost-push inflation |
| full-employment | wage-push variant |
| discouraged workers | supply-shock variant |
| natural rate of unemployment | real income |
| frictional unemployment | nominal income |
| structural unemployment | anticipated inflation |
| cyclical unemployment | unanticipated inflation |
| seasonal unemployment | cost-of-living adjustments (COLA) |

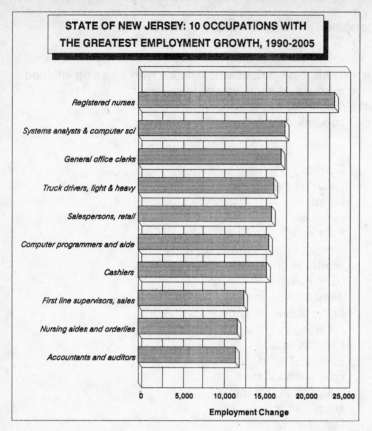

**STATE OF NEW JERSEY: 10 OCCUPATIONS WITH THE GREATEST EMPLOYMENT GROWTH, 1990-2005**

Registered nurses
Systems analysts & computer sci
General office clerks
Truck drivers, light & heavy
Salespersons, retail
Computer programmers and aide
Cashiers
First line supervisors, sales
Nursing aides and orderlies
Accountants and auditors

0   5,000   10,000   15,000   20,000   25,000

**Employment Change**

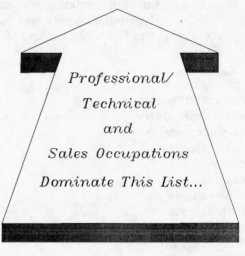

*Professional/ Technical and Sales Occupations Dominate This List...*

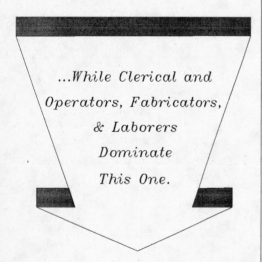

*...While Clerical and Operators, Fabricators, & Laborers Dominate This One.*

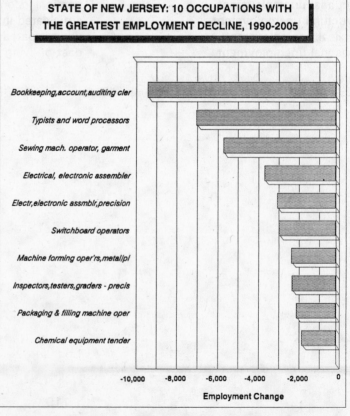

**STATE OF NEW JERSEY: 10 OCCUPATIONS WITH THE GREATEST EMPLOYMENT DECLINE, 1990-2005**

Bookkeeping, account, auditing cler
Typists and word processors
Sewing mach. operator, garment
Electrical, electronic assembler
Electr, electronic assmblr, precision
Switchboard operators
Machine forming oper'rs, metal/pl
Inspectors, testers, graders - precis
Packaging & filling machine oper
Chemical equipment tender

-10,000   -8,000   -6,000   -4,000   -2,000   0

**Employment Change**

Source: New Jersey Department of Labor, Division of Labor Market & Demographic Research.  January 1993.

## The Economics of Inflation and Unemployment

Table 8-1        Inflation in the United States 1967-1993
                 (Percentage Changes in Average Annual Consumer Price Index)

| YEAR | ANNUAL PERCENTAGE RATE OF INFLATION | YEAR | ANNUAL PERCENTAGE RATE OF INFLATION | YEAR | ANNUAL PERCENTAGE RATE OF INFLATION |
|------|------|------|------|------|------|
| 1967 | 2.9% | 1976 | 5.8% | 1985 | 3.8% |
| 1968 | 4.2  | 1977 | 6.5  | 1986 | 1.9 |
| 1969 | 5.4  | 1978 | 7.6  | 1987 | 3.7 |
| 1970 | 5.9  | 1979 | 11.5 | 1988 | 4.5 |
| 1971 | 4.3  | 1980 | 13.5 | 1989 | 4.8 |
| 1972 | 3.3  | 1981 | 10.2 | 1990 | 5.4 |
| 1973 | 6.2  | 1982 | 6.0  | 1991 | 4.2 |
| 1974 | 11.0 | 1983 | 3.8  | 1992 | 3.0 |
| 1975 | 9.1  | 1984 | 4.0  | 1993 | 3.4* |

*estimate

Table 8-2        Unemployment in the United States, 1967-1993

| YEAR | ANNUAL PERCENTAGE RATE OF UNEMPLOYMENT | YEAR | ANNUAL PERCENTAGE RATE OF UNEMPLOYMENT | YEAR | ANNUAL PERCENTAGE RATE OF UNEMPLOYMENT |
|------|------|------|------|------|------|
| 1967 | 3.7% | 1976 | 8.6% | 1985 | 7.1% |
| 1968 | 3.5  | 1977 | 6.9  | 1986 | 6.9 |
| 1969 | 3.4  | 1978 | 6.0  | 1987 | 6.2 |
| 1970 | 4.8  | 1979 | 5.8  | 1988 | 5.4 |
| 1971 | 5.8  | 1980 | 7.0  | 1989 | 5.3 |
| 1972 | 5.5  | 1981 | 7.5  | 1990 | 5.5 |
| 1973 | 4.8  | 1982 | 9.5  | 1991 | 6.7 |
| 1974 | 5.5  | 1983 | 9.0  | 1992 | 7.4 |
| 1975 | 8.3  | 1984 | 7.4  | 1993 | 6.7* |

*estimate

Source:        Bureau of Labor Statistics U.S. Department of Labor

### The Ups and Downs of Business

". . .the role of macro theory is to explain (and predict) the ups and downs of the economy. The challenge of macro policy is to even out the bumps in the road, while trying to satisfy a variety of different economic and budget goals. Neither job is as easy as it might appear."[1]

### An Idealized Business Cycle

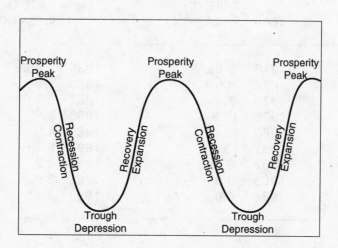

Recovery: the recession has run its course
- Businesses have cut costs
- Interest rates are at a low point
- New factory orders arrive

Faster Growth:
- Consumers and firms begin to spend and borrow again
- Businesses scramble to meet demand

Bursting the Bubble: as the economy expands, imbalances appear
- Shortages of skilled labor and raw materials
- Consumers become over-extended

Recession: the strains become too great
- Consumers retrench and save more income
- Businesses cut expenses

---------------------

1 Bradley B. Schiller, "News Flash: The Macro Outlook", The American University, Washington, D.C., September 5, 1986.

## PROBLEMS

1. As stated by the Port Authority of New York and New Jersey, in 1990 over 43,000 regional youths were high school dropouts and not in the labor force, almost 28,000 residing in New York City.  The region will face a major challenge in the 1990s of finding ways to employ it's untrained youthful population. It is a problem faced by other major cities in the U.S.  What implications do you see for our economy (labor costs, shortages, inflation, imports, etc.)?

2. How do we "read" the economy (what are the indicators to watch)?

3. What are two occupations expected to increase in New Jersey to 1995?
   In the United States?  Why?

4. What are two occupations expected to decline in New Jersey to 1995?
   In the United States?  Why?

5. List and explain the four phases of the business cycle.  Why do we have these imbalances?  Name at least three theories to explain business fluctuations.

6. If you were to compare the automobile industry with the agricultural industry, over the course of the business cycle, what changes would you encounter in comparing output, employment, and prices?

7. How is unemployment measured?  Explain why the employment rate may be          overstated or understated?

8. What are the economic and social costs of unemployment?

9. How is the Consumer Price Index (CPI) used to measure inflation?  In January of 1987, the BLS revamped the market basket with the aim of having it reflect consumers' spending patterns --how has it changed?

10. List and explain the costs and benefits of inflation.

<u>Self-Test</u>
1. Business cycles are defined as:
   a.   fluctuations which are recurrent and periodic.
   b.   ups and downs in certain industries.
   c.   fluctuations which are nonperiodic and recurrent
   d.   fluctuations that include seasonal and secular trends.

2. The GDP gap measures:
   a.   how much nominal GDP exceeds real GDP.
   b.   the difference between  and GDP.
   c.   the amount potential GDP exceeds actual GDP.
   d.   the amount actual GDP exceeds potential GDP.
3. The United States is considered to be at full-employment when:
   a.   frictional and structural employment equal zero.
   b.   cyclical unemployment is zero.
   c.   when 100% of the labor force is employment.
   d.   when every American, over age 16, is working.

4. Which of the following is <u>not</u> a type of unemployment?
   a.   frictional                          c.      structural
   b.   expectational                       d.      cyclical
5. If the rate of inflation is 10%, the price level will double in about:
   a.   12 years                            c.      7 years
   b.   10 years                            d.      4 years

6. Which of the following is <u>not</u> a type of inflation?
   a.   demand-pull                         c.      hyperinflation
   b.   cost-push                           d.      cyclical inflation

7. According to Okun's Law, for every 1% that the actual unemployment rate exceeds the national
   rate, what GDP gap is generated?
   a.   3.0%                                c.      .01%
   b.   2.5%                                d.      equilibrium
8. Which of the following does <u>not</u> measure inflation?
   a.   Rule of 70                          c.      producer price index
   b.   consumer price index                d.      GDP index

9. During a recession, you should expect:
   a.   durable goods' industries to cut output and employment, without changing the price level
   b.   durable goods industries to increase output and inventories and cut price
   c.   nondurable goods industries to raise the price since their goods are essential
   d.   nondurable goods industries to lower price, output, and employment

10.Which of the following will be hit the hardest by unanticipated inflation?
   a.   a homeowner                         c.      developer
   b.   a small business owner              d.      a retired person living on a fixed pension

# CHAPTER 17      "The Inflation - Unemployment Relationship"

## Chapter Orientation

For many years, the major economic problems facing our country have been inflation and unemployment. This chapter focuses on the tradeoffs between inflation and unemployment.

It was believed that we could expand output, employment, and income, up to full-employment, without raising the price level. However, pioneering work in the late 1950's and 1960's showed an inverse relationship between inflation and unemployment, which was named after British economist A.W. Phillips -- the "Phillips Curve". As demand for any commodity increases, its price rises, and unemployment falls. Hence, if unemployment is low, any increased demand for labor will result in rising wage rates. If unemployment is high, wages will rise less rapidly and may even fall.

One group of economists said the Phillips curve represented a long-run tradeoff between inflation and unemployment. Another group said that the Phillips curve was stable only in the short-run. Those economists stated that in the long-run, the "Phillips curve" is vertical at the natural or full-employment, level of output. People will adjust their expectations accordingly -- wages will "catch up" with inflation in the long-run.

Events of the 1970's and early 1980's were clearly at odds with the Phillips curve. Stagflation (slow growth, high unemployment, and rising prices) seemed to discredit the Phillips curve. What happened?

A series of cost-push or supply shocks occurred in the oil and agriculture industries, as well as a devalued dollar in 1971-73 which shifted the supply curve (which had been ignored in the demand-side models).

Economists began to wonder if there were ways to improve supply conditions. Ways were sought to control inflationary expectations, increase saving and investing, increase productivity, deregulation, etc. These ideas were not new (outgrowth of the Classical School), but they reflected an awareness that demand management was only half of a balanced policy -- not the whole!

Ronald Reagan won the presidency on a platform of cutting taxes to eliminate the deficits and getting the economy back on track. However, as George Bush learned the hard way, our economy is laden with deficits and only making a modest comeback with high unemployment.

## Learning Objectives

After reading this chapter in the text, and completing the following exercises in this concepts book, you should be able to:

1. Explain and contrast the typical Phillips Curve using the AD - AS model.
2. Discuss the rationale behind the Phillips Curve.
3. Define "stagflation" and discuss how "stagflation" may have discredited the Phillips Curve.
4. List the six supply-side shocks experienced by (the U.S. economy).
5. Explain how these "supply shocks" led to stagflation during the 1970's and early 1980's, using the AD - AS model.
6. Explain why demand-management policies cannot reduce or eliminate stagflation.

7. Illustrate the differences between the short-run and long-run Phillips Curve.
8. State the accelerationist hypotheses and the national expectations theory; and explain how economists use these tools to explain a vertical Phillips Curve.
9. Define the policy options proposed for fighting stagflation.
10. Contrast wage-price controls with wage-price guideposts.
11. Define incomes policies.
12. The supply-siders attribute stagflation to what cause?
13. List the four tax-transfer disincentives identified by the Supply-siders.
14. List and explain the four policies advocated by the Reagan administration in its economic recovery program.
15. List three observations which have emerged over the past fifteen or twenty years?

<u>Chapter Highlights</u>

I.  The Phillips Curve
   A.  The Phillips Curve:  Concept and Data
        1.      A more realistic approach is to use the upward sloping range of AS (Range II) and show AD shifting.
        2.      The intersection of AS and AD determines real national output (and employment) and the price level.
        3.      Therefore, the greater the growth of AD, the greater will be the resulting inflation and the greater growth of real national output (and lower unemployment).  This means that high rates of inflation should be accompanied by low rates of unemployment and vice versa (inverse relationship).
        4.      The period from the late 1950s through the 1960s verified the existence of this inverse relationship, known as the Phillips Curve (named after A.W. Phillips, who developed this concept in Great Britain).  See below.

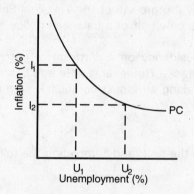

   B.  Logic of the Phillips Curve
        1.      Two reasons why inflation occurs before reaching full-employment:
            a.      Labor market imbalances -- shortages start to appear before full-employment is reached.
                (1)      Those unemployed workers may look for jobs elsewhere but bottlenecks occur -- time to train, relocate, obtain a license, etc.

        b.      Market Power -labor unions and business firms have market power rearing full-employment and a prosperous economy, hence, wages production costs, and prices increase.

C.    Stabilization Policy Dilemma

    1.     Although monetary and fiscal policies can be employed, to effect employment and inflation, they merely move the economy from one point on the Phillips Curve to another point along the same curve. Therefore, it is impossible to "full-employment without inflation".

    2.     In summation, movement along the Phillips Curve is caused by a change in fiscal or monetary policy. Shifts in the Phillips Curve (causing a new curve) would be caused by supply shocks (or changes in the natural rate of unemployment or the expected rate of inflation).

II. Stagflation:  A Shifting Phillips Curve?

A.    Definition -- slow growth, high unemployment, and rising prices; occurred during the 1970's and early 1980's in the United States. This contradicted the Phillips Curve.

B.    Causes of Stagflation

    1.     Supply shocks shifted AS to the left (decrease) to increase prices and unemployment. These experiences confirmed that the Phillips Curve is not a model for economic policy. The six supply shocks are:

        a.      OPEC and energy prices -- oil prices quadrupled which caused the cost of producing and distributing virtually every good and service to rise.

        b.      Agricultural shortfalls -- in 1972 and 1973 especially in Asia and the Soviet Union. As a result, American agricultural exports expanded sharply therefore higher prices at home.

        c.      Depreciated dollar -- in 1971-1973 helped ease the balance of payments (takes more dollars to buy foreign monies).

        d.      Demise of wage-price controls -- the 1971-1974 wage-price controls were lifted in 1974 (pushed prices upward to recoup lost revenue).

        e.      Productivity decline -- labor efficiency began to decline in the mid 1960's through the 1970's.

        f.      Inflationary expectations and wages -- demand for larger and larger nominal-wage increases, increased production costs, and shifted AS.

C.    Demand-management policies are not an effective means of treating stagflation.

D.    Stagflation's Demise:  1982-1988

    1.     Significant factors

        a.      Deep recession of 1981-82

        b.      Foreign competition 1982-88

        c.      Deregulation of industries

        d.      Decline in OPEC's monopoly power

    2.     Unemployment and inflation moved in the _same_ direction

III. The Natural Rate Hypothesis

A.    Definition - contends that the economy is stable in the long-run (vertical) at the natural rate of unemployment.

B.    Adaptive Expectations Theory

    1.     Definition - there may be a short-run tradeoff between inflation and unemployment, but in the long run no such tradeoff exists.

    2.     Nobel Prize winner, Milton Friedman, popularized the adaptive expectations theory.

    3.      Short-run Phillips Curve
        a.      When the actual rate of inflation is higher than expected, the unemployment rate will fall.
    4.      Long-run Phillips Curve
        a.      In the long-run, the traditional Phillips Curve does not exist: expansionary demand-management will shift the short-run Phillips Curve upward, resulting in increasing inflation with no permanent decline in unemployment.
        b.      Expansion of AD, through Keynesian policies, may _temporarily_ increase profits which increase output and employment. However, when wages "catch up", this lowers profits and therefore lowers output and employment (cancels out the stimulus).
    5.      Disinflation
        a.      Definition - reduction in the rate of inflation
        b.      Restrictive Keynesian stabilization policies can reduce inflation without creating permanent increases in unemployment.

C.    The Rational -- Expectations Theory
    1.      Definition -- businesses, consumers, and workers understand how the economy functions and effectively use available sources of information to protect or further their self-interest.
        a.      Rational expectations models have been developed which show that both fiscal and monetary policy are completely ineffective.

D.    Interpretation of the Phillips Curve have changed dramatically over the past three decades. The original theory of a stable tradeoff between unemployment and inflation gave way to the adaptive expectations view which stated that no such tradeoff existed in the long-run. Recently, the rational expectations theory stresses that macro policy is ineffective because it is anticipated by workers.

E.    Demand -- Management Policies
    1.      The accelerationist hypothesis and the rational -- expectations theory conclude that demand-management policies cannot influence real output and employment, but only the price level.

IV. Aggregate Supply Revisited
  A.    Definitions
    1.      The short-run is a period in which input prices (wages) remain fixed in the presence of a change in the price level.
        a.      Workers are unaware of price changes
        b.      Employee contracts
    2.      The long-run is a period in which input prices (wages) are fully responsive to the price level.

  B.    Short-run Aggregate Supply
    1.      The short-run AS Curve slopes upward because, assuming input prices are fixed, as the price level increases, profits increase, and therefore, real output increases. Likewise, when the price level decreases, profits decrease, and therefore, real output decreases.

  C.    Long-run Aggregate Supply
    1.      In the long-run, a price level increase, will result in an increase in nominal wages and thus a leftward shift of the short-run AS curve. Likewise, a decrease in the price level will produce a decline in nominal wages and a rightward shift of the short-run AS curve. The long-run AS curve is, therefore, vertical.

    D.    Keynesian vs. New Classical Implications
        1.    Unanticipated changes in the price level, called "price level surprises", do produce short-term fluctuations in real output. However, these changes are only temporary. In the long-run the economy is stable at the full-employment level of output.
        2.    Keynesians call for active use of stabilization policies to reduce the high costs associated with severe unemployment or inflation.
        3.    New classical economists, view the long-run as short, therefore, they advocate a hands-off policy by the government.

V. Demand-Pull and Cost-Push Inflation
    A.    Demand-Pull Inflation
        1.    Occurs when an increase in aggregate demand pulls up the price level.
        2.    In the short-run, demand-pull inflation will drive up the price level and increase real output; in the long-run, only the price level will rise.
    B.    Cost-Push Inflation
        1.    Arises from factors (or resources) which increase the cost of production at each price level - AS shifts leftward.
        2.    If the government attempts to maintain full-employment (under cost-push inflation) an inflationary spiral is likely to occur.
        3.    If the government takes a hands-off approach to cost-push inflation, a recession will probably occur.

VI. Policy Options
    A.    Given that demand-management policies are ineffective in coping with stagflation, what are our options?
    B.    Three categories of policies have been proposed: (1) market policies; (2) wage-price, or income policies; and (3) "supply-side" or "Reaganomics".
    C.    Market policies
        1.    Manpower policy -- intended to reduce or eliminate imbalances or bottlenecks in the labor market.
            a.    Vocational training
            b.    Job information
            c.    Nondiscrimination
        2.    Procompetition policy -- attempts to reduce the market power of unions and large corporations.
            a.    Apply existing antitrust laws more vigorously.
            b.    Remove legal restrictions in certain regulated industries.
            c.    Elimination of tariffs on imports.
            d.    Antimonopoly laws should be applied to unions or to decentralize collective bargaining.
    D.    Wage-price (incomes) policies -- restrict increases in wages and prices by utilizing guideposts (voluntary cooperation) or controls (force of law).
        1.    There have been five periods in our recent history where incomes policies have been applied: (1) comprehensive controls during WWII; (2) selective controls during the Korean War in the early 1950s; (3) guideposts during the early 1960's (Kennedy-Johnson administrations); (4)the Nixon administration wage-price freeze of 1971-1974; and (5) the Carter administration's guideposts of 1978.

   2.     Whether to employ incomes policy has been a heated debate centering on three issues: (1) workability and compliance; (2) allocative efficiency and rationing; and (3) economic freedom of choice.

   3.     Some economists argue that incomes policies would be more effective if special tax rebates (or penalties) be given for compliance (or noncompliance).

E.  Supply-side economics contend that aggregate supply must be recognized as an active force in determining both the level of inflation and unemployment.

   1.     Keynesians have neglected certain supply-side policies which might alleviate stagflation.

   2.     Taxes, according to the supply-siders, are a business cost and shifted forward to consumers in the form of higher prices.  Most taxes are a "wedge" between costs of resources and the price of a product.

   3.     Taxes and transfer payments have negative effects upon incentives to work, invest, innovate, and assume entrepreneurial risks.

   4.     Increased regulation of an industry has adversely affected costs and productivity.

F.  The Laffer Curve

   1.     The Laffer Curve (developed by supply-sider Arthur Laffer on a dinner napkin) depicts the relationship between tax rates and tax revenues.  His curve shows that if the economy is in the upper range (high tax rates), a decrease in tax rates will increase tax revenues.  This forms the foundation for supply-side economics.

   2.     Criticisms of the Laffer Curve

      a.     Impact of a tax reduction upon incentives will be minimal.

      b.     Tax reductions would increase AD (relative to AS) and, thereby creating large budget deficits and rapid inflation.

      c.     Where are we on the Laffer Curve?

      d.     Income inequality will increase substantially.

G.  Reaganomics (based upon the elements of supply-side economics) reflects the following four points in the "Economic Recovery Program" of early 1981:

   1.     Reduce government spending (except defense expenditures).

   2.     Reduce government regulation of private businesses.

   3.     Prevent the growth in the money supply from being inflationary.

   4.     Reduce the personal and corporate income tax rates.

VII. The Effects of Reaganomics

A.  Tight monetary controls lessened the effects of ERTA tax cuts (severe recession 1980-1986).

B.  Low inflation, caused by tight money policy (FED), as well as low oil prices.

C.  ERTA tax cuts were a primary cause of the huge budget deficits since 1982.

D.  The prediction of the Laffer Curve has not materialized to date.

E.  Large deficits may have "crowded-out" some unknown amount of private investment.

F.  There is no evidence which supports any significant impacts upon saving and investment rates or incentives to work.

G.  Time will tell the true impact of supply-side economics, but it hasn't been a "quick-fix" for stagflation.

VIII. Last Word:  "Real" Business Cycle Theory

Key Terms

| | |
|---|---|
| aggregate demand | Accelerationist Hypothesis |
| aggregate supply | Rational Expectations Theory |
| demand-pull inflation | market policies |
| cost-push inflation | wage-price (incomes) policy |
| premature inflation | wage-price guideposts |
| stagflation | wage-price controls |
| Phillips Curve | incomes policies |
| bottlenecks | tax-based incomes policy (TIP) |
| sticky prices | supply-side economics |
| supply shocks | tax "wedge" |
| stabilization policy dilemma | tax-transfer disincentives |
| inflationary expectations | Reaganomics |
| devalued dollar | Economic Recovery Tax Act (ERTA) |
| demand management policies | Laffer Curve |

Real World Example

## Straight Talk from Laura Tyson - Ann Reilly Dows and Carla Rapoport

*The Council of Economic Advisers sure has changed. While chairmen in the Reagan and Bush Administrations professed near-absolute faith in free markets and free trade, Laura D'Andrea Tyson believes that trade is not always free and that markets don't always produce the best results. A Ph.D. from MIT who taught economics at the University of California at Berkeley, Tyson is an advocate of economic and trade policies designed to spur U.S. competitiveness, particularly in high-tech industries. Tyson spoke with Fortune's Washington bureau chief, Ann Reilly Dowd, and European editor Carla Rapoport about Clintonomics and her convictions.*

**Why markets don't always work.** Even Adam Smith recognized that there are certain kinds of market failure. Education, research and development, immunization, and pollution are textbook cases in which privately desirable outcome. The only real difference between us and Reagan-Bush is that we see more potential for the government to do creative, effective things to realize socially desirable outcomes when the market fails.

**Steps Washington can take to help companies compete.** First, you have to get your macroeconomic policies right by addressing the budget deficit and shifting the focus of taxation and spending policies from consumption to investment. Second, you work to provide inputs from which all sectors of the economy can benefit--like improving manpower and training, education, and infrastructure. Third, you work on the market failures, like research and development. Finally, there are industry-specific policies, such as the government's support of Sematech [the semiconductor research consortium].

**Why Clinton wants to raise taxes.** There was no credible way to reduce the deficit without raising revenues. We looked for taxes that did essentially two things. One was to restore greater progressivity to the tax system. The other was to discourage energy consumption.

That's why it is correct to say that an energy tax will have an effect on energy-intensive industries. But remember, we'll introduce this tax gradually. Moreover, if you put the tax increases in the context of the overriding goal--to bring the deficit down, reduce borrowing rates, reduce the cost of capital, restore a higher long-term growth rate to the U.S. economy--then we would assume companies will benefit. And those benefits, over time, will offset the tax increases.

**Why health care price controls might work.** No one is going to pretend that if we did the price controls approach we would not have problems of enforcement, monitoring, and perpetuating distortions that currently exist. But there is one little-noted but interesting difference in this case: Normally, controls have been imposed in situations where there is a lot of inflation because of excess demand. That is not the case in the health care system. In many parts of the country we have excess supply--lots of doctors and MRI machines relative to the size of the population, and lots of hospital beds unutilized. So short-term controls are still an option we're examining.

**How to finance expanded health care coverage.** The notions of capping the deductibility of health care insurance by employers or requiring individuals to report insurance in excess of a set amount as income are attractive because they raise revenue and provide and incentives for people to use health care services more efficiently. Sin taxes are also interesting, because they would help finance access to health care while at the same time reduce the need for it. Usually we talk about cigarette taxes, where clearly the correlation between use and adverse health effects is very high. There is also compelling evidence that higher beer taxes save the lives of young adult males because they get into fewer care wrecks.

**Where Clinton is focusing his technology policy.** What we are trying to do is not so much increase the overall level of research and development spending as shift funding from defense to civilian technology. One area in which we have a national mission is space. Another is to improve environmental standards, which means dealing over the long run with automobile emissions by developing cleaner engine technologies. Other missions include an information superhighway, high-speed rail, and short-haul cargo or passenger planes. All this will be coordinated primarily through the Office of Science and Technology Policy and the Office of the Vice President.

**Why it's time to get tough on trade.** Trade isn't always free. And the choice of policymakers is often not between free trade and protectionism. It is somewhere in the middle, between one kind of manipulated trade and another.

In an ideal world, our competitive industries would not be meeting subsidized or protected industries abroad. but that is not the world we face So the question is, What should be our response? Do we want to be in the business of influencing market outcomes? It's a very hard call, and it is not one that I think any of take lightly. We would much rather start with an effort to try to reduce the subsidy or protectionist activity abroad. But I think we have to recognize that we may not be able to get far enough with that strategy.

There is no social or global justification for certain types of subsidies. Production subsidies like those the Europeans have given Airbus, for example, are simply market grabbing. But research and development subsidies may have the defense of at least possibly creating innovations.

**How to close the trade deficit with Japan.** The trade imbalance between the U.S.And Japan is primarily a macroeconomic phenomenon, the result of big U.S. budget deficits and big Japanese surpluses. The U.S. is now on an appropriate course, and it's time for the Japanese to get on one as well, by stimulating their economy. That's first.

Second, we must persuade the Japanese to work more actively to get the Uruguay Round completed. This is very important.

The third thing is sectoral talks. When you have negotiated and been unable to address the problem of structural barriers, and there is evidence that competitive opportunities in an industry are not being accorded to competitive producers, then moving to a set of quantitative marketshare indicators for foreign imports may be defensible. This should be a lest step.

But if you gave the Japanese some overall trade balance target that they had to reach, I'd be afraid they would be forced to manipulate the composition of their exports to us and their imports from us. I would much prefer those to be the outcomes of competitive forces.

# CHAPTER 17     "The Inflation - Unemployment Relationship"

## PROBLEMS

1. On graph paper, draw the aggregate demand (AD) curve and the aggregate supply (AS) curve. State what the AD and AS curves illustrate.

2. Explain the difference between demand-pull and cost-push inflation using the AD-AS model (draw two graphs).

3. Draw the Phillips Curve, what tradeoff is illustrated?  What are two reasons why prices increase before reaching full-employment?

4. What is "stagflation"?  What are the causes of "stagflation"?  When has it occurred in the United States?

5. List the six supply shocks and explain the impact of each on the U.S. economy.

6. Briefly explain the "Accelerationist Hypothesis" and the "Rational-Expectations Theory".  What have these theories concluded regarding the original Phillips Curve?

7. Given that demand-management policies are ineffective in coping with "stagflation", what are our options?

8. What is meant by the term "income policies"?  What are three issues surrounding this heated debate?

9. What are the major provisions of the Economic Recovery Tax Act (ERTA) of 1981?  What do the critics have to say about ERTA?

10. Has "Reaganomics" worked?  State your reasons why, or why not.

Self-Test
1. A Phillips Curve shows the relationship between:
   a.   consumption and savings
   b.   inflation and prices
   c.   inflation and unemployment
   d.   consumption and inflation
2. Short-run changes along a given Phillips Curve are accomplished through:
   a.   fiscal policies only
   b.   monetary policies only
   c.   competitive policies
   d.   both fiscal and monetary policies
3. The adaptive expectations theory suggest that in the long-run:
   a.   vertical Phillips Curve
   b.   horizontal Phillips Curve
   c.   full-employment and zero-inflation economy
   d.   a negative inflation rate
4. The immediate effect of an adverse supply shock, caused by an increase in the price of imported oil would include:
   a.   an upward shift of the AS curve
   b.   a downward shift of the AD curve
   c.   an upward shift of the AD curve
   d.   a leftward shift of the AS curve
5. With the AD curve held constant, an upward shift of the AS curve will cause:
   a.   demand-pull inflation          c.      falling unemployment
   b.   cost-push inflation            d.      decreasing prices
6. According to supply-side economists, lower tax rates can increase tax revenues because:
   a.   lower tax stimulate incentives to work
   b.   lower taxes motivate workers to come out of the underground economy
   c.   lower taxes encourage savings and investment
   d.   all of the above
7. "Reaganomics" advocates:
   a.   reduction in government spending
   b.   reduction in government regulation
   c.   reduction in personal and corporate income tax rates
   d.   all of the above
8. In the Keynesian expenditure-output model, it is impossible for the economy to experience:
   a.   full-employment                c.      unemployment and inflation
   b.   inflation                      d.      full-employment and stable prices
9. The full-employment rate, as seen by the accelerationists is:
   a.   4%                             c.      8%
   b.   6%                             d.      0%
10.     In the upper range of the Laffer Curve:
   a.   reductions in the tax rate will increase tax revenues
   b.   increases in the tax rate will increase tax revenues
   c.   reductions in the tax rate will decrease tax revenues
   d.   increases in the tax rate will not change tax revenues

# CHAPTER 13     "Money and Banking"

## Chapter Orientation

Chapter 13 discusses one of our favorite topics -- MONEY. We work hard to earn and spend money. According to the Federal Reserve, the story of money began when people learned they would trade for things they wanted -- but it was often difficult. For example, a fisherman couldn't get wheat from a farmer who didn't like fish.

So, prized ornaments -- beads, shells, stones, furs, etc. were items used as money. Because of the ease of carrying, and for its durability, "metal" money became popular. About 2,500 B.C. the Egyptians produced one of the first types of metal money in the form of rings. The Chinese used gold cubes about 400 years later. In Lydia, (western Turkey), the first metal coins were struck about 700 B.C. . . . some of the world's most beautiful coins were struck during the Golden Age of Greece -- 400 to 300 B.C. For centuries coins remained the favored medium of exchange.

Paper money is related to the clay tablets on which the Babylonians wrote due bills and receipts about 2,500 B.C. Marco Polo reported that the Chinese Emperor Kubla Khan issued mulberry bank paper notes bearing his seal and the signatures of his treasurers in 1273 A.D.

Metal coins lost some of their appeal during the Middle Ages as travel became more common. Their weight and the fear of robbery made coins impractical. Instead, travelers went to goldsmiths to exchange their coins for receipts that were valueless to a robber. The receipts could be exchanged for coins with a designated goldsmith in another city (paper money at work).

Our coins and coinage have changed many times since the Coinage Act of 1792, which adopted the dollar as our standard monetary unit and established the country's first Mint -- at Philadelphia (the Federal Reserve, "Coins and Currency").

What are the functions of money? What is the U.S. money (stock) supply? Why is there a demand for money? What is the framework of the U.S. financial system? What happened recently to our banking system, what is the "thrift bailout", and where are we headed? These questions will be addressed in this chapter.

## Learning Objectives

After reading this chapter in the text and completing the following exercises in this concepts book, you should be able to:

1. Discuss the earliest beginnings of money.
2. List and explain the three functions of money.
3. Define the money supply, M1.
4. Identify the four kinds of checkable deposits; and the four principal kinds of depository institutions.
5. Give examples of near-monies.
6. Define M2 and M3.
7. Explain what "back" the money supply in the United States.
8. Discuss why money has "value".
9. Explain the relationship between the value of money and the price level.
10. Explain how the government keeps the value of money relatively stable.

11. Identify two demands for money and the reasons behind each.
12. Explain what determines the equilibrium rate of interest.
13. Predict how changes in nominal GDP and in the money supply will affect the equilibrium rate of interest.
14. Discuss the framework of the American financial system.
15. Explain the roles of the district banks.
16. Define the Monetary Control Act of 1980.
17. Describe six functions of the Federal Reserve System and indicate which is the most important.
18. Discuss the recent banking difficulties, the thrift bailout and future reform.

Chapter Highlights
I. Functions of Money
    A.    Medium of exchange -- use to execute transactions.
    B.    Measure of value -- used as a yardstick for dollars.
    C.    Store of value -- holds purchasing power until you spend it.
II. The Money (Stock) Supply
    A.    Components of the money (stock) supply
        1.      M1 -- highly liquid, consists of currency (coins and paper) plus checkable deposits (deposits in which checks can be drawn).
        2.      All coins in circulation in the U.S. are "token money" (the value of the billion contained in the coin is less than its face value.
        3.      The Federal Reserve Board has abandoned its growth target for M1 for 1987.
        4.      The four principal types of financial institutions:
            a.      Commercial banks
            b.      Savings and loan associations
            c.      Mutual savings banks
            d.      Credit unions
        5.      Checkable deposits are the most important component (73% in September 1985) of M1. The types of checkable deposits are:
            a.      Demand deposits (checking accounts).
            b.      Automatic transfer of saving (ATS) accounts in commercial bank
            c.      Negotiable order of withdrawal (NOW) accounts in savings and loans.
            d.      Share drafts in credit unions.
        6.      Currency and checkable deposits owned by the government, the Federal Reserve Banks, commercial banks, or other financial institutions are excluded from M1 or any other broad measure of the money supply.
    B.    Liquid Assets
        1.      Liquid assets are assets which can be quickly turned into cash, with little loss of value. Cash is 100% liquid.
    C.    Near-monies: M2 and M3
        1.      Near-monies are highly liquid assets such as deposits in savings accounts, time deposits, short-term government securities, money market mutual fund shares, overnight repurchase agreements, small (under $100,000) time deposits.
        2.      M2 = M1 + noncheckable savings deposits + small time deposits.
        3.      M2 is a broader measure of the money (stock) supply.
        4.      M3 = M2 + large ($100,000 or more) time deposits.
        5.      M3 is the broadest measure of the money (stock) supply.

    6.     The existence of near-monies is important:
        a.     Effects willingness to spend.
        b.     Conversion of near-monies into money or vice versa affects our economic stability.
        c.     Near-monies expand the monetary base -- a broader perspective for monetary policy.
    7.     Credit cards or plastic money, are not money -- they are a loan (credit).

III. What Backs the Money (Stock) Supply
    A.   Debt
       1.     In the U.S. and other advanced economies, all money is essentially the debts of the government, commercial banks, and thrift institution.
    B.   Value of money
       1.     Acceptability -- confidence that we can exchange our money for goods and services when we choose to spend it.
       2.     Legal tender -- designated by the government.
          a.     Fiat money ("play money") is money because the government says its money -- not because it is backed by a precious metal.
          b.     The advantages of "fiat" money include: easily controlled by the government, less costly, and can possess all of the characteristics of "commodity" money (money which has value in addition to what it will buy).
       3.     Depends on the supply and demand of money.
       4.     The value of money is inversely related to the price level. (As prices increase, the value of a dollar decreases or loses purchasing power).
       5.     The government's responsibility in stabilizing the value of money (since it is not "backed" by any precious metal).
          a.     The application of appropriate fiscal policies.
          b.     The effective control over the supply of money.

IV. Demand for Money
    A.   Households and businesses need money for:
       1.     Transactions demand -- for cash-flow purposes -- day-to-day spending activities.
          a.     Influenced by the level of money (income) or nominal GDP (rather than by changes in the interest rate).
          b.     The transactions demand for money varies directly with nominal GDP.
          c.     Transactions demand for money (Dt) is shown as a vertical line because it is independent (unrelated) to changes in the interest rate. See Figure 13-1.
       2.     Asset demand -- money functions as a store of value. Included as part of a portfolio of investments.
          a.     The asset demand for money varies inversely with the rate of interest (when the interest rate is low, people will hold a large amount of money as assets; (when the interest rate is high, people will hold a small amount of money). See below.
    B.   The total demand for money is the sum of the transactions demand and the asset demand.

C. Where the total demand curve intersects the money supply curve is the equilibrium interest rate in the money market of the economy. See below -- Figure 13-1.

### FIGURE 13-1

Transaction Demand        Asset Demand        Total Demand

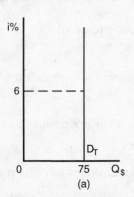 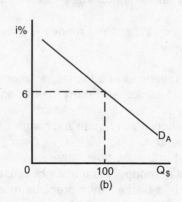 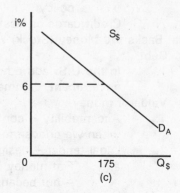

         (a)               (b)               (c)

V. The U.S. Financial System
  A. Early regulatory legislation deemed:
    1. Commercial banks provide checking accounts and make business consumer loans.
    2. Savings and loan associations -- accepted savings deposits and provide for mortgage lending.
    3. A variety of ways to "get around" this legislation provided the impetus for the deregulation of the banking system.
  B. The Depository Institutions Deregulated and Monetary Control Act (DIDMCA) of 1980
    1. Definition -- the "Monetary Control Act" of 1980 allowed banks to become more competitive by reducing the distinctions between them and the restrictions under which they operate.
    2. Provisions of the MCA included:
      a. <u>Uniform Reserve Standards</u> -- imposition of uniform (same) reserve requirements on <u>all</u> depository institutions (commercial banks, savings banks, savings and loan associations, credit unions, and industrial banks). (Previously, only member banks were subject to uniform reserve requirements).
      b. <u>Transaction Accounts</u> -- all depository institutions may hold interest-bearing checkable deposits, such as NOW accounts, checking accounts, etc. Increased FDIC coverage, from $40,000 to $100,000. (Prior to 1980, the only type of transaction account was a demand-deposit (no interest) account at a commercial bank).
      c. <u>Federal Reserve Services</u> -- access to the discount window by any depository institution that issues transaction accounts or nonpersonal time deposits. In addition, depository institutions can now purchase the Fed's services such as a check clearing and electronic transfer of funds. (Prior to 1980, only member banks could apply for loans from the Fed, they could receive its services free).
      d. <u>Thrift-Institution Banking Powers</u> -- expansion of lending powers of savings and loan associations and savings banks; limited authority to offer demand deposits and to make business loans. (Prior to 1982, only commercial banks could engage in such activities).

138

e.     <u>Elimination of usury ceilings</u> -- preemption of state usury ceilings on residential mortgage loans and elimination of usury ceilings on business and agricultural loans over $1,000. In addition, the 6-year phasing-out of interest rate ceilings on commercial banks and thrift institutions. (Prior to 1980, ceilings were in effect).

3.     State Banking

On January 1, 1988, according to the New Jersey Department of Banking, New Jersey opened to nationwide interstate banking. Bank holding companies in the state were permitted to enter any states that have reciprocal interstate banking laws with New Jersey. As of January 1, 1988 14 states (including New York) had interstate banking with Nw Jersey.

C.    Framework of the Federal Reserve System (The "Fed") see "Organization Chart of the Fed"

1.     Introduction

a.     At 6:00 p.m. on December 23, 1913, President Woodrow Wilson entered his office -- he was smiling . . . The President then sat down at his desk and, using four gold pens, signed into law the Federal Reserve Act . . . With this law, Congress established a central banking system which would enable the world's most powerful industrial nation to manage its money and credit far more effectively than ever before . . . the political and legislative struggle to create the Federal Reserve System was long and often extremely bitter, and the final product was the result of a carefully crafted yet somewhat tenuous political compromise. (The Federal Reserve Bank of Boston, "Historical Beginnings . . . the Federal Reserve").

2.     Structure of the Fed

a.     <u>Board of Governors</u> -- seven members, with fourteen-year terms staggered every two years -- appointed by the President with the confirmation of the Senate, which helps keep the Fed independent of the administration. The prime function of the Board is the formulation of monetary policy by determining reserve requirements and approving changes in the discount rate. The Board supervises and regulates member banks and bank holding companies. In addition, it oversees the 12 Federal Reserve Banks. The Chairman and the Vice Chairman of the Board are named for four-year terms by the President.

b.     <u>Federal Open Market Committee</u> -- is made up of the seven members of the Board plus five of the president's of the Federal Reserve Banks (one of whom is the president of the Federal Reserve Bank of New York; the other Bank presidents serve one-year terms on a rotating basis). Open market operations (buying and selling of government securities), are the principal instrument used by the Fed to implement monetary policy.

c.     <u>Federal Advisory Council</u> -- consists of twelve members (one member from each Federal Reserve District selected annually -- usually a prominent banker in the District). The Council confers with the Board of Governors on economic and banking developments and makes recommendations regarding the activities of the Federal Reserve System.

d.     <u>Twelve Federal Reserve Banks</u> -- for the purpose of carrying out day-to-day operations of the Federal Reserve System -- the U.S. has been divided into 12 districts, each with a Federal Reserve Bank. Branches of Reserve Banks have been established in twenty-five cities. Many of the services performed by the Reserve Banks for depository institutions (Bankers' Bank) for a fee are similar to services performed by banks and thrifts for the public.  These services include processing coins, currency, and checks, holding cash reserves and making loans, redeeming government securities, and act as fiscal agent for the U.S. Government.  They supervise and examine member banks for soundness and take primary responsibility for setting the Bank's discount rate (subject to review by the Board of Governors).  District banks are quasi-public banks in that they are a blend of private ownership and government control. They are not motivated by profit, as each year they return to the U.S. Treasury all earnings in excess of Federal Reserve operating and other expenses and statutory dividends paid on stock owned by member banks.  (In 1983 payments to the U.S. Treasury amounted to $14.2 billion -- about 95% of the net earnings).

      e.     <u>Commercial Banks</u> There are approximately 12,453 commercial banks.
- (a)     Roughly two-thirds are state banks -- commercial banks operating a under state charter.  (Prior DIDMCA state banks had the option of joining the Federal Reserve System).
- (b)     Roughly one-third are national banks -- commercial banks operating under a Federal charter (required by law to be a member of the Federal Reserve System).
- (c)     Dual Banking System -- commercial banks have the choice of having either a state or Federal charter.

      f.     <u>Thrift institutions</u>:
1.     There are approximately 2,250 Savings & Loans, 366 Mutual Savings Banks, and 14,141 Credit Unions.
2.     Thrift Institutions are regulated by agencies separate from the Board of Govenors and the District Banks.
3.     DIDMCA made the Savings and Loans subject to the same reserve requirements as other depository institutions.

## VI. Bank and Thrift Failures
  A.   Introduction
1.     Financial innovation and deregulation have enhanced competition among financial institutions and allocative efficiency.
2.     Deregulation and competition have also produced a rising tide of bank and thrift failures.

  B.   Commercial Bank Difficulties
1.     In the early 1980s mostly small banks operating in agriculture and energy producing regions failed.
2.     With the national recession in 1990, there were significant losses in some major banks.
3.     The FDIC was granted permission to borrow from the government.

  C.   Savings and Loan Collapse
1.     Savings and Loans were hit much harder, roughly one-third went out of business between 1987 and today.
2.     Reasons for Savings and Loans Collapse:
    a.     Deregulation and competition
    b.     Deposit insurance

          c.      Loan default and fraud
D.   The Thrift Bailout and Future Reform
      1.     In August of 1989 the Financial Institutions Reform, Recovery, and Enforcement Act (FIRREA) became law.  This new law established the Resolution Trust Corporation (RTC) to oversee the closing or sale of all failed Savings and Loans.  In addition, it increased premiums paid by banks and thrifts for deposit insurance and raised the thrift's capital requirements. Also, it permitted Savings and Loans to accept deposits from commercial businesses. Lastly, FIRREA allows bank holding companies to acquire healthy Savings and Loans.
      2.     FIRREA may be only the first phase of an overall reform of the banking industry.
VII.Last Word:  The Mystery of the Missing Money

## Key Terms

| | |
|---|---|
| medium of exchange | fiat money |
| standard of value | commodity money |
| store of value | depository institution |
| money supply | value of money |
| M1 | FDIC |
| currency | FSLIC |
| paper money | transactions demand for money |
| token money | asset demand for money |
| checkable deposit | total demand for money |
| ATS | Money market |
| NOW | DIDMCA |
| share draft | Board of Governors |
| commercial bank | Open Market Committee |
| thrift institution | Federal Advisory Committee |
| liquid asset | Federal Reserve Bank |
| intrinsic value | central bank |
| face value | bankers' bank |
| F.R. Note | quasi-public bank |
| time deposit | dual-banking system |
| overnight RPs | commercial bank |
| checking account | state bank |
| near-money | national bank |
| plastic money | member bank |
| M2, M3 | reserve requirement |
| noncheckable savings account | discount rate |
| legal tender | FIRREA |

## Federal Reserve System Map

■ Federal Reserve Bank city
▣ Board of Governors of the Federal Reserve System, Washingotn, D.C.
○ Federal Reserve Branch city, by District:
    (2) Buffalo; (4) Cincinnati, Pittsburgh; (5) Baltimore, Charlotte; (6) Birmingham, Jacksonville, Miami, Nashville; (7) Detroit; (8) Little Rock, Louisville, Memphis; (9) Helena; (10) Denver, Oklahoma City, Omaha; (11) El Paso, Houston, San Antonio; (12) Los Angeles, Portland, Salt Lake City, Seattle. District boundaries change periodically. The map shows the boundaries as of February 1993.

141

Source: Board of Governors

Real World Example

**Organization Chart of the Fed**

# The Federal Reserve System

**BOARD OF GOVERNORS**
*Seven members appointed by the President*
- Sets reserve requirements and approves the discount rate as part of monetary policy
- Supervises and regulates member banks, bank holding companies and foreign-owned banks operating in the United States
- Establishes and administers protective regulations governing consumer credit
- Oversees Federal Reserve Banks

The Board exercises general supervision over the Reserve Banks.

**ADVISORY COUNCILS**
- Consumer Advisory Council
- Federal Advisory Council
- Thrift Institutions Advisory Council

These councils advise the Board on various issues.

The members of the Board, along with five presidents from the Reserve Banks, compose the Federal Open Market Committee.

**FEDERAL OPEN MARKET COMMITTEE**
*Board of Governors and five Reserve Bank Presidents*
- Directs open market operations (the buying and selling of U.S. Government securities), the primary tool of monetary policy.

Twelve District Banks serve as the operating arms of the central bank. Five presidents from the Reserve Banks sit on the Federal Open Market Committee.

**FEDERAL RESERVE BANKS**
*Twelve district Banks serve as the operating arms of the central bank. Five presidents of the Reserve Banks sit on the Federal Open Market Committee.*
- Propose discount rate
- Hold reserve balances for depository institutions and lend them at the discount window
- Furnish currency and coin
- Collect, clear, and transfer funds for depository institutions
- Act as fiscal agent for Treasury Department

Source: Board of Governors

## PROBLEMS

1. Describe the earliest beginnings of money. What role did the goldsmiths play?

2. List and explain the three functions of money.

3. Define the money stock:  M1, M2, and M3.

4. What "backs" the U.S. dollar?

5. Name the four principal types of financial institutions and explain the role of each.

6. Why do households and businesses need money?

7. How is the equilibrium interest rate determined?

8. What are the most important recent developments in the U.S. banking system?

9. Discuss the framework of the American financial system.  Explain the role for each area.

10. Below is the demand schedule for money.

TABLE 13-1
Demand for Money (millions)

| Rates of interest | Asset demand for money | Total |
|-------------------|------------------------|-------|
| 20% | $25 | $_____ |
| 18% | $50 | $_____ |
| 16% | $75 | $_____ |
| 14% | $100 | $_____ |
| 12% | $125 | $_____ |
| 10% | $150 | $_____ |

a. If the transactions demand is $50, calculate the total demand for money.

b. On graph paper, plot the total demand for money (D$) at each rate of interest.

c. Assume the money supply (S$) is $150 million, plot this curve on the graph (in "b").

d. What is the equilibrium rate of interest?_____

e. If the money supply increased by $25 million, at each rate of interest, what is the new equilibrium rate of interest?  Show this change on the graph (also in "b").

11. Discuss the recent banking difficulties, the "thrift bailout", and future reform.

# CHAPTER 13     "Money and Banking"

<u>Self-Test</u>

1. The major component of the money supply (M1) is:
    a. currency
    b. coins
    c. gold certificates
    d. demand deposits
2. Which of the following items is a function of money?
    a. medium of money
    b. medium of value
    c. marketable good
    d. medium of barter
3. Which of the following is considered a near-money?
    a. a commercial bank time deposit
    b. a commercial bank demand deposit
    c. a General Motors bond
    d. a gold watch
4. Currently, the U.S. money supply is "backed" by:
    a. gold
    b. silver
    c. copper
    d. faith in the U.S. Government
5. The value of money is:
    a. directly related to the price level
    b. inversely related to the price level
    c. proportionally related to the price level
    d. equally related to the price level
6. Transactions demand for money (Dt) is graphed as:
    a. a vertical line when related to changes in the interest rate
    b. a horizontal line when related to changes in the interest rate
    c. shifts to the left when income increases
    d. an upward sloping curve when related to GDP.
7. When the quantity of money demanded is less than the quantity supplied:
    a. the interest rate will rise
    b. the interest rate will fall
    c. the market demand curve will shift to the left
    d. the money supply curve will shift to the right
8. The Monetary Control Act of 1980:
    a. reduced the competition among banks
    b. dropped fees for services rendered, since all banks must keep a reserve at the Fed
    c. allowed all depository institutions to offer interest-bearing checkable deposits
    d. exercised more control or regulation over depository institutions
9. The policy making arm of the Federal Reserve System is:
    a. the FOMC
    b. the Board of Governors
    c. the Federal Advisory Council
    d. the Federal District Banks
10. District banks are "quasi-public" banks because:
    a. they are a blend of private ownership and government control
    b. they deal only with foreign nations and do not have direct control with the American public
    c. they are able to earn and retain all net earnings
    d. they deal only with the thrift institutions and not the general public

# CHAPTER 14          "How Banks Create Money"

## Chapter Orientation

In the last chapter, money was defined by the components of the money (stock) supply. The most liquid form of money, M1, is currency in circulation plus the <u>checkable deposits</u> in depository institutions -- commercial banks have the largest volume.

What happens when a bank receives a demand deposit? Since, the United States operates under a fractional reserve banking system, some fraction of percentage less than 100% (called the required reserve ratio) must be legally held in reserve at the Federal Reserve District Bank or in vault cash. The balance is then placed into excess reserves, until it is invested or loaned out. For example, if a bank receives a demand deposit of $100, and has a 10 percent required reserve ratio, $10 will be the legal or required reserve and $90 would be placed into excess reserves until it is loaned out. Total (actual) reserves equals required reserves plus excess reserves.

Commercial banks create money whenever they increase the net amount of their loans. Monetary authorities (Board of Governors of the Federal Reserve System) utilize reserve requirements to influence the lending ability of commercial banks. Remember that a single commercial bank can expand (or contract) the money supply only by the amount of its excess reserves; the commercial banking system can expand the money supply by a magnified (money multiplier) amount.

An illustration given in the "Real World Example" shows that with an initial deposit of $1,000,000, and a reserve requirement of 12%, the expansion carried to the theoretical limit, would give rise to $7,333,333 of bank loans and investments. The initial $1,000,000 of reserves can support a total of $8,333,333 of new deposits under a 12% reserve requirement. The deposit expansion or money multiplier (m$), given an amount of excess reserves, is equal to the reciprocal of the required reserve ratio or 1/R.

We will examine the effects of various transactions on the quantity of money. The basic working tool is the "T" account, which gives us a simple step-by-step process on both the asset and liability sides of bank balance sheets.

## Learning Objectives

After reading this chapter in the text and completing the following exercises in this concepts book, you should be able to:

1. Recall the story of the goldsmiths and how they were a preclude to our present banking system.
2. Explain how banks "create" money.
3. Calculate a bank's required and excess reserves given the necessary balance-sheet information.
4. Discuss what is meant by a "fractional reserve system".
5. Explain the function or purpose of required reserves. Are the required reserves adequate to cover all depositors?
6. Describe how a check drawn against a bank and deposited in another bank, effects both the reserves and demand deposits for each bank.
7. Explain why commercial bank reserves are an asset to the commercial bank, but are a liability to the Federal Reserve bank holding them.

8. Illustrate what happens to the money supply when a commercial bank grants a loan (or buys securities); and what happens to the money supply when a loan is repaid (or a bank sells securities).

9. Explain what happens to a commercial bank's reserves and demand deposits after it has made a loan, a check has been written on the newly created demand deposit, deposited in another commercial bank, and cleared.  What happens to the reserves and demand deposits of the commercial bank in which the check was deposited?

10. Describe what would happen to a commercial bank's reserves if it made loans (or bought securities) in an amount greater than its excess reserves.

11. Explain the differences in the money-creating potential of a single commercial bank vs. the banking system.

12. Calculate the money multiplier (m$) and the total loan or investment potential, when given the necessary information.

13. List and explain the two leakages which effect the money-creating potential of the banking system.

14. Explain the need for monetary control.

Chapter Highlights

I.  The Balance Sheet of a Commercial Bank
   A.   Definition -- the purpose of a balance sheet is to show the assets, liabilities, and net worth (capital stock) of a bank.  In practice, total assets should equal total liabilities plus net worth.
II. Background Information
   A.   History of the goldsmiths
   B.   Prelude to our fractional reserve system of banking
        1.    Money creation
        2.    Bank "panics" and "runs"
III. Creation of a Single Commercial Bank and the Creation of Money
   A.   Steps in organizing a single commercial bank:
        1.    Birth of a bank
              a.    Secure a national or state charter
              b.    Sell shares of stock in return for cash ("vault cash" or "till money").
        2.    Becoming a going concern
              a.    Purchase property and equipment needed to run the bank
        3.    Accepting deposits
              a.    Depository cash in the bank does not change the total supply of money -- it merely changes the composition from currency in circulation (decreases) to demand deposits (increase).
        4.    Depository reserves in a Federal Reserve (District) Bank
              a.    All depository institutions with checkable deposits will have:
                    (1)    Legal (required) reserves -- some fraction less than 100% of the total deposit must be kept at the Federal Bank or vault cash.  Legal, or required reserves, cannot be used for meeting unexpected cash withdrawals.  Its purpose is a means in which the Board of Governors can influence the lending ability of commercial banks.
                    (2)    The reserve ratio (R) is a specified percentage that banks use to calculate legal reserves.
                    (3)    The actual reserves are the deposits of a commercial bank at the Federal Reserve Bank.
                    (4)    The excess reserves (E) equal the actual (total) reserves minus the

required reserves.
(5)     Commercial bank reserves are an asset to the commercial bank; but are a liability to the Federal Reserve Bank holding them.
5.     A check is drawn against the bank
a.     Effects -- whenever a check is drawn against a bank and deposited in another bank, the first bank loses (transfers) both reserves and deposits and the second gains both reserves and deposits.
6.     Granting a loan
a.     A single commercial bank in a multibank banking system can lend only an amount equal to its initial preloan excess reserves.
b.     Whenever a bank grants a loan, it creates money -- they create a demand (checkable) deposits which are money.  This increases the bank's deposit liabilities and the supply of money.
c.     When the loan is repaid, the bank's deposit liabilities and the supply of money decrease (currency held by bank is excluded from the money supply).
7.     Repaying a loan
a.     Money is credited when banks make a loan and it vanishes when bank customers pay off loans.
8.     Buying government securities
a.     When a commercial bank purchases securities, it increases its own deposit liabilities and the supply of money (when the securities dealer draws and clears the check, the bank will lose reserves and deposits in that amount).
b.     The selling of securities to the public will reduce the bank's deposit liabilities and the supply of money.
9.     A bank's balance sheet reflects the tradeoff between profits (making loans; purchasing securities) and safety (liquidity such as having excess reserves or vault cash).

IV. Banking System:  Multiple Deposit Expansion
A.     Definition of the demand-deposit expansion or money multiplier (m$)
1.     A single bank in a banking system can only lend the amount of its excess reserves. The banking system can lend (create money) a multiple of its excess reserves or (excess reserves x m$) because the reserves lost by a single bank are not lost to the banking system as a whole.
2.     Three underlying assumptions are made:
a.     Uniform reserve ratio
b.     All banks are "loaned up" no excess reserves
c.     Checks for the entire amount of the loan will be written and deposited.
B.     Complications to demand-deposit expansion
1.     Additional leakages
a.     Borrowers choose to be paid in cash (rather than a demand-deposit).
b.     Bankers choose to hold excess reserves (rather than lend the excess).
C.     Banks are procyclical in their lending
1.     During prosperity, banks happily extend credit to the maximum of their excess reserves.  Borrowers are working, the economy is expanding, so the thought of default is minimized.
2.     During a recession or depression, banks are extremely cautious in lending money (because of fear of default) and therefore retreat to the safety of liquidity (excess reserves) even at the expense of interest income.

3.      As a result of banks intensifying the business cycles, the Federal Reserve must use its "monetary tools", which are anticyclical, to stabilize the money supply.

V. Last Word:  The Bank Panics of 1930 - 1933

Key Terms

| | | |
|---|---|---|
| balance sheet | legal (required) reserve | FDIC |
| assets | reserve ratio | lending potential |
| liabilities | actual reserve | leakages |
| net worth (capital stock) | excess reserve | loaned-up |
| fractional reserve system | monetary (money) multiplier | anticyclical |
| vault cash (till money) | procyclical | promissory note |
| monetary tools | | |

Real World Example

Suppose the Federal Reserve wanted to expand the money supply to achieve its policy objectives. One way the central bank can initiate such an expansion is through the purchases of government securities in the open market -- at the trading desk located at the Federal Reserve Bank of New York.

Let's say the Fed buys $1,000,000 of Treasury bills from a securities dealer who in turn deposits the payment in his/her local Bank (#1). When the check clears, Bank #1 has $1,000,000 credit to its account at the Fed (the Fed has added $1,000,000 of securities to its assets).

Under current regulations, the reserve requirement is usually 12% against most transactions balances. Therefore, Bank #1 must keep 12% (or $120,000) in required reserves at the Fed or in vault cash and has $880,000 in excess reserves to be loaned out. (Stage 1).

Assuming that Bank #1 loans out the $880,00 of deposits created in Stage 1, then loans and deposits will rise by $774,400 in the second stage of expansion (Stage 2). We are assuming that the borrowers purchased something and the sellers in turn deposited the checks in Bank (#2). Since Bank #2 received $880,000 in deposits, they are in a position to hold approximately $105,600 in required reserves and loan out $774,400.

The process continues (see next page) until the total expansion of $7,333,333 of bank loans and investments takes place. The initial $1,000,000 of reserves can support a total of $8,333,333 of new deposits under a 12% reserve requirement.

### Deposit expansion
The amounts in the following illustrations are in thousands of dollars

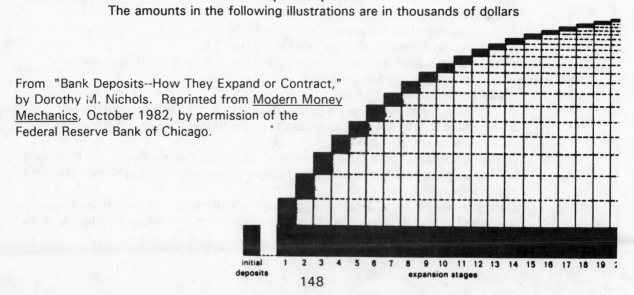

From "Bank Deposits--How They Expand or Contract," by Dorothy M. Nichols. Reprinted from <u>Modern Money Mechanics</u>, October 1982, by permission of the Federal Reserve Bank of Chicago.

## PROBLEMS

1. Discuss the process (steps) involved in forming a commercial bank.


2. Explain the differences in the money creating potential for a single commercial bank vs. the banking system as a whole.


3. Explain the function or purpose of required reserves. Are the required reserves adequate to cover all depositors?



4. Describe how a check drawn against a bank and deposited in another bank, effects both the reserves and demand deposits for each bank.



5.

### Simplified Bank Balance Sheet

| Assets | | Liabilities and Net Worth | |
|---|---|---|---|
| Total Reserves: | $_____ | Demand Deposits | $10,000 |
| Required | _____ | | |
| Excess | 0 | | |
| | | | |
| Loans | $8,000 | | |
| | | Total Liabilities | |
| Total Assets | $10,000 | and Net Worth | $10,000 |

a. Fill in the Balance Sheet above.

b. What is the required reserve ratio (R)?_____

c. If this bank received $10,000 in <u>new</u> deposits, its required reserves would become _____.

d. Construct a new balance sheet for part "c" above.

e. If all banks had the same required reserve ratio, what would the money multiplier (m$) be? _____

f. Therefore, this additional $10,000 in new deposits would expand loans and investments by _____.

## PROBLEMS

6. Suppose Bank #1 receives $2,000 as a new deposit in someone's checking account. Assuming a 20% reserve requirement, complete the balance sheet below.

BANK #1

| Assets | | Liabilities and Net Worth | |
| --- | --- | --- | --- |
| Total Reserves: | _____ | Demand Deposits | _____ |
| Required _____ | | | |
| Excess _____ | | | |
| | | | |
| | | Total Liabilities | |
| Total Assets | _____ | and Net Worth | _____ |

7. At this point, how much can Bank #1 loan out? _____

8. Suppose Denise W. borrows this entire amount from Bank #1 to pay for a rug she is buying from Michael B. Show the new balance sheet after the loan has been withdrawn.

BANK #1

| Assets | | Liabilities and Net Worth | |
| --- | --- | --- | --- |
| Total Reserves: | _____ | Demand Deposits | _____ |
| Required _____ | | | |
| Excess _____ | | | |
| Loans: | _____ | | |
| | | Total Liabilities | |
| Total Assets | _____ | and Net Worth | _____ |

## PROBLEMS

9. Michael deposits the money which he received for the rug in his checking account in Bank #2. Assume he has the only account and the reserve requirement ratio (R) is 20%, complete the balance sheet below.

BANK #2

| Assets | | Liabilities and Net Worth | |
|--------|--|---------------------------|--|
| Total Reserves: | _____ | Demand Deposits | _____ |
| Required _____ | | | |
| Excess _____ | | | |
| | | Total Liabilities | |
| Total Assets | _____ | and Net Worth | _____ |

10.    At this point, how much can Bank #2 loan out? _____

11.    Suppose Erin borrows this entire amount to buy a car from Valerie. Show the new balance sheet after Erin's money has been withdrawn from Bank #2.

BANK #2

| Assets | | Liabilities and Net Worth | |
|--------|--|---------------------------|--|
| Total Reserves: | _____ | Demand Deposits | _____ |
| Required _____ | | | |
| Excess _____ | | | |
| Loans | _____ | | |
| | | Total Liabilities | |
| Total Assets | _____ | and Net Worth | _____ |

Self-Test

1. Commercial banks increase the money supply when:
   a.    they accept deposits
   b.    the amounts of new loans exceed the old loans being paid off.
   c.    the amounts of old loans exceed the new loans being made.
   d.    they sell government securities.
2. If $1 of cash in a bank's vault (or at the Fed) can be used by a commercial bank to support $5 of new deposits:
   a.    the reserve ratio is .5.                    c.    the reserve ratio is .20.
   b.    the reserve ratio is .25.                   d.    every $1 reduction of cash must reduce reserves by .5.
3. If you borrow $1,000 from your local bank to buy a fur jacket, the transactions alone will:
   a.    increase the money supply by $1,000.
   b.    increase the money supply by more than $1,000.
   c.    increase the money supply by less than $1,000.
   d.    not change the money supply.
4. If the First National Bank has $10,000 in excess reserves and the reserve ratio is 25%, the bank must have:
   a.    $100,000 in demand deposits and $35,000 in total (actual) reserves.
   b.    $100,000 in demand deposits and $25,000 in total (actual) reserves.
   c.    $40,000 in demand deposits and $10,000 in total (actual) reserves.
   d.    $50,000 in demand deposits and $5,000 in total (actual) reserves.
5. The purpose of a reserve requirement is:
   a.    to cover the demand-deposits.              c.    to insure liquidity in the system.
   b.    to protect depositors.                     d.    for the Fed to control the money supply.
6. Commercial banks create money when they:
   a.    hold their excess reserves.
   b.    collect checks through the Fed.
   c.    increase the net amount of their loans.
   d.    accept repayment on a loan.
7. When commercial banks loan the maximum amount:
   a.    legal reserves will be zero.
   b.    legal reserves will equal actual reserves.
   c.    excess reserves will equal zero.
   d.    all of the above.
8. Practicing fractional reserve banking:
   a.    increases liabilities of the bank.         c.    attracts depositors to the bank.
   b.    reduces profits for the bank.              d.    increases profits for the bank.
9. Assume that $20,000 is deposited at a commercial bank which has a 25% reserve requirement and is fully loaned up. What is the total amount of new loans which can be made in the banking system?
   a.    $80,000                                    c.    $20,000
   b.    $60,000                                    d.    $10,000
10. A bank's balance sheet reflects the tradeoff between:
   a.    assets and liabilities                     c.    what you have and what you owe.
   b.    profits and safety.                        d.    all of the above.

## Chapter Orientation

Chapter 14 left us with a dilemma to solve -- banks actually intensify the business cycle (procyclical). As a result, the Board of Governors (policy-making arm) of the Federal Reserve System, must reverse or counteract these fluctuations by utilizing the major and minor monetary controls (tools) available. For example, what actions would the Fed take to counteract inflation? or recession? These questions will be addressed in Chapter 15.

In addition, the Keynesian viewpoint (cause-effect chain) of how monetary policy works will be presented step-by-step. The goal of monetary policy (and fiscal policy) is to stabilize the economy--to achieve a full-employment, noninflationary level of output. The effectiveness of monetary policy is determined by comparing the strengths and shortcomings of this system. Because monetary policy is implemented by the 12 Federal Reserve Banks, a consolidated balance sheet is examined.

Chapter 15 is a good "wrap-up" chapter for Fiscal and Monetary Policy because it reviews both and reaches the conclusion that although they are different, fiscal and monetary policy should be coordinated to maximize the goal of stabilizing the economy at a full-employment, non-inflationary level.

## Learning Objectives
After reading this chapter in the text, and completing the following exercises in this concepts book, you should be able to:

1. Explain the objectives of monetary policy.
2. Discuss the cause-effect chain between monetary policy and output and employment.
3. Explain the impact of interest rates on consumer investment (saving).
4. List and explain the two major assets and the three major liabilities of the Federal Reserve Banks.
5. Identify the three tools (or techniques) employed by the Board of Governors of the Federal Reserve System and explain how each can expand or contract the money supply.
6. State the most important (effective) tool that the Fed utilizes.
7. List and explain the three selective controls which supplement the major instruments of monetary policy.
8. Draw the demand and supply curves for money. Show how a change in the money supply will effect the interest rate, investment-demand, and equilibrium GDP.
9. Explain how the shape of the demand for money and the investment-demand curves influence the impact of a change in the money supply and on the equilibrium GDP.
10. Using the AS - AD model show the effect of changes in monetary policy.
11. Explain the three strengths and four shortcomings of monetary policy.
12. State the policy (or target) dilemma faced by the Fed and explain why it faces this dilemma.
13. Explain the Keynesian theory of employment and stabilization policies (text page 298).
14. Describe the problem of coordinating monetary and fiscal policy using Keynesian theory.

## Chapter Highlights
I. Objectives of Monetary Policy
   A.  Goal
       1.      To stabilize the economy by achieving a full-employment, noninflationary level of total output.

II. Consolidated Balance Sheet of the 12 Federal Reserve Banks
  A.   Assets
    1.      Securities (government bonds to adjust commercial bank reserves and therefore their ability to create money).
    2.      Loans to commercial banks (commercial banks increase their reserves in exchange for IOUs).
  B.   Liabilities
    1.      Reserves of commercial banks (deposits).
    2.      Treasury deposits (enables the Treasury to draw checks and pay obligations.
    3.      Federal Reserve Notes (our paper money supply consists of Federal Reserve Notes).
      a.      Federal Reserve Notes in circulation are liabilities for the Fed banks.
      b.      Those notes out of circulation (resting in the vault of the Fed) are neither an asset nor a liability.
III. Tools techniques of Monetary Policy
  A.   Major tools
    1.      Open-market operations -- (discussed in Chapter 17 under FOMC) -- the buying and selling of government securities by the Federal Reserve, in the open market.
      a.      Buying government securities increases the reserves ("Easy Money").
      b.      Selling government securities decreases the reserves ("Tight Money").
    2.      The Reserve ratio -- the percentage of deposit liabilities that a bank must maintain with the Federal Reserve Bank and vault cash.
      a.      Raising the reserve ratio reduces excess reserves and the money multiplier putting downward pressure on the money supply ("Tight Money").
      b.      Lowering the reserve ratio has the opposite effect (from 2a), "Easy Money".
    3.      The Discount rate -- the percentage charged on loans from the Federal Reserve Banks.
      a.      Raising the discount rate discourages borrowing (which discourages excess reserves) "Tight Money".
      b.      Lowering the discount rate encourages borrowing (which encourages excess reserves and loans to the public) "Easy Money".
  B.   A Preview:  Easy Money and Tight Money
    1.      "Easy Money"--to make credit cheaply and easily available.  To increase AE and employment.
    2.      "Tight Money"--to tighten the supply of money to reduce spending and control inflation.
  C.   Minor selective controls (to supplement the major tools listed previously)
    1.      Margin requirement -- a government restriction concerning the minimum down payment required to purchase stock from a financial institution (currently 50%) with the stock pledged as collateral.  Raising the margin requirements discourages investing in the stock market; lowering the margin requirement has the opposite effect.
    2.      Consumer Credit -- Congress may authorize the Board of Governors to invoke specific restraints on consumer credit. Tightening credit discourages spending; loosening credit has the opposite effect.
    3.      Moral suasion -- monetary authorities can use "jawboning" (oral statements) to influence lending policies of commercial banks.
IV. Cause-effect chain:  Keynesian view and the traditional view
  A.   The Federal Reserve Banks can accomplish the goal of monetary policy by:
    1.      Influencing the size of excess reserves which

      2.     Influences the supply of money

      3.     Influences the interest rate and bank credit which

      4.     Influences investment spending, output, employment and the price level.

  B.   The Board of Governors directs the Federal Reserve Banks to increase (or decrease) the excess reserves of commercial banks -- this starts the ball rolling . . .

  C.   Investment effect

      1.     The impact of the interest rate

          a.     Investment spending is very sensitive to change in the interest rates (long-term purchases are "locked-in").

          b.     Consumer spending is not quite as sensitive to changes in the interest rates (can refinance or "stretch" most payments over a longer time period).

V. Recap of the Equilibrium  and Monetary Policy

  A.   Effects of monetary policy

      1.     In the money market where the demand for money (transactions plus asset demand) equals the supply of money (determined autonomously by the Board of Governors) is the real interest rate; which is projected off the investment-demand curve; which plugs into the leakages-injections ("bathtub") model to determine the equilibrium GDP level.

      2.     The shapes of the demand for money and the investment-demand curves determine the impact on the money supply and the impact on the equilibrium GDP.

          a.     The steeper the demand for money curve and the flatter the investment-demand curve the greater the effect on equilibrium GDP.

      3.     Using the AS - AD model:  the flatter the AS curve, the greater is the effect of a change in the money supply on GDP, income and employment and the smaller is the effect on the price level.  The opposite effect occur with a steeper AS curve.

VI. Effectiveness of Monetary Policy

  A.   Strengths of monetary policy

      1.     Speed and flexibility -- monetary policy can be more quickly altered than fiscal policy.

      2.     Political acceptability -- monetary policy is more subtle and more politically conservative than raising taxes.

      3.     Monetarism -- economists who believe that changes in the money supply are the key determinants of the level of economic activity (called "Monetarists").

  B.   Shortcomings/problems of monetary policy

      1.     Cyclical asymmetry -- the power of a tight money policy <u>may</u> be greater than that of an easy money policy (Fed cannot <u>force</u> "easy money").

      2.     Changes in velocity

          a.     Velocity of money -- the number of times per year the average dollar is spent on goods and services.

          b.     Many Keynesians feel that velocity may change in opposite directions of the money supply.

      3.     The investment impact

          a.     Some economists believe that monetary policy only has a small impact upon investment spending in the economy.

  C.   The target (tradeoff) dilemma:  controls the money supply or the interest rate?

      1.     By controlling (stabilizing) the interest rate, the Fed will increase the supply of money, which may turn a healthy recovery into an inflationary boom (low interest rates).

      2.     Likewise to decrease the supply of money may turn the economy into a recession (because of the high interest rates).

    3.      History has shown that the Fed has switched from stabilizing interest rates to stabilizing the money supply, and from stabilizing the money supply to a middle-of-the-road policy in October of 1982.

  D.   Monetary Policy and the International Economy

      1.      International flows of financial capital in response to interest rate changes in the U.S., strengthen domestic monetary policy.

      2.      "Easy Money" Policy is compatible with the goal of correcting a trade deficit.

      3.      "Tight Money" Policy conflicts with the goal of correcting a balance of trade deficit.

VII. Fiscal and Monetary Policy

  A.   Fiscal Policy

      1.      Definition -- using the government's tools of spending and taxing to correct "problems" in the economy.

      2.      Discretionary and "built-in" stabilizers are part of fiscal policy

  B.   Fiscal and monetary policy

      1.      Interrelated and should be coordinated to maximize the effectiveness.

VIII. Last Word:  For the Fed, Life is a Metaphor

## Key Terms

| | |
|---|---|
| monetary policy | selective controls |
| cause-effect chain | moral suasion |
| monetarists | money market |
| treasury deposits | cyclical asymmetry |
| Federal Reserve Notes | velocity of money |
| open-market operations | cost-push inflation |
| easy money | fiscal policy |
| tight money | discretionary stabilizers |
| reserve ratio | built-in stabilizers |
| margin requirement | |

Real World Example

## Paul Volcker and the Fed
### Paul Volcker's reign at the Fed

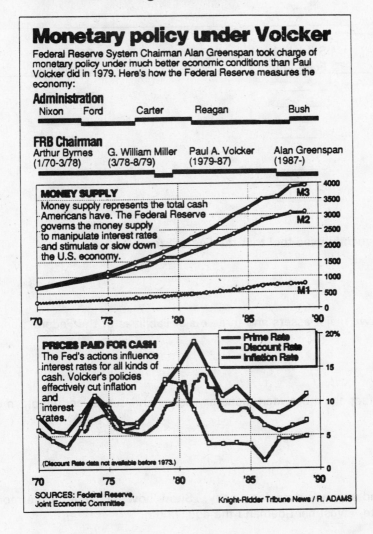

# Monetary policy under Volcker

Federal Reserve System Chairman Alan Greenspan took charge of monetary policy under much better economic conditions than Paul Volcker did in 1979. Here's how the Federal Reserve measures the economy:

**Administration**

Nixon  Ford          Carter          Reagan          Bush

**FRB Chairman**

| Arthur Byrnes (1/70-3/78) | G. William Miller (3/78-8/79) | Paul A. Volcker (1979-87) | Alan Greenspan (1987-) |

**MONEY SUPPLY**
Money supply represents the total cash Americans have. The Federal Reserve governs the money supply to manipulate interest rates and stimulate or slow down the U.S. economy.

M3  M2  M1

**PRICES PAID FOR CASH**
The Fed's actions influence interest rates for all kinds of cash. Volcker's policies effectively cut inflation and interest rates.

Prime Rate
Discount Rate
Inflation Rate

(Discount Rate data not available before 1973.)

SOURCES: Federal Reserve, Joint Economic Committee

Knight-Ridder Tribune News / R. ADAMS

| YEAR | M1 | M2 | M3 | discount AVG | Prime AVG | CPI | 30-YR MORTG avg |
|------|-----|------|------|------|------|------|------|
| 1977 | 335.3 | 1286.6 | 1472.5 | | | 6.8 | 9.0 |
| 78 | 363.0 | 1388.9 | 1646.4 | | | 9.0 | |
| 79 | 389.0 | 1497.9 | 1803.6 | 10.28 | 12.67 | 13.3 | 10.78 |
| 80 | 414.8 | 1631.4 | 1988.5 | 11.77 | 15.27 | 12.5 | 12.66 |
| 81 | 441.8 | 1794.4 | 2235.8 | 13.41 | 18.87 | 8.9 | 14.70 |
| 82 | 480.8 | 1954.9 | 2446.8 | 11.02 | 14.86 | 3.8 | 15.14 |
| 83 | 528.0 | 2188.8 | 2701.7 | 8.50 | 10.79 | 3.8 | 12.57 |
| 84 | 551.9 | 2367.2 | 2982.3 | 8.80 | 12.04 | 3.9 | 12.38 |
| 85 | 620.5 | 2567.4 | 3201.7 | 7.69 | 9.93 | 3.8 | 11.55 |
| 86 | 725.9 | 2811.2 | 3494.9 | 6.33 | 8.33 | 1.1 | 10.17 |
| 87 | 752.3 | 2909.9 | 3677.6 | 5.66 | 8.22 | 4.4 | 9.31 |
| 88 | 790.3 | 3069.3 | 3919.0 | 6.20 | 9.32 | 4.4 | 9.19 |
| 89 | 786.2 | 3079.4 | 3955.7 | 7.00 | 11.00 | 5.0 | 10.00 |

## PROBLEMS

1a.     Fill in the table below, based upon the correct policy actions by the Fed to stimulate or slow-down the economy.

| Tool | "Easy $" Stimulate Economy | "Tight $" Slow-down Economy |
|---|---|---|
| Government securities | _____ | _____ |
| Discount rate | _____ | _____ |
| Reserve requirement | _____ | _____ |
| Margin requirement | _____ | _____ |
| Interest rate on savings accounts | _____ | _____ |
| Consumer credit | _____ | _____ |
| Moral suasion | _____ | _____ |

b. What is the most frequently used tool that the Fed utilizes?

2. List and explain the two major assets and three major liabilities of the Federal Reserve Banks.

3. Discuss the cause-effect chain between monetary policy and output and employment.

4. Draw the demand and supply curves for money.  Show how a change in the money supply will effect the interest rate, investment-demand the equilibrium .

5. Discuss the strengths and shortcomings of monetary policy.

6. Explain the target, or tradeoff dilemma, faced by the Fed.

# CHAPTER 15      "The Federal Reserve Banks and Monetary Policy"

<u>Self-Test</u>

1. The Federal Reserve controls the level of _____ and hence greatly influences the _____.
   - a. bank reserves; money supply
   - b. income; money supply
   - c. prices; level of investment
   - d. prices; inflationary gap

2. A decrease in the money supply _____ the interest rate, and the new interest rate _____ investment spending.
   - a. lowers; lowers
   - b. raises; lowers
   - c. raises; raises
   - d. lowers; raises

3. The _____ the demand for money curve, and the _____ the investment-demand curve, the greater the effect on equilibrium GDP.
   - a. steeper; flatter
   - b. flatter; steeper
   - c. constant; more vertical
   - d. more horizontal; more vertical

4. Which of the following determines the position of the supply curve for money?
   - a. The Board of Governors of the Federal Reserve, through its control over bank reserves by monetary policy.
   - b. Congress, through control of the federal appropriations and its Money and Banking Committee.
   - c. The president of the Federal Reserve Banks who sit as a committee to formulate monetary policy.
   - d. The Council of Economic Advisers, through recommendations to the Congressional money and banking committees.

5. Which of the following is a true statement about the total demand for money?
   - a. The total demand for money is equal to the transaction demand plus total vault cash.
   - b. The total demand for money is equal to the asset demand plus the transaction demand for money.
   - c. The total demand for money is equal to the asset demand plus total vault cash.
   - d. The total demand for money is equal to the difference between transaction demand and asset demand for money.

6. If a commercial bank has demand deposits of $100, reserves of $75 and a required reserve ratio of 20%, it has excess reserves of:
   - a. $75
   - b. $55
   - c. $20
   - d. $100

7. The most frequently (day-to-day) monetary tool used by the Fed is:
   - a. the discount rate
   - b. the margin requirement
   - c. the reserve ratio
   - d. open-market operations

8. To establish a "tight money" policy, the Board of Governors of the Federal Reserve may:
   - a. increase the discount rate and lower the reserve ratio
   - b. increase the reserve ratio and sell government securities in the open market
   - c. increase the reserve ratio and lower the discount rate
   - d. sell government securities in the open market and lower the discount rate

9. Changing the required reserve ratio may be ineffective as an "easy money" policy because:
   - a. it takes large changes in the reserve ratio to offset a recession
   - b. banks are required to maintain a legal reserve
   - c. banks may hold excess reserves
   - d. Congress may overrule the Fed's decision

10. Which of the following is <u>not</u> considered an asset to a Federal Reserve bank?
   - a. Gold certificate account
   - b. Federal Reserve Notes
   - c. Loans to depository institutions
   - d. U.S. government securities

## Chapter 8 - "Macroeconomic Instability: Unemployment and Inflation"

I. Overview of the Business Cycles
    A. The historical record
    B. Definition
    C. Phases
        1. Peak
        2. Recession
        3. Trough
        4. Recovery
    D. Causation: A First Glance
        1. Major innovations
        2. Political and random events
        3. Monetary impact
        4. Aggregate expenditure
    E. Noncyclical variations
        1. Seasonal fluctuations
        2. Secular trends
    F. Cyclical impact: Durable and Nondurables
        1. Durable vs. nondurable goods
            a. Definitions
            b. Impact during a recession
            c. Impact during recovery
            d. Degree of competition
    G. NBER indicators
        1. Leading
        2. Coincident
        3. Lagging

II. Unemployment
    A. Types of unemployment
        1. Frictional (transitional)
        2. Structural
        3. Cyclical
        4. Seasonal
    B. Defining "full employment"
    C. Definition of unemployment
    D. Measurement of unemployment
        1. Bureau of Labor Statistics (BLS) conducts a random survey of 60,000 households each month.
        2. Unemployment rate
        3. Reliability of the unemployment rate
            a. Overstated
            b. Understated
        4. The "full-employment unemployment rate" or the "natural rate of unemployment".
    E. Economic Costs of unemployment
        1. Economic costs
            a. Definition
            b. Okun's Law

        c.      Unequal burdens
    2.    Noneconomic (social) costs
        a.      Definition
        b.      Employment Act of 1946
    3.    International Comparisons
        a.      Unemployment rate in U.S. and other industrialized countries.

III. Inflation: Defined and Measured
  A. Definition
  B. Measuring Inflation
    1.    Rate of Inflation
    2.    Rule of 70
  C. Indexes for measuring inflation:
    1.    Consumer Price Index (CPI)
    2.    Producer Price Index (PPI)
    3.    GNP deflator
  D. The Facts of inflation
    1.    Comparison of U.S. to other industrialized countries
  E. Causes: Theories of Inflation
    1.    Demand-pull inflation
        a.      Definition
        b.      Three ranges of the graph:
            (1)    Range I, Range II, Range III
    2.    Cost-push or supply-side inflation
        a.      Definition
        b.      Wage-push variant
        c.      Supply shock variant
  F. Redistributive Effects of Inflation
    1.    Real-income costs
    2.    Fixed income
    3.    Savers
    4.    Debtors/creditors
    5.    Anticipated
    6.    Government borrowing
    7.    Progressive tax structure
    8.    Balancing benefits and cost
  G. Output effect of Inflation
    1.    Demand-pull
    2.    Cost-push
    3.    Hyperinflation

## Chapter 17 "The Inflation-Unemployment Relationship"

I. The Phillips Curve
  A. The Phillips Curve: Concept and Data
    1.    Definition
    2.    A.W. Phillips (1914-1975)
  B. Logic of the Phillips Curve
    1.    Two reasons why inflation occurs before reaching full-employment.

    2.     Movement along the Phillips Curve (monetary and fiscal policies).

    3.     Shifts in the Phillips Curve (supply shocks).

  C.  Stabilization Policy Dilemma

II.  Stagflation

  A.  Definition

  B.  Causes of Stagflation

    1.     Six supply shocks

  C.  Demand-management policies are not effective in treating stagflation.

  D.  Stagflation's Demise 1982-1988

III.  The Natural Rate Hypothesis

  A.  Definition

  B.  Adaptive Expectations Theory

    1.     Definition

    2.     Short-run Phillips Curve

    3.     Long-run Phillips Curve

    4.     Disinflation

  C.  The Rational -- Expectations Theory

    1.     Definition

    2.     Impact on the economy.

  D.  Contradiction of the Phillips Curve

IV.  Aggregate Supply (revisited)

  A.  Definitions

  B.  Short-run AS

  C.  Long-run AS

  D.  Keynesian versus New Classical Policy Implications

V.  Demand-pull and Cost-push Inflation

  A.  Demand-pull

    1.     Definition

    2.     Short-run versus long-run

  B.  Cost-Push

    1.     Definition

    2.     Role of government

VI.  Policy Options

  A.  Market policies

    1.     Manpower policy

    2.     Procompetition policy

  B.  Wage-price (incomes) policies

    1.     Definition

    2.     Five periods of incomes policies in recent history

    3.     Three issues concerning incomes policies

    4.     Special tax rebates (or penalties) for compliance (or noncompliance).

  C.  Supply-side economics

    1.     Definition

    2.     Impact of AS alleviates stagflation.

    3.     Role of taxes and transfer payments

    4.     Impact of regulation

    D. Reaganomics
        1.     Definition
    E. The Laffer Curve
        1.     Definition
        2.     Arthur Laffer
        3.     Impact on supply-side economics
    F. Criticisms of the Laffer Curve.
        1.     Four criticisms
VII. The Effects of Reaganomics
    A. Pros and Cons

## Chapter 13 "Money and Banking"

I. Money
    A. History of money
    B. Functions of Money
        1.     Medium of exchange
        2.     Measure of value
        3.     Store of value
II. The Money (Stock) Supply
    A. Components of the money (stock) supply
        1.     Definition of M1
            a.     Currency (token money)
            b.     Types of checkable deposits
        2.     Four principal types of financial institutions:
            a.     Commercial banks
            b.     Savings and loan associations
            c.     Mutual savings banks
            d.     Credit unions
    B. Liquid Assets
        1.     Definition
        2.     Types
    C. Near-monies: M2 and M3
        1.     Definition
        2.     Types
        3.     Definition of M2
        4.     Definition of M3
        5.     Definition of credit cards (plastic money).
        6.     Reasons why near-monies are important (3).
III. "What Backs" the Money (Stock) Supply
    A. Debts of the government
    B. Value of money
        1.     Acceptability
        2.     Legal tender
            a.     Fiat money
            b.     Commodity money
        3.     Supply and demand of money.
        4.     Inverse relationship between the value of money and the price level.

5.      Government's role in stabilizing the value of money.

IV. Demand for Money
- A. Households and businesses need money for:
  - 1.     Transactions demand
    - a.     Definition
    - b.     Influenced by the level of money (income) or nominal GDP.
    - c.     Varies directly with nominal GDP.
    - d.     Shown as a vertical line.
  - 2.     Asset demand
    - a.     Definition
    - b.     Influenced by the rate of interest.
    - c.     Varies inversely with the rate of interest.
- B. Total demand for money
  - 1.     Definition
- C. Equilibrium
  - 1.     Where the total demand curve intersects the money supply curve.
  - 2.     Determines the rate of interest in the market.

V. The U.S. Financial System
- A. Early regulatory legislation deemed:
  - 1.     Roles for commercial banks and savings and loan associations.
- B. The Depository Institutions Deregulated and Monetary Control Act (DIDMCA) of 1980
  - 1.     Provisions
    - a.     Uniform Reserve Standards
    - b.     Transaction Accounts
    - c.     Federal Reserve Services
    - d.     Thrift-Institution Banking Powers
    - e.     Elimination of usury ceilings
- C. Framework of the Federal Reserve System (The "Fed")
  - 1.     Introduction
    - a.     background (beginning of the Federal Reserve System)
  - 2.     Structure of the Fed
    - a.     Board of Governors
      - 1.     responsibilities
    - b.     Federal Open Market Committee (FOMC)
      - 1.     responsibilities
    - c.     Federal Advisory Council
      - 1.     responsibilities
    - d.     Federal Reserve Banks
      - 1.     responsibilities
    - e.     Commercial Banks
      - 1.     State banks (operating under a state charter)
      - 2.     National banks (operating under a Federal charter).
      - 3.     Dual Banking System"
    - f.     Thrift institutions:
      - 1.     Savings and Loan Associations

VI. Bank and Thrift Failures
- A. Introduction

    B.  Commerical Bank Difficulties
    C.  Savings and Loan Collapse
    D.  The Thrift Bailout and Future Reform
        1.    FIRREA
        2.    Banking Reform

## Chapter 14 "How Banks Create Money"

I.  The Balance Sheet of a commercial bank
    A.  Definition of a balance sheet
II.  Background Information
    A.  History of the goldsmiths
    B.  Prelude to our fractional reserve system of banking
        1.    Money creation
        2.    Bank "panics" and "runs"
III.  Creation of a Single Commercial Bank and the Creation of Money
    A.  Steps in organizing a single commercial bank:
        1.    Birth of a bank
            a.    Secure a national or state charter
            b.    Sell shares of stock in return for cash ("vault cash").
        2.    Becoming a going concern
            a.    Purchase property and equipment
        3.    Accepting deposits
            a.    Depository a check does not alter the total money supply, merely changes its composition.
        4.    Depository reserves in a Federal Reserve (District) Bank
            a.    All depository institutions with checkable deposits will have:
                1.    Legal (required) reserves
                2.    Reserve ratio (R)
                3.    Actual (total) reserves
                4.    Excess reserves (E)
                5.    Reserves are assets and liabilities
        5.    A check is drawn against the bank
            a.    Effects -- transfers of reserves and deposits.
        6.    Granting a loan
            a.    A single commercial bank can loan up to its excess reserves.
            b.    The banking system can create money (checkable deposits).
            c.    Repayment of loan.
        7.    Repaying a loan
            a.    Money vanished when a loan is repaid
        8.    Buying government securities
            a.    When a commercial bank purchases securities:
                1.    It increases its own deposit liabilities
                2.    Increases the supply of money
                3.    When the securities dealer draws and clears the check, the bank will lose reserves and deposits in that amount.
            b.    When a commercial bank sells securities:
                1.    Reduce the bank's deposit liabilities.

              2.      Reduce the supply of money.
      9.     A bank's balance sheet reflects
            a.      The tradeoff between profits (making loans; purchasing securities) and safety (liquidity such as having excess reserves and vault cash).

IV. The Money Multiplier (M$) in the Banking System
    A. Definition of the demand-deposit expansion or money multiplier (m )
       1.     Three underlying assumptions
    B. Complications to demand-deposit expansion
       1.     Additional leakages
       2.     Holding of excess reserves
    C. Banks are procyclical in their lending
       1.     Policy during prosperity
       2.     Policy during a recession or depression
       3.     Anticyclical monetary tools by the Fed

## Chapter 15  "The Federal Reserve Banks and Monetary Policy"
I.  Objectives of Monetary Policy
    A. Goal
    B. Role of the Federal Reserve
    C. Investment effect (impact of the interest rate on investment spending and consumer spending).

II. Consolidated Balance Sheet of the 12 Federal Reserve Banks
    A. Assets
       1.     Securities
       2.     Loans
    B. Liabilities
       1.     Reserves of commercial banks
       2.     Treasury deposits
       3.     Federal Reserve Notes

III. Tools (techniques) of Monetary Policy
    A. Major tools
       1.     Open-market operations
            a.     Definition
            b.     "Easy Money" vs. "Tight Money"
       2.     Reserve ratio
            a.     Definition
            b.     "Easy Money" vs. "Tight Money"
       3.     Discount rate
            a.     Definition
            b.     "Easy Money" vs. "Tight Money"
    B. A Preview: Easy Money and Tight Money
    C. Minor selective controls
       1.     Margin requirement
            a.     Definition
            b.     Impact on the money supply
       2.     Consumer Credit
            a.     Definition

           b.       Impact on the money supply
- 3.      Moral suasion
  - a.      Definition
  - b.      Impact on the money supply

IV. Cause-effect chain: Keynesian View (steps) and traditional view

V. Recap of the Equilibrium NNP and Monetary Policy
- A. Effects of monetary policy
  - 1.      Where the demand for money equals the supply of money is the real interest rate; which is projected off the investment-demand curve; which plugs into the leakages-injections model to determine the equilibrium NNP level.
  - 2.      The shapes of the demand for money and the investment-demand curves determine the impact on the money supply and equilibrium NNP.
  - 3.      The AS - AD model illustrates the effect of a change in the money supply on NNP.

VI. Effectiveness of Monetary Policy
- A. Strengths of monetary policy
  - 1.      Speed and flexibility
  - 2.      Political acceptability
  - 3.      Monetarism
- B. Shortcomings/problems
  - 1.      Cyclical asymmetry
  - 2.      Changes in velocity
  - 3.      Investment impact
- C. The target (tradeoff) dilemma:
  - 1.      Definition
  - 2.      History of Fed policies
- D. Monetary Policy and the International economy
  - 1.      International flows of financial capital
  - 2.      Macro stability and the trade balance

VII. Fiscal and Monetary Policy
- A. Fiscal Policy
  - 1.      Definition
  - 2.      Discretionary and "built-in" stabilizers
- B. Fiscal and monetary policy
  - 1.      Interrelated and should be coordinated to maximize the effectiveness.

UNIT III

FORMULA SHEET

Unemployment rate = $\dfrac{\text{\# of unemployed}}{\text{Labor Force*}}$ x 100

\* may include the armed forces

Rate of Inflation = $\dfrac{P2 - P1}{P1}$ x 100

Rule of 70 = Approx. # of yrs. required to double = $\dfrac{70}{\text{\% annual increase}}$

Reserve ratio (R) = $\dfrac{\text{Required (Legal Reserves)}}{\text{Demand Deposits}}$

Legal (Required) reserves = reserve ratio x demand deposits

Actual (Total) reserves = the deposits of a commercial bank at the Federal Reserve Bank

Monetary (money) multiplier (M\$) = $\dfrac{1}{\text{Reserve Ratio}}$ = $\dfrac{1}{R}$

Maximum demand-deposit expansions = (Excess Reserves) X M\$ = E x M\$
     (or contractions)

# MICROECONOMICS

## UNIT I

**MICROECONOMICS CHAPTERS 1, 4, AND 5 ARE FOUND WITHIN THE MACROECONOMICS SECTION OF THIS WORKBOOK**

## Chapter Orientation

The study of elasticity of price is a refinement of supply and demand, which you studied in Chapter 4. Do you think it is important to know your customer's reaction if you raise or lower the price? (It is, if you are interested in maximizing your profits). Price elasticity means "sensitivity" or "responsiveness" to price changes.

When a product is sensitive to a price change, we say the product is "elastic". When consumers do not respond to a price change (and purchase almost the same quantity anyway) we say the product is "inelastic". When raising (or lowering the price) brings in the same total revenue, we say the product is "unit elastic". We will examine each of these in depth.

Price elasticities are utilized in analyzing consumer response, as well as seller response, in business and in the government. (We also want to determine how many sellers will enter or leave the industry due to changes in price).

The government measures price elasticity of a product(s) in order to determine which item(s) to tax and which to subsidize, for the greatest impact. Also, when a tax is imposed, the price elasticity of the buyer and the seller, determine which one, or both, will bear the burden of the tax.

In addition, two other types of elasticities (not fully covered in your text) will be presented in this concepts book. They are "income elasticity (Ey)" and "cross elasticity (Exy)". Income elasticity (Ey) measures the responsiveness of a change in demand to a change in one's income. Cross elasticity (Exy) measures the responsiveness of a change in demand for one good to a change in price of a different good.

## Learning Objectives

After reading this chapter in the text and completing the following exercises in this concepts book, you should be able to:

1.  Define the Law of Demand and the Law of Supply.
2.  Determine the equilibrium price and quantity.
3.  Define the price elasticity of demand (Ed) and explain the two techniques for calculating (Ed).
4.  Calculate the price elasticity of demand (Ed) and determine whether the product is elastic, inelastic, or unit elastic.
5.  Define elasticity of supply and compute (Es).
6.  Explain how time influences the elasticity of supply.
7.  List at least three factors that influence price elasticity.
8.  Explain the impact of price supports and price ceilings.
9.  Explain how elasticity of price influences the incidence of an excise tax.
10. Define and calculate income elasticity of demand (Ey).
11. Define and calculate cross elasticity of demand (Exy).

# CHAPTER 20        "Demand and Supply: Elasticities and Applications"

## Chapter Highlights

I.  Price Elasticity of Demand (Ed)
   A.  Definition: the percentage change in quantity demanded resulting from a one percent change in price. It measures consumers sensitivity to change in price.
   B.  Ways to calculate (Ed):
      1.  Mathematical formula

$$Ed^* = \frac{\% \triangle \text{ in Qd}}{\% \triangle \text{ in P}} = \frac{\dfrac{Q2 - Q1}{Q2 + Q1}}{\dfrac{P2 - P1}{P2 + P1}}$$

When   Ed > 1 relatively elastic
        Ed < 1 relatively inelastic
        Ed = 1 unit elastic

*(take the absolute value) or omit negative sign in the final answer)

      2.  The total revenue test (TR Test)
         a.  Total revenue = price x quantity demanded
         b.  The way total revenue changes with price changes, determines the price elasticity of a product.
   C.  Characteristics of Elasticity
      1.  Elasticity varies over different price ranges
      2.  Elasticity is not measured by the slope
   D.  Factors which influence price elasticity of demand:
      1.  Number of substitutes
      2.  Time period
      3.  Percentage of income
      4.  Luxuries vs. necessities
   E.  Applications (examples of price elasticity of demand):
      1.  Wage bargaining
      2.  Automation
      3.  Bumper crops
      4.  Airline deregulation
      5.  Excise taxes
      6.  Cocaine and street crime
      7.  Minimum wage

II. Price Elasticity of Supply (Es)
   A.  Definition: the percentage change in quantity supplied resulting from a one percentage change in price. It measures the sellers sensitivity to price changes. The main determinant is the amount of <u>time</u> which a producer has to respond.
   B.  Way to measure (Es)
      1.  Mathematical formula:

$$Es^* = \frac{\% \triangle \text{ in Qs}}{\% \triangle \text{ in P}} = \frac{\dfrac{Q2 - Q1}{Q2 + Q1}}{\dfrac{P2 - P1}{P2 + P1}}$$

When   Es > 1 relatively elastic
        Es < 1 relatively inelastic
        Es = 1 unit elastic

*(take the absolute value) or omit negative sign in the final answer
   be sure to use <u>quantity</u> supplied

C.  Factors that influence price elasticity of supply (Es)
    1.    Market period
    2.    Short-run vs. long-run
          a.    increasing-cost industry
          b.    constant-cost industry
          c.    decreasing-cost industry
D.  Price ceilings and price supports
    1.    Prevents price from performing the rationing function
    2.    Creates a surplus or shortage in the market
E.  Tax incidence
    1.    Specific tax incidence
          a.    Price elasticities of demand and supply determine the incidence of a specific tax.
    2.    The burden of the tax follows the path of least resistance (lowest elasticity).
    3.    Tax shifting (forward and backward)
    4.    Subsidies (negative taxes)
          a.    Opposite effect
          b.    Elasticity improves allocation of resources

III.  Income and Cross Elasticities
A.  Income Elasticity of Demand (Ey)
    1.    Definition:  measures the responsiveness of a change in demand to a change in income (judges the importance of a product).
    2.    Way to calculate Ey:
          a.    Mathematical formula:

$$Ey = \frac{\%\ \blacktriangle\ in\ Q}{\%\ \blacktriangle\ in\ Y} = \frac{\dfrac{Q2 - Q1}{Q2 + Q1}}{\dfrac{Y2 - Y1}{Y2 + Y1}}$$

Ey > 0  superior or normal good
Ey < 0  inferior good
Ey = 0  income unit elastic

B.  Cross Elasticity of Demand (Exy)
    1.    Definition:  measures the responsiveness of a change in demand for one good to a change in price of another good.
    2.    Way to calculate (Exy):
          a.    Mathematical formula:

$$Exy = \frac{\%\ \blacktriangle\ in\ Q\ Product\ X}{\%\ \blacktriangle\ in\ P\ Product\ Y} = \frac{\dfrac{QX2 - QX1}{QX2 + QX1}}{\dfrac{PY2 - PY1}{PY2 + PY1}}$$

Exy > 0    Substitute good
Exy < 0    Complementary good
Exy = 0    Independent good

IV.  Last Word:  The Troublesome Market for Health Care.

## Key Terms

| | |
|---|---|
| law of demand | market period |
| law of supply | short-run |
| equilibrium price and quantity | long-run |
| elasticity | increasing-cost industry |
| price elasticity | decreasing-cost industry |
| elastic demand/supply | constant-cost industry |
| inelastic demand/supply | price ceiling (cap) |
| unit elastic demand/supply | price floor (support) |
| total revenue | tax incidence |
| perfectly elastic | tax shifting |
| perfectly inelastic | subsidy |
| elasticity of supply | income elasticity of demand |
| elasticity coefficient | cross elasticity of demand |

## Real World Example

### "ELASTICITY OF DEMAND:  LEARN TO JUDGE IT RIGHTLY"

#### By Linda Ellis

IF YOUR DAILY newspaper goes up a nickel in price, do you cancel your subscription?  If gasoline begins flowing at higher prices, do you walk?  If your favorite bee hops up a quarter a six-pack, do you reach for a different brew?

Probably not.

Assume instead that the brand of bar soap you normally but took a price jump of a dime over other soaps.  Would you pay it rather than choose another kind?  Would you buy a ballpoint pen that looked the same but cost 50 percent more than similar products?  Probably not.

Soap and ballpoint pens are essentially generic, interchangeable and any brand will normally do.

ANOTHER WAY of putting this is that your demand for your daily paper or the gas in your car tank is inelastic.  There are no close substitutes and you aren't likely to respond negatively to a price hike.  The price of a roll of paper towels or a 98-cent pen is elastic.  There are a plethora of substitutes.

Elasticity defines the degree of responsiveness on the part of consumers to price changes.  If demand is inelastic, people will buy despite a price hike.  If elastic, they'll switch.

Don't think the owners of the newspaper or the oil distributors or the brewery middlemen don't know about demand elasticity and cross-substitution, seemingly esoteric laws of economics.  Sellers know within a defined range how many readers, drivers and guzzlers they will lose if they increase their prices.  They have done cost-benefit analyses that tell them the net effect for them will be positive, that they will earn more by the price change than they will lose in revenues.

I was reminded of all this when a notice appeared on the soda machine here at The Press that the price of a soft drink per can would rise to 50 cents from 45 cents in mid-January.  I asked myself how high it would have to go before I would switch to water, which is free, or office coffee, which is vile but unlimited if you chip in $5 every payday to be a member of the coffee club. I decided I would still drink more soda than I should until the price per can reached $1.  My demand for soda is inelastic.  Clearly, I'm an addict but even addicts have limits.

TIME FOR A QUIZ:

The demand for popcorn at the movies is (a) inelastic; (b) elastic.

The answer, of course, is (a). They could probably charge $5 for a medium-sized box of the stuff, probably the worst popcorn most people have ever eaten, and still sell it. There is no possible cross-substitution. They search your handbags these days at theaters for contraband, and popcorn from your own kitchen will be confiscated. Even if you hide it under your coat they'll smell it. You're stuck.

When politicians want to increase tax revenue and not take the heat, they pass higher "nuisance taxes." Economic studies have taught them that cigarette smokers will apparently pay whatever tax is imposed on tobacco and drinkers will fork over the cost of a fifth of whiskey, no matter how much of it goes for taxes. People won't decrease their driving much even if the tax on gasoline climbs. Luxury taxes on jewelry and furs won't stop the wealthy from indulging; in fact, any tax on a product that fits into the "If you have to ask you can't afford it" category will raise revenues without decreasing consumption enough to negate the price hike.

Generally, if there's no obvious substitute for a product that you like a lot, you're going to continue to buy it at higher and higher prices. There is of course a limit, and here come the economists again. They can, and do tell sports team owners how high ticket prices can go before they begin to see empty stands. They do that by writing down lots of partial differential equations and figuring out the breakpoint, the point beyond which even the most die-hard Giants or Nets fan will not go.

MOVIE THEATERS, as a case in point, either didn't hire the right economists or they didn't listen to the ones they had. They failed to figure out that if they raised the prices of movie tickets "too high" people would stay away in droves. "Too high" in this case was the point at which people began staying home to watch cable or rented movies for home video cassette recorders or just found some other way to be amused. The movie industry had some rough times in 1982 and 1983, and some companies are just barely hanging on this year. There is some degree of cross-substitution for the product and people went looking.

Businessmen who supply the Pentagon know all about inelasticity. They started a game some years called "How high can we go?"; the answer was apparently as high as they liked. The got caught charging $700 for a $2 bolt, but who knows what has gone unchallenged?

Detroit guessed wrong on elasticity and paid dearly for the mistake. U.S. automakers assumed that Americans would not switch en masse to imports after the Arab oil crunch of 1973-75, but would continue to pay more for gas-guzzling, higher-priced American models. We all know the end of that story.

# The Spectrum of Elasticity of Price

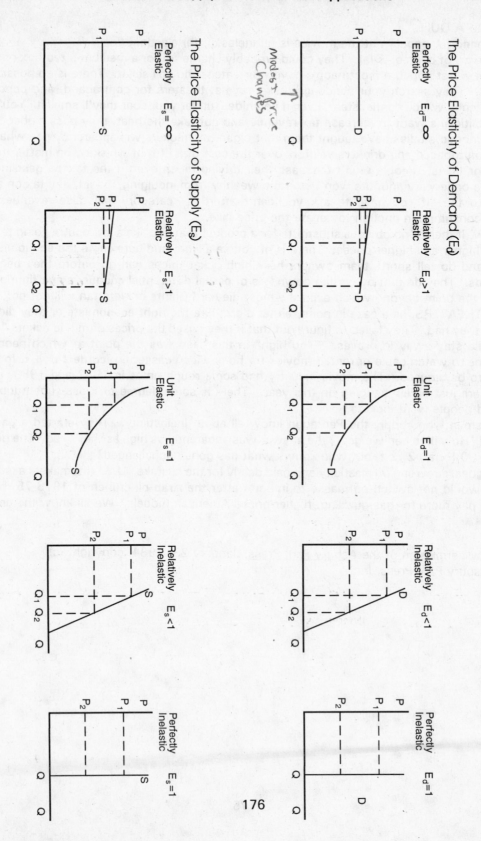

### PROBLEMS

1. A Ford dealer in Chicago cut his prices by 10 percent and sold 22 percent more cars. What is the Elasticity of Demand (Ed)? Label your answer "Elastic," Inelastic," or "Unit Elastic."

2. Suppose we are given the following demand schedule for a commodity:

| Points | Price | Quantity Demanded | Ed | Type of Elasticity |
|--------|-------|-------------------|------|--------------------|
| A | .20 | 50 | | |
| | | | 2.36 | ELastic |
| B | .15 | 100 | | |
| | | | 1.665 | Elastic |
| C | .10 | 200 | | |
| | | | .099 | INeLastic |
| D | .05 | 400 | | |

a. Calculate the (Ed) between points A and B, B and C, C and D.

b. Label your answers "Elastic," "Inelastic," or "Unit Elastic."

3. Fill the blank cell in each of the following rows:

| Price | Total Revenue | (Ed) |
|-------|---------------|------|
| Increases | decreases | >1  Elastic |
| Decreases | Decreases | <1  INelastic |
| Decreases | No Change | =1 |
| Increases | Increases | <1 |
| Increases | Decreases | >1 |
| Increases | No Change | =1 |

① $\dfrac{Q2-Q1}{Q2+Q1}$     $22 \div 10 = -2.2$   Elastic

$\dfrac{P2-P1}{P2+P1}$

② $\dfrac{100-50}{100+50} = \dfrac{50}{150} = .333$ _____ = 2.36

$\dfrac{.15-.20}{.15+.20} = \dfrac{-.05}{.35} = .143$

$\dfrac{200-100}{200+100} = \dfrac{100}{300} = .333$

$\dfrac{.10-.15}{.10+.15} = \dfrac{.05}{.25} = .2$ _____ = 1.665

$\dfrac{400-200}{400+200} = \dfrac{200}{600} = .333$

$\dfrac{.05-.10}{.05+.10} = \dfrac{-.05}{.15} = .333$

177

4. Assume that the Fisher family purchases the amounts shown of five commodities before and after Ms. Fisher gets a raise.

| Income per Month | Chicken | Quantity Purchased per Month (all in pounds) | | | |
| | | Peanut Butter | Steak | Hamburger | Bread |
| --- | --- | --- | --- | --- | --- |
| $1,200 | 10.0 | 5.0 | 3.0 | 9.0 | 5.0 |
| $1,600 | 11.4 | 4.5 | 5.2 | 11.0 | 5.0 |
| Ey | .454 | -.371 | 1.874 | .699 | 0 |
| | Normal good | INFERIOR FOOD | Normal good | normal good | unit income ELASTIC |

a. Calculate the income elasticity of demand (Ey) for each commodity and enter it in the table.

b. Which goods (if any) are superior, which (if any) are inferior, and which (if any) are unit income elastic -- enter it in the table.

5. After Ms. Fisher received the raise, the price of hamburger, which had been $2.00/lb., went up to $2.10/lb. Ms. Fisher adjusted her purchases of all commodities as shown below.

| Price per lb. of hamburger | Chicken | Quantities of Goods Purchased Other Things Remaining the Same | | | Hamburger Buns (doz.) |
| | | Peanut Butter | Ketchup | Bread | |
| --- | --- | --- | --- | --- | --- |
| $2.00 | 11.4 | 4.5 | 3.0 | 5.0 | 4.0 |
| 2.10 | 12.0 | 4.7 | 2.5 | 5.5 | 3.5 |
| Exy | 1.08 | .917 | -3.79 | 2 | -2.79 |
| | Substitute good | Substitute good | Complimentary good | substitute good | complimentary goods |

a. Calculate the cross elasticity of demand (Exy) for each product and enter it in the table.

b. Which goods are complements to, which are substitutes for, and which are independent of hamburger--enter it in the table.

## PROBLEMS (continued)

*This problem will be on test*

*Exact problem different numbers.*

6. Fill in the table below and check to see if the total revenue test and the price elasticity of demand (Ed) yield the same results.

*Price × Qty. Demanded*  →  *Total Revenue*

*Price Elasticity of Supply*

*Qty. Demanded*

*Price Elasticity of Demand*

| Es | Quantity Supplied | Price | Quantity Demanded | TR | TR Test | Ed |
|---|---|---|---|---|---|---|
| | 100 | $12 | 80 | $960 | | |
| 4.09 | | | | | R. Elastic | 1.37 |
| | 70 | $11 | 90 | $990 | | |
| 3.48 | | | | | R. Elastic | 1.10 |
| | 50 | $10 | 100 | $1,006 | | |
| 6.28 | | | | | R. Inelastic | .91 |
| | 25 | $9 | 110 | $990 | | |
| 7.27 | | | | | Rel. Inelastic | .73 |
| | 10 | $8 | 120 | $960 | | |

$$\frac{Q2 - Q1}{Q2 + Q1}$$
$$\frac{P2 - P1}{P2 + P1}$$

Price is the same for Es and Ed.

TR TEST

↑P ↓TR or ↓P ↑TR = Rel. Elastic > 1

↑P ↓P = Same TR        = Unit Elastic = 1

↑P ↑TR or ↓P ↓TR = Rel. Inelastic < 1

179

Self-Test

1.  If the government imposes a tax on a commodity to obtain tax revenues, what type of product should be selected to obtain the highest revenue?
    a.   perfectly elastic                    c.   unit elastic
    b.   perfectly inelastic                  d.   relatively inelastic

2.  If the government subsidizes a product in order to increase output, it would be the most successful if the supply curve is:
    a.   perfectly elastic                    c.   unit elastic
    b.   perfectly inelastic                  d.   relatively inelastic

3.  If the price of a product increases, and total revenue decreases then:
    a.   the demand for this product must be relatively elastic
    b.   the demand for this product must be relatively inelastic
    c.   the supply of this product must be relatively elastic
    d.   the supply of this product must be relatively inelastic

4.  If the cross elasticity for Products B and D is 2.6, then these products are:       Exy > 0
    a.   complementary                       c.   independent
    b.   substitutes                          d.   normal

5.  If the income elasticity for Products J and K is -1.7, then these products are:
    a.   inferior                            c.   independent
    b.   normal                              d.   complementary

6.  If the price elasticity of demand for products M and N is .8, then these products are:
    a.   relatively elastic                   c.   unit elastic
    b.   relatively inelastic                 d.   substitutes

7.  If the price of record albums falls from $8.00 to $6.00 and the quantity demanded increases from 500 to 750, we can conclude that:
    a.   demand is elastic                    c.   demand is unit elastic
    b.   demand is inelastic                  d.   unable to determine

8.  If the demand for ice cream is relatively elastic, a 5% decline in the price will:
    a.   increase the amount demanded by <u>less</u> than 5%
    b.   decrease the amount demanded by <u>less</u> than 5%
    c.   increase the amount demanded by <u>more</u> than 5%
    d.   decrease the amount demanded by <u>more</u> than 5%

9.  If the management of a theater wishes to lower the ticket prices for their plays, they are assuming that the demand for tickets is:
    a.   inelastic                           c.   unit elastic
    b.   elastic                             d.   shifting to the right

10. Assume the demand for wine is highly inelastic and the supply is highly elastic, who will bear the burden of the specific tax?
    a.   primarily by the consumer           c.   shared equally by consumers and sellers
    b.   primarily by the seller             d.   the wholesaler

# CHAPTER 21    "Consumer Behavior and Utility Maximization"

## Chapter Orientation

Chapter 4 introduced us to the law of demand. We learned that as the price of a good falls, consumers will purchase a higher quantity by substituting the cheaper good for something else (substitution effect). Also, when the price of a good decreases, your income will stretch further due to increased purchasing power (income effect) The opposite occurs when the price increases.

Utility analysis further clarifies the law of demand by explaining consumer decision making. How does the consumer choose among goods, services, and savings? It depends on the price of the product, the consumer's income, and how much he/she wants the product. We assume that every consumer wants to maximize his/her satisfaction. Utility is the ability or power of a good to satisfy a <u>want</u> -- not a need or usefulness. A "util" is a unit by which utility is measured. Determining how large one util of satisfaction is can be a difficult concept to quantify. But if you realize that we choose a starting point (how much satisfaction do you receive when you purchase a new album) and then compare the satisfaction you feel when you purchase another item (another album, or perhaps a tape). The concept is relative to the starting point.

As more and more of a product (or service) is consumed during a certain time period, total satisfaction (total utility) increases but at a slower and slower rate. This means that you are just not as satisfied as you were previously. This concept is known as "Diminishing Marginal Utility". The word marginal means a small increment change (or consuming one more).

Given your income, what combination of goods should you purchase to maximize satisfaction (consumer equilibrium)? You will be calculating this optimal solution, using utility analysis.

Do consumers really use this approach? Do we go into the mall shopping and say to ourselves, "how many "utils" does this pair of shoes give me?" Probably not, however don't you say to yourself, "given the money I have to spend, do I really want these shoes? Maybe I'll buy the shoes; but then again maybe I'll buy a pair sneakers instead -- or can I afford both? The wallets are on sale, maybe I'll purchase one since the price is so reasonable and I can afford it." We may not call this "utility analysis", but we are indeed trying to get the most out of our hard earned dollar.

## Learning Objectives

After studying this chapter in the text, and completing the following exercise in this concept book, you should be able to:

1. Define and distinguish between the income effect and the substitution effect as a result of a price change.
2. Define utility and state how it is measured.
3. Explain the concept of diminishing marginal utility.
4. List the four assumptions that are made in explaining consumer behavior.
5. Define the utility maximizing rule (or consumer equilibrium).
6. Derive a demand curve from data given.
7. Discuss the implications of time on consumer behavior.
8. Calculate the consumer expenditure and surplus in dollars and in utils.

# CHAPTER 21          "Consumer Behavior and Utility Maximization"

Chapter Highlights

I. Law of Demand
   A. Price changes yield a(n):
      1.     Income effect (change in purchasing power)
      2.     Substitution effect (replace more expensive good with a cheaper good)
II. Law of Diminishing Marginal Utility
   A. Definition - during a certain time period, as you consume successive units, eventually, the extra satisfaction decreases.
   B. Marginal Utility vs. Total Utility
III. Theory of Consumer Behavior
   A. Assumptions of consumer behavior
      1.     Rational behavior
      2.     Preferences
      3.     Budget restraint
      4.     Prices
   B. Utility Maximizing Rule (or Consumer Equilibrium)
      1.     Definition
      2.     Optimal mix or utility-maximizing combination
      3.     Formula Method
IV. Marginal Utility and the Demand Curve
   A. Substitution and Income Effects Revisited
V. Implications of time on consumer behavior.
VI. Calculation of consumer expenditure and consumer surplus (in dollars and in utils)
VII. Last Word: The Water-Diamond Paradox
IX. Appendix: Indifference Curve Analysis

Key Terms

income effect                         rational
substitution effect                   budget restraint
utility                               consumer optimum mix
utils                                 utility maximizing rule
law of diminishing marginal utility   consumer expenditure
marginal utility                      consumer surplus
indivisibility of products

Real World Example

   As discussed briefly under the "Chapter Orientation", do consumers use utility analysis when they go shopping?  Does utility analysis explain and predict real-world consumer behavior?
   Basically, the answer to both of those questions is "yes".  Whenever consumers go shopping and see something that they wish to purchase, they normally ask themselves (whether consciously or unconsciously), "is the price of the item worth it?"  The next question would be, "can I afford it?"  If the answer to both of those questions is positive, then we assume the consumer will purchase the item.  Likewise, if they decide they can't afford the item or the item isn't worth the selling price, then the consumer will not purchase the item and will continue to shop around.

182

Comparing this approach to utility analysis, we see that the effects of price, income and satisfaction/want determine whether the consumer will maximize his/her satisfaction by purchasing (or not purchasing) the item,. We also assume that consumers will continue spending their incomes as long as they continue to derive additional satisfaction from the product. When satisfaction declines (or diminishes) the consumer will look elsewhere-to spend or save.

From this perspective, we see that utility analysis helps to explain and predict consumer behavior.

## PROBLEMS

1.  a.  Fill in the following table:

| Number of artichokes consumed per month | Total utility (in utils) | Marginal utility (in utils) |
|---|---|---|
| 0 | 0 | 0 |
| 1 | 5 | 5 |
| 2 | 12 | 7 |
| 3 | 20 | 8 |
| 4 | 26 | 6 |
| 5 | 31 | 5 |
| 6 | 34 | 3 |
| 7 | 33 | -1 |
| 8 | 30 | -3 |

b.  Construct a graph of total utility (top half of graph paper).

c.  Construct a graph of marginal utility (bottom half of graph paper).

d.  When TU is at a maximum, MU is _____.

e.  MU is the _____ of the TU curve.

$$MU = \frac{\blacktriangle TU}{\blacktriangle Q}$$

## PROBLEMS (continued)

*money has no utility = spend all*
*money has utility = save all*

*Homework*
*9-21-93*

### CONSUMER EQUILIBRIUM

**Definition:**    To maximize your utility allocate, so MU per dollar spent on two commodities is equal. (Don't spend more $ than you earn).

Rule I:   $\dfrac{MU_a}{P_a}$   =   $\dfrac{MU_b}{P_b}$   =   MU$ (saved)

*Always Look For where the columns match-up.*

Rule II:  Spend and/or save all of your income

2. Two goods are available, pizza and suntan lotion, and money has no utility.  A pizza pie costs $3 and suntan lotion costs $2 per bottle.  Your income is $35.  How should you allocate your income?

| #Pies/Bottles | MU Pizza $3.00 | | MU Lotion $2.00 | |
|---|---|---|---|---|
| 4 | 24 | 8 | 20 | 10 |
| 5 | 21 | 7 | 18 | 9 |
| 6 | 18 | 6 | 16 | 8 |
| 7 | 15 | (5) | 10 | (5) |
| 8 | 12 | 4 | 8 | 4 |
| 9 | 9 | 3 | 4 | 2 |
| 10 | 3 | 1 | 2 | 1 |

4 BTLS. Lotion @ 10        4 pies @ 8
5 BTLS. Lotion @ 9         7 pies @ 7
6 BTLS. Lotion @ 8         6 pies @ 6
7 BTLS. Lotion @ 5         7 pies @ 5

7 Bottles Lotion @ 2.00 = $14.00
7 Pies        @ 3.00 = 21.00
                      $35.00

3. Assume that it is the day before payday, and all you have in your wallet is $10.00.  You decide to meet some friends at a local happy-hour.  A glass of wine costs $2.00/glass; a mug of beer costs $.50/mug; and a glass of soda costs $3.00 each.  The last column--MU$ shows your MU for savings.  To maximize your utility, what is your optimal combination?  How much will you save?

*will be on test*

| Units/$ | MU Wine $2.00 | | MU Beer $.50 | | MU Soda $3.00 | | MU $ (saved) |
|---|---|---|---|---|---|---|---|
| 1 | 20 | 10 | 10 | 20 | 3 | 1 | 14 |
| 2 | 16 | (8) | 8 | 16 | 1.5 | .5 | 12 |
| 3 | 10 | 5 | 6 | 12 | 0 | 0 | 10 |
| 4 | 6 | 3 | 4 | (8) | -1.5 | -.5 | (8) |
| 5 | 2 | 1 | 2 | 4 | -3 | -1 | 6 |

1 unit Beer @ 20
2 unit Beer @ 16
3 unit Beer @ 12
4 unit Beer @ 8

1 wine @ 10
1 wine @ 8

2 units of wine @ $2.00 = $4.00
4 units of Beer @ .50 = $2.00
                        $6.00
                        $4.00 saved.
                        $10.00

184

4.

**EXHIBIT I**

$\frac{\begin{array}{r}21\\14\end{array}}{35}$

**Demand Curve**

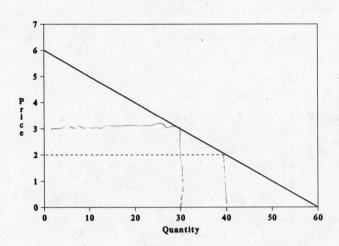
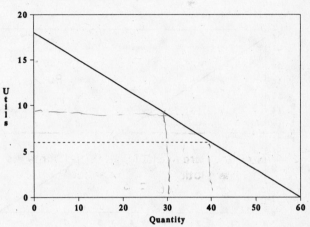

Answer the following questions, based upon Exhibit I.

a.  What is the <u>consumer surplus</u> (in dollars and in utils)?  $A = \frac{1}{2}b \times h$

$\frac{1}{2}\ of\ 2 = 1 \times h = 1 \times 5 = 5$

b.  What is the <u>total expenditure</u> (in dollars and in utils)?

$(2 \times 40) = 80\ dollars$

$(6 \times 40) = 240\ utils$

c.  Determine the <u>total expenditure</u> (in dollars and in utils) and the <u>consumer surplus</u> (in dollars and in utils) if the consumer purchases 30 units.

Total Exp. in dollars = $3 \times 30 = \$90$

Total Exp. in utils = $9 \times 30 = 270\ utils$

$\frac{1}{2}b \times h$

$\frac{1}{2}\ of\ 3 = 1.5$

$1.5 \times h = 1.5 \times 4 = \$6\ surplus$

$\frac{1}{2}\ of\ 9 = 4.5$

185

$4.5 \times h = 4.5 \times 11 = 49.5\ utils\ surplus$

# CHAPTER 21    "Consumer Behavior and Utility Maximization"

Answer questions 1 - 4 based upon Exhibit II (below).

## EXHIBIT II

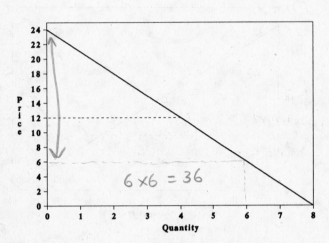
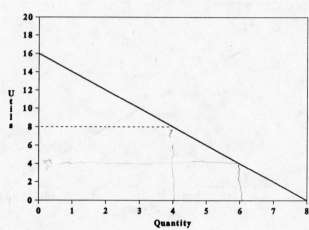

1. At a quantity of 6, the consumer expenditure in dollars is:
   a.  $24
   b.  $36
   c.  $48
   d.  $30

2. At a quantity of 6, the consumer surplus in dollars is:
   a.  $96
   b.  $108
   c.  $54
   d.  $36

   *½ of 6*    *Area of a triangle*
   *½ of 6 = 3 (6 is The base)*
   *A = ½ bh*    *h = 18 ( 24-6) 3 × 18 = 54*

3. At a quantity of 4, the consumer expenditure in utils is:
   a.  32 utils
   b.  24 utils
   c.  48 utils
   d.  16 utils

4. At a quantity of 4, the consumer surplus in utils is:
   a.  36 utils
   b.  24 utils
   c.  32 utils
   d.  16 utils

   *½ of 4 = 2*
   *h = 8 (16-8) 2 × 8 = 16 utils*

186

Self-Test (continued)

5. Assume your income is $48.00 and the price of product A is $5.00 each and the price of product B is $7.00 each. Assume saving money has no utility (satisfaction). What is your optimal combination (mix) to maximize your utility?

TABLE II

| Units | MUa | | MUb | |
|-------|-----|---|-----|---|
| 1 | 60 | *12* | 77 | *11* |
| 2 | 50 | *10* | 56 | *8* |
| 3 | 35 | *⑦ 3×5=15* | 49 | *⑦ 3×7=21* |
| 4 | 20 | *④ 4×5=20* | 28 | *④ 4×7=28* |
| 5 | 10 | *2* | 21 | *3* |

*4 units product "A" @ 5.00*
*4 units product "B" @ 7.00*
*+20*
*48*

6. If the marginal utility for Product A is 12 and the marginal utility for Product S is 40 and the prices are $4 and $10 respectively. To maximize total utility, the consumer would:
   a. buy more of Product A
   b. buy more of Product S
   c. buy equal amounts of each product
   d. unable to determine

7. When total utility is at a maximum; marginal utility is:
   a. increasing
   b. proportional
   c. zero
   d. unable to determine

8. We define utility as:
   a. how much we need a good
   b. how useful we find a good
   c. how much satisfaction a good gives us
   d. what the price of the product is

9. The income effect states that:
   a. as income increases, we purchase more goods and services
   b. when the price of a good falls, we purchase more of the cheaper good
   c. we replace the expensive good with the cheaper good
   d. our purchasing power is effected by changes in price

10. The "law of diminishing marginal utility" is defined:
    a. as the price of a product increases, we buy a smaller quantity
    b. as the price of a product decreases, we buy a larger quantity
    c. that at some point, we start experiencing less and less extra satisfaction from additional units of a product
    d. once we purchase a product, we are less and less happy with it and want to purchase something else

## Chapter 1 - "The Nature and Method of Economics"
I.  The Importance of Studying Economics
    A.  Definition of economics, macro, micro, ceteris paribus and comparative advantage
    B.  Reasons for study
II.  Deriving Economic Policy
    A.  The Scientific Method (positive economics)
        1.      Descriptive economics
        2.      Economic theory
            a.      Generalizations, assumptions, and abstractions
            b.      Forms of economic models
        3.      Test (inductive vs. deductive methods)
        4.      Economic policy
            a.      Predictions and implications for the real world
            b.      Steps
    B.  Potential "pitfalls" in economic models
III. Economic Goals
    A.  List of eight economic goals in our society
        1.      Some are complementary; others are mutually exclusive
IV.  Difficulties in Studying Economics
    A.  List of areas to beware in economics
V.  The Economic Perspective
    A.  Decision making (2)
VI. Appendix: Graphing and their Meaning
    A.  To express economic principles or models
    B.  Tools
        1.      Plotting points
        2.      Calculating the slope of a straight line and a nonlinear curve
        3.      Direct or inverse relationship

## Chapter 4 - "Understanding Individual Markets: Demand and Supply"
I.  Market
    A.  Definition of a Market
    B.  Examples
II.  Demand
    A.  Definition of Demand
    B.  Law of demand
        1.      Inverse relationship
        2.      Diminishing marginal utility
        3.      Income and substitution effects
    C.  Demand schedule and curve (individual and market)
    D.  "Change in quantity demanded" vs. "change in demand"
    E.  Non-price determinants of demand
III. Supply
    A.  Definition of Supply
    B.  Law of supply
        1.      Direct relationship
    C.  Supply schedule and curve (individual and market)
    D.  "Change in quantity supplied" vs. "change in supply"

    E.   Non-price determinants of supply

IV. Market Equilibrium
    A.  Equilibrium price and quantity
        1.      Rationing function
        2.      Effects of changes in demand and supply
    B.  Government's setting price in the market
        1.      Price floor (support)
        2.      Price ceiling (cap)
    C.  Word Problems

V. Application of Supply and Demand
    A.  The foreign exchange market
        1.      Depreciation and appreciation of currency
        2.      Economic consequences

**Chapter 5 - "The Private Sector and the Market System"**

I. Households as Income Receivers
    A.  Functional vs. Personal Distribution of Income

II. Households as Spenders
    A.  Personal Taxes
    B.  Personal Savings
    C.  Personal Consumption Expenditures

III. The Business Population
    A.  Terms:  Plant, firm, conglomerate, industry, horizontal and vertical combinations.

IV. Legal Forms of Business
    A.  Sole Proprietorship
        1.      Definition
        2.      Advantages/Disadvantages
    B.  Partnership
        1.      Definition
        2.      Advantages/Disadvantages
    C.  Corporation
        1.      Definition
        2.      Advantages/Disadvantages
        3.      Decision to Incorporate

V. Industrial Distribution and Bigness
    A.  Type of Industries
    B.  Impact of Big Business

VI. The Foreign Sector
    A.  Volume, Pattern, and Linkages of U.S. Trade
    B.  Economic Implications

VII. The Competitive Market System
    A.  Definition

VIII. The Five Fundamental Questions
    A.  "<u>What</u> is to be produced?"
        1.      Calculation of profit
        2.      Profits and losses are industry "signals"
            a.     Expanding industry
            b.     Declining industry

      3.      Consumer sovereignty (dollar votes)

      4.      Derived demand

  B.   "How is production organized?"

      1.      Profitability insures resources

      2.      Economic efficiency

      3.      Least-cost production

  C.   "Who receives the output?"

      1.      Resource prices determine money income

      2.      Prices for goods and services are set in the market

      3.      Ability (income) to pay for these goods and services

  D.   "How much should be produced?"

  E.   "Adapt to change?"

      1.      Guiding function of prices

      2.      Invisible hand

      3.      Technological advances

      4.      Capital accumulation

IX. The Case for the Market System

  A.  Merits of the Market System

      1.      Efficiently allocates scarce resources

      2.      Emphasizes personal freedom

**Chapter 20** - "Demand and Supply:  Elasticities and Applications"

I.  Price Elasticity of Demand (Ed)

  A.  Definition of Ed

  B.  Definition of elastic, inelastic, unit elastic and elasticity coefficient

  C.  Ways to calculate Ed

      1.      Mathematical formula

      2.      The total revenue test

  D.  Characteristics of elasticity (2)

  E.  Factors that influence Ed (4)

  F.  Applications of Ed

II.  Price Elasticity of Supply (Es)

  A.  Definition

  B.  Way to measure (Es)

      1.      Mathematical formula:

  C.  Factors that influence Es

  D.  Price ceilings and price supports

  E.  Tax incidence

      1.      Specific tax

      2.      Burden of tax

      3.      Tax shifting

      4.      Subsidies

III.Income Elasticity of Demand (Ey)

  A.  Definition

  B.  Way to calculate Ey

      1.      Mathematical formula:

IV.   Cross Elasticity of Demand (Exy)

  A.  Definition

    B.  Way to calculate Exy
       1.      Mathematical formula:

## Chapter 21 - "Consumer Behavior and Utility Maximization"

I. Law of Demand
    A.  Price changes yield a(n):
       1.      Income effect
       2.      Substitution effect

II. Law of Diminishing Marginal Utility
    A.  Definition
    B.  Marginal utility vs. total utility

III. Consumer Behavior
    A.  Assumptions of consumer behavior (4)
    B.  Utility Maximizing Rule (or Consumer Equilibrium)

IV. Marginal utility and the demand curve

V. Implications of time on consumer behavior.

VI. Calculation of consumer expenditure and consumer surplus (in dollars and in utils)

## FORMULA SHEET

$$SLOPE = \frac{\blacktriangle Y}{\blacktriangle X} = \frac{rise}{run} = \frac{Y2 - Y1}{X2 - X1}$$

$$Ed = \frac{\dfrac{Q2 - Q1}{Q2 + Q1}}{\dfrac{P2 - P1}{P2 + P1}} = Es$$

$$Ey = \frac{\dfrac{Q2 - Q1}{Q2 + Q1}}{\dfrac{Y2 - Y1}{Y2 + Y1}}$$

$$Exy = \frac{\dfrac{Qx2 - Qx1}{Qx2 + Qx1}}{\dfrac{Py2 - Py1}{Py2 + Py1}}$$

$$MU = \frac{\blacktriangle TU}{\blacktriangle Q} \qquad \frac{MUa}{Pa} = \frac{MUb}{Pb} = \frac{MU\$ \text{ saved}}{}$$

$$TR = (P) \times (Q)$$

Area of Triangle = 1/2 (bh)        Area of Rectangle = lw

# REVIEW SHEET: UNIT I MICROECONOMICS

## Elasticity Review Sheet

I. **Price Elasticity of Demand** (Ed)

   A. Definition: the percentage change in quantity demanded, resulting from a one percent change in price.

   B. Ways to calculate (Ed):

      1. $\quad Ed^* = \dfrac{\% \triangle \text{ in Qd}}{\% \triangle \text{ in P}} = \dfrac{\dfrac{Q2 - Q1}{Q2 + Q1}}{\dfrac{P2 - P1}{P2 + P1}}$

               When    Ed > 1 relatively elastic

                              Ed < 1 relatively inelastic

                              Ed = 1 unit elastic

          *(take the absolute value) or omit negative sign in the final answer

      2. The total revenue test (TR test)

          Total revenue = price x quantity demanded = (P x Qd)

          ↑P ↓TR or ↓P ↑TR       Relatively Elastic (opposite directions)

          ↑P ↓ P = same TR         Unit Elastic (same TR)

          ↑P ↑TR or ↓P ↓TR       Relatively Inelastic (same direction)

II. **Price Elasticity of Supply** (Es)

   A. Definition: the percentage change in quantity supplied resulting from a one percentage change in price.

   B. Way to measure (Es)

       $Es^* = \dfrac{\% \triangle \text{ in Qs}}{\% \triangle \text{ in P}} = \dfrac{\dfrac{Q2 - Q1}{Q2 + Q1}}{\dfrac{P2 - P1}{P2 + P1}}$

               When    Es > 1 relatively elastic

                              Es < 1 relatively inelastic

                              Es = 1 unit elastic

          *(take the absolute value) or omit negative sign in the final answer

          be sure to use quantity supplied

III. **Income Elasticity of Demand** (Ey)

   A. Definition: measures the responsiveness of a change in demand to a change in income.

   B. Way to measure (Ey):

       $Ey = \dfrac{\% \triangle \text{ in Q}}{\% \triangle \text{ in Y}} = \dfrac{\dfrac{Q2 - Q1}{Q2 + Q1}}{\dfrac{Y2 - Y1}{Y2 + Y1}}$

                           Ey > 0 superior or normal

                           Ey < 0 inferior good

                           Ey = 0 income unit elastic

IV. **Cross Elasticity of Demand** (Exy)

   A. Definition: measures the responsiveness of a change in demand for one good to a change in price of another good.

   B. Way to calculate (Exy):

       $Exy = \dfrac{\% \triangle \text{ in Q Product X}}{\% \triangle \text{ in P Product Y}} = \dfrac{\dfrac{QX2 - QX1}{QX2 + QX1}}{\dfrac{PY2 - PY1}{PY2 + PY1}}$

Exy > 0 Substitute good

Exy < 0 Complementary good

Exy = 0 Independent good

# MICROECONOMICS

## UNIT II

Chapter Orientation

Economists have long been interested in the market and in what determines value. Since market prices reflect value, they seek to analyze the facts that influence the relative market prices of goods and services. These prices also give us information about the allocative efficiency of our economy.

The market price is determined by the forces of supply and demand. In previous chapters, factors which influence consumer demand were examined. Chapter 22 focuses on the seller or supplier. Supply was defined (in Chapter 4) as the amount of a commodity that the sellers are willing and able to make available for sale, at alternative prices, during a certain time period, all other things remaining the same.

Supply depends upon the costs of production (cost is a sacrifice, whether tangible or intangible). Economists view costs quite differently from expenses in accounting, because they include opportunity cost (value of the best alternative -- what you gave up). We will be computing and graphing costs in both the short-run and long-run.

For the most part, the goal of business is to maximize profit. Profit is the difference between total revenue (price x quantity) received by a firm and the total costs (fixed plus variable) incurred. As a profit maximizer, a business needs to know when diminishing returns begins and where the most efficient level of production is located.

Chapter 22 serves as a foundation for analyzing the four markets structures -- pure competition, pure monopoly, monopolistic competition, and oligopoly. Therefore, it is extremely important that you have a clear understanding of all the terms, and be able to explain the shape of each of the cost curves in both the short-run and the long-run.

Learning Objectives

After reading this chapter in the text, and completing the following exercises in this concepts book, you should be able to:

1.  Define opportunity cost (economic cost).
2.  Distinguish between implicit and explicit costs.
3.  Explain the difference between normal profit and economic  profit.
4.  Explain why normal profit is a cost but economic profit is not a cost.
5.  Define the law of diminishing returns.
6.  Distinguish between the short-run and the long-run in economics.
7.  Using the Input/Output Model, compute and graph average product (AP) and marginal product (MP)
8.  Explain the relationship between MP and AP.
9.  Define the total costs: fixed costs, (TFC), variable costs, (TVC) and total costs, (TC). Graph each curve and explain the shape of each curve.
10. Define the average costs:  average fixed costs (AFC), average variable cost (AVC), average total cost (ATC).Graph each curve and explain the shape of each curve.
11. Define the marginal cost curve (MC) and graph an MC curve and explain its shape.  Compare the MP curve with the MC curve.
12. Compute TFC, TVC, TC, AFC, AVC, ATC, and MC when given the necessary data.

13. State the relationship between AVC and AP.
14. Explain the shape of the long-run average total cost curve based upon economies and diseconomies of scale.
15. Indicate the relationship between economies and diseconomies of scale and the size and number of firms (competitiveness) in an industry.
16. Discuss how the "planning curve" in the long-run determines the most efficient level of production.

## Chapter Highlights

I. Economic Costs
 A. Definition of opportunity cost -- the value of the benefit that is given up to produce one economic good as opposed to another.
 B. Definition of economic cost -- payments a firm must make to secure resources.
  1. Explicit costs -- tangible expenses; out-of-pocket expenditures such as wages, materials, telephone, etc.
  2. Implicit costs -- nonexpenditures which include a "normal" profit such as foregone wages, interest, rental income, etc.
  3. Economic Cost = Explicit Cost + Implicit Cost
 C. When the total revenue received by a firm, equals the economic cost, a normal profit has been realized.
  1. A normal profit is a cost, because without it, resources cannot be secured.
 D. Economic (pure) profits are surplus or excess profits.
  1. Economic profits are not a cost because they are over-and-above what is needed to secure the resource.
  2. Economic profits differ from accounting profits because economic profits include implicit costs.
  3. Total Revenue
     - Explicit Cost          or     Total Revenue
       Accounting Profit              - Economic Costs
     - Implicit Cost                  Economic Profit*
       Economic Profit

   *  when economic profit equals zero, a normal profit has been realized.
 E. Short-run vs. long-run costs
  1. The short-run refers to a period of time where at least one cost is fixed and there is not enough time to change plant capacity.
  2. The long-run refers to a period of time where all costs are variable including plant capacity.

II. Production Costs in the short-run
 A. Law of Diminishing Returns -- a property of a production process which states that when one factor is fixed, adding successive units of a variable resource will result in declining output (returns) beyond some point.
  1. The "Production Function" or "Input/Output Model
   a. Total product (TP)--combining output at each level of input.
   b. Marginal product (MP) -- how much output was achieved by adding one more worker (input).

   $$MP^* = \frac{\Delta\ TP}{\Delta\ \text{units of labor}}$$

   * graphed at the midpoints

    c.    Average product (AP)--shows the output per worker (per unit)

$$AP = \frac{TP}{\text{units of labor}}$$

    d.    MP is the slope of the TP curve. When TP is at a maximum, MP is equal to zero.

    e.    When MP is greater than AP, AP is rising; when MP is less than AP, AP is falling; therefore MP intersects AP at its maximum point (See below).

Figure 1
"The Production Function"
The Law of Diminishing Returns

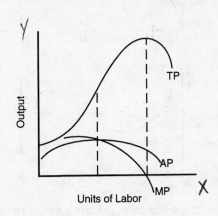

B.  **Total cost curves**

    1.    Fixed costs (TFC) or "sunk costs" are those costs that do not change with output -- starts at zero quantity (overhead costs).

    2.    Variable costs (TVC) are those costs that vary or change with output (operating costs). In the beginning, variable costs will increase at a decreasing rate (volume), but at some point (diminishing returns), variable costs will switch to an increasing rate.

    3.    Total cost (TC) is the sum of fixed and variable costs at each level of output.

        TC = TFC + TVC

        Once TFC is satisfied, TC resembles the TVC curve. (See total curves below).

C.  **Average or "per unit" cost curves**

    1.    Average Fixed Cost (AFC) -- is the fixed cost per unit of output.

$$\frac{TFC}{Q}$$

    2.    Average Variable Cost (AVC) -- is the variable cost per unit of output.

$$\frac{TVC}{Q}$$

3.      Average Total Cost (ATC) -- is the total cost per unit of output.

ATC = $\dfrac{TC}{Q}$ = AFC + AVC

(see average curves below)

Figure 2        Summary of Cost Curves

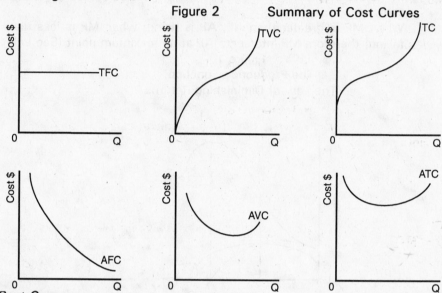

D.  Marginal Cost Curve

1.      Definition -- marginal cost is the extra cost incurred in the production of one more unit of output.

$$\dfrac{\blacktriangle\ TC}{\blacktriangle\ Q}$$

2.      The marginal cost curve (MC) intersects both ATC and AVC at their minimum points (when the cost of adding one more unit is less than the average, it pulls the average down; when it is greater than the average, it pulls the average up).

3.      The MC curve reflects the law of diminishing returns.

4.      The MC curve is a mirror reflection of the marginal product (MP) curve -- when MP is increasing, MC is decreasing and vice versa.

5.      The "most efficient level of production" is where MC = ATC or where ATC is at its minimum point, (at 15 units in Figure 3).

(See relationships below).

Figure 3
"Relationship between MC, ATC and AVC"

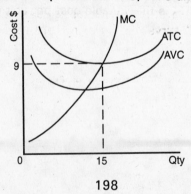

E. Shifting the cost curves
   1. Reasons: changes in resources, prices or technology
III. Long-run Production Costs
   A. Definition -- the long-run refers to a period of time in which the firm can vary all inputs, as well as plant capacity, in order to produce at the most efficient (profitable) level of output.
      1.    The long-run average total cost curve (LRATC) is an "envelope" of all the short-run curves for the firm.
            a.    The LRATC curve indicates the minimum cost possible (by varying all inputs, including firm size) to produce any given output.
            b.    The LRATC curve is U-shaped over an entire range of output, because of economies and diseconomies of scale.
            c.    The LRATC curve is the firm's "planning curve". (See below).
            Figure 4                                              Figure 5

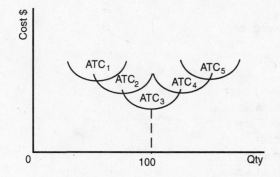
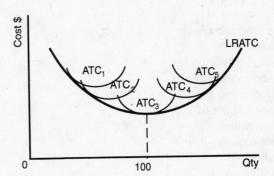

   B. Economies and diseconomies of scale
      1.    Definition -- refers to the effects on unit costs for a firm, as it increases its scale or plant size over the long-run.
            a.    Economies of scale imply decreasing units costs as plant size increases due to increased specialization (labor and management); technological factors (capital goods); financial advantages (discounts given to larger buyers of resources); and by-products (effective utilization of secondary product obtained during manufacture of principal commodity). (See next page).
            b.    Diseconomies of scale imply increasing unit costs as plant size increases, primarily due to the managerial problems encountered. (See next page).
            c.    Constant returns to scale imply that unit costs stay the same as plant size expands (see next page).
      2.    The LRATC curve can have different shapes (slopes), depending upon the industry. The shape of the LRATC curve can be significant in determining the structure and competitiveness of an industry.
   C. MES and Industry Structure
      1.    The minimum efficient scale (MES) is the smallest level of output which a firm can minimize long-run average total costs.
      2.    Natural Monopoly

199

Figure 6

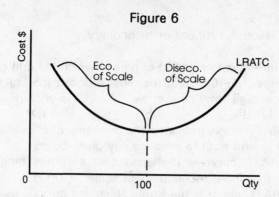

IV.Last Word:  Economies of Scale and Industrial Concentration
Key Terms

| | |
|---|---|
| economic cost | marginal product |
| explicit cost | fixed cost |
| implicit cost | variable cost |
| accounting profit | total cost |
| economic profit | average fixed cost |
| normal profit | average variable cost |
| tangible | average total cost |
| intangible | marginal cost |
| short-run | planning curve |
| long-run | economies of scale |
| Law of diminishing returns | diseconomies of scale |
| production function | by-product |
| total product | minimum efficient scale (MES) |
| average product | natural monopoly |

Real World Example

## SEARS HAS LOST MORE THAN JUST CUSTOMERS
### By Robert Hordt

I had a neighbor who used to boast that he had one-and only one-credit card.  It was a Sears charge card.

"If Sears doesn't have it, I don't need it," he used to say.  A Madison Avenue ad man could not have written better copy.

I haven't seen my old neighbor in a few years, but I'd be willing to bet that by now he's got a few more cards.

Sears Roebuck and Co., of course, is not the company it once was.  In the last decade, the giant retailer has stumbled and has been overtaken by more nimble competitors.  Once, it was the undisputed heavyweight of retailers.  Now, as measured by sales, Sears ranks third  behind Wal-Mart and Kmart.

If we needed yet another reminder of Sears' fading glory, we got it last week-in spades.  Sears announced it was closing 113 stores, eliminating 50,000 jobs and discontinuing its famous catalog.

Of the three, it is interesting that the decision to scuttle the catalog, the so-called "big book," got the most media attention.  Perhaps, we've become so accustomed to hearing about mass layoffs that the loss of 50,000 jobs almost seemed incidental.

Richard Fronapfel will tell you differently.

The 50-year-old Allenhurst resident is one of several thousand Sears employees whose lives have been upended by a company that once had his loyalty but today has his disdain.

Fronapfel went to work for Sears in 1965 at what was then its Neptune store on Route 66.  The store has since moved across the highway into Seaview Square shopping mall in Ocean Township.

Two years after he started, Fronapfel went full time.  He described what it was like to work for Sears as a salesman back then:

"When I started, it was a big, happy family.  It was a fun place to work, and I enjoyed it.  I made money.  Sears made money.  Everybody was happy.  You knew you were never going to be rich, but you felt you had job security."

About 10 years ago, Fronapfel said the culture at Sears began to change.  Whereas providing the best possible service to its customers had always been its guiding light,  Sears seemed to be increasingly interested in finding ways to cut costs.

The reason was simple.  Sears was already under siege, losing its share of the big-ticket, hard-goods market to discounters like Wal-Mart, while losing its share of the soft-goods market to specialty stores like The Gap and The Limited.

During the 1980s, Sears began reinventing itself every few years.  It bought Allstate Insurance and the Dean Witter brokerage, putting financial salesmen on its selling floor.  It opened Brand Central, where it began selling appliances and electronics from major manufacturers.  Then ;there was Sears' highly touted "Everyday Low Prices" campaign, which turned into a bust when the prices didn't prove to be all that low.

At one point in the 1980s, Sears also tried to upgrade its clothing line, signing on model Cheryl Tiegs as one of its  spokespersons.  It even ran its ad in high fashion magazines such as Vogue, Glamour and Cosmopolitan.

The strategy misfired.  The people who could afford the clothing couldn't bring themselves to shop at Sears and the people who had been shopping at Sears couldn't afford the clothing.

"That's when they started losing customers," Fronapfel said.  "That's when they started losing Mr. and Mrs. Middle America."

At the same time that Sears was losing business, it began losing the respect of its employees.  Sears changed its commission structure for many of its veteran salespeople.  Between the new pay structure and declining business, Fronapfel said his annual salary dropped from $38,000 to $22,000 over four years.  Morale plummeted.

When Sears finally offered him early retirement last year, Fronapfel said he had only one question: "Where do I sign?  It wasn't a question of can I afford to.  I couldn't afford to stay there."

Fronapfel was not alone.  All but three of the 16 eligible workers at the Seaview Square Sears took the early retirement offer.

Fortunately for Fronapfel, he had seen the signs early.  A few years ago he went back to college part time.  After he left Sears he went back full time, earned his bachelor's degree and is now pursuing his master's in education.  He hopes to teach in elementary school after graduation.

Sears may have been doomed to its fate by a changing marketplace, but Fronapfel is not about to let management off the hook that easy.

"It's disappointing to see a company so great destroyed by managers that don't know what's going on," he said.  "They're insulated from the real world."

**CHAPTER 22**    **"The Costs of Production"**

## PROBLEMS

1. You are given the following information for a firm that can produce different levels of output by varying the amount of one input, all other inputs remaining constant.
   Fill in the last two columns of the table.

| (Q) Units of Resource | (TP) Total Product | (AP) Average Product | (MP) Marginal Product |
|---|---|---|---|
| 0 | 0 | 0 | |
| | | | 3 |
| 1 | 3 | 3 | |
| | | | 5 |
| 2 | 8 | 4 | |
| | | | 7 |
| 3 | 15 | 5 | |
| | | | 5 |
| 4 | 20 | 5 | |
| | | | 3 |
| 5 | 23 | 4.6 | |
| | | | -3 |
| 6 | 20 | 3.33 | |

$\frac{TP}{Q}$    $\frac{\Delta TP}{\Delta Q}$

a. Plot all three product curves.

b. Answer the following questions with reference to the graphs you have drawn:

   (1) When marginal product is greater than average product, average product is (rising/constant/falling).  *rising*

   (2) When marginal product is less than average product, average product is (rising/constant/falling).  *Falling*

$$AP = \frac{TP}{Q}$$

$$MP = \frac{\Delta TP}{\Delta Q}$$

   (3) Label the three phases.

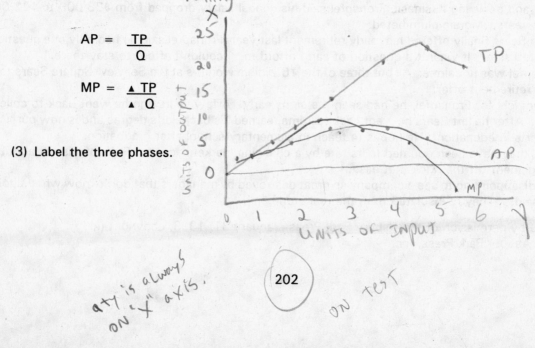

*qty is always on "x" axis.*

*ON TEST*

10/19          Homework

## PROBLEMS (continued)

2. The Fiasco Company is a perfectly competitive firm whose costs of production in the short-run are as follows:

| Output per day (Q) | TFC | TVC | TC ($TVC + TFC$) | ATC ($\frac{TC}{Q}$) | AVC ($\frac{TVC}{Q}$) | MC ($\frac{\Delta TC}{\Delta Q}$) |
|---|---|---|---|---|---|---|
| 0 | 14 | 0 | 14 | 0 | 0 | |
| 1 | 14 | 2 | 16 | 16 | 2 | 2 |
| 2 | 14 | 4 | 18 | 9 | 2 | 2 |
| 3 | 14 | 6 | 20 | 6.66 | 2 | 2 |
| 4 | 14 | 10 | 24 | 6 | 2.5 | 4 |
| 5 | 14 | 16 | 30 | 6 | 3.2 | 6 |
| 6 | 14 | 24 | 38 | 6.33 | 4 | 8 |
| 7 | 14 | 34 | 48 | 6.86 | 4.86 | 10 |
| 8 | 14 | 46 | 60 | 7.5 | 5.75 | 12 |
| 9 | 14 | 60 | 74 | 8.22 | 6.66 | 14 |
| 10 | 14 | 76 | 90 | 9 | 7.6 | 16 |

Total Fixed Costs are $14 per day. ✲

AVC          ATC          MC

a. On graph paper plot and label the average variable cost, average total cost and marginal cost curves.

b. How would you interpret the vertical distance between the average total cost and the average variable cost curves?

c. Why does average total cost (ATC) decline first, and then start rising?

d. What is the most efficient level of production?   where MC = ATC (6 units)

**"The Costs of Production"**   *✱ problem will be on Exam*

3. Assume a firm has fixed costs of $80 and variable costs as indicated below:

TC = TVC + FC

| QTY. | TFC | | TVC | TC | AFC $\frac{FC}{Q}$ | AVC $\frac{VC}{Q}$ | ATC $\frac{TC}{Q}$ | MC $\frac{\Delta TC}{\Delta Q}$ |
|------|-----|---|-----|-----|-----|-----|-----|-----|
| 0 | 80 | + | $0 | 80 | 0 | 0 | 0 | |
| 1 | 80 | + | 110 | 190 | 80 | 110 | .190 | ½ 110 |
| 2 | 80 | + | 150 | 230 | 40 | 75 | 115 | 1½ 40 |
| 3 | 80 | + | 180 | 260 | 26.2 | 60 | 86.2 | 2½ 30 |
| 4 | 80 | + | 220 | 300 | 20 | 55 | 75 | 3½ 40 |
| 5 | 80 | + | 270 | 350 | 16 | 54 | 70 | 4½ 50 |
| 6 | 80 | + | 340 | 420 | 13.2 | 56.4 | 56.67 | 5½ 70 |
| 7 | 80 | + | 440 | 520 | 11.3 | 62.6 | 74.3 | 100 |
| 8 | 80 | + | 580 | 660 | 10 | 72.4 | 72.5 | 140 |

a. Complete the table above.

b. On graph paper, plot and label the AVC, ATC, and MC curves on one graph.

c. What is the most efficient level of production?   5 units
where MC = ATC

d. Shade in the AFC area.

TC = TVC + TFC

$$AVC = \frac{VC}{Q}$$

$$MC = \frac{\Delta TC}{\Delta Q}$$

$$AFC = \frac{FC}{Q}$$

$$ATC = \frac{TC}{Q} = AFC + AVC$$

Self-Test

1. Implicit costs:
   a. are utilized by accountants to calculate total expenses
   b. are regarded as costs by accountants and by economists
   (c.) plus explicit costs are equal to economic cost
   d. are an expenditures cost

2. A firm will, in the short-run, incur:
   a. only fixed costs
   (b.) both fixed and variable costs
   c. only variable costs
   d. only costs related to expanding plant capacity

3. The difference between the average total cost (ATC) and total cost (TC) concepts is that:
   a. TC refers to both fixed and variable cost, while ATC refers to variable cost only
   b. TC refers to losses, while ATC is equivalent to price
   (c.) TC is the sum of all costs incurred in the production process, while ATC is the cost per unit
   d. TC is a long-run concept, while ATC is a short-run concept

Answer the following four questions based upon Table I below:

Table I

| Output | TFC | TVC | TC | $\frac{FC}{Q}$ AFC | $\frac{VC}{Q}$ AVC | $\frac{TC}{Q}$ ATC | $\frac{\Delta TC}{\Delta Q}$ MC |
|--------|-----|-----|-----|-----|-----|-----|-----|
| 0 | 100 | 0 | 100 | 0 | 0 | 0 | 0 |
| 1 | 100 | 12 | 112 | 100 | 12 | 112 | 12 |
| 2 | 100 | 16 | 116 | 50 | 8 | 58 | 4 |
| 3 | 100 | 21 | 121 | 33.3 | 7 | 40.3 | 5 |
| 4 | 100 | 32 | 132 | 25 | 8 | 33 | 11 |
| 5 | 100 | 45 | 145 | 20 | 9 | 29 | 13 |

4. When output increases from 2 to 3, marginal costs is:
   a. 2                    (c.) 5
   b. 4                    d. 11

5. When output increases from 4 to 5, marginal cost is:
   a. 4                    c. 11
   b. 5                    (d.) 13

6. At an output level of 4, ATC is:
   a. 58                   (c.) 33
   b. 29                   d. 112

7. At an output level of 5, AFC is:
   (a.) 20                 c. 50
   b. 25                   d. 100

Figure 7

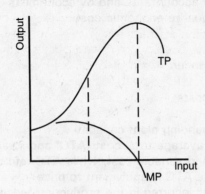

8. In Figure 7 (above), diminishing returns first occurs at _____ and negative returns first occurs at _____.
   a. 0;     100
   b. 100;   200
   c. 100;     0
   d. 200;   100

9. The "most efficient" level of production is where:
   a. MC equals ATC
   b. per unit costs are at their minimum
   c. ATC is at its lowest point
   d. all of the above.

10. Economies and diseconomies of scale help to explain the shape of the:
    a. MC curve
    b. MR curve
    c. AFC curve
    d. LRATC curve

Figure 8

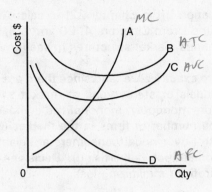

11. In Figure 8 (above), curves A, B, C, and D represent the:
    a.  MC, AVC, ATC, and AFC curves respectively.
    b.  AFC, AVC, ATC, and MC curves respectively.
    c.  MC, ATC, AVC, and AFC curves respectively.
    d.  AVC, ATC, AFC, and MC curves respectively.

12. Average fixed cost decreases with increased output because:
    a.  output rises as more costs are incurred
    b.  total fixed cost is divided by larger and larger numbers
    c.  it is always cheaper to produce on a larger scale
    d.  none of the above

13. Which of the following would <u>not</u> represent a fixed cost to a firm in the short run?
    a.  the rent owed on the plant
    b.  salary of the company president
    c.  mortgage payments on the land
    d.  overtime pay to machine operators

14. A recording company has an output of 1.5 million records in the short-run.  During the same period its total variable cost is $450,000.  Its average variable cost for a record is:
    a.  Three dollars
    b.  Thirty cents
    c.  Thirty dollars
    d.  Three cents

    $$\frac{450,000}{1,500,000} \qquad \frac{VC}{Q}$$

15. The relationship between MC and MP is:
    a.  when MP is increasing, MC is increasing
    b.  when MP is decreasing, MC is decreasing
    c.  when MP is increasing, MC is decreasing
    d.  there is no real relationship

# CHAPTER 23      "Price and Output Determination: Pure Competition"

## Chapter Orientation

Now that we have the foundation (from Chapter 22) to calculate the costs of production and an understanding of consumer demand (from Chapters 4, 20 and 21), we can now bring the sellers and the consumers together under various market structures to see how price and output are determined.

Although no two industries are exactly alike (and since there are so many to examine), economists have developed certain basic models or stereotypes of market structures. The four basic market models are: pure competition, pure monopoly, monopolistic competition, and oligopoly. Each model will be analyzed by looking at the number of firms in the market (competition); the type of product (standard or differentiated); control over price (consumers are elastic, inelastic); conditions of entry (into the market); and nonprice competition (advertising). Decisions will be made (in the short-run and long-run) regarding maximizing profit or minimizing loss.

Chapter 23 opens with a brief description of each market model to give you an overall idea of the spectrum which will be covered. Then from that point, the chapter moves into the first market model and focuses on pure competition. Although, in the real-world, it is difficult to cite an industry that is operating under all the conditions of pure competition, the concept is important because it provides us with a standard of comparison with real-world market structures.

## Learning Objectives

After reading this chapter in the text, and completing the following exercises in this concepts book, you should be able to:

1. List the four basic market structures and explain the major characteristics.
2. Distinguish between the demand curve facing an individual firm and the industry demand curve.
3. Compute total revenue (TR), average revenue (AR) and marginal revenue (MR) when given the necessary data.
4. Graph demand, price, average revenue (AR) and marginal revenue (MR) on one line and explain the relationship.
5. Explain why a "purely competitive" firm is a price-taker.
6. Determine the profit maximizing or loss minimizing output (in the short-run) using the three approaches.
7. Derive a short-run supply curve under pure competition, using the cost and revenue curves given.
8. Determine the long-run equilibrium price and output given short-run curves.
9. Explain why a firm might stay open, in the short-run, even when incurring a loss.
10. Explain the close (shut) down point.
11. Discuss how the entry and exit of firms in a purely competitive market, determines the long-run equilibrium.
12. Compare the long-run supply curves for constant-, increasing-, and decreasing-cost industries.
13. Distinguish between productive efficiency (P = AC) and allocative efficiency (P = MC).
14. Explain the shortcomings of a purely competitive price system.

## Chapter Highlights
I. Market Models (See table 23-1 in your text)
   A. Four basic market models (overview)

1.    Pure (perfect) competition
   - a.    A very large number of firms, producing a standardized product (price-taker). New firms can enter (or exit) the industry easily. No one firm has an impact on market price or output.
2.    Pure monopoly
   - a.    One firm is the sole producer of a unique (differentiated) product and there are no close substitutes (price-maker). Entry into the industry is blocked by patents, economies of scale, etc.
3.    Monopolistic competition
   - a.    many sellers with a differentiated product, which gives each firm a "partial monopoly" (based upon elasticity). Product differentiation lends itself to advertising. Entry (or exit) into (from) the industry is relatively easy.
4.    Oligopoly
   - a.    A few sellers, with either a standardized or differentiated product. Each firm is affected by the price and output decisions of the other firms (mutual interdependence). Entry into the industry is difficult because of significant obstacles such as licensing boards, zoning, etc.
5.    Imperfect competition covers monopoly, monopolistic competition, and oligopoly.

II. Pure (perfect) competition
   A. Characteristics
     1.    Very large number of firms
     2.    Standardized product (no need for nonprice competition -- advertising)
     3.    "Price-taker" -- no one firm can control price or output in the market
     4.    Free entry and exit -- no significant obstacles
   B. Example
     1.    Agriculture in America approximates a purely competitive market -- gives us a standard, or norm, to judge real-world industries.
   C. Demand (short-run) under pure competition
     1.    One firm -- the demand curve is perfectly elastic (no one firm can control price, as a result, the firm must accept the going-market price. A firm cannot get a higher price by cutting output and it can sell all that it wants at the market price, so there is no need to lower price).
     2.    The industry is faced with a downward sloping demand curve (it can only sell a larger quantity by lowering price). See demand curves in Figure 1 below.
     3.    For a single firm, therefore, price does not change ($6 in the example below).

Figure 1

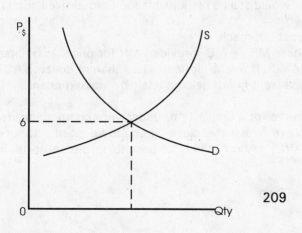

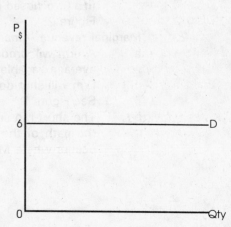

    D.  Revenue curves
       1.      Total revenue (TR) -- the sum of all the receipts of a firm in a given time period.
             TR = Price x Quantity
            a.      Since the price stays the same for a firm under pure competition, TR increases at a constant rate.
       2.      Average revenue (AR) -- the "per unit" receipt (money) from each unit sold.

$$AR = \frac{TR}{Q}$$

            a.      Since the price stays the same, for a purely competitive firm, the "per unit" revenue will be the same as price. ($6 in Figure 1).
       3.      Marginal revenue (MR) -- the extra receipt (money) from selling one more unit.

$$MR = \frac{\blacktriangle TR}{\blacktriangle Q}$$

            a.      Since the price stays the same for a purely competitive firm, the money received by selling one more unit will be the same as price ($6 in Figure 1).
       4.      Under pure competition: D = P = AR = MR
       5.      Total economic profit (or loss) is the difference between TR and TC (also called, "net revenue" or "gross profit").
             Total profit (or loss) = TR - TC

III. Profit Maximization (or loss minimization), in the short-run, under Pure Competition.
    A.  Difference between the "most efficient" level (MC = ATC) and the "most profitable level" of output (three techniques below).
       1.      A firm may be operating at its most efficient level (lowest per unit cost) but may not be at its most profitable level.  This can occur because potential profits might be lost when the selling price of the product is compared to its cost.  The per unit cost may be rising (diminishing returns) but, when the selling price is higher and offsets the inefficiency, more profits are realized.
    B.  Three techniques for determining profit maximization or (loss minimization) in the short-run:
       1.      **Total revenue -- total cost approach**
            a.      Where the difference between TR and TC is the greatest (profit maximization) or the smallest (loss minimization) provided TR is greater than total variable costs -- a firm more than covers the cost of materials and chips away at fixed cost.
            b.      When TR is greater than TC an economic profit is realized; when TR is equal to TC a normal profit is realized; when TR is less than TC a loss is incurred.
            c.      A firm will stay open, even when losing money in the short-run, if the firm is minimizing that loss by staying open -- the loss is less than the total fixed cost (if a firm closed-down it would still be responsible for its total fixed costs).  See Figure 2.
       2.      **Marginal revenue -- marginal cost approach**
            a.      A firm will produce where MR = MC, provided MR (or price) is greater than average variable cost (AVC). If the MR (price) is less than or equal to AVC, the firm will shut-down because it is not helping itself by staying open. See Figure 2.
            b.      The short-run supply curve for a single firm, under pure competition, follows the path of the MC curve above the close-(shut) down point.  (Shut-down occurs where MC = AVC).  Another way of describing the short-run supply

curve is to say that it is that portion of the MC curve above AVC.  (See Figure 2).  A step-by-step derivation is found under the "Problems" section of this concepts book.

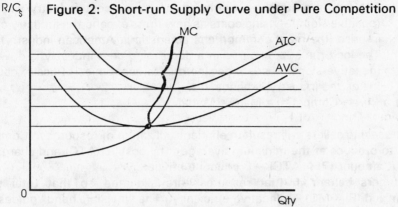

Figure 2:  Short-run Supply Curve under Pure Competition

3.      **Total economic profit (or loss) approach** or where Net Revenue is at a maximum.
   a.      A firm will produce where total economic profit (or loss) is at its maximum point.  Total profit (or loss) = TR - TC = NR
   b.      This technique is similar to technique 1, but it shows only one curve.
   c.      Also called "net revenue" and "gross profit".
4.      The industry supply curve (which is the sum of all the individual supply curves) and the total demand for the product, determine the short-run price and equilibrium output for the industry:  the firms in the industry may be prosperous (profitable) or unprosperous (loss) in the short-run.

IV. Profit Maximization, (or loss minimization) in the long-run under, Pure Competition
   A.  Long-run
      1.      Firms in an industry can either expand or contract their plant capacities.
      2.      The number of firms in the industry can increase or decrease (entry and exit within the industry).
   B.  Model
      1.      The existence of economic profits (when average revenue exceeds average total cost) induces firms to enter an industry.  As a result, the market supply increases causing price to decrease (eliminating the economic profits).
      2.      Once the economic profits are exhausted, the incentive to enter the industry disappears and long-run equilibrium has been restored.
      3.      As a result of declining consumer demand, prices drop (causing losses to be incurred) and when average total cost is greater than average revenue firms exit from an industry.
      4.      Competition forces each firm (in the long-run) under pure competition, to end up with an optimum plant size, earning normal profits, (MC = P = MR = AR = ATC = LRATC).
      5.      The long-run supply curve under pure (perfect) competition.
         a.      The industry's long-run supply curve is shaped by the number of firms entering or exiting the industry.
         b.      Equilibrium for the industry (in the long-run) is reached when no firm wishes to enter or leave the industry.

      c.      The long-run supply curve in a **constant-cost** industry is horizontal (perfectly elastic) -- no increases in costs as new firms expand the industry and prices remain the same.

      d.      The long-run supply curve in an **increasing-cost** industry is upward sloping (positive slope) -- rising costs as new firms expand the industry cause increases in price (the most common characteristic in American industry).

      e.      The long-run supply curve in a **decreasing-cost** industry is downward sloping (negative slope) -- costs decline due to economies of scale, causing prices to fall as the industry expands.

V.  Pros and Cons of a Purely Competitive Market Model

    A.  Pros

        1.      Profit-seeking sellers will result in efficient utilization of resources.  Competition forces firms to produce at the minimum average total cost (LRATC) and charge a price equal to that amount (P = ATC) -- productive efficiency.

        2.      Consumers benefit in that resources are allocated so that total satisfaction is maximized (P = MC) -- allocative efficiency.  The "invisible hand" guides a competitive market through self-interest.

    B.  Cons

        1.      The income distribution problem -- the price system efficiently allocates resources to those who have the money to buy them.

        2.      Market failure:  spillovers and public goods -- the price system does not measure spillovers or externalities.

        3.      Productive techniques -- large-scale production is lost due to the large number of sellers in a competitive market as well as the ability of small firms to keep up technologically.

        4.      Range of consumer choice -- since the competitive market structure entails a standardized product, it presents a limited choice for consumers (no product differentiation), and is not progressive in developing new products.

VI. Last Word:  The Theory of Contestable Markets

Key Terms

| | |
|---|---|
| pure competition | marginal revenue - marginal cost approach |
| pure monopoly | close-(shut) down point |
| monopolistic competition | MR = MC rule |
| oligopoly | short-run supply curve for a single firm |
| imperfect competition | standardized product |
| price-taker | short-run equilibrium |
| nonprice competition | total profit approach |
| total revenue | industry supply curve |
| average revenue | long-run equilibrium |
| marginal revenue | long-run supply curve |
| total economic profit | constant-cost industry |
| net revenue | increasing-cost industry |
| profit maximization | decreasing-cost industry |
| loss minimization | productive efficiency |
| break-even point | allocative efficiency |
| total revenue - total cost approach | self-interest |
| externalities (spillovers) | |

Real World Example

# FARMERS RESILIENT IN FACE OF PRESSURES

## By Melanie E. Eversley

With communities bearing bucolic names like Cream Ridge, and scenes less complicated that those found in urban areas, one might be hardpressed to view the region's farm country as troubled.

But local farms, with most in western Monmouth and Ocean counties, remain in danger of failing, in spite of continued efforts such as the state's Farmland Preservation Program.

"Right now, its really our only tool," Karen Fedosh, senior environmental specialist with Monmouth County, said of the program, set into motion by former Gov. Thomas H. Kean a decade ago.

The program provides funds that counties use toward purchasing from farmers their rights to develop.  The property may then be used for only farming, and the farmers are permitted to remain.

But despite voters' approval in November of a $50-million bond to keep farmland preservation going, farmers remain in danger of losing their livelihood, even those who have already sold their development rights.  The recession has helped keep farmers hungry for more business, said Thomas Lamb, a nursery farmer in Cream Ridge.

"We're just trying to trudge along," said Lamb, 32, who co-owns B & J Nursery with his father, wife, and daughter.

The family sold off the development rights of the 34-year-old, 100-acre farm on Holmes Mill Road about five years ago.  While the move did prevent the Lambs from having to sell to one of several interested developers, the recession has meant struggle for them, Lamb said.

"Last year, we broke even," he said.  "Most farmers have been through it before and it's kind of an up-and-down thing."

In Ocean County, the Board of Freeholders last September agreed to buy development credits from owners of two Plumstead Township farms that together total 540 acres.  In Monmouth County, about 1,500 acres of farmland have been preserved, and about 450 more could be, depending on what the county Agriculture Development Board decides on pending applications, Fedosh said

But K. Edward Jacobi, chairman of that board said the Legislature has not yet appropriated the money from November's vote, meaning that it cannot yet be spent.

In Burlington County, farmers continue to participate in the transfer of development rights, a pilot program in which farmers hold financial credits for maintaining their properties as farmland and developers must purchase those credits in order to build somewhere else.  But so far, no other municipalities or counties have sought to try the program, Fedosh said.

The farming business overall, however, has shown resiliency, said Richard Obal, an agricultural agent for Monmouth County.  A May 1992 frost that was predicted to devastate farmers' crops actually did little damage, Obal said.

However, one branch of the industry that has suffered markedly during the recession is sod farming and landscaping, Obal said.  "So much relies on new construction," he said.  "Many of the (sod and landscape) producers reported their worst year in the last 20 over the last year."

The key to beating hard times is diversity, said Robert Sickles, a Little Silver farmer  who not only runs a garden center but who also earns income through a fruit and vegetable stand.

Aside from an estimated $15,000 to $20,000 loss caused by a wet period that destroyed a crop of tomatoes, last year was a good one for the Sickles family.

"The garden center business is actually good," said Sickles, 36, whose family's farm was created out of a 17th-century land grant from the king of England.  "I think with people traveling less, they spend more time at home and they take the time to fix up their homes.  And a lot of people are trying to sell their homes, so they'll try to fix it up."

Rupert H. Freiberger, a dairy and grain farmer in Upper Freehold Township, said he had a better year than most last year, but has become accustomed to business being rocky in recent years.

"Yields on soybeans were probably higher than we ever had and corn was very good also," Freiberger, 44, said from his 185-acre farm, but he added, "Things aren't exactly super rosy."

State government should lend more support to farmers, in the way of lessening pesticide and other regulations, or permitting them to pay workers less than minimum wage, in order to help farmers stay afloat, Sickles said.  "Essentially, farm laborers in New Jersey are the highest paid in the country."

Fedosh said more options must be developed to help preserve the state's farmland.  "The more solutions, the more likely you are to find something that will work."

## PROBLEMS

1. **Profit Maximization in the Short-Run**

   a.  Fill in the table and determine, as the production manager, how many items you would produce in each of the three cases above.  Are you earning a profit or a loss in the short-run?

### A. Case 1

| QTY | Price | TR ($P \times Q$) | TVC | TFC | TC ($TVC + TFC$) | MR ($\frac{\Delta TR}{\Delta Q}$) | MC ($\frac{\Delta TC}{\Delta Q}$) | NR ($TR - TC$) |
|-----|-------|------|-----|-----|-----|------|------|------|
| 0 | $5.99 | 0 | $0 | $5 | 5 | | | -5 * |
| 1 | | 5.99 | 6 | | 11 | 5.99 | 6 | -5.01 |
| 2 | | 11.98 | 14 | | 19 | 5.99 | 8 | -7.02 |
| 3 | | 17.97 | 24 | | 29 | 5.99 | 10 | -11.03 |
| 4 | | 23.96 | 36 | | 41 | 5.99 | 12 | -17.04 |

Produce "0" units

### B. Case 2

| QTY | Price | TR | TVC | TFC | TC | MR | MC | NR |
|-----|-------|------|-----|-----|-----|------|------|------|
| 0 | $6.01 | 0 | $0 | $5 | 5 | | | -5 |
| 1 | | 6.01 | 6 | | 11 | 6.01 | 6 | -4.99 * |
| 2 | | 12.02 | 14 | | 19 | 6.01 | 8 | -6.98 |
| 3 | | 18.03 | 24 | | 29 | 6.01 | 10 | -10.97 |
| 4 | | 24.04 | 36 | | 41 | 6.01 | 12 | -16.96 |

Produce "1" unit

### C. Case 3

| QTY | Price | TR | TVC | TFC | TC | MR | MC | NR |
|-----|-------|------|-----|-----|-----|------|------|------|
| 0 | $10.01 | 0 | $0 | $5 | 5 | | | -5 |
| 1 | | 10.01 | 6 | | 11 | 10.01 | 6 | -.99 |
| 2 | | 20.02 | 14 | | 19 | 10.01 | 8 | 1.02 |
| 3 | | 30.03 | 24 | | 29 | 10.01 | 10 | 1.03 * |
| 4 | | 40.04 | 36 | | 41 | 10.01 | 12 | .96 |

Produce "3" units

### PROBLEM

2.

| QTY | Price | TR (PxQ) | TFC | TVC | TC (TC-TFC) | AFC ($\frac{FC}{Q}$) | AVC ($\frac{VC}{Q}$) | ATC ($\frac{TC}{Q}$) | MC ($\frac{\Delta TC}{\Delta Q}$) | MR ($\frac{\Delta TR}{\Delta Q}$) | NR (TR-TC) |
|---|---|---|---|---|---|---|---|---|---|---|---|
| 0 | $9 | 0 | 1 | 0 | 1 | 0 | 0 | 0 | | | -1 (Breakeven) |
| | | | | | | | | | 8 | 9 | |
| 1 | | 9 | 1 | 8 | 9 | 1 | 8 | 9 | | | 0 |
| | | | | | | | | | 7 | 9 | |
| 2 | | 18 | 1 | 15 | 16 | .5 | 7.5 | 8 | | | 2 |
| | | | | | | | | | 8 | 9 | |
| 3 | | 27 | 1 | 23 | 24 | .333 | 7.67 | 8 | | | 3 |
| | | | | | | | | | 10 | 9 | |
| 4 | | 36 | 1 | 33 | 34 | .25 | 8.25 | 8.5 | | | 2 |
| | | | | | | | | | 11 | 9 | |
| 5 | | 45 | 1 | 44 | 45 | .2 | 9 | 9 | | | 0 |
| | | | | | | | | | 13 | 9 | |
| 6 | | 56 | 1 | 57 | 58 | .166 | 9.67 | 9.67 | | | -1 |
| | | | | | | | | | 17 | 9 | |
| 7 | | 63 | 1 | 74 | 75 | .143 | 10.71 | 10.71 | | | -12 |

A. Complete table.

B. Graph #1 - Graph TR and TC

   #2 - Graph MC, MR, and ATC

   #3 - Graph NR

C. What is our profit maximum quantity? Label.   MC= ATC  3 units

D. What is Total Fixed Cost (TFC) in the above problem?  1

FORMULAS:

TR = P x Q          MR = $\frac{\Delta TR}{\Delta Q}$          NR = TR - TC

TC = TVC + TFC      MC = $\frac{\Delta TC}{\Delta Q}$

on Test

216

## PROBLEM

3.  Short Run Supply Curve
    A.  Below are the cost and revenue curves for a perfectly competitive firm.
        1.       Label the cost curves
    B.  For <u>each selling price (MR)</u> determine the following: (show all work)
        1.       Label the profit max. (loss min.) price--Pe and quantity--Qe
        2.       State whether an economic profit, normal profit, or a loss has occurred and give the
                 per unit and the total dollar amounts.
        3.       Should you shut-down?
    C.  At what selling price (MR) should you shut-down?  $2.⁰⁰ MR₅
    D.  Shade the AFC area.
    E.  Where is the short-run supply curve?  (highlight on graph)

MC = supply curve down To
            Shutdown point -

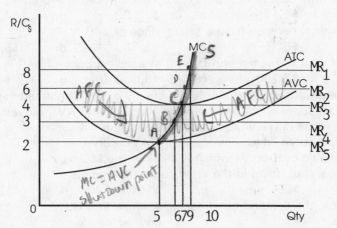

Long term - Point "A"  Shut Down point (Covering VC noT FC)
            Point "B"  Stay in Business  (covering All VC/some FC) minimizing Losses
            Point "C"  Breakeven point  (covering All VC and All FC)
<u>HINTS</u> (if you need them):  Point "D"  Profit  (Economic profit)
            Point "E"  Profit  (Economic profit)

Step 1-Determine the profit max.(loss min.) price and quantity-MC=MR
    2-Calculate the profit (or loss) per unit:
        Pe--Selling price (Demand Curve)
        <u>-CP</u>--Cost price (ATC Curve)
        Economic Profit (or loss)*  when Economic Profit = 0 (normal return)
                        * loss incurred by staying open.
    3-Should the firm shut down when its earning a loss (or are you minimizing losses by staying
    open)?
        AVC--(Average Variable Cost)
        <u>+AFC</u>--(Average Fixed Cost)**
        ATC--(Average Total Cost)

    ** Incur the Average Fixed Cost when you <u>shut down</u>.

217 + 218
combination of 2 problems
ON Test.

Self-Test

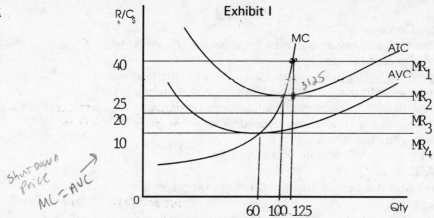

Exhibit I

*Handwritten notes near graph:* SHUT DOWN PRICE  MC=AVC

*Handwritten notes at right:* 40 x 125 = 5000 TR / 15 x 125 = 1875 EP / #3125 TC

1.  In Exhibit I, the firm's total cost of producing at a selling price of $40 is:
    a.  $2,200       b.  $3,125       c.  $2,500       d.  $4,500
2.  In Exhibit I, the firm's total revenue from a selling price of $40 is:
    a.  $4,000       b.  $600         c.  $2,200       d.  $5,000
3.  In Exhibit I, the firm's total economic profits (NR) at a selling price of $40 is:
    a.  $1,875       b.  $2,200       c.  $5,000       d.  $600
4.  In the short-run, the individual competitive firm's supply curve is that segment:
    a.  of the marginal cost curve which lies between the ATC and AVC curves.
    b.  of the marginal revenue curve which lies below the demand curve.
    c.  of the marginal cost curve which lies above the AVC curve.
    d.  of the average variable cost curve which lies below the MC curve.
5.  In Exhibit I, the firm will shut down in the short-run if the price is:
    a.  $20          b.  $25          c.  $10  MC=AVC   d.  $30
6.  Under pure competition, the demand curve facing a single firm is:
    a.  perfectly inelastic            c.  downward sloping
    b.  perfectly elastic              d.  vertical
7.  A purely competitive firm will stay open, even if it is incurring a loss in the short-run if:
    a.  the firm is minimizing that loss
    b.  total fixed cost is greater than the loss
    c.  MR is greater than AVC
    d.  all of the above
8.  A purely competitive firm sells its output for $25 when it produces 100 units.  At that output MC
    = $25 and is rising, AVC = $30 and ATC = $50.  In this situation, the firm should:
    a.  increase output                c.  maintain output
    b.  decrease output                d.  close- (shut) down
9.  A purely competitive industry will earn:
    a.  normal profits in both the short-run and long-run.
    b.  economic profits in both the short-run and long-run.
    c.  economic profits in the short-run and normal profits in the long-run.
    d.  normal profits in the short-run and economic profits in the long-run.
10. The long-run supply curve in an increasing-cost industry will  be:
    a.  negatively sloped.             c.  perfectly elastic.
    b.  positively sloped.             d.  downward sloping.

218

# CHAPTER 24     "PRICE AND OUTPUT DETERMINATION:  PURE MONOPOLY"

## Chapter Orientation

Economic activity is carried on in various types of market situations.  In the last chapter, the foundations of pure (or perfect) competition were presented.  This chapter deals with another type of market model -- the monopoly market.

Although it is difficult to cite examples of a pure monopoly, by studying this model we can use it as a basis for comparison since it is at the opposite end of the spectrum.  There are industries that approximate a pure monopoly, and these industries produce over 5% of the GDP (currently over $5 trillion).

Chapter 24 opens with the definition of pure monopoly are how a monopolistic firm remains "alone and loving it" (through barriers to entry); how price and output are determined using the MC = MR rule; and evaluate the monopoly model as compared to the competitive model.

In addition, the chapter explains how the monopolist discriminates by price to maximize profits.  Lastly, since there is no competition in a monopoly market to keep prices in line, the government has a dilemma as to which pricing policy to follow.

## Learning Objectives

After reading this chapter in the text, and completing the following exercises in this concepts book, you should be able to:

1.  Define pure monopoly and list the key characteristics.
2.  List and explain six barriers to entry.
3.  Describe the demand curve facing the pure monopolist.
4.  Compare the demand curves for pure competition and pure monopoly.
5.  Explain why price exceeds marginal revenue under a pure monopoly.
6.  State the technique used to determine price and output under a monopoly; locate the equilibrium price and output on a monopoly graph.
7.  Describe the effects of pure monopoly on the price of a product, the quantity of a product, and the allocation of resources.
8.  Explain why economies of scale and X-inefficiency affects the cost structure.
9.  Define technological progress (or dynamic efficiency) in pure competition and pure monopoly.
10. Explain the effects of monopoly on the distribution of income in the economy.
11. Define price discrimination; list the three conditions necessary for successful price discrimination; and explain two economic consequences of price discrimination.
12. Compare the socially optimum (marginal-cost) price; fair return (full-cost) price; and the monopolist's (profit max) price.
13. Explain the dilemma which the regulatory agency encounters in setting price.

## Chapter Highlights
I.  Pure Monopoly
   A.  Market model
      1.     Definition of pure monopoly -- a market situation in which there is only one seller or producer of a product or service and there are no close substitutes.

2.    Characteristics of a pure monopoly
   a.    Single seller -- or one-firm industry, therefore the firm and the industry are one and the same.
   b.    No close substitutes -- the buyer must purchase the product from the monopolist or do without the product.
   c.    "Price-maker" -- the monopolist sets the price by manipulating the quantity supplied.
   d.    Blocked entry -- high barriers to entry into the industry such as economic, legal, or technological barriers.
   e.    Advertising -- since there is no competition, if a monopolist advertises it will be for public relations or good will.
   f.    Examples -- utilities, DeBeers Diamond syndicate, etc. approximate pure monopolies.

II. Barriers to entry
   A.  A natural monopoly exists when economies of scale are so great in an industry that only one firm can efficiently serve the market.  As a result the government grants to the industry exclusive franchises and in return reserves the right to regulate the industry.
   B.  A monopoly firm might have exclusive ownership or control of a basic new material or other factors of production.
   C.  A monopoly firm might control patents on production equipment and techniques, or may utilize tying agreements to extend monopoly power.  A patent is the exclusive right to control a product for seventeen years.
   D.  A monopoly firm might engage in unfair competitive practices designed to exclude new competitors.
   E.  The monopolist might be so well established that it might have exceptional advantages or economies arising:  from the ability to raise money more easily and cheaply, from long-term advertising, and from efficient policies and personnel.
   F.  Although barriers to entry are high, it is possible for a firm to enter a monopoly market (just look at MCI Communications).  Also, the question of efficiency arises when there is a lack of competition in the market (perhaps too much time is wasted keeping the competition out).

III. Determining Price and Output for a Pure Monopolist
   A.  Monopoly demand
   1.    Definition--the demand curve for a monopolist is the same as the industry demand curve because the monopoly firm is the only seller in the market.
   2.    The industry demand curve is a downward sloping because of the inverse relationship between price and quantity (the monopolist must lower prices to increase the quantity demanded).
      a.    As a result of lowering price to increase sales, marginal revenue is less than price (= AR) for every level after the first one.  The reason for this is because when you drop the price, for example by a dollar, the marginal effect (or change will be a dollar, the average effect will be the dollar divided by the number of units (therefore once the number of units is greater than 1, AR or price will be greater than MR).  See Table 24-1 and Graph 24-1.

Table 24-1

| Q | Price | TR | AR | MR |
|---|-------|-----|-----|-----|
| 0 | $10 | 0 | -- | |
| | | | | 9 |
| 1 | 9 | 9 | 9 | |
| | | | | 7 |
| 2 | 8 | 16 | 8 | |
| | | | | 5 |
| 3 | 7 | 21 | 7 | |
| | | | | 3 |
| 4 | 6 | 24 | 6 | |

Graph 24-1

-□- AR = D    -*- MR

3.  All imperfect market firms have a price policy because they can influence total supply which in turn effects price.
4.  The monopolist will try to operate in the elastic range of the demand curve.  As a rational producer, the monopolist will not produce where an increase in output lowers revenue (inelastic demand).
5.  To maximize profit (or minimize loss) in the short-run, the monopolist will produce where:
    a.    MC = MR output
    b.    The difference between TR and TC is the greatest (profit maximization) or the smallest (loss minimization).
    c.    Total profit (or net revenue) is at its highest point. (See illustration:  "Profit Maximization for a Pure Monopolist" in this concepts book).
  B.  Misconceptions concerning monopoly pricing
    1.    Highest price -- the monopolist chooses to maximize overall profits not charge the highest price.
    2.    Max unit profits -- the monopolist chooses to maximize total profits not unit profits.
    3.    Economic profits -- it is possible for the monopolist to incur a loss (not guaranteed economic profits).
    4.    Supply Curve - the pure monopolist has no supply curve.
IV. Effects of Monopolies
  A.  The existence of a pure monopoly has significant effects on the economy as a whole.
    1.    A monopolist keeps prices high by restricting output, as a result, there is a misallocation of resource (as compared to a competitive market).
    2.    The justification for a monopoly is that consumers benefit because of lower per unit costs due to economies of scale -- is that true?
      a.    If there are economies of scale present in the production process than the monopolist can produce the good or service at a lower long-run average total cost than smaller firms under pure competition.
      b.    However, a monopolist is more susceptible to X-inefficiency than are competitive producers because the monopolist is shelter from competitive forces which put pressure on a firm to be internally efficient to survive.
      c.    Looking at dynamic efficiency (focuses on the question of whether monopolists are more likely to develop more efficient production techniques overtime than

are competitive firms), competitive firms have the motivation to employ efficient production techniques -- their survival depends upon it!  Under the monopoly model presents two schools of thought -- the first being that with the absence of competition the monopolist has every reason to be satisfied with the status quo and "file" any new advances.  In addition, any cost reductions will add to the monopolist's profit, only a small amount, if any, will be passed along to the consumer.  The second idea is that technological advance will increase profits.  In addition, research and technological advance can be used as a barrier to entry.

       d.     Since corporate stock ownership is in the hands of upper income groups, monopolistic profits contribute to income inequality in the economy.

V.  Price Discrimination
   A.  Definition -- price discrimination occurs when a firm sells a product to two different buyers at different prices without justification by differences in cost.
   B.  Conditions required for price discrimination to be profitable
      1.     The seller must have control over price and quantity.
      2.     The seller must classify (segment) customers into groups according to their elasticity of price.
      3.     Resale of the product must be nonexistent
   C.  Consequences of price discrimination
      1.     A monopolist can increase profits by practicing price discrimination (knowing how far you can "push" your customers).
      2.     A discriminatory monopolist will produce a larger output because for example, when the price is lowered it only applies to the additional units sold - not the prior units.
   D.  Examples of Price Discrimination
      1.     Different electric rates to residential and industrial users.
      2.     Higher adult movie ticket prices  as compared to children's movie ticket prices.
      3.     Different rates for airline passengers who are business or vacation travelers.

VI.  Pricing Policies for a Monopolist
   A.  Monopolist's price (or profit maximizing price)
      1.     Where MR = MC
      2.     Since MC is less than price, there is a misallocation of resources (See Graph 24-3).
   B.  Socially optimum price (or marginal cost price)
      1.     Where P = MC (the standard of perfect competition).
      2.     At the intersection of P = MC a ceiling price is established which resolves the underallocation issue.
      3.     Price may be so low that ATC is not always covered (loss for firm).  (See Graph 24-3).
   C.  Fair return price (or full-cost price)
      1.     Where P = ATC.

2.   Covers all costs and includes a normal profit but may underallocate resources. (See Graph 24-2).
3.   Price which the government is likely to impose.

Graph 24-2                                          Graph 24-3

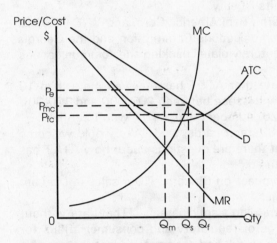

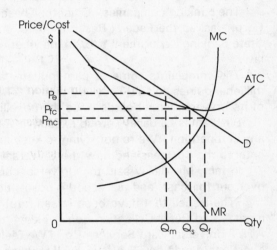

**VII. Dilemma of Regulation**
   A. Tradeoffs of pricing policies
      1.   The dilemma of regulation is that the socially optimum price may cause losses for the monopolist; a fair-return price results in underallocation of resources.
      2.   Price regulation can offset the tendency of monopolists to earn economic profits by underallocating resources.
**VIII. Long-run for a Monopolist**
   A. Economic profits depend on
      1.   Barriers to entry
      2.   Demand for the product
      3.   Government regulation
   B. A monopoly produces higher long-run profits, as compared to the other market models.
**IX. Last Word: Monopolies in the National Parks**

<u>Key Terms</u>

pure monopoly                          misallocation of resources
barrier to entry                       X-inefficiency
price-maker                            dynamic efficiency
natural monopoly                       price discrimination
tying agreement                        monopolist's price
unfair competition                     socially optimum price
economies of being established         fair-return price
monopoly demand                        dilemma of regulation

<u>Real World Example</u>

### As AT&T Credit Card Charges Ahead, Banks Fight Back

By John J. Keller and Robert Guenther

NEW YORK - With American Telephone & Telegraph Co.'s new credit card attracting strong consumer interest, four of the nation's largest card issuers attacked its legality.

The banking companies - Citicorp, Chase Manhattan Corp., BankAmerica Corp. and MNC Financial Corp. - asked the Federal Reserve Board, the Federal Communications Commission and the Georgia State Banking Department to examine whether the AT&T venture violates banking and communications law.

The complaints come as card-industry analysts estimate that AT&T has received more than 10 million inquiries so far.  They say that AT&T has approved and issued between 200,000 and 300,000 of its Universal credit cards since the unveiling on March 26, numbers that AT&T won't confirm.

But James L. Bailey, group executive for Citicorp's U.S. credit cards, said, "We would welcome any competition.  We're not trying to keep anyone out.  But there are questions about how AT&T has entered the business and how the Universal Bank is structured."

In fact, Mr. Bailey said the Universal card has had no impact on Citicorp.  "Our sales in May are over our forecast, and our account acquisitions are on target."

"The issues that have been raised [are] nothing that we didn't anticipate.  ...[They] are without merit," said Peter Gallagher, senior vice president in charge of regulatory and consumer affairs for AT&T Universal Card Services Co.  "We feel we did our homework and anticipated what the possible questions would be.  We're in this business to stay."

AT&T has teamed up with the second-largest processor of credit cards in the country, Total Systems Services Inc., a subsidiary of Synovus Financial Corp., a Columbus, Ga., bank holding company.  Another Synovus subsidiary, Universal Bank, is the issuer of the cards and handles billing on card transactions.

The banks have charged that AT&T, in effect, controls Universal Bank and is therefore violating federal banking laws, which forbid commercial and industrial companies from owning commercial banks.  AT&T owns a small stake in Universal Bank and buys the bank's credit card receivables.

The banks also allege that Universal Bank is no more than a funding vehicle for an unregulated affiliate, namely AT&T, and that Universal is grossly undercapitalized, given that it has only $3 million in capital, but has ambitions to reach five million customers in the next few years.

In the FCC complaint, the banks argue that the 10% discount on long-distance call that AT&T is giving its cardholders amount to "predatory pricing" against other telecommunication providers and a tariff reduction that the FCC hasn't sanctioned.  What's more, say the banks, if giving the discount, then the banks would argue Universal is reselling long-distance service without FCC sanction.

AT&T has refused to give figures on how many of its customers have been issued the cards.  But Mr. Gallagher said the company received 250,000 inquiries from its customers in the 24-hour period after announcing its Universal bank card, about 15 times what it had been expecting the first day.

"From March 26 to May 17, our expectations have been exceeded by 250%," Mr. Gallagher said.  "It has exceeded our wildest expectations."

The big challenge for AT&T will be to turn these Universal card customers into late-paying credit card customers.  The company already has 46 million users of its long-distance calling card, but its customers are notorious on-time payers, an enanthema to a credit issuer that seeks to profit from finance charges.

Moreover, the big banks have a huge head start over AT&T.  Citicorp is the largest issuer of credit cards, with more than 37 million card holders world-wide.  Chase, BankAmerica and MNC, the parent of Maryland National Bank, are second, third and sixth, respectively.

Still, some experts expect AT&T to be one of the top players within a few years.  AT&T Universal Card has set up an operation in Jacksonville, Fla., that can handle the back-office telemarketing needs of a financial services company with millions of customers.

"AT&T won't make any money on this for two to three years," said Spencer Nilson, who publishes the Nilson Report, a newsletter on the credit industry.  But "within five years, they'll have 35 million cardholders.  They're terrible efficient.  I'd say they're issuing about 7,500 cards a day.  I got my card within seven days, compared with more than three weeks with some other cards."

At least one credit card expert saw the bank action as an attempt to stifle the card's success.  "It's a harassment action,"  said Elgie Holstein, executive director of the Bankcard Holders of America, a non-profit consumer credit, education and advocacy group.  "This is an attempt to do in a major new competitor by ... companies that are engaged in acquiring portfolios of smaller and medium-sized players.  They're the primary movers increasing the consolidation and decreasing competiveness of the industry."

## PROBLEMS

1. The following is a table for a monopolist:

   A. Complete the table below.

   B. Prepare three graphs:
      Graph #1 - Graph TR and TC
            #2 - Graph MC, MR, and ATC
            #3 - Graph NR

   C. Label the profit-maximizing or loss-minimizing quantity and price.

| Quantity Per day | AR = P | TR (P×Q) | TC | ATC (TC/Q) | MC (ΔTC/ΔQ) | MR (ΔTR/ΔQ) | NR (TR−TC) |
|---|---|---|---|---|---|---|---|
| 0 | $12 | 0 | $20 | 0 | | | −20 |
| | | | | | 4 | 11 | |
| 1 | 11 | 11 | 24 | 24 | | | −13 |
| | | | | | 3 | 9 | |
| 2 | 10 | 20 | 27 | 13.5 | | | −7 |
| | | | | | 5 | 7 | |
| 3 | 9 | 27 | 32 | 10.67 | | | −5 * |
| | | | | | 7 | 5 | |
| 4 | 8 | 32 | 39 | 9.75 | | | −7 |
| | | | | | 10 | 3 | |
| 5 | 7 | 35 | 49 | 9.8 | | | −14 |
| | | | | | 14 | 1 | |
| 6 | 6 | 36 | 63 | 10.5 | | | −27 |
| | | | | | 20 | −1 | |
| 7 | 5 | 35 | 83 | 11.86 | | | −48 |

## PROBLEMS

2.  The following is a table for a monopolist:

A.  Complete the table below.

B.  Prepare three graphs:
    Graph  #1 - Graph TR and TC
           #2 - Graph MC, MR, and ATC
           #3 - Graph NR

C.  Label the profit-maximizing or loss-minimizing quantity and price.

| Quantity Per day | AR = P | $P \times Q$ TR | TC | $\frac{TC}{Q}$ ATC | $\frac{\Delta TC}{\Delta Q}$ MC | $\frac{\Delta TR}{\Delta Q}$ MR | TR-TC NR |
|---|---|---|---|---|---|---|---|
| 0 | $21 | 0 | $22 | 0 | | | -22 |
| 1 | 20 | 20 | 37 | 37 | 15 | 20 | -17 |
| 2 | 19 | 38 | 42 | 21 | 5 | 18 | -4 |
| 3 | 18 | 54 | 45 | 15 | 3 | 16 | 9 |
| 4 | 17 | 68 | 47 | 11.75 | 2 | 14 | 21 |
| 5 | 16 | 80 | 50 | 10 | 3 | 12 | 30 |
| 6 | 15 | 90 | 54 | 9 | 4 | 10 | 36 |
| 7 | 14 | 98 | 59 | 8.43 | 5 | 8 | 39 |
| 8 | 13 | 104 | 65 | 8.125 | 6 | 6 | 39 |
| 9 | 12 | 108 | 72 | 8 | 7 | 4 | 36 |
| 10 | 11 | 110 | 80 | 8 | 8 | 2 | 30 |
| 11 | 10 | 110 | 89 | 8.1 | 9 | 0 | 21 |
| 12 | 9 | 108 | 99 | 8.25 | 10 | -2 | 9 |

227

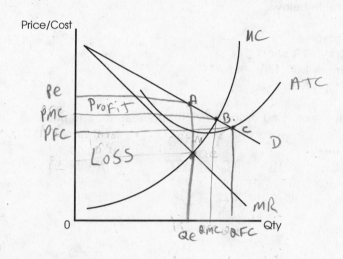

3.  The accompanying diagram refers to a monopolist.
    a.  Label all of the curves.

$MC = MR$ b.  Show the level of output that the unregulated monopolist will sell and label it (Qe). " A "
       Show the price at which the unregulated monopolist will sell and label it (Pe).

    c.  Shade in the area that shows the monopolist's profit or loss.

$MC = D$

    d.  Show the level of output that the regulated monopolist would produce if it followed the " B "
        marginal cost pricing (socially optimum pricing) and label it (Qmc) and also the price level and
        label it (Pmc).

$MC = D$ e.  Show the level of output and pricing if the regulated monopolist followed the full-cost or fair-
       return pricing approach and label it (Qfc) and (Pfc).        " C "

$ATC = D$
    f.  Compare the three levels of pricing.

    g.  Does the profit-maximizing monopolist produce at a level of output which optimally uses its
        plant?  Explain.
                 NO


        Optimize at  P = MC      "Point B"

                    MC = D

228

Self-Test

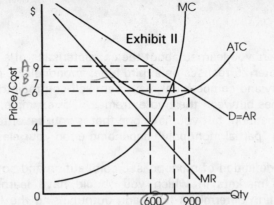

1.  In Exhibit II, the profit-maximizing (or loss-minimizing) level of output for this pure monopolist is:
    a.  400 units per day              c.        850 units per day
    b.  600 units per day              d.        900 units per day
2.  In Exhibit II, the maximum total economic profit that this pure monopolist can earn is approximately:     9-6=3  3×600=1800
    a.  $6,900        b.      $3,600        c.      $1,800        d.      -$1,800
3.  In Exhibit II, what is the profit maximizing price?
    a.  $9.00         b.      $7.00         c.      $6.00         d.      $4.00
4.  In Exhibit II, the full-cost or fair-return price allowed by the government is:
    a.  $6.00         b.      $7.00         c.      $8.00         d.      $4.00
5.  In Exhibit II, following the socially optimum pricing policy, the price would be set at approximately:
    a.  $6.00         b.      $7.00         c.  $8.00            d.      $4.00
6.  A monopolist normally makes output decisions:
    a.  in the inelastic range of the demand curve
    b.  at the point of unit elasticity on the demand curve
    c.  in the elastic range of the demand curve
    d.  without reference to the price elasticity of demand
7.  The demand curve for a firm in a monopolistic industry is:
    a.  always a straight line              b.      slightly less than the industry curve
    c.  perfectly elastic                   d.      the same as the industry demand curve
8.  If a firm is enjoying economic profits over the long-run, it is safe to say that:
    a.  it is too big                       b.      it is being efficiently managed
    c.  it is efficiently allocating resources   d.   it is not a perfectly competitive market
9.  Which of the following describes the relationship of the marginal revenue curve to the demand (average revenue) curve in a monopoly situation?
    a.  The marginal revenue curve is above and has a steeper slope than the average revenue curve.
    b.  The marginal revenue curve falls below and has a steeper slope than the average revenue curve.
    c.  The average revenue curve is above and has a steeper slope than the marginal revenue curve.
    d.  The average revenue curve falls below and has steeper slope than the marginal revenue curve.
10. Which of the following is not a condition necessary for successful price discrimination?
    a.  The seller must have control over price and quantity.
    b.  The buyer must be relatively inelastic to price changes.
    c.  The seller must segment customers.
    d.  Resale of the product is nonexistent.

# CHAPTER 25 "PRICE AND OUTPUT DETERMINATION: MONOPOLISTIC COMPETITION"

## Chapter Orientation

In the previous two chapters you learned about the characteristics of a purely competitive market and a monopoly market. Chapter 25 focuses on a third type: monopolistic competition. Seeing those two words together (monopoly and competition) may seem self-contradictory or a paradox, however, we will see that this market lies between the two extremes. For example, there are lots of Mexican restaurants in your area (competition) but you have <u>one</u> that is your favorite (monopoly). As a result, your favorite restaurant has a "partial monopoly" depending upon your elasticity of price.

Chapter 25 opens with a definition of monopolistic competition and covers its characteristics, as compared to the other two markets in which you should have learned. In addition, how a monopolistically competitive firm determines price and output using the MC = MR rule, the profit picture in both the short-run and the long-run; and the "wastes" of monopolistic competition will be examined. Lastly, nonprice competition, such as product developments and advertising will be evaluated.

Since many firms in the United States fall under monopolistic competition, an understanding of this market will help explain how price, product, and advertising are manipulated to maximize profits.

## Learning Objectives

After reading this chapter in the text, and completing the following exercises in this concepts book, you will be able to:

1. Define monopolistic competition.
2. List and explain the characteristics of monopolistic competition.
3. Determine the price and output for a monopolistically competitive firm wishing to maximize profits (minimize loss) in the short-run, when given the necessary information.
4. Explain why a monopolistically competitive firm usually earns a normal profit in the long-run.
5. Explain and identify the "wastes" of monopolistic competition.
6. Explain why product differentiation may offset these "wastes".
7. List the types of nonprice competition.
8. Present the pros and cons of advertising.
9. Compare monopolistic competition with the other two markets (pure competition and pure monopoly).
10. Discuss the elasticity of demand as compared to the other markets.

## Chapter Highlights

I. Monopolistic Competition
   A. Market model
      1. Definition of monopolistic competition--a market characterized by many sellers in a market where the product of each seller is similar in nature, but differentiated in other ways. Because there are so many sellers, no one seller has much influence over price and, therefore, must differentiate its product in order to gather a large share of the market.

    2.    Characteristics
        a.    Large number of sellers--each with a small percentage of the market.  As a result, no collusion, no mutual interdependence among firms.
        b.    Product differentiation--a product is similar to other products, but not identical.  Therefore, consumers have preference for certain products which give specific sellers, within limits, higher prices.
        c.    Nonprice competition--rivalry on product quality, advertising, etc.  Since products are differentiated, it is natural to advertise their attributes.
        d.    Entry into the market is relatively easy due to the fact that sellers are typically small-sized firms.
        e.    Examples--most clothing items, such as shoes, dresses, and various food products, etc.

II.  Price and Output Determination
    A.  The firm's demand curve
        1.    Highly (but not perfectly) elastic due to the fact that there are substitutes available (perhaps not your favorite brand).
        2.    The demand curve of a monopolistically competitive firm is less elastic than that of a purely competitive firm (product differentiation); but more elastic than that of a pure monopoly firm (substitutes available).
    B.  Short-run profits (or losses)
        1.    In the short-run, a firm will maximize profits (or minimize losses), by producing the output designated by the intersection of MC and MR.
        2.    A firm under monopolistic competition can incur economic profits in the short-run (as well as normal profits or losses).
    C.  Long-run profits or losses
        1.    The tendency in the long-run is to earn a normal profit (or break even).
        2.    The entry and exit of firms will tend to change the profit (or loss) picture.
        3.    Whenever firms enjoy short-run economic profits, other firms see this market as lucrative and the entry of these new firms causes economic profits to be competed away.  The demand curve will fall and become more elastic (because each firm has a smaller share of total demand and faces more close-substitutes).  This causes the disappearance of economic profits because eventually price is equal to ATC.
        4.    Whenever firms are realizing a loss, this will cause firms to exit or leave the industry until normal profits are restored in the long-run.

III.  Wastes of Monopolistic Competition
    A.  Excess plant capacity
        1.    With the existence of too many sellers, there is an underallocation of resources (under pure competition, fewer firms would produce the same total output at a lower price).
        2.    Since there are so many sellers, products are differentiated (due to competition), which gives consumers a variety from which to choose (to maximize satisfaction).

IV.  Nonprice Competition
    A.  Product differentiation
        1.    Consumers are offered a wide range of types, styles, brands, quality, etc. of products from which to choose.
    B.  Product development
        1.    Spurs rivals to copy or improve on a technological advantage.

    2.    Profits realized from successful product development can be applied to further research.

    3.    Critics argue that many product alterations are superficial (example: a flashier container). Also, development may have "planned obsolescence".

  C.  Product differentiation and product development may offset the "wastes" of monopolistic competition.

V.  The Economics of Advertising

  A.  There are two views of advertising: the "traditional" and the "new perspective"

  B.  Major issues in favor of advertising: (Traditional)

    1.    Provides information

    2.    Finances national communications

    3.    Stimulates product development

    4.    Expands production resulting in economies of scale (lower per unit costs even including the cost of advertising)

    5.    Promotes competition

    6.    Promotes full-employment

  C.  Major issues against advertising: (New Perspective)

    1.    Objective of advertising is to persuade (not much relevant information is given).

    2.    Advertising expenditures are relatively unproductive, therefore, it represents inefficient use of scarce resources

    3.    Significant external costs are entailed by advertising.

    4.    Much advertising is self-canceling (advertising war).

    5.    Advertising leads to less competition

    6.    Most economists are reluctant to accept advertising as an important determinant of the levels of output and employment.

  D.  Empirical evidence

    1.    Empirical evidence does not reach a consensus as to the economic impact of advertising.

  E.  The monopolistically competitive firm must adjust price, product and its promotion of the product to achieve profit maximization.

    1.    Each situation presents a different demand and cost schedule. the optimum combination must be found by the process of trial and error.

VI. Last Word: The Market For Principles of Economics Textbooks

Key Terms

| | |
|---|---|
| monopolistic competition | nonprice competition |
| partial monopoly | product development |
| noncollusion | external costs |
| product differentiation | self-canceling |
| nonprice competition | empirical evidence |
| wastes of monopolistic competition | anti- and procompetitive view of advertising |

Real World Example

## Retailers Fighting Tide of Discounters

### By William Conroy

Almost all of the new additions to the area's retail landscape in the past 12 months have been warehouse clubs and discounters, and that  pattern will continue this year.

Existing stores in the area have had to modify their own approaches to cope with the added competition.  This pattern will continue, too.

The warehouse clubs and the discounters ;had the money and the credibility with lenders to expand aggressively while others struggled to survive the recession.  Despite the comeback most retailers experienced this past Christmas season, no major new players except discounters have announced plans to add stores in Monmouth and Ocean counties this year.

Indeed, previously announced plans for new Macy and Stern's anchors to be added to the Freehold Raceway Mall this fall have been put on hold indefinitely.

Meanwhile, three new warehouse clubs joined the local market in 1992:  BJ's Wholesale Club in Ocean Township, Pace Membership Warehouse in Freehold Township, across from the mall, and Price Club in Brick Township.  Price Club pioneered the concept locally with the opening  of its Hazlet Township store in November 1991.

Even one of these acknowledged the local market is not limitless for such clubs: Pace, a subsidiary of Kmart Corp., abandoned a plan to add a store in Lakewood.

"Some of our competitors coming into the same area were able to build before we were able to get in there," said Pace spokesman Douglas Hock.  "We just felt it would not be a good idea to go into the market at (this) point."

The stores that warehouse clubs compete with most directly are supermarkets.  They have responded by adapting the warehouse club tactic of offering bargain prices on items bought in bulk.

"Clearly, we've increased the number of 'big deals' (to respond to the warehouse clubs)," said Larry Salinas, vice president of public affairs and research for Supermarkets General, which owns 146 Pathmark stores, including 62 in New Jersey.

Big deals are multi-pack items, such as 24-can cases of soft drinks, he said.

Pathmarks are also putting more emphasis on in-house and "no frills" brands to meet the warehouse club challenge, Salinas said.  Consumers who compare per-ounce costs on these items and sale items with what is available in warehouse clubs see that they compare favorably, he said.

Other new retail players joining the field in the last 12 months include Staples Inc., billed as "The Office Superstore," which opened its first area store in Toms River in October.  The Framingham, Mass.-based chain plans to pen its first store in Monmouth County in West Long Branch Feb. 22.

The arrival of Staples has already hastened changes at Charney's stationery store, a local family-owned landmark since 1931.

A month after Staples opened, Simon Schwartz sold Charney's to American Office Products Corp., Parsippany.  The company has been buying up such independent businesses in belief that by combining several office products and services into one company, it can compete with the discount office chains.

Kmart Corp.'s office product division, Office Max, plans to open its first area store in the spring, in Holmdel Town Center on Route 35.

Another Kmart subsidiary, The Sports Authority, added its first store in the area in West Long Branch in December, at the same shopping center, Consumer Centre on Route 36, in which Staples will open.

Bob Kislin's, a sporting goods retailer at the Shore since 1946, plans no big changes to cope with the new megastore challenge. The three-store chain has units in Ocean Township, Toms River and Pleasantville.

Wal-Mart Stores Inc., Betonville, Ark., plans to open its first two stores in the area this year.

No exact dates are set, but the opening of the Wal-Mart in Toms River is scheduled for the spring, said Wal-Mart spokeswoman Sandy Brummett, and the Wal-Mart in Stafford Township is expected to pen in late spring or early summer.

"You can't compete with Wal-Mart on price," said Don R. Clarke, chairman and chief executive officer of Caldor Corp., Norwalk, Conn. "The key for us is to be different."

Reprinted by permission of the Asbury Park Press, January 31, 1993, copyright (c) 1993 by Asbury Park Press, Inc.

# CHAPTER 25 "PRICE AND OUTPUT DETERMINATION: MONOPOLISTIC COMPETITION"

## PROBLEMS

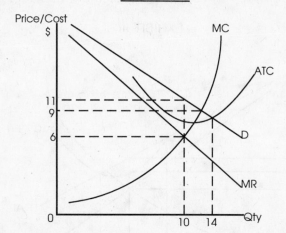

1. Shown above are the cost and revenue curves for a monopolistically competitive firm.
   a. The firm will produce approximately ___*10*___ units of output and charge approximately
      $___*11*___ per unit. *11-9=2 ×10 =20*
   b. The firm's net revenue is approximately $ _*20*_ . The firm is thus earning (normal profit,
      economic profit, or a loss) _*Economic profit*_ .
   c. In the long run, new firms (will tend to/will not tend to) _*Will tend to*_ enter the
      industry.
   d. In the long run, each firm (will/will not) _*Will*_ tend to earn a normal profit.

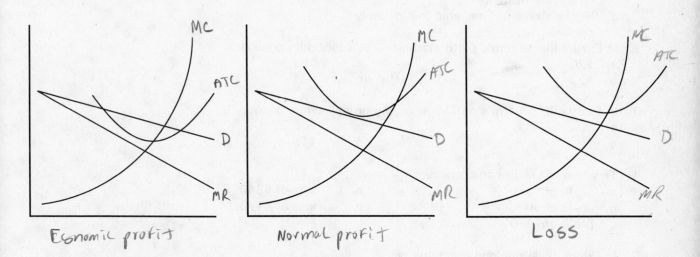

2. Shown above are the profit/loss positions for a firm under monopolistic competition.
   a. Label all the curves and the X and Y axis.
   b. Label the profit maximizing (or loss minimizing) price (Pe), output (Qe) and cost price (CP).
   c. Indicate whether an economic profit, a normal profit, or a loss has occurred.
   d. Shade in the area of profit or loss.

Self-Test

EXHIBIT III

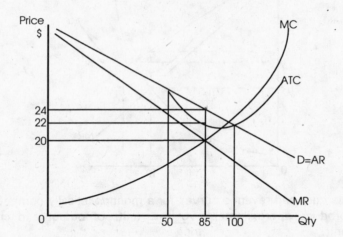

1. The monopolistically competitive firm views its demand curve as being:
   a. Unimportant in relation to other firms
   b. Highly inelastic as compared to Monopoly
   c. Of unitary elasticity
   d. Highly elastic as compared to Monopoly

2. In Exhibit III, the firm's profit-maximizing or equilibrium price is:
   a. $20
   b. $22
   c. $23
   d. $24

3. In Exhibit III, the firm's profit-maximizing or equilibrium quantity is:
   a. 50
   b. 85
   c. 100
   d. 115

4. This firm will realize an economic:
   a. profit of $340
   b. profit of $0
   c. profit of $170
   d. loss of $340
   e. loss of $170

5. In Exhibit III, in the long run, firms will:
   a. enter the market causing a normal profit.
   b. enter the market causing economic profits.
   c.. leave the industry due to loss.
   d. no way to tell from this graph.

Self-Test (continued)

6. Purely competitive markets and monopolistically competitive markets are similar in that there are:
   a. identical products sold by all firms in each market
   b. a large number of small producers in each market
   c. a small number of large producers in each market
   d. none of the above

7. Entry of the new firms into the industry in response to short-run economic profits will cause:
   a. demand to increase for the firm
   b. demand to shift downward and to the left and become more elastic for the firm
   c. demand to remain constant for the firm
   d. none of the above

8. Which of the following is the correct ranking, from highest to lowest, of the relative price equilibrium for a given industry under monopolistic, purely competitive, and monopolistically competitive market situations, assuming the same cost structures?
   a. monopolistic; monopolistically competitive; and purely competitive
   b. purely competitive; monopolistically competitive; monopolistic
   c. monopolistically competitive; monopolistic; purely competitive
   d. purely competitive; monopolistic; monopolistically competitive

9. Short-run equilibrium in a monopolistically competitive industry requires a firm to produce at that point where:
   a. any difference between average revenue and average cost is computed away
   b. marginal revenue equals marginal cost
   c. no cost exists in the short-run
   d. the demand curve is perfectly elastic

10. The three basic forms of monopolistic competition are:
    a. price competition, product variation, and the costs of production
    b. price competition, product differentiation, and product promotion
    c. advertising, consumer satisfaction, and product variation
    d. none of the above

<u>Chapter Orientation</u>

An oligopolistic market structure characterizes much of American industry.  For example, the airline, automobile, cigarette, soft drink, and cereal industries all operate under oligopolistic market conditions.

In Chapter 26, you will learn the distinctive features of an oligopolistic market and be able to distinguish oligopoly from the other market structures -- pure competition, pure monopoly, and monopolistic competition.  The chapter opens with a definition of an oligopoly market, then presents the underlying feature: mutual interdependence.  This condition leads to behavior which is different from all the other models and therefore is difficult for economists to stereotype into a specific market structure (so four models to explain oligopoly behavior are presented -- Kinked Demand Curve, Collusive, Price Leadership, and Cost-plus pricing).

How the profit maximizing (or loss minimizing) price and output are determined; the role of nonprice competition; and the economic impact of oligopoly market will be examined.  Lastly, a real-world oligopoly market (the automobile industry) will be illustrated.

<u>Learning Objectives</u>

After reading this chapter in the text and completing the following exercises in this concepts book, you will be able to:

1.  Define oligopoly.
2.  List and explain the characteristics of an oligopoly market.
3.  Distinguish between homogeneous and differentiated  oligopolies.
4.  Define concentration ratio and give an example of a highly  concentrated industry.
5.  State the underlying causes of an oligopoly market.
6.  Explain why mutual interdependence complicates the  prediction of price and output by an oligopolist.
7.  Compare and contrast the four models used to explain  oligopoly behavior.
8.  Discuss why oligopolists may choose to emphasize nonprice  competition.
9.  Explain the three forms of nonprice competition.
10. Compare the Schumpeter-Galbraith view with the traditional view of oligopoly and discuss the empirical evidence.
11. Compare the American automobile industry to the characteristics of an oligopoly market.

<u>Chapter Highlights</u>

I.  Oligopoly
    A.  Market model
        1.      Definition -- an oligopoly market consists of relatively few sellers of a standardized or differentiated product.  Because there are only a small number of firms in the market, the actions of each firm affect the other firms which cause them to be mutually interdependent.  High barriers to entry helps to prevent new firms from entering the market.

2.    Characteristics of an oligopoly
    a.    Fewness -- a market situation where there are very few sellers -- several firms dominating the entire industry so that these firms are in a position to set price.
    b.    Type of product
        1.    Homogeneous oligopolies produce a standardized product.
        2.    Differentiated oligopolies produce a differentiated product.
    c.    Concentration ratio
        1.    Definition -- the percentage of all sales contributed by the leading four firms in an industry (measures "fewness").  Generally when it is greater than 40 percent or more the industry is oligopolistic.
        2.    Shortcomings of concentration ratios:
           (a)    Pertains to the entire nation (regional measurement might be more applicable).
           (b)    Interindustry competition is ignored (competition between two products of different industries).
           (c)    Data is for American producers only (does not include import competition).
           (d)    Herfindahl Index
           (e)    Actual market performance is ignored.
    d.    Reasons for market concentration
        1.    Economies of scale (especially as a result of technological progress).
        2.    Other barriers such as effective advertising, patents, and control of raw materials.
        3.    Merger -- combining two or more formerly competing firms may increase a firm's market share and enable economies of scale ("horizontal merger").

II.  Oligopoly Behavior:  Game Theory Overview
  A.  Definition of Game Theory
  B.  Mutual interdependence
    1.    Oligopoly is a market situation where there are few sellers.  As a result, each seller knows that the other sellers will react to its changes in price and quantity.
    2.    Sellers will quickly follow a price cut (touch off a price war), but are reluctant to raise price (lose market share).

III.  Price and Output Determination
  A.  Difficulties in explaining oligopoly behavior
    1.    Many types of oligopolies make it difficult to develop one generalized market model.
    2.    Mutual interdependence (see above) -- the inability of a firm to predict with certainty the reactions of its rivals, makes it impossible to estimate the demand or marginal revenue data which interferes with setting price and quantity.
    3.    Use the MC = MR Approach (to maximize profit or minimize loss).
    4.    "Sticky" prices -- under an oligopolistic structure prices change less frequently than under the other three markets.

IV.  Models to Explain Oligopoly Behavior
  A.  The Kinked demand curve
    1.    Oligopoly behavior is illustrated by a demand curve with a "bend" and a corresponding marginal revenue curve with a "step".

239

2.    These two curves are based upon elasticity of price, mutual interdependence, and noncollusion.  (See Figure 26-1a below).

Figure 26-1    The Kinked Demand Curve

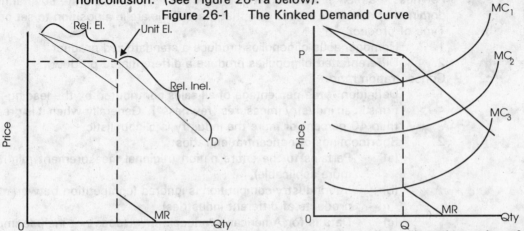

3.    To maximize profits (or minimize loss) the oligopolist will produce where MC = MR.

4.    The equilibrium price and quantity are relatively stable, as compared to the other markets, because once the price and output have been established, the individual firm is reluctant to raise price (in the elastic range of the demand curve; TR decreases) or lower price (in the inelastic range of the demand curve; TR decreases).  Hence, for any marginal cost in the "step" area of the MR curve (see MC1 to MC3 in Figure 26-1b) the selling price and quantity will remain stable.

5.    When MC falls outside the "step" of the MR curve, selling price and quantity will have to change, however, profits will not be as high (as at the "kink").

6.    It is possible for an oligopolist to earn an economic profit in the long-run because of high barriers to entry.

7.    The shortcomings of the kinked-demand model:

   a.    Price rigidity may not fit every oligopolistic industry.

   b.    Does not explain the entry/exit idea.

   c.    No insight into how the equilibrium price was established.

   d.    Does not explain how prices change.

B.   Collusion and Cartels

1.    Firms in an oligopoly coordinate activities for profit maximization (also called a "shared monopoly").   An agreement, usually secret, among competitors to engage in anticompetitive practices is in violation of the Sherman Act -- which declares any contract, combination, or conspiracy in restraint of trade, illegal.

2.    Given similar cost and demand conditions the oligopolistic firms will collude and strive for the same price and output as a monopoly (MC = MR).

3.    Identical price policies are not themselves evidence of collusion. More revealing are the measures taken to ensure compliance with price and output decisions.  A "cartel" typically involves a formal written agreement with respect to both price and production.  This tight-knit agreement involves pressuring member firms to comply (Example: OPEC).

4.    A "gentlemen's agreement" is an informal verbal agreement (perhaps made at a cocktail party or on the golf course) on price, leaving market shares to the individual seller to determine.

5.    Obstacles to collusion
   a.    Demand and cost differences -- make it difficult to agree on price.
   b.    Number of firms -- the larger the number, the more difficult to collude.
   c.    Cheating -- price concessions can be used by buyers as a leverage for a better deal.
   d.    Recession -- a down turn in the economy, causes markets to slump and therefore the temptation to cut price is great.
   e.    Legal obstacles:  antitrust -- as mentioned earlier, collusion and price-fixing are illegal in the United States.
6.    OPEC in disarray

C.  Price Leadership:  tacit collusion
   1.    An informal situation in which the dominant or largest firm in an industry acts as a leader in setting a price that other firms in the industry will follow.
   2.    Tactics used by a price leader:
      a.    Infrequent price adjustments.
      b.    Price will only be changed due to cost and demand conditions.
      c.    Price does not necessarily reflect short-run profits for the industry.

D.  Cost-plus pricing
   1.    A pricing policy in which a profit rate is predetermined by the firm, and the price is set equal to the cost per unit plus the established profit rate (markup).
   2.    Advantage of cost-plus pricing
      a.    Useful for firms with multiproducts.
      b.    May result in similar prices among firms in the industry.

V.  Role for Nonprice Competition
   A.  Use of nonprice competition
      1.    Since price cuts can be easily matched, nonprice competition can have permanent advantages.
      2.    Oligopolists are in a financial position to support advertising and product development.

VI.  Oligopoly and Economic Efficiency
   A.  To compare the efficiency of an oligopolist with that of a pure competitor is difficult, barrier two distinct views have evolved:
      1.    The traditional view contends that since an oligopoly is a "shared monopoly" it reacts in the same way as a monopoly.
      2.    The Schumpeter-Galbraith view contends that large oligopolistic firms are needed for technological progress (dynamic efficiency).
   B.  Empirical evidence is not conclusive, however, it appears that inventors, acting independently, created the majority of inventors.
      1.    Certain oligopolistic industries may lend themselves more easily to technological progress than others.

VII.  Case Study:  The Automobile Industry
   A.  Oligopoly behavior
      1.    The automobile industry "fits" the oligopoly market model because there are a few large firms; high barriers to entry; price leadership; product differentiation; and competition from foreign producers.

VIII.  Last Word:  The Beer Industry -- Oligopoly Brewing?

## Key Terms

| | |
|---|---|
| oligopoly | collusive oligopoly |
| fewness | shared monopoly |
| homogeneous oligopoly | Sherman Act |
| differentiated oligopoly | cartel |
| concentration ratio | gentlemen's agreement |
| interindustry competition | tacit collusion |
| horizontal merger | cost-plus pricing |
| mutual interdependence | price leadership |
| price war | nonprice competition |
| sticky prices | traditional view |
| kinked demand curve | Schumpeter-Galbraith view |
| noncollusion | |

# SOME LEADERS IN MARKET VALUE DO A DISAPPEARING ACT

**20 largest companies worldwide, by stock market valuation, in billions**

| 1972 | | 1982 | | 1992 | |
|---|---|---|---|---|---|
| 2 AT&T | 29.2 | 2 AT&T | 52.2 | 1 EXXON | $75.8 |
| 3 EASTMAN KODAK | 23.9 | 3 EXXON | 25.7 | 2 GENERAL ELECTRIC | 73.9 |
| | | 4 GENERAL ELECTRIC | 21.6 | 3 WAL-MART | 73.5 |
| 5 EXXON | 19.6 | | | 4 ROYAL DUTCH/SHELL¹ | 71.8 |
| | | 6 ROYAL DUTCH/SHELL¹ | 16.9 | 5 NIPPON TEL. & TEL. | 71.4 |
| 7 GENERAL ELECTRIC | 13.3 | 7 EASTMAN KODAK | 14.2 | 6 PHILIP MORRIS | 69.3 |
| 8 XEROX | 11.8 | 8 SCHLUMBERGER | 13.4 | 7 AT&T | 68.0 |
| 9 TEXACO | 10.2 | 9 TOYOTA MOTOR | 12.6 | 8 COCA-COLA | 55.7 |
| 10 MINNESOTA MINING & MFG. | 9.7 | 10 AMOCO | 11.7 | 9 MITSUBISHI BANK | 53.5 |
| 11 PROCTER & GAMBLE | 9.1 | 11 CHEVRON | 10.9 | 10 MERCK | 50.3 |
| 12 ROYAL DUTCH/SHELL¹ | 9.1 | 12 MOBIL | 10.7 | 11 INDUS. BANK OF JAPAN | 46.5 |
| 13 COCA-COLA | 8.9 | | | 12 SUMITOMO BANK | 45.6 |
| 14 DU PONT | 8.4 | 14 ATLANTIC RICHFIELD | 10.2 | 13 TOYOTA MOTOR | 44.1 |
| 15 FORD MOTOR | 8.0 | 15 HITACHI | 9.9 | 14 FUJI BANK | 41.8 |
| 16 AVON PRODUCTS | 7.9 | 16 PROCTER & GAMBLE | 9.8 | 15 DAIICHI KANGYO BANK | 41.8 |
| 17 MOBIL | 7.5 | 17 MATSUSHITA ELECTRIC IND. | 9.6 | 16 SANWA BANK | 37.9 |
| 18 JOHNSON & JOHNSON | 7.4 | 18 GENERAL ELECTRIC CO. (U.K.) | 9.3 | 17 BRITISH TELECOM. | 37.8 |
| 19 CHEVRON | 6.8 | 19 JOHNSON & JOHNSON | 9.3 | 18 PROCTER & GAMBLE | 36.4 |
| 20 MERCK | 6.6 | 20 BRITISH PETROLEUM | 8.7 | 19 GLAXO HOLDINGS | 36.1 |
| | | | | 20 BRISTOL-MYERS SQUIBB | 35.1 |

*FORTUNE TABLE / SOURCES: MORGAN STANLEY; WILSHIRE ASSOCIATES*

*Sic transit gloria*: IBM, General Motors, and Sears were stars in total market value in 1972, but after two decades they were conspicuously absent from the Big 20. Morgan Stanley data show IBM ranking 26th at year-end 1992, with about $29 billion in value; GM 40th, with $22 billion; and Sears (gulp!) 81st, with not quite $16 billion. And all that in the face of a crisply rising stock market—the S&P 500 was up 269% over the 20 years. The lists, natch, show infiltration by the Japanese—they were shut out in 1972 but held eight spots in 1992. A churning market this year has also created a Japanese champ: As of April 2, Nippon Telegraph & Telephone had leaped to $137 billion in value and No. 1 in rank. Philip Morris had dropped from 6th to 16th, Merck from 10th to 19th, and P&G, Glaxo, and Bristol-Myers from the top 20 entirely.

¹The figure combines the market values of Royal Dutch Petroleum and Shell Transport & Trading.

From "Dinosaurs?" by Carol J. Loomis. Reprinted by permission from <u>Fortune</u>, May 3, 1993, copyright (c) 1993 by Time, Inc.

## PROBLEMS

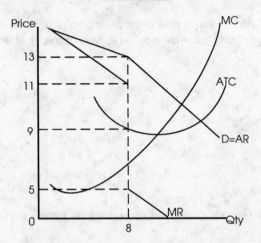

1.  Shown above are the cost and revenue curves for an oligopolistically competitive firm.

    a.  To maximize profit, the oligopolist will produce approximately ___8___ units of output and charge approximately $__13__ per unit. The net revenue <u>per unit</u> will be approximately $__4__ , and the <u>total</u> profit/loss will be approximately $__32__ .

    b.  If the oligopolist sold 7 units of output, his profit/loss <u>per unit</u> would be approximately $_3.25_ , and the <u>total</u> profit/loss would be approximately _22.75_ .

    c.  If the oligopolist sold 9 units of output, his profit/loss <u>per unit</u> would be approximately $_3.50_ , and the <u>total</u> profit/loss would be approximately _31.50_ .

    d.  Assume that the oligopolist's MC curve shifts upward. He/she would continue to produce 8 units of output as long as MC at 8 units were no greater than $__11__ . If it were greater than this, he/she would (reduce/increase) _reduce_ output and (reduce/increase) _increase_ price. Similarly, he/she would continue to produce 8 units of output as long as MC at 8 units dropped to no less than $__5__ . If it were less than this, he/she would (reduce/increase) _increase_ output, and (reduce/increase) _reduce_ price. Hence, according to the kinked demand curve model, prices charged by oligopolists (do/do not) __do__ tend to be rigid.

## PROBLEMS

2.  What are the types of collusion?  What role does collusion play in an oligopoly market?  Is collusion legal in the United States?  Why or why not?  Do you think that American businesses collude?  Why or why not?

3.  Compare and contrast the four models used to explain oligopoly behavior.  Why don't economists choose just one model?

4.  What is a concentration ratio?  What does it tell us?  Give an example of a highly concentrated industry.  What are the shortcomings of concentration ratios?

5.  Define mutual interdependence.  Cite an industry that is currently involved with a "price war" or where all the firms are currently raising prices.  What is the impact on the consumer?

Self-Test

Exhibit IV

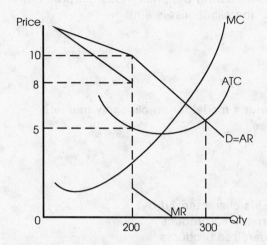

1. In Exhibit IV, the equilibrium price and output is:
   a. $8;    200                   c. $10;   200
   b. $5;    200                   d. $5;    100

2. In Exhibit IV, the economic profit realized at the equilibrium output is:
   a. $1,000                       c. $2,000
   b. $600                         d. $1,600

3. In Exhibit IV, the firm's total revenue at its most profitable output is:
   a. $200                         c. $2,000
   b. $1,000                       d. $1,600

4. Which of the following industries is an illustration of a homogeneous oligopoly?
   a. soaps and detergents         c. aluminum
   b. typewriters                  d. cigarettes

5. The kinked demand curve of an oligopolist is based on the assumption that:
   a. other firms will determine their pricing and output policies in collusion with the given.
   b. competitors will ignore a price cut but follow a price increase.
   c. competitors will match both price cuts and price increases.
   d. competitors will follow a price cut but are reluctant to follow a price increase.

Self-Test (continued)

6.  When an oligopolist considers raising the price of his/her product, and expects the other firms in the industry to follow suit, the oligopolist is a(n):
    a.  shared monopolist
    b.  collusive cartel
    c.  noncollusive oligopolist
    d.  price leader

7.  Which of the following is not a model for an oligopoly market?
    a.  mutual interdependence
    b.  kinked demand curve
    c.  price leadership
    d.  cost-plus pricing

8.  An oligopoly market model is characterized by:
    a.  many firms with differentiated product
    b.  many firms with standardized products
    c.  few firms with differentiated products
    d.  few firms with standardized or differentiated products

9.  Concentration ratios:
    a.  measures the percentage of all sales contributed by the leading four or eight firms
    b.  measures "fewness"
    c.  are limited because interindustry competition is ignored
    d.  all of the above

10. The Schumpeter-Galbraith view states:
    a.  oligopolists act as "shared monopoly"
    b.  oligopoly is less desirable than monopoly because it is not subject to government regulation
    c.  the oligopoly market gives only an outward appearance of competition
    d.  large oligopolistic firms are needed for technological progress

# REVIEW SHEET: UNIT II MICROECONOMICS

<u>Chapter 22</u> **The Costs of Production**
I.   Economic Costs
    A.  Definition of opportunity cost
    B.  Definition of economic cost
        1.      Implicit
        2.      Explicit
    C.  Normal profit
    D.  Economic (pure) profit
    E.  Accounting profit
    F.  Short-run versus long-run costs
II.  Production Costs in the short-run
    A.  Law of Diminishing Returns
        1.      Definition
        2.      The "Production Function" or Input/Output Model
              a.      Total product (TP)
              b.      Marginal product (MP)
              c.      Average product (AP)
              d.      Relationship between MP and AP
              e.      Relationship between MP and TP
    B.  Total cost curves
        1.      Fixed cost (TFC) -- "sunk cost"
              a.      Definition
              b.      Graphic presentation
        2.      Variable cost (TVC)
              a.      Definition
               b.      Graphic presentation
        3.      Total cost (TC)
              a.      Definition
              b.      Formula
              c.      Graphic presentation
    C.  Average or "per unit" cost curves
        1.      Average fixed cost (AFC)
              a.      Definition
              b.      Formula
              c.      Graphic presentation
        2.      Average variable cost (AVC)
              a.      Definition
              b.      Formula
              c.      Graphic presentation
        3.      Average total cost (ATC)
              a.      Definition
              b.      Formula
              c.      Graphic presentation
    D.  Marginal cost (MC) curve
        1.      Definition
        2.      Formula
        3.      Graphic presentation

    4.      Relationship between MC and ATC, AVC
    5.      Relationship between MC and MP
    6.      Depicts the "most efficient level of production"
  E.  Shifting the cost curves

III. Long-run Production Costs (LRATC)
  A.  Definition of long-run
  B.  Definition of the LRATC or "planning curve"
    1.      Determining the LRATC curve
    2.      "U" shape of the LRATC curve depicts economies and diseconomies of scale
  C.  Economies and diseconomies of scale
    1.      Definition of economies of scale
        a.      Reasons why economies of scale exist in business
    2.      Definition of diseconomies of scale
        a.      Reasons why diseconomies of scale exist in business
    3.      Economies and diseconomies of scale form the "U" shape of the LRATC curve depending upon the industry (significant to the structure and competitiveness).
    4.      Definition of constant returns to scale
    5.      Minimum efficient scale (MES)
        a.      Definition
        b.      Natural Monopoly

**Chapter 23  Price and Output Determination:  Pure Competition**
I.  Market Models (See Table 23-1 in your text)
  A.  Four basic market models (overview)
    1.      Pure (perfect) competition
        a.      Definition of market structure
    2.      Pure monopoly
        a.      Definition of market structure
    3.      Monopolistic competition
        a.      Definition of market structure
    4.      Oligopoly
        a.      Definition of market structure
    5.      Imperfect competition covers pure monopoly, monopolistic competition and oligopoly
II.  Pure (perfect) Competition
  A.  Characteristics
    1.      Very large number of firms
    2.      Standardized product
    3.      "Price-taker"
    4.      Free entry/exit
  B.  Example: agriculture
  C.  Demand (short-run)
    1.      Single firm demand curve -- perfectly elastic (firm must accept the going-market price).
    2.      Industry demand curve -- downward sloping (must lower price to sell a higher quantity).
  D.  Revenue curves
    1.      Total revenue (TR)
        a.      Definition and formula
    2.      Average revenue (AR)
        a.      Definition and formula

3. Marginal revenue (MR)
   a. Definition and formula
4. Under pure competition: $D = P = AR = MR$
5. Total economic profit (or loss) is the difference between TR and TC (also called "net revenue" or "gross profit").

III. Profit Maximization (or loss minimization) in the Short-run under Pure Competition.
   A. Difference between the "most efficient level" ($MC = ATC$) and the "most profitable level" (three techniques below) of output.
   B. Three techniques to determine profit maximization (or loss minimization) in the short-run:
      1. Total revenue -- total cost approach
      2. Marginal revenue -- marginal cost approach
         a. The short-run supply curve
      3. Total economic profit (or loss) approach
   C. Equilibrium price and quantity in the short-run
   D. Short-run Supply Curve under Pure Competition (shut-down point)

IV. Profit Maximization (or loss minimization) in the Long-run under Pure Competition
   A. Long-run
      1. Expand or contract plant capacity
      2. Entry/Exit industry
   B. Model
      1. Economic profits are signals to enter the industry
      2. Losses are signals to leave the industry
      3. Competition forces each firm (in the long-run) to earn a normal profit--
         $MC = P = MR = AR = ATC = LRATC$
      4. The industry's long-run supply curve is shaped by the number of firms entering or exiting the industry.
         a. Equilibrium is achieved when no firm wishes to enter or leave the industry.
         b. Constant-cost industry
         c. Increasing-cost industry
         d. Decreasing-cost industry

V. Pros and Cons of a Purely Competitive Market Model
   A. Pros
      1. Productive efficiency ($P = ATC$)
      2. Allocative efficiency ($P = MC$)
   B. Cons
      1. The income distribution problem
      2. Market failure: spillovers and public goods
      3. Productive techniques (technological changes)
      4. Range of consumer choice

**Chapter 24  Price and Output Determination: Pure Monopoly**

I. Pure Monopoly
   A. Market Model
      1. Definition of pure monopoly
      2. Characteristics
         a. Single seller
         b. No close substitutes
         c. "Price-maker"

        d.      Blocked entry  
        e.      Goodwill advertising  
        f.      Examples

II. Barriers to Entry  
    A. Definition of a natural monopoly  
    B. Exclusive ownership  
    C. Patents  
    D. Unfair competitive practices  
    E. Well-established firm  
    F. Overcoming barriers

III. Determining Price and Output for a Pure Monopolist  
    A. Monopoly Demand Curve  
        1.      Definition  
        2.      Shape  
            a.      Marginal revenue is less than price  
        3.      Price policy  
        4.      Elasticity  
        5.      Three techniques to maximize profit (or minimize loss)  
    B. Misconceptions concerning monopoly pricing (4)

IV. Effects of Monopolies  
    A. Existence of pure monopolies has significant effects on the economy  
        1.      Pros and cons

V. Price Discrimination  
    A. Definition  
    B. Conditions required  
    C. Consequences  
    D. Examples

VI. Pricing Polices for a Monopolist  
    A. Monopolist's price (or profit maximizing price) - unregulated  
    B. Socially optimum price (or marginal cost price) - regulated  
    C. Fair-return price (of full-cost price) - regulated

VII. Dilemma of Regulation  
    A. Tradeoffs of pricing policies

VIII. Long-run for a Monopolist  
    A. Factors that influence economic profit  
    B. Higher long-run profits

## Chapter 25 Price and Output Determination: Monopolistic Competition

I. Monopolistic Competition  
    A. Market Model  
        1.      Definition of monopolistic competition  
        2.      Characteristics  
            a.      Large number of sellers  
            b.      Product differentiation  
            c.      Nonprice competition  
            d.      Easy entry into the market  
            e.      Examples

II. Price and Output Determination
   A. The firm's demand curve
      1. Highly elastic
      2. Less elastic than pure competition; more elastic than pure monopoly
   B. Short-run profits (or losses)
      1. A firm will produce where MC = MR.
      2. A firm under monopolistic competition can earn economic profits in the short-run (also normal profits or losses).
   C. Long-run profits (or losses)
      1. Tendency to earn a normal profit (or break even)
      2. The entry/exit of firms changes the profit (loss) picture.
      3. Economic profits signal firms to enter the industry competing away economic (pure) profits in the long-run.
      4. Losses are signals to firms to exit or leave the industry until normal profits are restored in the long-run.
      5. Profits or losses affect the demand curve.
III. Wastes of Monopolistic Competition
   A. Excess plant capacity
      1. Too many sellers causes underallocation of resources.
      2. Too many sellers causes differentiation (competition).
IV. Nonprice Competition
   A. Product differentiation
      1. Definition
   B. Product development
      1. Definition
   C. Product differentiation and produce development may offset "wastes" of monopolistic competition.
V. The Economics of Advertising
   A. Major issues in favor of advertising
   B. Major issues against advertising
   C. Empirical evidence
      1. Traditional vs. New Perspective
      4. Price, product, and its promotion must be adjusted by the monopolistically competitive firm through trial and error, to maximize profits.

Chapter 26  Price and Output Determination:  Oligopoly
I. Oligopoly
   A. Market Model
      1. Definition
      2. Characteristics of an oligopoly
         a. Fewness
         b. Type of product
         c. Concentration ratio
            (1) Definition
            (2) Shortcomings
         d. Reasons for market concentration

**REVIEW SHEET: UNIT II MICROECONOMICS**

II.  Oligopoly Behavior:  A Game Theory Overview
    A.  Definition of Game Theory
    B.  Mutual Interdependence
III. Price and Output Determination
    A.  Difficulties in explaining oligopoly behavior
        1.      Many types of oligopolies
        2.      Mutual interdependence
        3.      Use MC = MR approach
        4.      "Sticky prices"
IV.  Models to Explain Oligopoly Behavior
    A.  Kinked Demand Curve
        1.      Shape of the demand and marginal revenue curves
        2.      Curves based upon the elasticity of price, mutual interdependence, and noncollusion.
        3.      Use the MC = MR approach
        4.      The equilibrium price and quantity are relatively stable.
        5.      Economic profits are possible in the long-run because of high barriers to entry.
        6.      Shortcomings of the kinked demand curve (4).
    B.  Collusion and Cartels
        1.      Definition of collusion
        2.      Use MC = MR approach (strive for same price and output as monopoly).
        3.      Cartel (OPEC)
        4.      Gentleman's agreement
        5.      Obstacles to collusion (5)
    C.  Price leadership:  tacit collusion
        1.      Definition of price leader
        2.      Tactics used by a price leader (3)
    D.  Cost-plus pricing
        1.      Definition
        2.      Advantages (2)
V.  Role of Nonprice Competition
    A.  Use of nonprice competition
        1.      Advantages
VI.  Oligopoly and Economic Efficiency
    A.  Comparison of the efficiency of an oligopolist with a pure competitor.
        1.      Traditional view
        2.      Schumpeter-Galbraith view
    B.  Empirical evidence
VII. Case Study:  The Automobile Industry
    A.  Oligopoly behavior
        1.      "Fit" of the automobile industry to an oligopoly market model

## Formula Sheet

$$MP = \frac{\blacktriangle \ TP}{\blacktriangle \ Units \ of \ Labor} \qquad AP = \frac{TP}{Units \ of \ Labor}$$

$$TC = TVC + TFC \qquad TR = Price \times Quantity$$

$$AFC = \frac{TFC}{Q} \qquad AVC = \frac{TVC}{Q}$$

$$ATC = \frac{TC}{Q} = AFC + AVC \qquad MC = \frac{\blacktriangle \ TC}{\blacktriangle \ Q}$$

$$MR = \frac{\blacktriangle \ TR}{\blacktriangle \ Q} \qquad AR = \frac{\blacktriangle \ TR}{Q}$$

Total profit (or loss) = TR - TC = NR

### NOTES ON MONOPOLY

1.  The demand curve facing a monopolist is the same as the industry demand curve.
2.  Monopoly may not be highly profitable (not guaranteed economic profits).
3.  Price is not determined by supply and demand as in perfect competition.
4.  By adhering to MC = MR Rule, a monopolist will guarantee either maximum profits or minimum losses.
5.  A monopolist must lower price to increase sales, therefore MR < P( = AR).
6.  Pricing policies for a monopolist include: (1) monopolist's price (2) socially optimum price (3) fair-return price.
7.  A monopoly produces less than under perfect competition, misallocation of resources (MC < P).
8.  A necessary condition for effective price discrimination is that products for sale must be separable among buyers or markets, according to their elasticity.
9.  A necessary condition for effective price discrimination is that resale is nonexistent.
10.  Economic profits are possible in the long-run.

### NOTES ON OLIGOPOLY AND MONOPOLISTIC COMPETITION

1.  Monopolistic competition is characterized by many firms and products that are differentiated. Oligopoly has a few large firms ("Big 4 or Big 8") with a standardized or differentiated product.
2.  In monopolistic competition, the demand curve facing a firm will become more elastic the greater the number of sellers (greater # of substitutes available).
3.  The entry of new firms into a monopolistically competitive industry is fairly easy in most instances. Difficult to enter an oligopoly market.
4.  Comparing long-run equilibrium costs between a monopolistic competitive firm as compared with a perfectly competitive firm, price is higher and output is smaller in monopolistic competition. The oligopolist charges a higher price with a smaller output.
5.  The effect of advertising on a firm's ATC curve is to raise it (however economies of scale may actually lower a firm's costs on the average).
6.  Selling costs are expenditures made by a firm for the purpose of adapting the buyer to the product.
7.  The expression "wastes of monopolistic competition" refers to tendency of monopolistic competitive firms to suffer from overcrowding and inefficiency.
8.  Those firms that survive in monopolistic competition tend to earn normal profits in the long run; oligopolists may earn economic profits in the long run.
9.  Monopolistic competition leads to underutilization of firms, due to the large number of firms.

# REVIEW SHEET: UNIT II MICROECONOMICS

1. For each market model shown,
   a. Label all of the revenue and costs curves.
   b. Label the profit maximizing (or loss minimizing) price--Pe and quantity--Qe.
   c. State whether an "economic profit", a "normal profit", or a "loss" has occurred.
   d. Shade the profit/loss area.

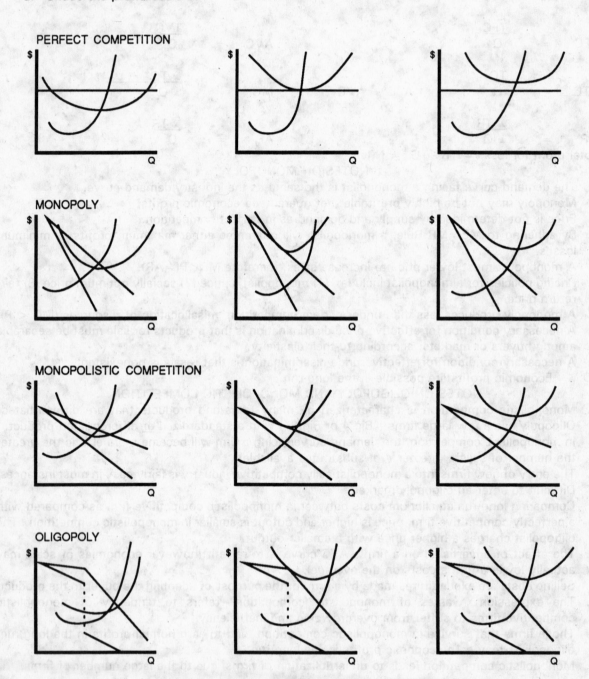

PERFECT COMPETITION

MONOPOLY

MONOPOLISTIC COMPETITION

OLIGOPOLY

2. Fill in the following table based upon the information which you have learned.

TABLE I

"Comparing Market Structure"

| Market Model: | Pure Competition | Monopolistic Competition | Oligopoly | Pure Monopoly |
|---|---|---|---|---|
| Number of Sellers: | | | | |
| Unrestricted entry\exit | | | | |
| Product Differentiation | | | | |
| Ability to set price | | | | |
| Non price Competition | | | | |
| Long-run Economic Profits | | | | |
| Examples: | | | | |

# MICROECONOMICS

## UNIT III

# CHAPTER 27          "PRODUCTION AND THE DEMAND FOR RESOURCES"

## Chapter Orientation

Up to this point, you have studied the supply and demand for <u>final</u> goods and services.  Now we will complete the circular flow and examine the supply and demand for the factors of production -- land, labor, capital and entrepreneurial ability -- that are needed to create the final product.

In the input markets, businesses now determine the demand curve for resources (there is an inverse relationship between wage and units of a resource).  Consumers now determine the supply curve for resources (there is a direct relationship between wage and units of a resource).

Labor receives wages; owners of land receive rent; the price paid for capital is interest, and entrepreneurs receive profit.  How is the price paid to these factors determined?

In a purely competitive market the price paid is determined by the forces of supply and demand.  It gets a bit more complicated when big unions or big business try to manipulate the competitive price to their own advantage (imperfect market).

You will find that many of the concepts and analytical tools which you used in determining the profit maximizing (or loss minimizing) price and quantity in the output markets can also apply to the input markets -- factor demand and supply.  Also, many of the terms will remain the same except that a word might be added to denote the input market rather than the output markets.

## Learning Objectives

After reading this chapter in the text and completing the following exercises in this concepts book, you will be able to:

1. List the major reasons for studying resource pricing.
2. Define the marginal productivity theory.
3. Explain the factor markets using a simple circular flow diagram.
4. State the ways a firm determines the "worth" of an employee.
5. Explain in the input markets who "demands" and who "supplies".
6. Define marginal product (MP) and explain how this concept illustrates the law of diminishing returns.
7. Define marginal revenue product (MRP) and calculate MRP when given data from a purely competitive market.
8. Define and calculate average revenue product (ARP) when given the necessary information.
9. Explain why the demand for resources is derived demand.
10. Define and calculate the marginal resources cost (MRC) when given the necessary data.
11. State the technique used by a profit-maximizing firm to determine how much of a resource it will employ and apply it when you are given the necessary data.
12. Explain what curve represents the demand curve in a competitive market.
13. List three reasons which would cause a change in factor demand (shift the curve), and explain their impact.
14. State what effect the elasticity of resources and causes a "change in quantity demanded" for the factor.

15. State the rule employed by a firm to determine the least-cost combination of resources and apply this rule when given the necessary data to determine the quantities to purchase.
16. State the pros and cons of marginal productivity theory.

Chapter Highlights

I.  Introduction of the Input Markets
    A.  Background
        1.  You will recall from the simple circular flow model that the flow of money and goods/services between households and businesses are carried out in the two markets: resource and product.  In the out put markets, we determined the product price and quantity (product market). In the input market we will determine the factors price and quantity (resource market). This will complete our understanding of the simple circular flow model.  (See Figure 27-1 below).

Figure 27-1
Simple Circular Flow Model

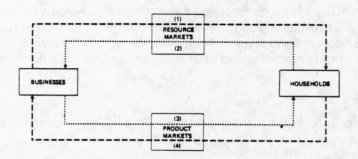

    B.  Marginal productivity theory -- in a purely competitive market, a worker is paid a wage rate that is equal to his/her marginal output (marginal productivity).
    C.  Reasons for studying resource pricing
        1.  Money incomes -- resource prices influence the size of individual incomes.
        2.  Resource allocation -- resource prices allocate scarce resources among businesses.
        3.  Cost minimization -- resources represent a cost to the firm (takes away from profits), therefore to maximize profit the most efficient (least cost) combination should be purchased.
        4.  Policy issues -- resource prices bring up the question of equity between profits and wages.
II. Complexities of Resource Pricing
    A.  Economists are in substantial agreement with the basic principle of resource pricing.  But, because these principles are effected by policies of the government, business firms, labor unions, etc., it becomes extremely complex.
    B.  As stated earlier, businesses now determine the demand curve for resources (inverse relationship) and consumers now determine the supply curve for resources (direct relationship).

III. Marginal Productivity Theory of Resource Demand
   A.   Terms
      1.      Derived demand -- factor demand is taken from the demand for the final good or
              service, which resources help produce.
           a.      A firm determines the demand for a resources based upon productivity, the
                   going-market rate, and the value of the final product produced.
      2.      Marginal product (MP) -- the change in output resulting from an additional unit of a
              resource (the amount each resource demands).

MP = $\dfrac{\blacktriangle \text{ Total Product}}{\blacktriangle \text{ Units of Resource}}$

           a.      MP declines because of the law of diminishing returns.
           b.      MP is graphed at the midpoints.
      3.      Marginal revenue product (MRP) -- the change in total revenue resulting from an
              additional unit of a resource (value each resource adds).

MRP = MP x Product's price = $\dfrac{\blacktriangle \text{ Total Revenue}}{\blacktriangle \text{ Units of Resource}}$

           a.      Combines the MP (production added) and the price of the product (value
                   added) to determine the "worth" of a resource.  In a competitive market a
                   resources is paid what it's worth (MRP = resource price).
           b.      Since the MRP curve determines a resources' worth to a business, the MRP
                   curve is the demand curve for a firm (it indicates the number of units a
                   business will hire at alternative prices or wages).
           c.      MRP is graphed at the midpoints.
      4.      Average revenue product (ARP) -- is the "per unit" revenue received by a firm.

ARP = $\dfrac{\text{Total Revenue}}{\text{Units of Resource}}$

      5.      Marginal resource cost (MRC) -- the change in total resource cost resulting from an
              additional unit of a resource (cost each resource adds).

MRC = $\dfrac{\blacktriangle \text{ Total Resource Cost}}{\blacktriangle \text{ Units of Resource}}$

           a.      MRC is graphed at the midpoints.
   B.   Profit maximization (or loss minimization)
      1.      Use the MRP = MRC rule (similar to the MR = MC rule in the output markets).
      2.      It will be profitable for a firm to hire additional units of a resource up to the
              point where MRP equals MRC.  Another technique which will give the same
              results in the TR - TRC approach where the difference between TR and TC is
              the greatest (profit max) of the smallest (loss min).
IV. Market Demand for a Resource
   A.   Purely competitive markets
      1.      The MRP curve is the resource demand curve for a purely competitive seller.  Because
              of diminishing returns (MP decreases) the resource demand curve is downward sloping
              (product price is constant).
   B.   Imperfect competition
      1.      The MRP curve is also the resource demand curve under imperfect competition.
              The resource demand curve is downward sloping because of diminishing
              returns and because the product price is falling as output increases.

C.  Market demand
    1.      The market demand curve can be found by summing together all of the individual
            resource demand (or MRP) curves. (See Figure 27-2 below).

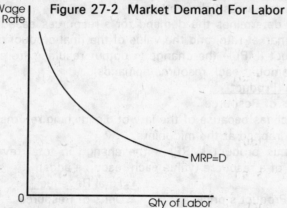

Figure 27-2  Market Demand For Labor

V.  Changes in Resource Demand
    A.  A change in resource demand (new demand curve -- See Figure 27-3 below).
        1.      The resource demand curve will shift due to:
                a.      Changes in product demand -- (shifts the curve in the same direction).
                b.      Productivity changes -- (shifts curve in the same direction).
                c.      Change in the price of a substitute factor -- (the substitution and output effects
                        work in opposite directions).  If the substitution effect outweighs the output
                        effect, the demand for labor will move in the same direction, and in the
                        opposite direction.  If the output effect outweighs the substitution effect.
                d.      Change in the price of a complementary factor -- (shifts in the opposite
                        direction).

Figure 27-3                                           Figure 27-4
Change in Resource Demand                    Change in Quantity Demanded

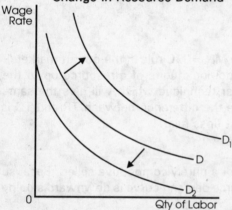

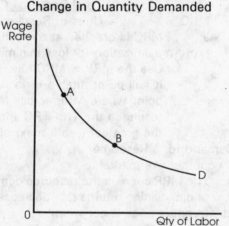

VI. Elasticity of Resource Demand
    A.  A change in the "quantity" of resource demand
        1.      Movement along the resource demand curve due to changes in the price (wage) of a
                factor -- (See Figure 27-4 above).
                a.      The rate of decline of the MP.

262

      b.      The number of resource substitutes available.

      c.      The elasticity for the output (final product).

      d.      The labor cost - total cost ratio.

VII. Optimum Combination of Resources

  A. The least-cost rule

    1.    Since in the long-run all resources are variable, we need to calculate the least-cost combination of resources of a firm will select to maximize profits. This approach is similar to the idea of consumer equilibrium measured in "utils" of satisfaction per dollar.

    2.    $$\frac{\text{MP of labor}}{\text{Price of labor}} = \frac{\text{MP of capital}}{\text{Price of capital}} = 1$$

        The cost of any output is minimized when the ratio of the MP of a resource to its price is the same for all the resources the firm employs.

    3.    To maximize profits, a firm in a competitive market would hire where the MRP of each resource is equal to the price of each resource.

    4.    A numerical example in the text (page 528) illustrates how the least-cost and profit-maximizing rules apply in a perfectly competitive market.

    5.    Under imperfect competition, when the resource price is raised to attract new resources, that higher price is also paid to the current resources. This causes MRC to be higher than the resource price.

      a.      As a result of this higher MRC curve our least-cost and profit-maximizing formula must be adjusted to reflect this change.

          $$\frac{\text{MP of labor}}{\text{MRC of labor}} = \frac{\text{MP of capital}}{\text{MRC of capital}} = 1$$

VIII. Marginal Productivity Theory of Income Distribution

  A. Shortcomings

    1.    Inequality -- ownership of the factors are not justly distributed among people.

    2.    Noncompetitive markets -- factors will not receive wages (prices) based on their productivity when there is monopsony or monopoly in the resource markets.

IX.    Last Word: Input Substitution -- The Case of Cabooses

Key Terms

| | |
|---|---|
| marginal productivity theory | marginal resource cost (MRC) |
| circular flow model | MRP = MRC rule |
| factors of production | substitution effect |
| derived demand | output effect |
| marginal product (MP) | least-cost rule |
| law of diminishing returns | profit-maximizing rule |
| marginal revenue product (MRP) | monopsony |
| average revenue product (ARP) | |

# EXECUTIVE PAY: THE PARTY AIN'T OVER YET

John A. Byrne and Chuck Hawkins

## THE 20 HIGHEST-PAID CHIEF EXECUTIVES...

| | 1992 salary and bonus | Long-term compensation | Total pay |
|---|---|---|---|
| | | Thousands of dollars | |
| 1. **THOMAS F. FRIST JR.** Hosp. Corp. of America | $1,068 | $125,934 | $127,002 |
| 2. **SANFORD I. WEILL** Primerica | 2,752 | 64,883 | 67,635 |
| 3. **CHARLES LAZARUS** Toys 'R' Us | 7,025 | 57,206 | 64,231 |
| 4. **LEON C. HIRSCH** U.S. Surgical | 1,695 | 60,476 | 62,171 |
| 5. **STEPHEN A. WYNN** Mirage Resorts | 1,505 | 36,500 | 38,005 |
| 6. **ANTHONY J.F. O'REILLY** H.J. Heinz | 1,318 | 35,600 | 36,918 |
| 7. **MARTIN J. WYGOD** Medco Containment | 807 | 29,400 | 30,207 |
| 8. **WILLIAM A. ANDERS** General Dynamics | 7,849 | 21,166 | 29,015 |
| 9. **RONALD K. RICHEY** Torchmark | 2,136 | 24,432 | 26,568 |
| 10. **LOUIS F. BANTLE** UST Inc. | 2,701 | 21,901 | 24,602 |
| 11. **REUBEN MARK** Colgate-Palmolive | 2,002 | 20,816 | 22,818 |
| 12. **WALTER J. SANDERS III** Advanced Micro Devices | 2,965 | 19,391 | 22,356 |
| 13. **JOHN F. WELCH JR.** General Electric | 3,500 | 14,470 | 17,970 |
| 14. **LEE A. IACOCCA*** Chrysler | 1,528 | 15,380 | 16,908 |
| 15. **EUGENE P. GRISANTI** Int'l Flavors & Fragrances | 900 | 15,575 | 16,475 |
| 16. **ALAN C. GREENBERG** Bear Stearns | 15,832 | — | 15,832 |
| 17. **ROBERTO C. GOIZUETA** Coca-Cola | 3,201 | 12,017 | 15,218 |
| 18. **WALTER E. BARTLETT** Multimedia | 856 | 13,966 | 14,822 |
| 19. **CHARLES N. MATHEWSON** Int'l Game Technology | 625 | 14,170 | 14,795 |
| 20. **PHILLIP B. ROONEY** Wheelabrator Technologies | — | 11,216 | 11,216 |

*Retired

## ...AND 10 WHO AREN'T CEOS

| | 1992 salary and bonus | Long-term compensation | Total pay |
|---|---|---|---|
| | Thousands of dollars | | |
| 1. **DONALD R. KEOUGH** Pres., Coca-Cola | $2,141 | $38,630 | $40,771 |
| 2. **R. DEREK FINLAY** Sr. VP, H.J. Heinz | 542 | 32,024 | 32,566 |
| 3. **TURI JOSEFSEN** Exec. VP, U.S. Surgical | 964 | 26,362 | 27,326 |
| 4. **WILLIAM MURRAY** Pres. & COO, Philip Morris | 1,608 | 22,251 | 23,859 |
| 5. **ROGER A. ENRICO** Chmn., PepsiCo Worldwide Foods | 1,221 | 14,524 | 15,745 |
| 6. **JAMES E. CAYNE** Pres., Bear Stearns | 14,729 | — | 14,729 |
| 7. **JAMES R. MELLOR** Pres., General Dynamics | 3,853 | 10,422 | 14,275 |
| 8. **BEVERLY F. DOLAN** Chmn., Textron | 2,230 | 7,876 | 10,106 |
| 9. **JACK O. BOVENDER JR.** COO, Hosp. Cp. of Am. | 382 | 9,637 | 10,019 |
| 10. **JEFFREY H. BROTMAN** Chmn., Costco Wholesale | 509 | 8,749 | 9,258 |

DATA: STANDARD & POOR'S COMPUSTAT SERVICES INC.

Reprinted from the April 26, 1993 issue of <u>Business Week</u> by special permission, copyright (c) 1993 by McGraw-Hill, Inc.

## PROBLEMS

1a.    Complete the following table:

| Units of Resource | TP | MP | Product Price | TR | ARP | MRP |
|---|---|---|---|---|---|---|
| 1 | 17 |  | $2 | 34 | 34 |  |
|  |  | 14 |  |  |  | 28 |
| 2 | 31 |  |  | 62 | 31 |  |
|  |  | 12 |  |  |  | 24 |
| 3 | 43 |  |  | 86 | 28.67 |  |
|  |  | 10 |  |  |  | 20 |
| 4 | 53 |  |  | 106 | 26.5 |  |
|  |  | 7 |  |  |  | 14 |
| 5 | 60 |  |  | 120 | 24 |  |
|  |  | 5 |  |  |  | 10 |
| 6 | 65 |  |  | 130 | 21.67 |  |

b.    Assume the cost of labor is $10 per person per day.  Calculate the TRC and MRC per day. (Use chart below).

c.    Assume the cost of labor is $20 per person per day.  Calculate the TRC' and MRC' per day. (Use chart below).

| Units of Resource | Wage Rate | TRC | MRC | Wage Rate | TRC' | MRC' |
|---|---|---|---|---|---|---|
| 1 | $10 | ___ |  | $20 | ___ |  |
| 2 |  | ___ | ___ |  | ___ | ___ |
| 3 |  | ___ | ___ |  | ___ | ___ |
| 4 |  | ___ | ___ |  | ___ | ___ |
| 5 |  | ___ | ___ |  | ___ | ___ |
| 6 |  | ___ | ___ |  | ___ | ___ |

d.    Prepare two (2) separate graphs.
      Graph #1 - Graph TR and TRC, TRC'   Graph #2 - Graph MRP and MRC, MRC'

e.    How many persons would you hire at $10 per day?  How many at $20 per day?

$$MP = \frac{\triangle TP}{\triangle \text{Units of Resource}} \qquad ARP = \frac{TR}{\text{Units of Resource}}$$

$$TR = TP \times \text{Product Price} \qquad TRC = \text{Units of Labor} \times \text{Wage Rate}$$

$$MRP = \frac{\triangle TR}{\triangle \text{Units of Resource}} \qquad MRC = \frac{\triangle TRC}{\triangle \text{Units of Resource}}$$

266

# CHAPTER 27      "PRODUCTION AND THE DEMAND FOR RESOURCES"

## PROBLEMS

2. The productivity of labor and capital is shown in Table 27-1 (below). The output for these resources sells in a purely competitive market for $1 per unit. The price paid to labor is $2 and to capital $4 in a purely competitive market.

### Table 27-1

| Units of Labor | | MP of Labor | | Units of Capital | | MP of Capital |
|---|---|---|---|---|---|---|
| 0 ___ | | -- | ___ | 0 ___ | | -- |
| 1 ___ | | 18 | ___ | 1 ___ | | 24 |
| 2 ___ | | 16 | | 2 ___ | | 20 |
| 3 ___ | | 14 | | 3 ___ | | 16 |
| 4 ___ | | 12 | | 4 ___ | | 12 |
| 5 ___ | | 10 | | 5 ___ | | 8 |
| 6 ___ | | 2 | | 6 ___ | | 4 |

    a.    What is the least-cost combination of labor and capital to produce 84 units of output? Explain.

    b.    What is the profit-maximizing combination of labor and capital? Explain. What is the economic profit?

    c.    Is your answer in "2b" also the least-costly way of producing? Explain.

Self-Test

1. Which of the following statements best explains why we can say that demand for a factor input is a "derived" demand?
   a. The demand for factor inputs is based on the demand for the final product.
   b. The demand for factor inputs is based on the productivity of the factor inputs.
   c. The demand for factor inputs is developed from the relative availability of the factor inputs.
   d. The demand for factor inputs is based on changes in demand resulting from advanced technology.

2. Which of the following statements best describes the relationship between "marginal product" and "diminishing returns"?
   a. Increasing marginal product is indicative of diminishing returns from increasing the units of resource.
   b. Decreasing marginal product reflects diminishing returns from increasing the units of resources.
   c. Decreasing marginal product is the result of diminishing returns from decreasing the units of resource.
   d. Decreasing marginal product reflects diminishing returns from the units of resource, which are always constant.

3. Which of the following best accounts for the shape of the resource demand curve in imperfect competition?
   a. A factor demand curve will have an initial positive slope due to the increase in demand for a product.
   b. A factor demand curve will have a downward slope due to the slope of the demand curve for the final product.
   c. A factor demand curve will be downward sloping due to the diminishing returns associated with factor productivity and the downward slope of the demand curve for the final product.
   d. A factor demand curve has a shape which depends solely on the shape of the demand curve for the final product.

4. Which of the following statements best defines marginal revenue product of a resource?
   a. The additional value to final product contributed by the average of all factor inputs.
   b. The value obtained by multiplying MP by total revenue.
   c. The additional value to total revenue contributed by an additional unit of resource.
   d. The additional output contributed by an additional unit of a resource.

5. Select from the alternatives below the one that correctly completes the following sentence:  "Since the demand for butter is _____ because of the availability of margarine, the demand for resource factors that produce butter tends to be _____.
   a. elastic; inelastic
   b. elastic; available
   c. elastic; elastic
   d. inelastic;inelastic

6. Which of the following is not a justification for studying resource pricing:
   a. Resource prices influence the size of individual incomes.
   b. Resource prices allocate scarce resources.
   c. Resources represent a cost to the firm.
   d. Resources bring about equality in a competitive market.

<u>Self-Test</u>

7. The circular flow model helps to explain
   a.   The price and quantity of goods and services
   b.   The price and quantity of the factors of production.
   c.   The interaction of households and businesses in the product and resource markets.
   d.   All of the above.

8. The MRP curve is the:
   a.   demand curve for the competitive seller.
   b.   demand curve for the imperfectly competitive seller.
   c.   demand curve for the market.
   d.   all of the above.

9. Which of the following will cause a change in resource demand?
   a.   the rate of decline of MP.
   b.   productivity changes.
   c.   a change in the wage rate.
   d.   the percentage of total production costs.

10. The least-cost approach states that:
   a.   when given a specific output, the least-cost approach will also be the profit-maximizing combination.
   b.   the profit-maximizing combination will also be the least-cost approach
   c.   the least-cost approach is a separate formula and therefore, independent of the profit-maximizing combination.
   d.   to maximize profits, a firm must minimize costs.

# CHAPTER 28   "THE PRICING AND EMPLOYMENT OF RESOURCES: WAGE DETERMINATION"

## Chapter Orientation

Since Chapter 27 has laid the foundation for the input (resource) market, we can now build on these concepts and apply them to the price (wage) and quantity of labor in six different kinds of labor markets.

Chapter 28 opens with the definition of wages and explain why wages in the U.S. rank near the top as compared to the rest of the world. The chapter then details specific labor markets and how the wage rate and quantity of labor are determined. You should have an understanding of each of the markets and be able to distinguish one market from another. The first market will be a competitive market based upon supply and demand. The remaining markets will be based upon who has the economic power (clout)? Having this "edge" tilts the direction of the wage rate, rather than wages being based upon supply and demand in the marketplace.

In addition, the chapter discusses minimum-wage laws (a "hot topic" now in Congress); wage differentials that exist among occupational groups; and human capital investment -- any action that improves the productivity of workers. Lastly, see the "Real World Example" in this chapter, which shows how the rich are getting richer.

## Learning Objectives

After reading this chapter in the text and completing the following exercises in this concepts book, you will be able to:

1. Define wages (or wage rate); distinguish between nominal wages and real wages.
2. List the factors that have contributed to the high level of real wages in the U.S.
3. Explain how the wage rate and quantity of labor are determined in a competitive and in monopsonistic labor market (use graphs for each).
4. Explain how the unions seek to raise wage rates and the impact of these actions on the employment of labor.
5. Compare the wage rate and the level of employment in a competitive labor market with what happens when the industrial workers become unionized (use one graph).
6. Use a graph to explain the wage rate and level of employment under a bilateral monopoly.
7. Discuss the controversy over minimum-wage (pros and cons) and present the empirical evidence.
8. Define wage differential and explain the three major factors that influence this inequity.
9. Define investment in human capital.
10. Discuss the cause-effect chain in the theory of human capital.
11. Present the criticisms of the human capital theory.

## Chapter Highlights

I. Meaning of Wages
   A. Definition of wages (or the wage rates) -- are the prices paid to secure labor. Nominal wages (or money wages) represent the amount of money a worker receives per hour, per week, etc. Real wages represents the purchasing power of wages.
   B. Definition of earnings -- the wage rate multiplied by the amount of time worked are equal to earnings.

# CHAPTER 28 "THE PRICING AND EMPLOYMENT OF RESOURCES: WAGE DETERMINATION"

II. The General Level of Real Wages
  A. The U.S. is among the highest in the world because the demand for labor in the U.S. has been strong compared to the supply of labor.
  B. The demand for labor in the U.S. has been high because labor has been highly productive due to:
    1. Capital goods -- workers are utilized with large amounts of capital goods.
    2. Natural resources -- the U.S. is richly endowed with natural resources.
    3. Technology -- not only do American workers use capital equipment, their technology is superior.
    4. Labor quality -- American workers have both the background needed and proper work attitude.
    5. Other factors such as the efficiency of American management; the social, business and political environment; and the vast size of our domestic market.
  C. The real income per worker can increase only at about the same rate as output per worker.
  D. Although the American population and the labor force have grown significantly over the decades, those increases have been more than offset by the demand for labor as a result of increased productivity. The result has been a long-run (secular) increase in wage rates.

III. Wages in Particular Labor Markets
  A. Types of market models
    1. We will be examining six different labor market models:
      a. Competitive market
      b. Monopsony market
      c. Increasing the demand for labor (attempt by union)
      d. Exclusive or Craft Unionism (union restricts the supply of labor)
      e. Inclusive or Industrial Unionism (union threatens a strike to secure a wage rate above the equilibrium)
      f. Bilateral monopoly market
    2. The wage rate and the level of employment depends upon the supply and the demand for labor and the competitiveness of the market.
  B. **Pure Competition**
    1. The wage rate and level of employment is determined by the intersection of the labor demand and labor supply curves in the market.
      a. Market demand is found by summing the individual MRP curves in the market.
      b. The <u>market</u> supply curve is upward sloping, because the wage must rise to attract more workers.
        (1) Once the going-rate has been established, the individual <u>firm</u> faces a perfectly elastic supply curve.

(2)   An <u>individual</u> worker's supply curve is "backward bending", due to the tradeoffs between work and leisure hours. The "substitution effect" says that in the beginning you will replace leisure hours with more work hours. The income effect says that at a certain point, a worker will tradeoff work hours for more leisure hours. (See Figure 28-1).

Figure 28-1
A Competitive Model of Wage Determination

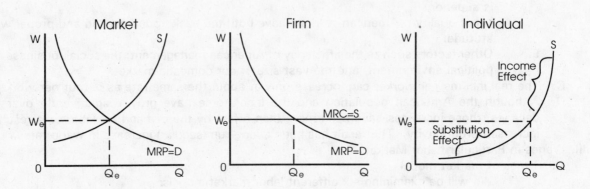

C.  **Monopsony** (from the Greek word meaning "single buyer")
1.   Definition -- one buyer (employer) in a populated nonunionized area.
2.   Examples of monopsony markets: nurses, professional athletes, or a "company town", etc.
3.   Definition of oligopsony -- three of four firms may each hire a portion of the supply of labor in a particular market.
4.   A monopsonist must increase wages to attract new workers and must also increase the wages of the present employees (or else suffer low morale). Therefore the MRC is higher than the wage rate (the cost of hiring a new worker (MRC) his/her rate plus the extra amount for the present workers). (See Figure 28-2).

Figure 28-2
Monopsony

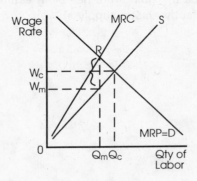

5.  The relationship of a monopsonist is similar to a monopolist's demand and marginal revenue curves.

6.  The monopsonist will hire until MRC = MRP. In Figure 28-2 MRC crosses MRP at point "R" (our reference point). From point "R" go to the quantity of labor (X-axis) to determine the number of workers (Qm). How much will a monopsonist pay these workers? Go up to the height of the supply curve (point X) for the wage rate (Wm), on the y-axis.

7.  Compare the monopsonists wage rate and quantity of labor with that of a purely competitive market where the wage rate is Wc (higher) and the quantity of labor hired is Qc (higher).

8.  The difference between the reference point (R) and the wage rate (x) is called "monopsonistic exploitation".

D.  **Union models**

1.  Unions seek many goals, but the basic objective is to raise wage rates. Three models are illustrated.

2.  **Increasing the demand for labor** - unions seek to raise wage rates by increasing the demand for labor. (See Figure 28-3 below).

Figure 28-3 Increasing Labor Demand

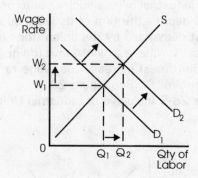

a.  A union will attempt to increase labor demand by:

(1)  Increasing the demand for the product or service (derived demand) by advertising or by political lobbying.

(2)  Enhancing labor productivity -- more union involvement in establishing joint labor-management committees to increase labor productivity.

(3)  Alter the prices of other related goods -- increase the price of substitute resources (example: increase the minimum wage) or reduce the price of a complementary resource.

b.  In reality, unions are actually trying to protect declines (rather than increases) in the demand for labor.

3.   **Exclusive or craft unionism** -- by limiting the supply of labor, unions may increase wage rates, "also called labor monopoly".  (See Figure 28-4).

Figure 28-4 Craft Unionism

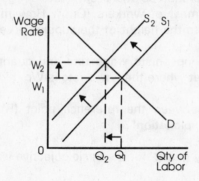

a.   A union will restrict the labor supply by:
 (1)   Supporting legislation which restricts the supply of labor
 (2)   Adopting techniques to limit membership (exclusive unionism) or lobbying for licensing of trades (occupational licensing).

4.   **Inclusive or industrial unionism** -- most unions week to organize <u>all</u> potential workers (a characteristic of industrial unions such as automobile workers).  A "strike threat" by <u>all</u> the workers will deprive the firm of its labor supply.  If no workers will work for a wage less than that demanded by the union (for example $12) the labor supply curve with a "strike threat" will have a "kink" in it (point "K").  To attract additional workers after point "K", a firm must increase the wage rate.  Hence, the shape of the labor supply curve will be WuKS. (See Figure 28-5).

Figure 28-5 Inclusive or Industrial Unionism

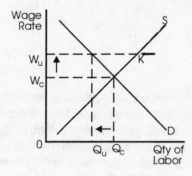

      a.      The result of this "strike threat" will be fewer workers demanded (hired) by business.

    5.      Empirical evidence has shown that union members receive a wage advantage over nonunion members (on the average of 10-15 persons). However, the actions of exclusive (restricts labor supply) and inclusive ("strike threat") unionism causes unemployment within the ranks because the union seeks such a high wage rate, as compared to the competitive rate. Two ways the unemployment impact can be offset are:

      a.      Growth of the economy spurs demand for labor over time.

      b.      The size of the unemployment impact is based upon the elasticity of demand for labor.

  E.  **Bilateral monopoly** -- "a monopsonist buys from a monopolist". For example: "Big labor clashes with big business". A bilateral monopoly is a market in which there is only one seller of a resource (labor monopoly) and only one buyer (monopsonistic or a combination of oligopsonistic employer(s)).

    1.      The union will seek a wage rate above the equilibrium (Wu) and the monopsonist will seek a wage rate of (Wm). The outcome is indeterminant (based upon collective bargaining), but will fall somewhere between Wu and Wm depending on which side has the advantage. (See Figure 28-6, below). The two monopoly powers tend to offset each other resulting in competitive or near-competitive results (no exploitation).

Figure 28-6 Bilateral Monopoly

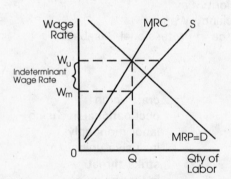

    2.      The minimum-wage controversy

      a.      Pros -- in certain markets wages can increase without causing unemployment; also it increases worker productivity.

      b.      Cons -- minimum-wage causes firms higher costs which results in the hiring of fewer workers or closing down the business.

      c.      Empirical evidence suggest that the minimum-wage does cause unemployment (especially among teenagers), however, those who are employed have a better standard of living with the higher rate.

IV. Wage Differentials

  A.  Definition of wage differentials -- differences in wage rates that occur either for rational or nonrational reasons.

    B.  Reasons for wage differentials
       1.     Noncompeting groups -- both the capacity and the opportunity for education and training are unequally distributed, hence persisting wage differentials.
       2.     Equalizing differences -- wage differentials are paid to compensate for the nonmoney differences among jobs.  (For example:  risk, danger, night shift, etc.).
       3.     Market imperfections -- because workers are not perfectly mobile (reluctant to leave their home; lose their union card or license by moving to another state) or because the are in a minority group (sociological factor) wage differentials persist.

V.  Investment in Human Capital
    A.  Theory of human capital -- noncompeting groups (causing wage differentials) exist to a large extent because of differing amounts of investment in human capital.  A human capital investment is any action that improves the productivity of workers; the expenditures on education, improving health and the mobility of workers.

VI.  Pay and Performance
    A.  Principal Agent Problem
       1.     Definition -- a conflict of interest arises when agents (workers) pursue their own objectives to the detriment of the principal (employer's goals).
       2.     Ways to Remedy
          (a)     Monitor workers
          (b)     Incentive Pay Plan
              (1)     Piece Rates
              (2)     Commissions and Royalties
              (3)     Bonuses and Profit Sharing
              (4)     Seniority Pay
              (5)     Efficiency Wages

VII. Last Word:  Pay and Performance in Professional Baseball

## Key Terms

| | |
|---|---|
| wage (rate) | craft union |
| earnings | occupational licensing |
| nominal wage | labor monopoly |
| real wages | inclusive unionism |
| marginal resource cost (MRC) | strike threat |
| competitive labor market | industrial union |
| "backward bending supply curve" | bilateral monopoly |
| substitution effect | indeterminant wage |
| income effect | minimum-wage |
| monopsony | wage differentials |
| oligopsony | noncompeting groups |
| monopsonistic exploitation | equalizing differences |
| exclusive unionism | theory of human capital |
| cost-benefit analysis | cause-effect chain in human capital |
| principal agent problem | |

Real World Example

## IMPACT OF MINIMUM WAGE DEBATED

### The Associated Press

TRENTON - While some business experts claim increasing the state's minimum wage to $5.05 has had a devastating impact, the authors of a recent study believe its effects have been exaggerated in many industries.

"We found on of the main effects of the minimum wage increase was who gets what slice of the pie, not the size of the pie," Princeton University professor Alan Krueger said in a telephone interview from Berlin, Germany.

New Jersey increased its minimum wage in April 1992, to $5.05 from $4.25 an hour, making it the second-highest minimum wage in the nation.  The federal minimum wage is $4.25 an hour for employers involved in interstate commerce.  No states have a lower minimum wage, but some have set higher rates.

Krueger wrote a study with fellow Princeton economics professor David Card comparing 410 fast-food restaurants in New Jersey and Pennsylvania for two months before the increase and nine months afterward.  Pennsylvania has held its minimum wage to $4.25.

The study found that the increase has not significantly impacted hiring.  It did show that the prices of fast-food meals increased more in New Jersey than in Pennsylvania.

"But within New Jersey, we find no evidence that the prices increased more in stores that were most affected by the minimum-wage rise," the study said.

"We were somewhat surprised because the typical economic model predicts a negative effect," Krueger said.  "But the way the labor market works is more abstract than a model."

State Labor Commissioner Ray Bramucci said he was not surprised by the study's results.

"The minimum wage has little bearing to the hiring wage for most jobs.  It's a symbol, an heirloom," Bramucci said.  "By artificially lowering wages, we're not helping anyone.  How many people in New Jersey are making the minimum wage?  It's not too many.

The commissioner conceded that the wage increase may have hurt the agricultural filed.  He noted there were fewer seasonal crop workers in 1992 than in 1991.  But Bramucci said poor weather conditions last year also contributed to a difficult season for farmers.

The prevailing opinion among farmers is that the increase has hurt the agricultural business in the state.

"The impact has been very severe," said Peter Furey, executive director of the New Jersey Farm Bureau.  "The additional costs increased labor costs by 20 to 25 percent.  A few dozen farms probably went of business.  That may be the tip of the iceberg if things don't get better."

"It's eventually going to put all of us out of business," said Russell Marino, a fruit and vegetable farmer in South Harrison Township in Gloucester County.  "It cost me about $90,000 more to pay this wage.  That means we don't have money to repair or replace equipment.  That'll eventually catch up to us."

Bramucci said some have made the minimum wage a scapegoat for business problems.

"People who fasten on the minimum wage as a way to look at economic health and failure have to look at something else," he said.

But other business leaders strongly object to the argument that an increase in the minimum wage does not have an adverse effect on the economy.

"Think about all those jobs that may have been created that weren't, especially lower-level and entry-level jobs," said Richard Duprey, the director of government relations for the Commerce and Industry Association of New Jersey.

"If the minimum wage has no impact, why don't you just make it $100?" Duprey asked. "It's an unnecessary interference in the market place. You shouldn't artificially inflate the minimum rate."

Some managers from around the state reported the increase had no significant impact on their businesses.

"The minimum wage increase hasn't hurt us," said John Pawlicki, the manager of Williams Sunoco auto service station in the Short Hills section of Millburn Township.

Pawlicki said his only employees that earn minimum wage are the people who pump gas, and the manager has continued hiring at the same level.

But the increase has affected prices at the Summit Car Wash. Manager Dan Maietta said he had to increase the price of a car wash by 25 cents, to $7, after the new minimum wage went into effect.

"The customers are the ones who pay," Maietta said.

# CHAPTER 28 "THE PRICING AND EMPLOYMENT OF RESOURCES: WAGE DETERMINATION"

## PROBLEMS

1. Table 28-1 below shows the cost a revenue schedule for a Monopsonist.

### Table 28-1

| Quantity of Labor Supplied | Wage Rate | TRC | MRC | MRP |
|---|---|---|---|---|
| 1 | $3.02 | $ 3.02 | | |
| | | | 3.06 | 14.25 |
| 2 | 3.04 | 6.08 | | |
| | | | 3.10 | 14.20 |
| 3 | 3.06 | 9.18 | | |
| 150 | 6.00 | 900 | | |
| | | | 9.02 | 9.02 )  MRC = MRP |
| 151 | 6.02 | 909.02 | | |
| | | | 9.06 | 9.00 |
| 152 | 6.04 | 918.08 | | |
| 200 | 7.00 | 1400 | | |
| | | | 11.02 | 7.00 |
| 201 | 7.02 | 1411.02 | | |
| | | | 11.06 | 6.90 |
| 202 | 7.04 | 1422.08 | | |

Formulas:

TRC = Wage Rate x Quantity of Labor

MRC = $\dfrac{\blacktriangle \text{ TRC}}{\blacktriangle \text{ Units of Resource}}$

a. Fill in the table above.

b. On one graph, plot MRC, the supply curve and MRP.

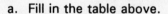

c. What will be the wage rate and quantity of labor for this monopsonist?

$6.00   150 people

d. Under competitive circumstances, what would be the wage rate and quantity of labor?

$7.00   200 people

279

## PROBLEMS

2. Answer the following questions based on Figure 28-7 below.

Figure 28-7

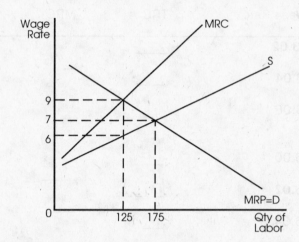

1. In equilibrium, the perfectly competitive employer will pay a wage rate of: *INTERSECTION OF supply & Demand curves*

    a.  $4              b.  $6              c.  ($7)              (d.)  $9

2. In equilibrium, the perfectly competitive employer will hire how many workers?

    a.  100            b.  150            c.  200            (d.)  175

3. In equilibrium, the monopsonistic employer will pay a wage rate of:              *Hire up. till*
                                                                                                                *MRC = MRP*
    a.  $4            (b.)  $6            c.  $7            (d.)  $9

4. In equilibrium, the monopsonistic employer will hire how many workers?

    a.  100            b.  150            c.  200            (d.)  125

5. The amount of "monopsonistic exploitation" in the wage rate is:

    a.  $1            b.  $2            (c.)  $3            d.  $4

6. Under a bilateral monopoly, the wage rate will be:

    a.  $2            b.  $4            c.  $6            (d.)  Indeterminant

280

## PROBLEMS

3.  Answer the following questions based on Figure 27-8 below.

Figure 27-8

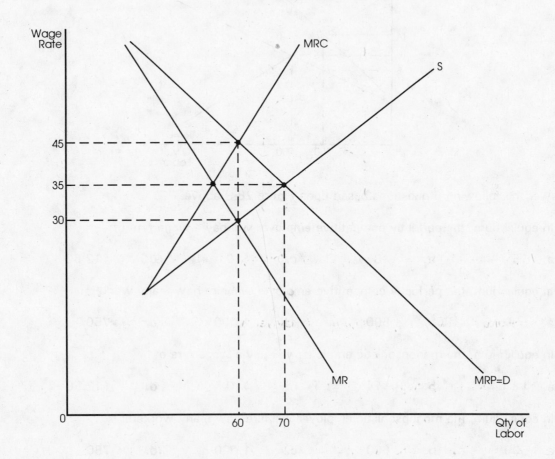

1.  Under perfect competition, an employer would hire ___70___ persons and pay $ 35 per hour.

2.  Under monopsony, an employer would hire ___60___ persons and pay $ 30 per hour.

3.  Under a bilateral monopoly, the wage will be between ___30___ and ___45___.

4.  The amount of "monopsonistic exploitation" in the wage rate is:

    a.   $10          b.     $13          c.     $15          d.     $18

Self-Test

### Figure 28-9

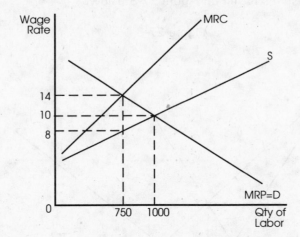

Answer the following 6 questions based upon Figure 28-9 above.

1. In equilibrium, the perfectly competitive employer will pay a wage rate of:

   a. $5          b.    $8          c.    $10          d.    $12.50

2. In equilibrium, the perfectly competitive employer will hire how many workers:

   a. 500          b.    600          c.    1,000          d.    750

3. In equilibrium, the monopsonistic employer will pay a wage rate of:

   a. $8          b.    $14          c.    $10          d.    $12.50

4. In equilibrium, the monopsonistic employer will hire how many workers:

   a. 500          b.    600          c.    1,000          d.    750

5. Under monopsony, with no union, the equilibrium wage rate in this market would be:

   a. $8.00          b.    $10          c.    $12.50          d.    $14

6. If a labor union successfully bargained for a wage of $10 per hour, what would happen to total employment (based upon question #5) demanded?
   a. it would increase by 250 workers
   b. it would not change
   c. it would decrease by 250 workers
   d. no way to tell from the diagram

Self-Test (continued)

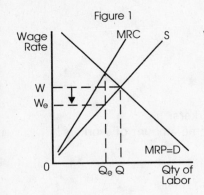

Figure 1

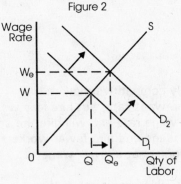

Figure 2

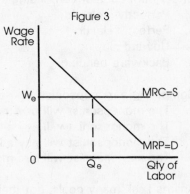

Figure 3

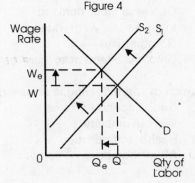

Figure 4

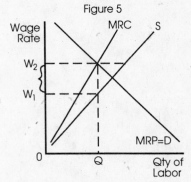

Figure 5

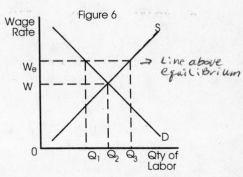

Figure 6

7. What model does Figure 1 represent?
   a. Bilateral monopoly
   b. Monopsony
   c. Inclusive unionism
   d. Craft unionism

8. What model does Figure 2 represent?
   a. Pure competition
   b. Inclusive unionism
   c. Craft unionism
   d. Increasing demand for labor

9. What model does Figure 3 represent?
   a. Inclusive unionism
   b. Increasing labor demand
   c. Pure competition
   d. Bilateral monopoly

10. What model does Figure 4 represent?
    a. Craft unionism
    b. Increasing demand unionism
    c. Pure competition
    d. Monopsony

11. What model does Figure 5 represent?
    a. "Strike threat"
    b. Craft unionism
    c. Bilateral monopoly
    d. Monopsony

12. What model does Figure 6 represent?
    a. Craft unionism
    b. Bilateral monopoly
    c. Pure competition
    d. Inclusive unionism

ONLY model with a wage rate
above equilibrium

Line above
equilibrium

problem on test

Self-Test (continued)

13. Under pure competition, a single firm faces a supply curve that is:
    a. Perfectly inelastic
    b. Perfectly elastic
    c. Upward sloping
    d. Backward bending

14. Comparing a monopsonist with a purely competitive market:
    a. The monopsonist will pay the same wage rate, but hire less workers.
    b. The monopsonist will pay a lower wage rate and will hire the same amount of workers.
    c. The monopsonist will pay a lower wage and hire fewer workers.
    d. The monopsonist will hire more workers at a lower wage.

15. Unions seek many goals, but their main objective is to:
    a. Decrease labor demand
    b. Increase the wage rates
    c. Go on strike
    d. Give management a "hard time".

16. Which of the following is a reason for wage differentials?
    a. Noncompeting groups
    b. Worker mobility
    c. Health and nutrition
    d. All of the above

# CHAPTER 29 "THE PRICING & EMPLOYMENT OF RESOURCE: RENT, INTEREST AND PROFITS"

## Chapter Orientation

Up to this point, we have studied the four factors of production -- land, labor, capital, and entrepreneurial ability. However, we have really only focused on the demand and supply of labor to determine the wage rate and quantity of their respective payments -- rent, interest, and profits will now be examined in Chapter 29.

Rental payments for land, interest payments for capital, and profits received by entrepreneurs, are similar to wage payments made to labor. Land, as a productive factor, includes all natural resources. Land is in fixed supply or perfectly inelastic because it will be there regardless of whether it has a building, a house, or is left idle. Therefore, the owner earns (pure) economic went because no income was necessary to "create" the land.

The interest rate is the price paid for the use of money (to buy capital goods). The theory of interest is that the interest rate is determined by the supply (the Federal Reserve System) and demand (consumers, businesses, the government) for money.

Profits are "rewards" or surpluses over and above all costs. The justification for earning a profit is because of bearing risk or because of creating new products. Why would anyone be motivated to take a risk or try something new if there wasn't a potential for profits? Profits are signals for entry into (or exit from) a market.

After analyzing these three areas: rent, interest, and profits, Chapter 29 looks at the current and historical trends and discusses their significance.

## Learning Objectives

After reading this chapter in the text, and completing the following exercises in your concepts book, you will be able to:

1. Distinguish between economic rent and pure economic rent.
2. Explain what determines the amount of economic rent paid.
3. Discuss why economic rent is a surplus and the plans that Henry George had in mind.
4. Explain why the owners of land do not all receive the same economic rent.
5. Discuss if economic rent is a surplus, why a firm must pay rent.
6. Define the interest rate and discuss why interest rates vary.
7. Identify the two demand for money and state the role that each plays in determining the interest rate.
8. Distinguish between real and nominal interest rates.
9. Explain how the real interest rate effects investment decisions; the equilibrium level of GDP; and the allocation of capital goods.
10. Distinguish between economic profit, normal profit and business (accounting) profit.
11. State the reasons economists give to explain why economic profits occur.
12. Discuss the general function of profits in the American economy.
13. State the current relative size of labor's and of the capitalists' share of national income.
14. Describe the historical trend of wages and salaries.

# CHAPTER 29 "THE PRICING & EMPLOYMENT OF RESOURCE: RENT, INTEREST AND PROFITS"

<u>Chapter Highlights</u>

I. Economic Rent
   A. Definition -- the price paid for use of land and other natural resources which are completely fixed in supply (perfectly inelastic). (See Figure 29-1 below).

Figure 29-1
Economic Rent
Perfectly Inelastic Supply

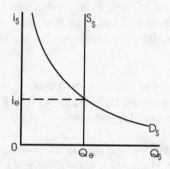

   B. Single-tax movement
      1. Henry George (1839-1897) in his book <u>Progress and Poverty</u> he stated that a single-tax on land, which is equal to the surplus that landowners receive from their land, should be placed on the land, to finance government expenditures. He felt that increases in land rent belonged to the society as a whole and should be taxed away (up to 100%) and spent for public uses.
      2. George's book gained support in the United State, during the late nineteenth century, causing a single-tax movement.
      3. Criticisms of the single-tax on land
         a. A single-tax on land would not bring in enough revenue to finance all government expenditures.
         b. Most income payments fall into the interest, rent, wages, and profits categories. Capital improvements made on the land, cannot be separated from economic rent.
         c. Unearned income is not limited to just land.
      4. Those in favor of a tax on land argue that:
         a. Landowners typically are a high-income minority who receive high incomes with little or no expenditure of effort or money.
         b. A tax on land does not contribute to a misallocation of resources -- it does not have the same effect as high property taxes.
   C. Productivity Differences
      1. Differing productivities of land causes varying economic rent. This is due to soil, fertility, climatic factors, location, etc.
   D. Alternative Uses and Costs
      1. From society's standpoint, land is to be used by society (no alternative), therefore rents are a surplus; however, land does have alternative uses and therefore payments must be made by business to attract that land from alternative uses, as a result, rental payments are a cost.

II. Interest
- A. Definition of interest -- the price paid for the use of money.  Because the use takes place over time, interest must be expressed as a rate per unit ($1) over time (usually one year).  In 1968, Congress passed the Truth in Lending Act which requires full disclosure of the rates on finance charges and other consumer credit transactions.
  - 1. Money is not an economic resource; it does not produce goods and services; however money "buys" capital goods.
- B. Determining the interest rate
  - 1. The "pure" rate of interest is the rate of interest paid on virtually riskless bonds (Example:  U.S. government securities).
  - 2. There exists a wide range of interest rates based upon risk, maturity, loan size, taxability and market imperfections, such as a small country bank monopolizing the local economy.
  - 3. The intersection of the demand curve for money and the supply curve for money determines the equilibrium rate of interest.
    - a. Total demand for money is comprised of:
      - i. Transactions demand (directly related to the level of money GDP).
      - ii. Asset demand -- (inversely related to the rate of interest).
    - b. The supply of money is controlled by the Federal Reserve System.
        Figure 29-2   Supply and Demand for $

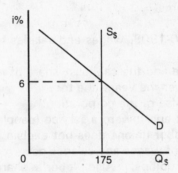

  - 4. The nominal interest rate is the interest rate expressed in current dollars; the real interest rate is adjusted for inflation and is expressed in real dollars (or the nominal rate minus the rate of inflation).  Investment decision-making is based upon the real rate of interest.
  - 5. The interest rate effects investment, which in turn effects the level of output, employment, and prices.
  - 6. The interest rate allocates money (which buys capital goods) to those industries which are the most productive and profitable (they can afford it) and therefore impacts on society as a whole.  However, large oligopolistic borrowers are in a better position than a small purely competitive firms so the interest rate's allocation of capital is not without some faults.

III. Business Profits and Economic Profits
- A. Economic profits vs. business (accounting) profits
  - 1. Recall from Chapter 22, that accountants take revenues minus expenses (or explicit

costs) to calculate business (accounting) profit. Economists go one step further and subtract implicit costs (such as a normal profit, opportunity cost, etc.) to get economic profits which are excess or pure profits.

B. Profit is the reward or payment to the entrepreneur for operating in a dynamic economy. (Signal for entry/exit).

C. Sources of Economic Profits:
1. Uncertainty and uninsurable risks.
2. Innovation -- new products or new methods of production.
3. Monopoly power -- an innovative firm can enjoy economic profits, minimize risk, and become a monopoly. However, bearing risk in a dynamic and uncertain economy and the undertaking of innovations and more socially desirable than monopoly profits based upon the cutting output to drive prices up.

D. Functions of Profits
1. Investment and Domestic Output
2. Profits and Resource Allocation

IV. Income Shares
A. Current Shares
1. Looking at 1982-1990:
a. Wages and salaries comprise 75% of national income; using a broader definition, they comprise 80% of national income.
b. The capitalist share (corporate profits, plus interest, plus rent) as only 20% of national income.

B. Historical trends
1. Since the years 1900-1909, wages and salaries have gone from 55% to 75%.
2. Structural changes
a. Labor's share and the capitalist share of national income has remained about the same, over the years due to:
i. The rise of the corporation.
ii. The trend toward a service (people-oriented) economy.
3. The growth of the labor unions does not explain the expanding wage share because much of the growth of wages and salaries occurred during a different time frame from the growth of the unions. Also, labor's share has grown more rapidly in the nonunionized sectors (such as the service industries).

V. Last Word: Determining the Price of Credit

Key Terms

| | |
|---|---|
| economic rent | real interest rate |
| incentive function | economic (pure) profit |
| single-tax movement | implicit cost |
| interest | explicit cost |
| Truth in Lending Act | normal profit |
| "pure" interest rate | business (accounting) profit |
| theory of interest | static economy |
| transactions demand for money | dynamic economy |
| asset demand for money | uninsurable risk |
| nominal (money) interest rate | capitalist's share |

<u>Real World Example</u>

**Magazine Says World's Richest Getting Richer**

**The Associated Press**

NEW YORK-Many of the world's tycoons rode surging stock prices to more riches over the past year, but the average net worth of the 101 wealthiest people and families increased only slightly, Fortune magazine reports.

The average net worth of the wealthiest people rose 2.27 percent, to $4.5 billion from $4.4 billion, the semimonthly business magazine estimates in its June 28 issue, available Monday. The increase was less than the U.S. inflation rate, which was about 3 percent during the same period.

the Sultan of Brunei led the list again with a fortune of $37 billion in real estate and energy holding, the same as last year. The Walton family, which owns 38 percent of Wal-Mart Stores, was second at $23.5 billion, about a half-billion less than last year.

The Mars family's ownership of the candy company was worth $14 billion, $1 billion more than a year earlier, putting it in third place.

Among the more notable increases, legendary investor Warren Buffet's holdings in the stock of his Berkshire Hathaway conglomerate increased his wealth 33 percent to $6.4 billion.

In Hong Kong, real estate magnate Li Kashing's 35 percent stake in Cheung Kong Holdings increased in value by $2 billion, bringing his trove to $5.8 billion.

"The most prosperous, unlike the rest of us in these difficult economic times, have more money then they had last year," the magazine.

Fortune, which calculated wealth for the year ended in April, confined this year's list to the top 101 billionaires, rather than listing all the world's billionaires as it has in years past. The list had grown from 98 individuals and families in 1987 to 233 last year.

"Frankly, the club was getting less exclusive," the magazine said.

The worth of the 101 billionaires totals $455 billion, just less than the gross domestic product of Spain, Fortune said. Of the 101, 26 are Americans.

## America's Wealthiest

The top five American entries in Fortune magazine's 1993 list of world billionaires, with name, home, source of wealth and estimated value in billions of dollars:

1. Helen R. Walton, S. Robson Walton, James C. Walton, Alice L. Walton, Arkansas: John T. Walton, California; Wal-Mart stores; $23.5.
2. Forrest Mars Sr., Nevada; Forrest Mars Jr., John Mars, Virginia; Jacqueline Mars Vogel, New Jersey; Mars, Inc.; $14.
3. Samuel I. Newhouse Jr., Donald E. Newhouse and family, New York; publishing and broadcasting; $10.
4. John Werner Kluge, Virginia; communications, real estate; $8.8.
5. William Gates, Washington state; Microsoft computer software; $6.7.

# CHAPTER 29 "THE PRICING & EMPLOYMENT OF RESOURCE: RENT, INTEREST AND PROFITS"

## PROBLEMS

1. Henry George felt that a single-tax on land would be appropriate because land rent is considered pure economic rent. Discuss the pros and cons of this theory.

2. What is interest and what is the economic function of interest rates?

3. What is the economic function of profits? How do economists differ from accountants in their view of profits?

### Table 29-1

| Rent per acre | Quantity Demanded |
|---|---|
| $500 | 2,000 |
| 400 | 4,000 |
| 300 | 6,000 |
| 200 | 8,000 |
| 100 | 10,000 |

4. Assume that the number of acres of land available in a particular area is 8,000 and the demand schedule is illustrated in Table 29-1.

   a. What is the total amount of pure economic rent (per acre)? _$200_

   b. How many acres will be rented based upon Table 29-1? _8,000_

   c. Graph the supply and demand curves for this land and label the equilibrium rent/acre (Re) and number of acres (Qe).

   d. If the landowners were taxed (Henry George's idea), $200/acre, the number of acres rented would be _8,000_.

5. Describe the current and historical trends of wages and salaries.

6. What structural changes have impacted on labor's and the capitalist share of national income? Discuss.

7. Currently, our interest rates are extremely low, what impact does that have on the economy?

8.  After reading the "Real World Example", what are your feelings about the "rich getting richer".
    What impact does this have on the economy?

Figure 29-3

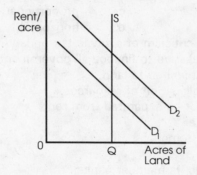

9.  In Figure 29-3, at Demand (D1):

    a.  Shade in the area of economic rent.

    b.  Label the graph economic rent or pure economic rent.

    c.  Label the rent/acre (Re) and the number of acres rented (Qe).

10. Discuss the two functions of profits.

<u>Self-Test</u>

1. Which of the following best defines the term "economic rent"?
   a. the returns on any factor of production which is elastic in supply.
   b. payments made for the use of capital borrowed to increase production.
   c. the price paid for the use of land and other natural resources in fixed supply.
   d. Payments made to an owner for use of a dwelling or equipment.
2. Under pure economic rent, the supply curve is:
   a. perfectly elastic.     c.    proportional
   b. perfectly inelastic.     d.    horizontal.
3. Which of the following is <u>not</u> a criticism of a single-tax on land?
   a. does not bring in enough revenue to finance all government expenditures.
   b. unearned income is not just limited to land.
   c. does not contribute to misallocation of resources.
   d. capital improvements cannot be separated from rent.
4. The pure interest rate is the rate:
   a. banks lend to their best customers.
   b. banks lend to each other.
   c. the Federal Reserve lends to its member banks.
   d. paid on U.S. government securities.
5. Which of the following describes "profit"?
   a. reward or payment to an entrepreneur.
   b. signals to enter/exit an industry.
   c. the prime energizer of the capitalist economy.
   d. all of the above.
6. Which of the following is <u>not</u> a justification for economic profits?
   a. innovation.     c.    monopoly power.
   b. risk.     d.    static economy.
7. Economic profits differ from business profits because:
   a. they measure revenues minus expenses.
   b. they include explicit cost.
   c. they include implicit cost.
   d. they exclude opportunity cost.
8. The pursuit and escape theory describes:
   a. stockholders with the Board of Directors.
   b. insider trading on Wall Street.
   c. labor unions with businesses.
   d. labor with the unions.
9. Wages and salaries are a share of GDP received for:
   a. all labor services.
   b. blue-collar labor services.
   c. administrative labor services.
   d. entrepreneurial labor services.
10. Profits are defined by economists as:
    a. a residual from sales revenue after costs of production have been met.
    b. the money return on capital.
    c. the return to management.
    d. none of the above.

# CHAPTER 36   "LABOR MARKET ISSUES: UNIONISM, DISCRIMINATION, & IMMIGRATION"

## Chapter Orientation

In Chapter 28 you studied how labor unions attempt to raise wage rates.  Organized labor is involved with more than just wages -- it has an impact on its rank-and-file, the business, and the economy.  Chapter 36 focuses on American unionism, by opening with a brief history, followed by a discussion of present and future membership, and closes with the economic effects of unions.

Basically, there are three phases of the history of American unionism: (1) Repression phase; (2) Encouragement phase; (3) Intervention phase.  It is interesting to see how legislation has swung from pro-management to pro-union and back again.  When one side was/seemed too powerful, laws were passed to protect the other side.  After this brief history the chapter discusses labor-management relations and the process of collective bargaining.

Lastly, the economic effects of labor unions on wages, efficiency and productivity, the distribution of earnings, and the price level (inflation) will be explored.

## Learning Objectives

After reading this chapter in the text, and completing the following exercises in this concepts book, you will be able to:

1. Discuss the earliest beginnings of American unionism.
2. Describe the attitude and behavior of the courts and business toward labor unions during the repression phase.
3. Define the three fundamental ideas of Samuel Gompers.
4. Explain the Norris-LaGuardia Act (1932).
5. Explain the Wagner Act (1935) or the National Labor Relations Act.
6. Define the role of the National Labor Relations Board (NLRB).
7. Contrast Samuel Gompers and the AFL with John E. Lewis and the CIO.
8. Discuss the provisions of the Taft-Hartley Act of 1947.
9. Define the objectives of the Landrum-Griffin Act of 1959.
10. State what the trend has been in regard to union memberships over the past thirty years, and present three hypotheses to explain this occurrence.
11. Define the collective bargaining process and explain the four basic areas usually covered.
12. Discuss the impact unions have on the wage rates for their members, on the wages of nonunion workers and on the average level of real wages in the American economy.
13. Describe and evaluate the pros and cons concerning the impact of unions on efficiency and productivity and give the empirical evidence.
14. Compare the demand-pull and cost-push models of inflation.  Explain how unions effect the "cost-push" model.
15. List the causes of inflation in the American economy from the 1970s to present.
16. Discuss discrimination and its economic effect on the American economy.
17. Discuss the pros and cons of immigration and explain what the U.S.'s position should be on immigration.

# CHAPTER 36 "LABOR MARKET ISSUES: UNIONISM, DISCRIMINATION, & IMMIGRATION"

## Chapter Highlights

I. Brief History of American Unionism

   A. Introduction -- The Industrial Revolution, in the late 1700s, changed the nature of our work force  Prior to the Industrial Revolution, the labor force was composed of mostly farmers, since our economy was largely agricultural. Growth of mass production and factories lured workers into the cities, where they found themselves highly exploited, because of poor working conditions ("sweat shops").

   B. Repression phase: 1790 to 1930

      1. Although these conditions were horrible for all workers, including children, progress, was very slow in forming unions to protect the workers.

      2. Local craft unions (shoemakers, printers, carpenters, etc.) were the only labor unions that were able to survive. Skilled workers were few in number and they were able to control their own numbers by requiring union membership as a necessary condition for admission to apprenticeship in the trade.

      3. By contrast, the supply of unskilled labor was much more plentiful and was continually fed by immigrants. As a result, any union of unskilled labor was quickly undercut by unskilled nonunionized workers.

      4. In addition, the hostility of the courts toward labor unions and the reluctance of American businesses to recognize and bargain with unions contributed to the slow progress in organizing the labor force.

      5. Some of the obstacles to unionization were: the criminal conspiracy doctrine (unions were guilty of criminal conspiracy and hence illegal), injunctions (a restraining order which stipulated that an action -- such as a strike -- not be carried out), discriminatory discharge and black listing (effected present and future employment), lockout (management closes up shop for a while), yellow-dog contracts (workers agreed not to join a union as a condition of employment), and company unions or paternalism (a labor union dominated or controlled by management).

      6. From 1869 up until 1911, the Knights of Labor was the first national union for all workers.

      7. In 1886, the American Federation of Labor (AFL) was founded by Samuel Gompers -- "the father of the American Labor movement". His fundamental ideas were:

         a. Business unionism (higher wages and better working conditions)

         b. Political neutrality (not tied to one party)

         c. Trade autonomy (organized by craft)

   C. Encouragement phase: 1930 to 1947

      1. With the onset of the Great Depression, the public's attitude toward big business fell. The federal government passed two prolabor acts:

        (a) Norris-LaGuardia Act of 1932 -- declared yellow-dog contracts illegal and made it more difficult to obtain an injunction.

        (b) Wagner Act of 1935 (officially called the National Labor Relations Act) -- guaranteed labor the right of self-organization and the right to bargain collectively with employers. The act listed several "unfair labor practices on the part of management and set up the National Labor Relations Board (NLRB) or "Labor Board" which investigates unfair labor practices and conducts elections among employees to determine if they want to become unionized and which union they want to represent them.

2.      As a result of these two acts, union membership grew at a rapid pace.  In addition, the Wagner Act made it easier to organize unskilled, as well as skilled labor.

(a)      John E. Lewis contended that unions should shift from craft unions to industrial unions, which would include skilled and unskilled labor in a particular industry or a group of related industries.

(b)      Congress of Industrial Organization (CIO) was formed in 1936.  It was a highly successful union especially in the auto and steel industries.

D.  Intervention phase:  1947 to date

1.      After World War II, the favorable treatment of labor was attacked, and Congress again turned its attention and passed the Taft-Hartley Act of 1947, officially called the "Labor-Management Relations Act".

(a)      Outlined and prohibited certain "unfair union practices".

(b)      Regulated the internal administration of unions.

(c)      Specified the collective bargaining process; abolished the closed shop and made state right-to-work laws legal.

(d)      Set up a procedure for national emergency strikes.

2.      In the 1950s the progress of the labor movement slowed down; membership grew slowly.  Congress again turned its attention on organized labor and didn't like what it saw:  corrupt unions, links with organized crime, and the unions did not seem to be benefitting their rank-and-file.

(a)      In 1959, Congress passed the Landrum-Griffin Act, or officially called, the "Labor-Management Reporting and Disclosure Act".  Financial practices, elections, officers, constitutions, member rights, etc. came under this law, and the unions were required to be more responsive to the membership.

II. Unionism's Decline

A.  Merger of the AFL-CIO

1.      In 1955, the AFL and CIO merged to improve its political influence and because a unified effort was needed to organize nonunion firms and industries.

2.      The marriage of the AFL-CIO has not brought about a resurgence of organized labor currently, about 17 million workers or 15% of the labor in 1985 were organized.  In 1980 that figure was 22 million workers or 25% of the labor force.

B.  Reasons for the decline of union membership

1.      The structural-change hypothesis -- a variety of structural changes have taken place such as the shift from manufacturing to services; import competition; and the composition of the labor force -- women, youths, and part-time workers are difficult to organize.

2.      The managerial-opposition hypothesis -- management's opposition to unions has become more aggressive lately, as a result of the increased union wage advantage which causes union firms to be less profitable than nonunion firms.  Legal and illegal tactics, by management, have helped reduce union membership.

III. Collective Bargaining

A.  The collective bargaining process

1.      Definition -- collective bargaining is a process by which decisions regarding wages, hours, and conditions of employment are determined by the interaction of workers (acting through their unions) and employers usually brought about by compromise rather than by strikes or violence.

2.    Collective bargaining agreements usually cover four basic areas:
    (a)    Degree of recognition and status accorded the union and the prerogatives of management (See Figure 36-1 below).
    (b)    Wages and hours
    (c)    Seniority and the control of job opportunities.
    (d)    Procedure for settling grievances.

---

Figure 36-1
Union Security

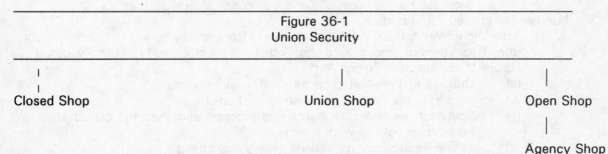

Closed Shop                    Union Shop                    Open Shop

                                                                                    Agency Shop

Closed Shop -- strongest union protection -- makes union membership a precondition to employment. The Taft-Hartley Act (1947) outlawed closed shops except in certain circumstances (union hiring halls).

Union Shop -- stipulates that all workers must belong to the union that represents their bargaining unit upon employment (after a grace period, usually 30 days). The Taft-Hartley Act (1947) modifies union shops and permits its prohibition by individual states in "right-to-work" laws (currently 19 states have "right-to-work laws).

Open Shop -- a situation in which the employer is free to hire without considering an applicant's union status and the worker's under no obligation to join a union. The open shop does not give the union any security -- they must seek out the workers and recruit them on a voluntary basis.

Agency Shop -- exists when workers in a bargaining unit are not required to join the union, but must make a payment equal to the dues. Thus shop eliminates the "free rider" problem in which nonunion workers benefit from the union representation. Agency shops are particularly important to the union in states with right-to-work laws.

---

3.    Implications of collective bargaining:
    a.    Concerned with security and the status of the union itself, in addition to wage rates.
    b.    Collective bargaining is a continuous process.
    c.    Provides short-run temporary adjustments to our dynamic environment.
IV. The Economic Effects of Unions
    A.  The unions wage advantage -- empirical evidence suggests that union workers do receive a higher wage and better fringe benefits than do nonunion workers. (Today, the focus is on job security).
    1.    Unions have had little impact on the average level of real wages received by the total labor force because union gains have been at the expense of nonunion workers. (Fewer union workers are hired at the higher wage -- those unemployed may seek employment in nonunion labor markets).

   B.   Efficiency and productivity
      1.   Unions exert a negative impact upon efficiency by:
         (a)   Featherbedding and work rules
         (b)   Strikes
         (c)   Fostering labor misallocation
      2.   Unions exert a positive impact upon efficiency by:
         (a)   Shock effect on managerial performance
         (b)   Reduced worker turnover
         (c)   Seniority and informal training
      3.   Empirical evidence is not clear on a conclusion regarding the effect of unionization on efficiency and productivity -- some industries have increased, while others have decreased.
   C.  Distribution of earnings
      1.   There is also no consensus as to the effect unions have on the distribution of earnings among the workers.
         (a)   Some economists argue that unions increase earnings and reduce employment in unionized labor markets (which leads to unemployed seeking out nonunionized employment). This results in an inequality of earnings.
         (b)   Other economists feel that unions seek uniformity in the wage rates for the same jobs within a firm; as well as among firms. This leads to income equality.
   D.  Unions and inflation
      1.   There is also not agreement as to whether unions generate cost-push inflation.
      2.   Demand-pull inflation is caused by consumer spending, wage increases are an effect (or symptom) not a cause.
      3.   Cost-push models allow for union wage increases, without increases in productivity, to push up labor costs which in turn will effect product prices.
      4.   Most economists blame increase in government spending in the late 1960s; supply shocks due to OPEC, etc. with causing inflation rather than as a result of union wage-setting. However, unions due seem to perpetuate existing inflation because of long-term contracts (Example: three-years) which anticipate future inflation and labor market conditions.
V. Discrimination
   A.  Definition of economic discrimination
   B.  Dimensions of discrimination
      1.   Wage discrimination
      2.   Employment discrimination
      3.   Human-capital discrimination
      4.   Occupation discrimination
   C.  Occupational Segregation:  The Crowding Model
      1.   Definition of occupation segregation
      2.   The "Crowding Model" illustrates that society gains from a more efficient allocation of resources when discrimination is abandoned.
   D.  Costs of Discrimination
      1.   One estimate of economic and social policies were successful output would rise by four percent (or $181 billion in 1988)

E.  Addenda
    1.      Comparable with doctrine
    2.      Nondiscriminating factors
            a.      Some of the differences in male-female earnings due to considerations other than discrimination by gender.
VI. Immigration
    A.  History and Policy
        1.      History of immigration in the U.S.
        2.      Current immigration laws
        3.      Impact of illegal immigrants
    B.  Economics of Immigration
        1.      Supply and Demand analysis suggests that the movement of migrants from a poor to a rich country will:
                a.      increase the national income
                b.      reduce the average level of wages
                c.      increase business incomes in the receiving country
        2.      The opposite effects will occur in the sending country, but the world as a whole can expect to realize a larger total output.
    C.  Complications and Modifications
        1.      Cost of migration
                a.      Explicit and implicit costs vs. (expected) benefits
        2.      Remittances and backflows
                a.      Causes an altering of gains and losses through time
        3.      Full employment vs. unemployment
                a.      When a country has unemployed workers (collecting unemployment compensation, it might benefit from migration.
        4.      Fiscal aspects
                a.      Evidence suggests that immigrants are net contributors to the fiscal system of the host country.
                b.      Direct social welfare costs of illegals are low because of fear of detection and most illegals are working.
    D.  Economics and Beyond
        1.      The issues involved in determining the economic aspects of immigration are complex. Much depends upon the character of the immigrants themselves and the economic conditions of the host country.

VII.Last Word:  Racism in Professional Basketball?

# CHAPTER 36 "LABOR MARKET ISSUES: UNIONISM, DISCRIMINATION, & IMMIGRATION"

## Key Terms

criminal-conspiracy doctrine
injunction
lockout yellow-dog contract
company union
business unionism
AFL
Norris-La Guardia Act
Wagner Act
NLRB
CIO
Taft-Hartley Act
Landrum-Griffin Act
structural change hypothesis
managerial-opposition hypothesis
jurisdictional strike
discriminatory discharge
blacklisting
sympathy strike
occupational segregation
comparable worth doctrine

secondary boycott
feather bedding
closed shop
open shop
agency shop
nonunion shop
right-to-work law
managerial prerogative
COLA
grievance procedure
seniority
fringe benefit
collective voice
exit mechanism
voice mechanism
craft union
industrial union
wage, employment, occupational, and human-capital discrimination
legal and illegal immigrants

## Real World Example

### Strike, Lockouts Continue

### By Dennis P. Carmody

NO PROGRESS was made in the talks held yesterday and Monday between four supermarket chains and the union that is striking them, union and management spokesmen said.

The two sides talked for 16 1/4 hours Monday and started up again at 11 a.m. yesterday, said Donald C. Vaillancourt, spokesman for the combined management of Foodtown, Grand Union, Pathmark and ShopRite. It appeared last evening that they would continue working late into the night, as they have done several times before.

"There's not progress to report, but they're still talking, so I guess that's important," said union spokesman Frank Margiotta.

Meanwhile, management unlocked some more stores where members of the Clifton-based United Food and Commercial Workers Local 1262 had been previously locked out, Vaillancourt said. The union planned to strike those unlocked stores, Margiotta said.

Vaillancourt would not say how many or which stores were being unlocked because revealing that would hurt management's strategy, he said. However, telephone calls to the 40 previously locked stores in Monmouth, Ocean and Middlesex counties found 16 had ended their lockouts yesterday only to see the union strike those stores.

Previously, every time the union struck a new store, management locked out union members from all nearby stores, ensuring that all four chains would share the burden and no unstruck store would get extra business at the expense of nearby struck stores.

Margiotta said the union is striking those unlocked stores because it believes management is trying to fool the public and the union members into thinking the dispute is abating and that management is being conciliatory. He said management is only acting because it fears losing an unfair labor practices complaint filed by the union in federal district court last week.

Vaillancourt denied that, saying it simply made no sense to continue the lockouts in areas relatively unaffected by the strike. Margiotta said he did not know when the hearing on that complaint will be held.

The new strike tactics do not seem to have made much of a difference at ;the bargaining table in the latest round of talks scheduled by federal mediator Thomas Ervin. The strike started May 7. After the first round failed May 14, the strike spread from 18 to 58 stores and the lockouts spread from 23 to 71 stores. When the second round failed Thursday, the strike spread from 69 to 108 stores and the lockouts spread from 79 to 117 stores.

When asked why he kept scheduling talks despite the lack of progress, Ervin responded, "My job is to bring people together. As long as I can get people to get together, thing get settled."

Beyond scheduling the talks, Ervin can do little else. "I don't have any power to make anyone do anything they don't want to do," he said.

The two side remain stuck over health care costs. Management has stressed that its new managed care plan would not take any deductions from the workers' paychecks. The union says despite that the higher deductibles and maximum out-of-pocket expenses for full-timers would be too high, especially for workers who decide to use a doctor or hospital outside the managed care network.

Single full-timers outside the network will see their deductibles climb from $150 to $300, said Michael Kinsora, a union negotiator. Full-timers with families will see their deductibles rise from $300 to $600, he said.

After that, the workers will pay 35 percent of the additional cost, not 20 percent, like those in the network. Vaillancourt said that percentage is still under negotiation.

Maximum out-of-pocket expenses for single full-timers outside the network would rise from $550 to $1,200, Kinsora said. For full-timers with families, it would rise from $1,500 to $2,400, he said. Vaillancourt disagreed with that, saying the cost for families would actually drop from $1,500 to $1,400, but did not provide any more details.

# CHAPTER 36   "LABOR MARKET ISSUES: UNIONISM, DISCRIMINATION, & IMMIGRATION"

## PROBLEMS

1. Define the four shops in union security.

2. What impact did the Taft-Hartley Act have on the shops listed above?

3. Explain what brought about unionism in the United States.

4. Discuss the three phases of unionism: repression phase, encouragement phase, and the intervention phase.

5. What is the current status of union membership in the United States? What do you predict for the future? Why?

6. What is collective bargaining? What are the four basic areas usually covered in collective bargaining?

7. Compare the demand-pull and cost-push models of inflation. Explain how unions effect the cost-push model.

8. From a wage standpoint, is a worker better off belonging to a union? Discuss.

9. Briefly define the Norris-LaGuardia Act, the Wagner Act, and the Landrum-Griffin Act.

10. What are the three theories to help explain the trend in union membership? Define each theory and state which one(s) you agree with.

11. Define "economic discrimination" and explain the four areas of discrimination. What does the "crowding out model" tell us about discrimination?

12. Discuss the pros and cons of immigration. In your opinion, what should be the U.S.'s immigration policy?

Self-Test
1. Which is the best description of the rationalization for lockouts?
    a.  to reduce output in response to decreased demand for the product.
    b.  to minimize property damage during periods of unrest.
    c.  to disrupt production and weaken management's bargaining position.
    d.  to discontinue workers' income and weaken labor's bargaining position.
2. A company union is:
    a.  the duly elected representative of labor in any firm.
    b.  the bargaining agent for management in labor disputes.
    c.  a labor union dominated or controlled by management.
    d.  an organization of companies designed to give management strength in conflicts with labor unions.
3. The rationalization for the formation of company unions is:
    a.  to provide labor with a bargaining agent in its endeavors to get favorable wage contracts.
    b.  to protect workers from outside agitators who may make unreasonable demands on management.
    c.  to weaken the strength of other labor unions which may obtain wage contracts favorable to labor.
    d.  to provide labor a legitimate channel of communications.
4. Which of the following would management be most likely to support?
    a.  legislation legalizing the closed shop.
    b.  legislation prohibiting strikes for union recognition.
    c.  legislation requiring that workers in certain skill categories pass union requirements.
    d.  legislation legalizing union shops in all states.
5. Which of the following is not a complication of immigration?
    a.  explicit and implicit costs           c.      remittances
    b.  "cheap" labor                         d.      backflows
6. Which of the following pieces of legislation declared yellow-dog contracts illegal and made it more difficult to obtain an injunction?
    a.  Wagner Act.                           c.      Taft-Hartley Act
    b.  Norris-LaGuardia Act.                 d.      Landrum-Griffin Act.
7. Which of the following pieces of legislation declared that financial practices, elections, constitutions, member rights, etc. came under the law?
    a.  Wagner Act.                           c.      Taft-Hartley Act
    b.  Norris-LaGuardia Act.                 d.      Landrum-Griffin Act.
8. Which of the following pieces of legislation guaranteed labor the right of self-organization and the right to bargain collectively?
    a.  Wagner Act.                           c.      Taft-Hartley Act
    b.  Norris-LaGuardia Act.                 d.      Landrum-Griffin Act.
9. Which of the following pieces of legislation outlined and prohibited certain "unfair union practices"; specified the collective bargaining process and abolished the closed shop, etc.?
    a.  Wagner Act.                           c.      Taft-Hartley Act
    b.  Norris-LaGuardia Act.                 d.      Landrum-Griffin Act.
10.The National Labor Relations Board was established by:
    a.  Wagner Act.                           c.      Taft-Hartley Act
    b.  Norris-LaGuardia Act.                 d.      Landrum-Griffin Act.

## Chapter 27  Production and the Demand for Economic Resources
I.   Introduction of the Input Markets
   A. Background
      1.     Simple circular flow model
   B. Definition of marginal productivity theory
   C. Reasons for studying resource pricing (4)
II.  Complexities of Resource Pricing
   A. Outside impact from Government, unions, etc.
   B. Businesses determine the resource demand curve; consumers determine the resource supply
      curve
III. Marginal Productivity Theory of Resource Demand
   A. Terms
      1.     Derived demand
          a.     Definition
      2.     Marginal product (MP)
          a.     Definition
          b.     Law of diminishing returns
          c.     Graphed at the midpoints
      3.     Marginal revenue product (MRP)
          a.     Definition
          b.     Determines "worth"
          c.     MRP is the demand curve for a firm
          d.     Graphed at the midpoints
      4.     Average revenue product (ARP)
          a.     Definition
      5.     Marginal resource cost (MRC)
          a.     Definition
          b.     Graphed at the midpoints
   B. Profit maximization (or loss minimization)
      1.     Use the MRP = MRC rule
      2.     TR - TRC Approach
IV.  Market Demand for a Resource
   A. Purely competitive markets
      1.     MRP is the resource demand curve for a purely competitive seller
          a.     Diminishing returns (MPP decreases) causes a downward sloping resource
               demand curve (product price is constant).
   B. Imperfect competition
      1.     MRP is also the resource demand curve under imperfect competition.
          a.     Diminishing returns and falling product price causes a downward sloping
               resource demand curve.
   C. Market demand
      1.     The market demand curve can be found by summing together all of the individual
          resource demand (or MRP) curves.
V.   Determination of Resource Demand
   A. A change in resource demand (new curve)
      1.     Factors that cause the resource demand curve to shift (4)

VI. Elasticity of Resource Demand
   A. A change in the "quantity" of resource demand
      1.    Factors that cause a movement along the resource demand curve (sensitivity to price-- elasticity) -- (4)
VII. Optimum Combination of Resources
   A. The least-cost rule
      1.    Definition
      2.    Formula
      3.    Maximization of profits under pure competition
      4.    Numerical example in text
      5.    Maximization of profits under imperfect competition
         a.     New formula
VIII. Marginal Productivity Theory of Income Distribution
   A. Shortcomings
      1.    Inequality
      2.    Noncompetitive markets

**Chapter 28**  **The Pricing and Employment of Resources: Wage Determination**
I.   Meaning of Wages
   A. Definition of wages
   B. Definition of earnings
II.  The General Level of Real Wages
   A. Real Wages in the U.S. are among the highest in the world.
   B. Reasons for the productivity of the American workforce (5)
   C. Real income per worker increases at approximately the same ratio as output per worker.
   D. Population increases offset by productivity increases
III. Wages in Particular Labor Markets
   A. Types of market models
      1.    Competitive market
         a.    Wage and output determined through the forces of supply and demand.
         b.    Supply curves for the market, the single firm, and the individual
         c.    Graphic presentation: wage and output determination
      2.    Monopsony
         a.    Definition
         b.    Examples
         c.    Graphic presentation: wage and output determination
         d.    Comparison of Monopsony to the purely competitive market
      3.    Union models -- models that seek to raise wage rates:
         a.    Increasing the demand for labor
            (1)    Definition
            (2)    Graphic presentation: wage and output determination
            (3)    Techniques used to increase labor demand (3)
         b.    Exclusive or craft unionism (labor monopoly)
            (1)    Definition
            (2)    Graphic presentation: wage and output determination
            (3)    Techniques used to restrict the labor supply (2)
         c.    Inclusive or industrial unionism
            (1)    Definition

             (2)     Graphic presentation (with a strike threat): wage and output determination

             (3)     Techniques used to raise the wage rate

        d.     Empirical evidence regarding wage rates of union workers versus nonunion workers

             (1)     Tradeoff high wages versus unemployment

    4.     Bilateral monopoly

        a.     Definition

        b.     Graphic presentation: wage and output determination

        c.     End results of the two monopolies

    5.     The minimum wage controversy

        a.     Pros

        b.     Cons

        c.     Empirical evidence

IV. Wage Differentials

  A. Definition

  B. Reasons for wage differentials (3)

V. Investment in Human Capital

  A. Theory of human capital

    1.     Definition

VI. Pay and Performance

  A. Principal-Agent Problem

    1.     Definition

    2.     Ways to Remedy

**Chapter 29** **The Pricing & Employment of Resources: Rent, Interest and Profits**

I.  Economic Rent

  A. Definition

  B. Graphic presentation

  C. Single-tax movement

    1.     Henry George

    2.     Criticisms of the single-tax movement (3)

    3.     Benefits of a single-tax on land

  D. Productivity differences

  E. Alternative uses and costs

II.  Interest

  A. Definition

    1.     Truth in Lending Act

    2.     Money is not an economic resource

  B. Determining the interest rate

    1.     Definition of the "pure" rate of interest

    2.     Reasons for differing interest rates

    3.     Determining the equilibrium interest rate:

        a.     Total demand for money = Transactions + assets demand

        b.     The supply of money controlled by the Federal Reserve System

    4.     Nominal versus real interest rates

    5.     Cause and effect chain

    6.     Allocates resources

III. Business Profits and Economic Profits
  A. Economic profits versus business (accounting) profits
    1.    Definitions of economic profit, normal profit and business (accounting) profits
  B. Profits are rewards or payments to the entrepreneur
  C. Sources of economic profits
  D. Profits are energizers; motivators to innovation and efficiency; allocative signals, and a means to finance expansion
IV. Income Shares
  A. Current shares
    1.    Percentage of wages/salaries and the capitalist's share (corporate profits + interest = rent) to national income
  B. Historical trends
    1.    Trend of wages/salaries since 1900-1909
    2.    Structural changes have kept labor's share and the capitalist's share relatively stable
    3.    Growth of the labor unions and their impact on the labor's wage share

**Chapter 36  Labor Market Issues:  Unionism, Discrimination and Immigration**
I.   History of American Unionism
  A. Introduction
    1.    Earliest beginnings
  B. Repression phase:  1790 to 1930
    1.    Local craft unions
    2.    Hostility of the courts
    3.    Obstacles to unionization
    4.    American Federation of Labor (AFL)
      a.    Samuel Gompers
      b.    Fundamental ideas (3)
  C. Encouragement phase:  1930 to 1947
    1.    Favorable (prolabor) legislation
      a.    Norris-LaGuardia Act of 1932
      b.    Wagner Act of 1935
    2.    Congress of Industrial Organization (1936)
      a.    John E. Lewis
      b.    Fundamental ideas
  D. Intervention phase:  1947 to present
    1.    Taft-Hartley Act of 1947
    2.    Landrum-Griffin Act of 1959
II.   Unionisms Decline
  A. Merger of the AFL-CIO in 1955
    1.    Reasons behind the merger (2)
  B. Reasons for the decline in union memberships (2)
III. Union Security (4)
IV. Collective Bargaining
  A. The collective bargaining process
    1.    Definition
    2.    Four basic areas covered
    3.    Implications of collective bargaining (3)

V. The Economic Effects of Unions
  A. The union wage advantage
    1.     Wage rate for union workers versus nonunion workers
    2.     Impact on the average level of real wages
  B. Efficiency and productivity
    1.     Negative impact (3)
    2.     Positive impact (3)
    3.     Empirical evidence
  C. Distribution of earnings
    1.     Pros and cons of union's impact on wage inequality
    2.     Empirical evidence
  D. Unions and inflation
    1.     Demand-pull inflation effects
    2.     Cost-push inflation effects
    3.     Reasons for inflation in the 1960s, 1970s and 1980s
    4.     Union's effect on perpetuating inflation
    5.     Empirical evidence
VI. Discrimination
  A. Definition
  B. Dimensions of discrimination (4)
  C. Occupational segregation: The Crowding Model
  D. Costs of Discrimination
  E. Addenda
    1.     Comparable worth doctrine
    2.     Nondiscriminatory factors
VII. Immigration
  A. History and Policy
  B. Economics of Immigration
  C. Complications and Modifications
  D. Economics and Beyond

## Formula Sheet

Marginal Product (MP) = $\dfrac{\blacktriangle \text{ TP}}{\blacktriangle \text{ Units of Resource}}$

Marginal Revenue Product (MRP) = MP x Product's Price = $\dfrac{\blacktriangle \text{ TR}}{\blacktriangle \text{ Units of Resource}}$

Total Revenue (TR) = TP x Product's price

Average Revenue Product (ARP) = $\dfrac{\text{TR}}{\text{Units of Resource}}$

Total Resource Cost (TRC) = Units of resource x wage rate

Marginal Resource Cost (MRC) = $\dfrac{\blacktriangle \text{ TRC}}{\blacktriangle \text{ Units of Resource}}$

# FACTS ABOUT U.S. MONEY

Source: U.S. Treasury Department

In the early days of our nation, before United States money was issued, there were in circulation English shillings, French louis d'ors, and Spanish doubloons, along with other units of those nations' money. This caused confusion and slowed up trade. The dollar was adopted (1785) by the Congress existing under the Articles of Confederation as the unit of our money, and the decimal system as the method of reckoning. In 1792 the United States monetary system was established, and the U.S. Mint began coining money at Philadelphia in 1793.

Many changes in the laws governing coinage and the denominations themselves have been made since the original 1792 act. Coins no longer in use include the half-cent, two-cent, three-cent, and 20-cent pieces, as well as the silver half dime. The five-cent nickel coin was introduced in 1866. Gold coins were struck from 1795 through 1933, in denominations ranging from $1 to $20. The minting and issuance of gold coins were terminated by Section 5 of the Gold Reserve Act of 1934.

President Johnson signed (July 23, 1965) an historic bill providing for the first major change in U.S. coinage in more than a century. Silver was eliminated altogether from the dime and quarter and substanially reduced in the half dollar.

On Dec. 31, 1970, President Nixon signed the Bank Holding Company Act calling for the removal of all silver from silver dollars and half dollars. This legislation also authorized a silver dollar with a design emblematic of the symbolic eagle of the Apollo 11 landing on the Moon. Once adopted, a coin design may not be changed more often than once in 25 years without specific legislation.

The selection of coin designs is usually made by the Director of the Mint, with the approval of the Secretary of the Treasury. However, Congress has, in a few instances, prescribed them. For example, as a part of the bicentennial celebration of Washington's birth in 1932, Congress declared that the likeness of our first President should appear on the quarter dollar.

The Lincoln penny was the first portrait coin of a regular series minted by the United States. The 100th anniversary of Lincoln's birth aroused sentiment sufficiently strong to overcome a long-prevailing popular prejudice against the use of portraits on coins. A new reverse design was adopted in 1959, when the sesquicentennial of Lincoln's birth was observed. The familiar likeness on the obverse remains unchanged. Others which followed are the 25-cent coin, with Washington's profile, first minted in 1932; the five-cent piece honoring Jefferson, adopted in 1938; the FDR dime, introduced in 1946, and in 1971 the Eisenhower silver dollar, manufacture of which was discontinued in December 1978.

In July 1979, a new, smaller dollar coin was introduced whose size is between the half dollar and the quarter; its smaller size will save in the cost of dollar bill production and help the circulation of the little-used dollar coin. This coin bears the likeness of women's suffrage leader Susan B. Anthony.

Portraits of living persons on American coins are extremely rare and confined to a few commemorative issues of limited minting.

The year 1976 marked the 200th anniversary of American Independence. One of the most far-reaching Government observances was the issuance of specially designed dollars, half dollars, and quarters. Circulation commenced on July 4, 1975, and production ended on December 31, 1976.

The design selection used for American paper currency, including the selection of portraits, is a respon-sibility of the Secretary of the Treasury, who acts with the advice of the Director of the Bureau of Engraving and Printing, the Treasurer of the United States, and others. By tradition, portraits used on present paper money are those of deceased statesmen of assured historical significance.

The first regular issue of United States currency, the Demand notes that were issued in 1861, carried the portraits of Alexander Hamilton (first Secretary of the Treasury) on the $5 denomination and of Abraham Lincoln on the $10 denomination.

Those design features of U.S. paper currency that have historical or idealistic significance, as distinct from purely ornamental or security implications, include the following:

(1) The New Treasury Seal: Approved on January 29, 1968, the seal of the Department of the Treasury is found on the face of each note. Balance scales, a key, and a chevron with 13 stars appear on the seal, along with the date "1789," the year the Department was created.

(2) The obverse and reverse of the Great Seal of the United States are reproduced on the backs of $1 bills.

(3) Portraits of great Americans used on the face of currency.

(4) Pictures of famous buildings, monuments or events used on the back of currency.

All notes of the same denomination bear the same portrait. Designs on U.S. currency (Federal Reserve Notes) now in circulation are as follows:

| Denomination and Class | Portrait | Back |
|---|---|---|
| $1 Fed. Reserve Note | Washington | Obverse and reverse of Great Seal of U.S. |
| $2 Fed. Reserve Note | Jefferson | John Trumbull's "Declaration of Independence" |
| $5 Fed. Reserve Note | Lincoln | Lincoln Memorial |
| $10 Fed. Reserve Note | Hamilton | U.S. Treasury Building |
| $20 Fed. Reserve Note | Jackson | White House |
| $50 Fed. Reserve Note | Grant | U.S. Capitol |
| $100 Fed. Reserve Note | Franklin | Independence Hall |

Notes of the higher denominations ($500, $1,000, $5,000, and $10,000) have not been printed for many years. As they are returned to Federal Reserve banks, they are removed from circulation and destroyed. The portraits selected for these small-sized notes were McKinley for the $500, Cleveland for the $1,000, Madison for the $5,000, and Chase for the $10,000.

The motto "In God We Trust" owes its presence on U.S. coins largely to the increased religious sentiment existing during the Civil War. Salmon P. Chase, then Secretary of the Treasury, received a number of appeals from devout persons throughout the country urging that the Deity be suitably recognized on our coins as it was on the coins of other nations.

The approved motto first made its appearance on the two-cent coin, authorized by Act of Congress (April 22, 1864), but its use has not been uninterrupted. In 1866 the motto was introduced on the double eagle, eagle, and half eagle gold coins and on the silver dollar, half dollar, and the quarter dollar pieces. It was included in the nickel five-cent design from 1866 to 1883, when it was dropped and not restored until the introduction of the Jefferson nickel in 1938. The motto has been in continuous use on the penny since 1909 and on the dime since 1916.

A law passed by the 84th Congress and approved by the President on July 11, 1955, provides that "In God We Trust" shall appear on all United States paper currency and coins.

By a joint resolution of the 84th Congress, approved by the President on July 30, 1956, "In God We Trust" was declared to be the official motto of the United States.

**Assets:** Everything a corporation owns or has outstanding: cash, investments, money due it, materials and inventories (current assets); buildings and machinery (fixed assets); and patents and good will (intangible assets).

**Averages:** Various ways of measuring the trend of securities prices, the most popular of which is the Dow-Jones average of 30 industrial stocks listed on the New York Stock Exchange. The numbers are not true numerical averages, but take into account such factors as past splits, etc.

**Balance Sheet:** A condensed statement showing the nature and amount of a company's assets, liabilities, and capital on a given date. In dollar amounts, the balance sheet shows what the company owned, what it owed, and the ownership interest in the company of its stockholders.

**Bear:** Someone who believes the market will decline.

**Blue Chip:** Common stock in a company known nationally for the quality and wide acceptance of its products or services and its ability to make money and pay dividends.

**Bond:** Basically an IOU or promissory note of a corporation, usually issued in multiples of $1,000 or $5,000. A bond is evidence of a debt on which the issuing company usually promises to pay the bondholders a specified amount of interest for a specified length of time, and to repay the loan on the expiration date. In every case a bond represents debt—its holder is a creditor of the corporation and not a part owner as is the shareholder.

**Book Value:** An accounting term. Book value of a stock is determined from the company's records, by adding all assets (generally excluding intangibles), then deducting all debts and other liabilities, plus the liquidation price of any preferred issues. The sum arrived at is divided by the number of common shares outstanding and the result is book value per common share. Book value may have little or no significant relationship to market value.

**Bull:** One who believes the market will rise.

**Capital Gain or Capital Loss:** Profit or loss from the sale of a capital asset. Under current federal income tax laws, a capital gain may be either short-term (12 months or less) or long-term (more than 12 months). A short-term capital gain is taxed at the reporting individual's full income tax rate. A long-term capital gain is subject to a lower tax.

**Capitalization:** Total amount of the various securities issued by a corporation. Capitalization may include bonds, debentures, preferred and common stock. Bonds and debentures are usually carried on the books of the issuing company in terms of their par or face value. Preferred and common shares may be carried in terms of par or stated value. Stated value may be either an arbitrary figure decided upon by the directors, or may represent the amount received by the company from the sale of the securities at the time of issuance.

**Cash Flow:** Reported net income of a corporation plus amounts charged off for depreciation, depletion, amortization, extraordinary charges to reserves, which are bookkeeping deductions and not paid out in actual dollars and cents.

**Common Stock:** Securities that represent an ownership interest in a corporation. If the company has also issued preferred stock, both common and preferred have ownership rights, but the preferred normally has prior claim on dividends and, in the event of liquidation, assets. Claims of both common and preferred stockholders are junior to claims of bondholders or other creditors of the company. Common-stock holders assume greater risk than preferred-stock holders, but generally exercise greater control and may gain greater reward.

**Conglomerate:** A corporation that has diversified its operations usually by acquiring enterprises in widely varied industries.

**Convertible:** A bond, debenture, or preferred share that may be exchanged by the owner for common stock or another security, usually of the same company, in accordance with the terms of the issue.

**Dealer:** An individual or firm in the securities business acting as a principal rather than as an agent. Typically, a dealer buys for his own account and sells to a customer from his own inventory. The dealer's profit or loss is the difference between the price he pays and the price he receives for the same security.

**Discretionary Account:** An account in which the customer gives the broker or someone else discretion, which may be complete or within specific limits, as to the purchase and sales of securities or commodities including selection, timing, amount and price to be paid or received.

**Dollar Cost Averaging:** A system of buying securities at regular intervals with a fixed dollar amount. Under this system the investor buys by the dollars' worth rather than by the number of shares. If each investment is of the same number of dollars, payments buy more when the price is low and fewer when it rises. Thus temporary downswings in price benefit the investor if he continues periodic purchases in both good times and bad and the price at which the shares are sold is more than their average cost.

**Dow Theory:** A theory of market analysis based upon the performance of the Dow-Jones industrial and transportation stock price averages. The Theory says that the market is in a basic upward trend if these averages advance above a previous important high. When the averages dip, there is said to be a downward trend.

**Fiscal Year:** A corporation's accounting year. Due to the nature of their particular business, some companies do not use the calendar year for their bookkeeping.

**Growth Stock:** Stock of a company with prospects for future growth—a company whose earnings are expected to increase at a relatively rapid rate.

**Investment Banker:** Also known as an underwriter. He is the middleman between the corporation issuing new securities and the public. One or more investment bankers buy outright from a corporation a new issue of stocks or bonds. The group forms a syndicate to sell the securities to individuals and institutions. Investment bankers also distribute very large blocks of stocks or bonds.

**Investment Company:** A company or trust which uses its capital to invest in other companies. There are two principal types: the closed-end and the open-end, or mutual fund. Closed-end shares are readily transferable in the open market and are bought and sold like other shares. Open-end funds sell their own new shares to investors, stand ready to buy back their old shares, and are not listed.

**Legal List:** A list of investments selected by various states in which certain institutions and fiduciaries, such as insurance companies and banks, may invest.

**Liquidity:** The ability of the market in a particular security to absorb a reasonable amount of buying or selling at reasonable price changes. Liquidity is one of the most important characteristics of a good market.

**Listed Stock:** The stock of a company that is traded on a securities exchange and for which a listing application and a registration statement, giving detailed information about the company and its operations, have been filed with the Securities & Exchange Commission (SEC), unless otherwise exempted, and the exchange itself. The various stock exchanges have different standards for listing.

**Load:** The portion of the offering price of shares of open-end investment companies in excess of the value of the underlying assets which cover sales commissions and all other costs of distribution. The load is incurred only on purchase, there being, in most cases, no charge when the shares are sold (redeemed).

**Margin:** The amount paid by the customer when he uses his broker's credit to buy a security. Under Federal Reserve regulations, the initial margin required in the past years has ranged from 50 percent of the purchase price all the way to 100 percent.

**NASD:** The National Association of Securities Dealers, Inc., an association of brokers and dealers in the over-the-counter securities business.

**NYSE Common Stock Index:** A composite index covering price movements of all common stocks listed on the "Big Board." It is based on the close of the market December 31, 1965, as 50.00 and is weighted according to the number of shares listed for each issue. The index is computed continuously by the Exchange's Market Data System and printed on the ticker tape each half hour. Point changes in the index are converted to dollars and cents so as to provide a meaningful measure of changes in the average price of listed stocks. The composite index is supplemented by separate indexes for four industry groups: industrials, transportation, utilities, and finances.

**Option:** A right to buy (call) or sell (put) a fixed amount of a given stock at a specified price within a limited period of time. The purchaser hopes that the stock's price will go up (if he bought a call) or down (if he bought a put) by an amount sufficient to provide a profit greater than the cost of the contract and the commission and other fees required to exercise the contract. If the stock price holds steady or moves in the opposite direction, the price paid for the option is lost entirely.

**Over-the-Counter:** A market for securities made up of securities dealers who may or may not be members of a securities exchange. Thousands of companies have insufficient shares outstanding, stockholders, or earnings to warrant application for listing on a stock exchange. Securities of these companies are traded in the over-the-counter market between dealers who act either as principals or as brokers for customers. The over-the-counter market is the principal market for U.S. Government bonds and municipals.

**Par:** In the case of a common share, a dollar amount assigned to the share by the company's charter. Par value may also be used to compute the dollar amount of the common shares on the balance sheet. Par value has little significance so far as market value of common stock is concerned. Many companies today issue no-par stock, but give a stated per share value on the balance sheet. In the case of preferred shares and bonds, however, par is important. It often signifies the dollar value upon which dividends on preferred stocks and interest on bonds are figured. The issuer of a 6% bond promises to pay that percentage of the bond's par value annually.

**Point:** In the case of shares of stock, a point means $1. In the case of bonds, a point means $10.

**Portfolio:** Holdings of securites by an individual or institution. A portfolio may contain bonds, preferred stocks and common stocks of various types of enterprises.

**Preferred Stock:** A class of stock with a claim on the company's earnings before payment may be made on the common stock, usually also entitled to priority over common stock if the company liquidates. It is usually entitled to dividends at a specified rate before payment of a dividend on the common stock.

**Price-Earnings Ratio:** The price of a share of stock divided by earnings per share for a twelve-month period.

**Principal:** The person for whom a broker executes an order, or a dealer buying or selling for his own account. The term "principal" may also refer to a person's capital or to the face amount of a bond.

**Puts and Calls: see Option**

**Quotation:** Often shortened to "quote." The highest bid to buy and the lowest offer to sell a security in a given market at a given time. A "quote" on a stock might

be "45¼ to 45½." This means that $45.25 is the highest price any buyer would pay at the time the quote was given on the floor of the Exchange, and that $45.50 was the lowest price that any seller would take at the same time.

**REIT:** Real Estate Investment Trust, an organization similar to an investment company but concentrating its holdings in real estate. The yield is generally liberal since REIT's are required to distribute as much as 90% of their income.

**Registration:** Before a public offering may be made of new securities by a company, or of outstanding securities by controlling stockholders—through the mails or in interstate commerce—the securities must be registered under the Securities Act of 1933. Registration statement is filed with the SEC by the issuer. It must disclose pertinent information relating to the company's operations, securities, management, and purpose of the public offering. Securities of railroads under jurisdiction of the Interstate Commerce Commission (ICC), and certain other types of securities, are exempted.

**Round Lot:** A unit of trading or a multiple thereof. On the New York Stock Exchange, the unit of trading is generally 100 shares in stocks and $1,000 par value in the case of bonds. In some inactive stocks, the unit of trading is 10 shares.

**Short Sale:** A person who believes a stock will decline and sells it though he does not own any has made a short sale. Your broker borrows the stock so he can deliver the 100 shares to the buyer. The money value of the shares borrowed is deposited by your broker with the lender. Sooner or later you must cover your short sale by buying the same amount of stock you borrowed for return to the lender. If you are able to buy at a lower price than you sold it for, your profit is the difference between the two prices—not counting commissions and taxes. Stock exchange and federal regulations govern and limit the conditions under which a short sale may be made on a national securities exchange.

**Specialist:** A member of the New York Stock Exchange who has two functions: First, to maintain an orderly market in the stocks in which he is registered as a specialist. The Exchange expects the specialist to buy or sell for his own account, to a reasonable degree, when there is a temporary disparity between supply and demand. Second, the specialist acts as a broker's broker. When a commission broker on the exchange floor receives a limit order, he cannot wait at the particular post where the stock is traded until the price reaches the specified level. He leaves the order with the specialist, who will try to execute it in the market if and when the stock declines to the specified price. The specialist must always put his customers' interests first.

**Split:** The division of the outstanding shares of a corporation into a larger number of shares. A 3-for-1 split by a company with 1 million shares outstanding would result in 3 million shares outstanding. After the 3-for-1 split, each holder of 100 shares would have 300 shares.

**Take-Over:** The acquiring of one corporation by another — usually in a friendly merger but sometimes marked by a "proxy fight."

**Yield:** Also known as return. The dividends or interest paid by a company expressed as a percentage of the current price. A stock with a current market value of $40 a share paying dividends at the rate of $2.00 is said to return 5% ($2.00 ÷ $40.00).

## WALL STREET INDEXES

**Dow Jones Industrial Average:** The addition of closing prices for 30 stocks divided by the current divisor. The divisor is never the number of stocks listed, but by reflecting splits, mergers, and bankruptcies, it is constantly revised.

**NASDAQ Composite Index:** The measure of all domestic common issues traded over-the-counter included in the NASDAQ System, exclusive of those listed on an exchange and those with only one market maker. The index is market value-weighted, in that the importance of each stock is proportional to its price times the number of shares outstanding.

**New York Stock Exchange Common Stock Index:** The current aggregate market value (sum of all shares times the price per share) divided by the adjusted base market value and multiplied by 50. The adjusted value reflects additions or deletions of listings, but remains unaffected by stock splits and dividends.

**Standard and Poor's Index:** The aggregate market value (price of each share times the number of shares) for 425 industrial stocks, expressed as one-tenth the percentage of the average market value relative to the average market value during the years 1941-43.

Reprinted by permission of the Hammond Almanac, copyright (c) 1987 by Hammond, Inc.

# ANSWERS TO
# SELF-TEST QUESTIONS
# AND SELECTED PROBLEMS

**Chapter 1: "The Nature and Method of Economics"  Self-test Questions**

1. B; 2. B; 3. B; 4. D; 5. D; 6. B; 7. B; 8. C; 9. A; 10. C

## 1.1 GRAPH OF X VERSUS Y
### Slope = 1

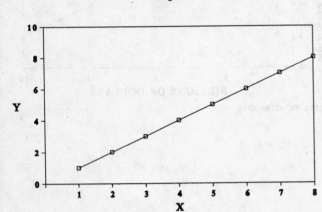

## 1.2 GRAPH OF X VERSUS Y
### Slope = -1

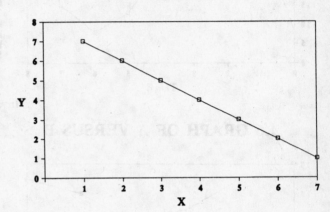

## 1.3 GRAPH OF X VERSUS Y
### Slope = 2

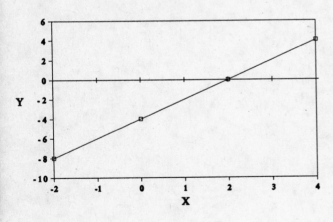

## 1.4 GRAPH OF X VERSUS Y
### Slope of D = -1 Slope of S = 1

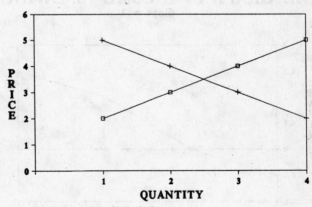

**Point of Intersection (2.5, 3.5)**

## 1.5 GRAPH
## TIME (t) VS HOG PRICES (P)

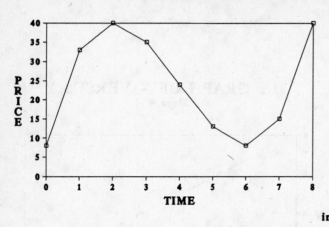

## 1.8 GRAPH % RATE V. BILLIONS $
### Slope = -.4

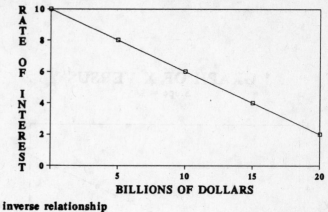

inverse relationship

## 1.6 GRAPH OF A VERSUS B

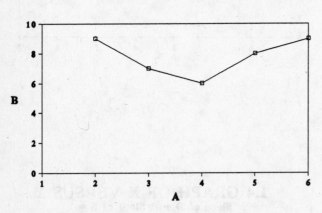

## 1.7 GRAPH OF INCOME VS. SAVING
### Slope = .2

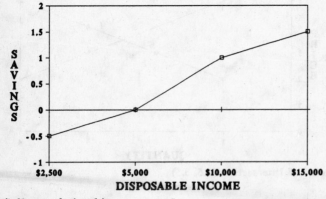

(c) direct relationship

## GRAPH 1.1 PROBLEM # 1
### Slope = -.1

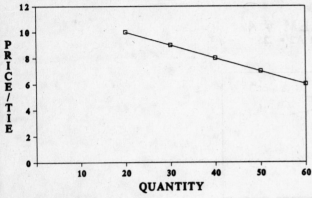

nverse Relationship

## GRAPH 1.2 PROBLEM # 2
### Slope = .4

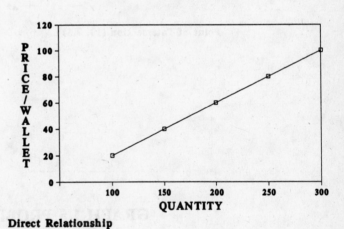

Direct Relationship

## 1.3 GRAPH PROBLEM # 3
### Slope = 1

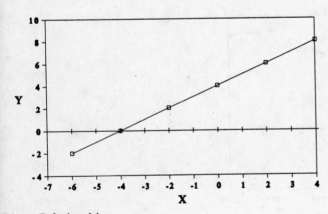

Direct Relationship

315

# 1.4 GRAPH PROBLEM # 4
### Slope of A1 = -.25 Slope of A2 = .25

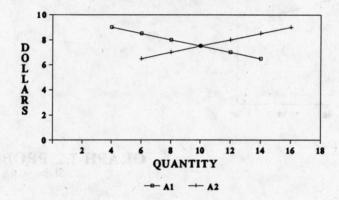

**Point of Intersection (10, 7.5)**

# GRAPH 1.5 PROBLEM # 5

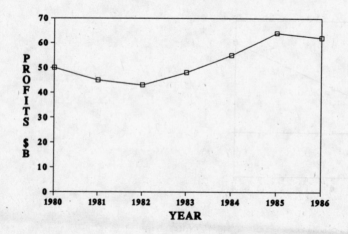

## 2.1 PRODUCTION POSSIBILITIES CURVE

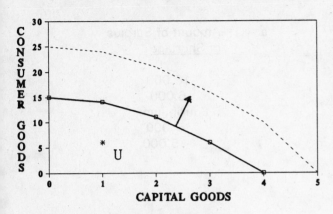

**CONSUMER GOODS** (vertical axis, 0–30)

**CAPITAL GOODS** (horizontal axis, 0–5)

*U

**CONSUMER GOODS** (vertical axis, 0–16)

**CAPITAL GOODS** (horizontal axis, 0–4)

T

R

a. Sacrifice of Consumer
   <u>goods for Capital goods</u>

   -1
   -3
   -5
   -6

b. See graph
c. See graph
d. See graph

e. The Law of Increasing Costs:
   As you trade-off resources
   from one good to another, the
   sacrifice becomes greater and
   greater because resources are
   not perfectly shifted. This
   is illustrated by the "bow"
   shaped PPC Curve.

Problem 2:  C; Problem 3: D; Problem 4: D; Problem 5:  A

**Chapter 3: "Pure Capitalism and the Circular Flow"**     **Self-test Questions**
1. C; 2. B; 3. B; 4. B; 5. D; 6. D; 7. D; 8. A; 9. D; 10. B

Problem 1

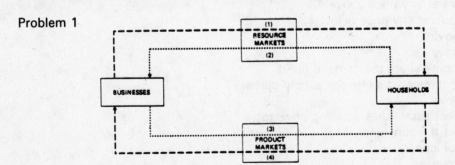

Counterclockwise flow of resources and goods and services; clockwise flow of money income
and consumption expenditures. Households are the resources owners (supply-side) and
Businesses are the buyers of resources (demand-side). Households purchase the finished
goods and services (demand-side) and businesses are the suppliers (supply-side).

1. A; 2. C; 3. C; 4. B; 5. B; 6. B; 7. $10, 75; 8. SURPLUS, 50; 9. Shortage, 50; 10. $6; 11. $6; 12. C; 13. A; 14. Ceiling

## Problem 1

a.  Amount of Surplus
    or Shortage

    10,000
    6,000
    Equilibrium
    -7,000
    -15,000

### 4.1 SUPPLY AND DEMAND
#### (Macro)

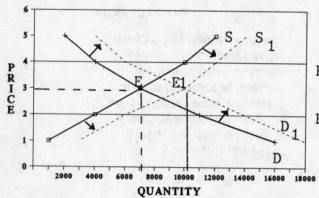

Price floor (support)

Price Ceiling (cap)

b.  $3; 7,000 bushels
c.  Surplus occurs at any price above $3
    Shortage occurs at any price below $3
d.  See graph above
e.  See graph above
    Change in income shifts the demand curve
    Change in resource cost shifts the supply curve
f.  See graph above
    The government establishes a ceiling price to:
    1.    protect the consumer
    2.    control inflation
g.  See graph above
    The government establishes a floor price to:
    1.    protect the seller
    2.    insure an ample supply and competition

318

Problem 2

a.   Total Market Demand
2
5
9
13
20

b.   See graph

c.   Increase in demand (demand curve shifts to the right), see graph.

## 4.2 (Macro)Market Demand Curve

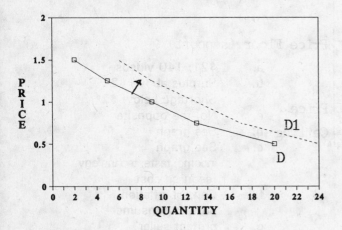

Problem 3

See answer on next page (same as micro)

MICRO Self-test Questions
1. A; 2. C; 3. C; 4. D; 5. A; 6. C; 7. $15,000; 8. Shortage, 50; 9. Surplus, 50; 10. $20; 11. $20; 12. C; 13. A; 14. Ceiling

Amount of Surplus
or Shortage

100
50
Equilibrium
25
75
125

## 4.1 SUPPLY AND DEMAND
### (Micro)

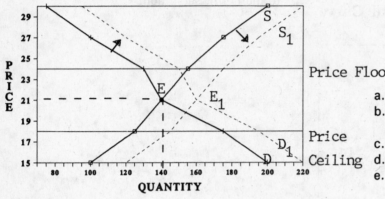

Price Floor (support)

a.  $21; 140 videos
b.  Surplus above $21
    Shortage below $21
c.  No, the opposite
d.  See graph
e.  See graph
    income; taste; technology
    resource cost
f.  Control inflation
    protect consumer
g.  protect seller
    insure an ample supply
h.  surplus of 75
i.  $18; 175 videos

Problem 2

## 4.2 MARKET DEMAND CURVE
### (MICRO)

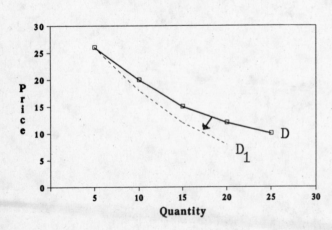

Total Market Demand
2
5
11
17
23
b.  See graph
c.  Inverse relationship

Revised Total Market Demand
2
4
9
13
18
d.  See graph
    demand has decreased

320

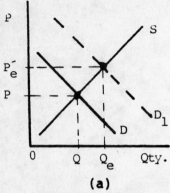

**(a)**

Increase in demand
Increase in qty. supplied

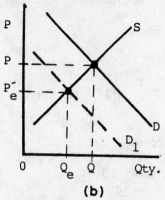

**(b)**

Decrease in demand
decrease in qty. supplied

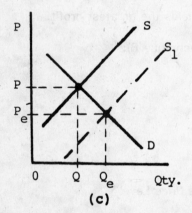

**(c)**

Increase in qty. demanded
Increase in supply

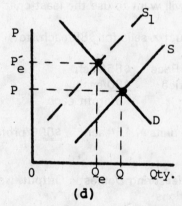

**(d)**

Decrease in qty. demanded
Decrease in supply

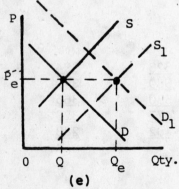

**(e)**

Increase in demand
Increase in supply

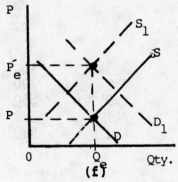

**(f)**

Increase in demand
Decrease in supply

**Chapter 5: "The Private Sectors and the Market System"     Self-test Questions**
1. D; 2. C; 3. A; 4. D; 5. C; 6. C; 7. C; 8. B; 9. B; 10. C

Problem 1:     Least-cost Problem

1a.     Technique A costs:

     Labor   5 x $10  =  $50
     Capital 8 x $4   =  $32
          Total Cost $82          (for 100 units of product X)


     Technique B costs:

     Labor   4 x $10  =  $40
     Capital 5 x $4   =  $40
          Total Cost $80          (for 100 units of product X)

     Technique B reprsents the least-cost combination

b.     Firms will want to use the least-cost technique because it yields the greatest profit.

c.     If product X sells for $85/each, total profit will be (using Technique B):

     Selling Price     $85/each
     Cost Price        $80/each
                       $5/profit each

     or 100 units X $5/each  =  $500 profit


**Chapter 7: "Measuring Domestic Output, National Income, and the Price Level"**
**Self-test Questions**
1. A; 2. C; 3. B; 4. C; 5. A; 6. B; 7. C; 8. $392.86; 9. $480; 10. $559.26; 11. Deflation; 12. C; 13. B; 14. B; 15. B; 16. A

Problem 1

## COUNTRIES

|      | 1   | 2   | 3   | 4   | 5   | 6   |
|------|-----|-----|-----|-----|-----|-----|
| GDP  | 210 | 305 | 400 | 307 | 623 | 394 |
| NDP  | 200 | 280 | 390 | 255 | 580 | 380 |
| NI   | 180 | 250 | 350 | 233 | 530 | 365 |
| PI   | 165 | 244 | 340 | 228 | 477 | 326 |
| DPI  | 150 | 220 | 320 | 190 | 462 | 288 |

Chapter 7

Problem 2

**Real GDP (billions)**
$1974.6
2879.5
3776.8
4539.9
4837.6
4847.7

Problem 3

    a.      Complete the table below (hypothetical data)

    b.      This economy has been characterized by _Inflation_.

| Year | Qty. | Price | Price Index | Current $ | Constant $ |
|------|------|-------|-------------|-----------|------------|
| 1 | 3 | $2 | .5 or 50% | $6 | $12 |
| 2 | 5 | 4 | 1.0 or 100% | 20 | 20 |
| 3 | 6 | 5 | 1.25 or 125% | 30 | 24 |
| 4 | 8 | 6 | 1.5 or 150% | 48 | 32 |
| 5 | 9 | 8 | 2.0 or 200% | 72 | 36 |

**Chapter 8: "Macroeconomic Instability: Unemployemnt and Inflation" Self-test Questions**
1. C; 2. C; 3. B; 4. B; 5. C; 6. D; 7. B; 8. D; 9. A; 10. D

Problems (see "Chapter Highlights" in this workbook)

2.     Indicators such as the inflation rate, unemployment rate, GNP, housing starts, and the Government's Index of Leading Economi Indicators help to "read" the economy. The three types of indicators are leading, lagging, an coincident.

4.     On the decline (to 1995) in New Jersey are stenographrs and machine operators. In the U.S., are stenographers and shoe repairers.

6.     The auto industry represents a durable goods industry, whereas, the farm industry is characterized by nondurable goods. Durable goods experience wide swings in output, employment and income--price remains relatively stable. Nondurable goods have very small (stable) swings in outpt, employment and income. However, there is usually much competition and therefore, large changes in prices.

8.     The economic cost of unemployment are the lost "potential" goods and services (as measured by Okun's Law). The social cost of unemployment is measured by the social trauma it causes.

10.     Briefly, the benefits of inflation are that if you have borrowed money you are paying back with cheaper dollars and property, for example, escalates tremendously. The costs of inflation are that inflation redistributes income and wealth arbitrarily, hurts those of fixed incomes, and inflation effects every consumer.

### Problem 1

| Savings | APC | APS | MPC | MPS |
|---------|-----|-----|-----|-----|
| $-400 | 1.13 | -.13 | | |
| | | | .8 | .2 |
| -200 | 1.05 | -.05 | | |
| | | | .8 | .2 |
| 0 | 1.00 | 0 | | |
| | | | .8 | .2 |
| 200 | .97 | .03 | | |
| | | | .8 | .2 |
| 400 | .94 | .06 | | |
| | | | .8 | .2 |
| 600 | .92 | .08 | | |

f.  $5,000
g.  Slope of consumption function = .8
h.  Slope of the savings function = .2

## 10.1 CONSUMPTION CURVE/ SAVINGS CURVE

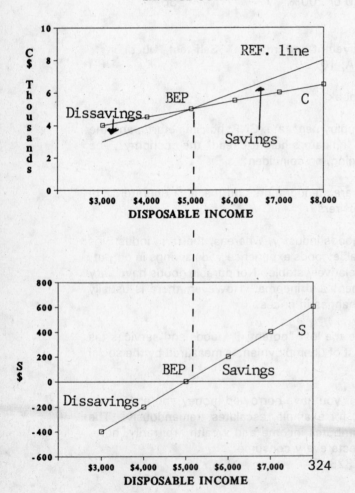

324

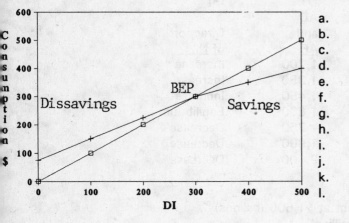

a.  See graph
b.  $300 is the BEP
c.  Savings occurs at greater than $300
d.  Dissavings occurs at less than $300
e.  $75 is autonomous
f.  Induced begins at greater than 0 of DI
g.  At $400, APC = .94, APS = .06
h.  MPC = .75 from $100 to $200
i.  MPS = .25 from $200 to $300
j.  Slope = .75
k.  See graph
l.  See graph

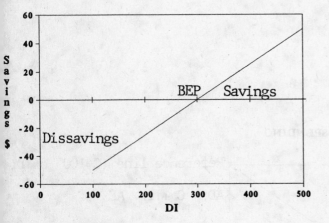

## Problem 3

See "Economic Schools of Thought" on page 68 in this workbook.

Problem 1

## Table 11-1

| (4)<br><br>Planned<br>Savings | (6)<br>Unplanned<br>Inventory<br>Changes | (7)<br>AD<br>and<br>AE | (8)<br><br>Direction<br>of NI |
|---|---|---|---|
| -100 | -200 | 1,200 | Increase |
| -50 | -150 | 1,350 | Increase |
| 50 | -50 | 1,450 | Increase |
| 100 | 0 | 1,600 | Equilibrium |
| 150 | 50 | 1,750 | Decrease |
| 200 | 100 | 1,900 | Decrease |
| 300 | 200 | 2,000 | Decrease |

b.    $1,600 (billions)
c.    Planned Savings equals Planned Investment at $1,600 (billions)
d.    The equilibrium employment level is 20 (million)
e.    See graph

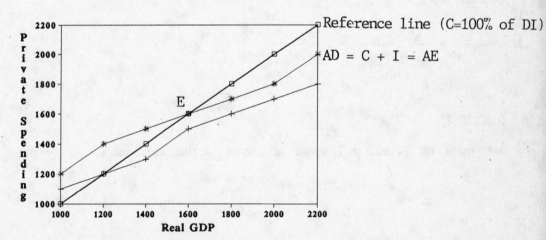

**GRAPH 11.1 PRIVATE SPENDING**

Problem 2

| MPC | M | MPC | M |
|-----|-----|-----|-----|
| .9 | 10 | .2 | 5 |
| .8 | 5 | .5 | 2 |
| .75 | 4 | .4 | 2.5 |
| .5 | 2 | .1 | 10 |
| .6 | 25 | .05 | 20 |
| .95 | 20 | | |

Problem 3

| AS | AD |
|-----|-----|
| 100 | 180 |
| 200 | 260 |
| 300 | 340 |
| 400 | 420 |
| 500---------------500 |
| 600 | 580 |
| 700 | 660 |
| 800 | 740 |
| 900 | 820 |

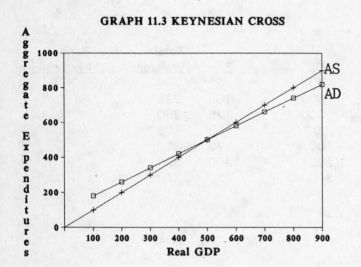

**GRAPH 11.3 KEYNESIAN CROSS**

Problem 4

| T. Leakages | Pl. Injection |
|-----|-----|
| -35 | 45 |
| -15 | 45 |
| 5 | 45 |
| 25 | 45 |
| 45---------------45 |
| 65 | 45 |
| 85 | 45 |
| 105 | 45 |
| 125 | 45 |

**GRAPH 11.4 LEAKAGES-INJECTIONS APPROACH**

c. The eqiulibrium GDP level = 500
d. Either technique yields the same equilibrium GDP level (see above).

327

Problem 1

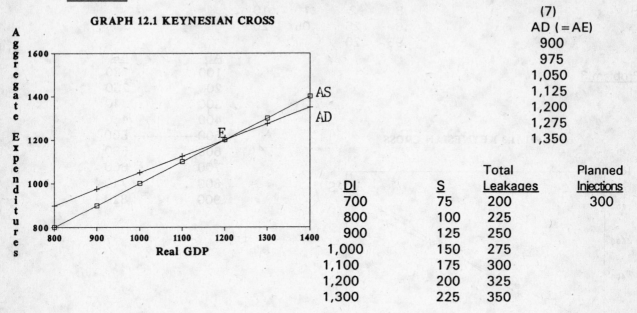

**GRAPH 12.1 KEYNESIAN CROSS**

(7)
AD ( =AE)
900
975
1,050
1,125
1,200
1,275
1,350

| DI | S | Total Leakages | Planned Injections |
|---|---|---|---|
| 700 | 75 | 200 | 300 |
| 800 | 100 | 225 | |
| 900 | 125 | 250 | |
| 1,000 | 150 | 275 | |
| 1,100 | 175 | 300 | |
| 1,200 | 200 | 325 | |
| 1,300 | 225 | 350 | |

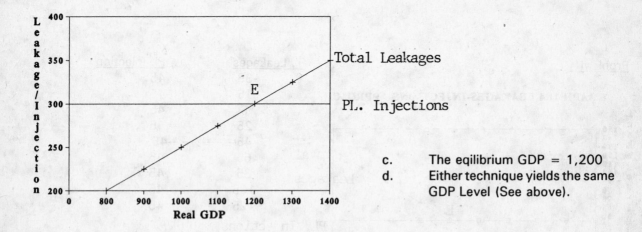

**GRAPH 12.2 LEAKAGES-INJECTIONS**

c.     The eqilibrium GDP = 1,200
d.     Either technique yields the same GDP Level (See above).

<u>Problem 10</u>

**GRAPH 13.1 DEMAND FOR MONEY**

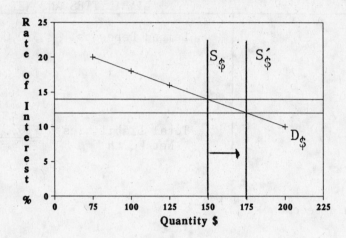

**Chapter 14: "How Banks Create Money" Self-test Questions**
1. B; 2. C; 3. A; 4. A; 5. D; 6. C; 7. C; 8. B; 9. B; 10. D

Problem 5: Simplified Bank Balance Sheet

| ASSETS | | LIABILITIES AND NET WORTH | |
|---|---|---|---|
| Total Reserves: | 2,000 | Demand Deposits | $10,000 |
| Required | 2,000 | | |
| Excess | 0 | | |
| Loans | 8,000 | Total Liabilities & Net Worth | $10,000 |
| Total Assets | 10,000 | | |

b. R = 20%

c. Required Reserves would become $4,000.

| ASSETS | | LIABILITIES AND NET WORTH | |
|---|---|---|---|
| Total Reserves: | 12,000 | Demand Deposits | $10,000 |
| | | | 10,000 |
| Required | 4,000 | | |
| Excess | 8,000 | | |
| Loans | 8,000 | Total Liabilities & Net Worth | $20,000 |
| Total Assets | 20,000 | | |

d. $M_\$ = \frac{1}{R}$

$= \frac{1}{.2} = 5$

e. $40,000 = 8,000 x 5 additional expansion

**Chapter 15: "The Federal Reserve Banks and Monetary Policy"     Self-test Questions**
1. A; 2. B; 3. A; 4. A; 5. B; 6. B; 7. D; 8. B; 9. C; 10. B

<u>Problem 1:</u>     Tools utilized by the Fed

a.

| Stimulate <br> <u>Economy</u> | Slow-down <br> <u>Economy</u> |
|---|---|
| Buy | Sell |
| Lower | Raise |
| Lower | Raise |
| Lower | Raise |
| Raise | Lower |
| Relax | Tighten |
| Positive remarks | Negative remarks |

b.     The most frequent means to control the money supply is through the open market operations.


**Chapter 17: "The Inflation-Unemployment Relationship"**
1. C; 2. D; 3. A; 4. D; 5. B; 6. D; 7. D; 8. C; 9. B; 10. A

<u>Problems</u>

See graphs and explanations under "Chapter Highlights" in this workbook.


**Chapter 18: "Budget Deficits and the Public Debt"     Self-test Questions**
1. D; 2. B; 3. C; 4. C; 5. B; 6. D; 7. B; 8. C; 9. D; 10D

<u>Problems</u>

See graphs and explanations under "Chapter Highlights" in this workbook.

Problem 3:

| Price | Total Revenue | $E_d$ |
|-------|---------------|-------|
| Increases | Decreases | $>1$ |
| Decreases | Decreases | $<1$ |
| Decreases | No Change | $=1$ |
| Increases | Increases | $<1$ |
| Increases | Decreases | $>1$ |
| Increases | No Change | $=1$ |

Problem 4:

Chicken
$E_y = .45$
Superior

$$E_y = \frac{\frac{11.4-10}{11.4+10}}{\frac{1,600-1,200}{1,600+1,200}} = \frac{.065}{.143} = .45$$

Peanut Butter
$E_y = -.37$
Inferior

$$E_y = \frac{\frac{4.5-5}{4.5+5}}{\frac{1,600-1,200}{1,600+1,200}} = \frac{-.053}{.143} = -.37$$

Steak
$E_y = 1.87$
Superior

$$E_y = \frac{\frac{5.2-3}{5.2+3}}{\frac{1,600-1,200}{1,600+1,200}} = \frac{.268}{.143} = 1.87$$

Hamburger
$E_y = .7$
Superior

$$E_y = \frac{\frac{11-9}{11+9}}{\frac{1,600-1,200}{1,600+1,200}} = \frac{.1}{.143} = .70$$

Bread
$E_y = 0$
Unit Income
  elastic

$$E_y = \frac{\frac{5-5}{5+5}}{\frac{1,600-1,200}{1,600+1,200}} = \frac{0}{.143} = 0$$

## Problem 5:

chicken  
$E_{xy} = 1.08$  
substitute

$$E_{xy} = \dfrac{\dfrac{12-11.4}{12+11.4}}{\dfrac{2.10-2.00}{2.10+2.00}} = \dfrac{.026}{.024} = 1.08$$

Peanut Butter  
$E_{xy} = .92$  
substitute

$$E_{xy} = \dfrac{\dfrac{4.7-4.5}{4.7+4.5}}{\dfrac{2.10-2.00}{2.10+2.00}} = \dfrac{.022}{.024} = .92$$

Ketchup  
$E_{xy} = -3.7$  
complement

$$E_{xy} = \dfrac{\dfrac{2.5-3}{2.5+3}}{\dfrac{2.10-2.00}{2.10+2.00}} = \dfrac{-.091}{.024} = -3.79$$

Bread  
$E_{xy} = 2.0$  
substitute

$$E_{xy} = \dfrac{\dfrac{5.5-5}{5.5+5}}{\dfrac{2.10-2.00}{2.10+2.00}} = \dfrac{.048}{.024} = 2.0$$

Hamburger Buns  
$E_{xy} = -2.79$  
complement

$$E_{xy} = \dfrac{\dfrac{3.5-4}{3.5+4}}{\dfrac{2.10-2.00}{2.10+2.00}} = \dfrac{-.067}{.024} = -2.79$$

## Problem 6:

| $E_s$ | TR | TR Test | | $E_d$ |
|-------|-----|---------------|---|------|
| 4.09 | 900 | Rel. Elastic | > | 1.37 |
| 3.48 | 990 | Rel. Elastic | > | 1.10 |
| 6.28 | 1,000 | Rel. Inelastic | > | .91 |
| 7.27 | 990 | Rel. Inelastic | > | .73 |
| | 960 | | | |

$$TR = P \times Q_D$$

TR TEST

$\uparrow$ P $\downarrow$ TR or $\downarrow$ P $\uparrow$ TR  Rel. Elastic

$\uparrow$ P $\downarrow$ P = same  TR  Unit Elastic

$\uparrow$ P $\uparrow$ TR or $\downarrow$ P $\downarrow$ TR  Rel. Inelastic

$$E_d = \frac{\frac{90-80}{90+80}}{\frac{11-12}{11+12}} = \frac{.059}{-.043} = -1.37 = 1.37 \quad \text{Rel. Elastic}$$

$$E_d = \frac{\frac{100-90}{100+90}}{\frac{10-11}{10+11}} = \frac{.053}{-.048} = -1.10 = 1.10 \quad \text{Rel. Elastic}$$

$$E_d = \frac{\frac{110-100}{110+100}}{\frac{9-10}{9+10}} = \frac{.048}{-.053} = -.91 = .91 \quad \text{Rel Inelastic}$$

$$E_d = \frac{\frac{120-110}{120+110}}{\frac{8-9}{8+9}} = \frac{.043}{-.059} = -.73 = .73 \quad \text{Rel. Inelastic}$$

$$E_s = \frac{\frac{70-100}{70+100}}{\frac{11-12}{11+12}} = \frac{-.176}{-.043} = 4.09 \quad \text{Rel. Elastic}$$

$$E_s = \frac{\frac{50-70}{50+70}}{\frac{10-11}{10+11}} = \frac{-.167}{-.048} = 3.48 \quad \text{Rel. Elastic}$$

$$E_s = \frac{\frac{25-50}{25+50}}{\frac{9-10}{9+10}} = \frac{-.333}{-.053} = 6.28 \quad \text{Rel. Elastic}$$

$$E_s = \frac{\frac{10-25}{10+25}}{\frac{8-9}{8+9}} = \frac{-.429}{.059} = 7.27 \quad \text{Rel. Elastic}$$

334

## 21.1 GRAPH
## TOTAL & MARGINAL UTILTIES

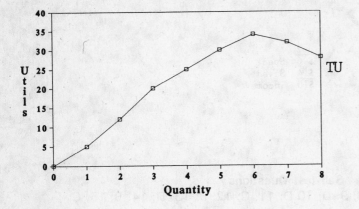

| Marginal Utility |
| --- |
| 5 |
| 7 |
| 8 |
| 6 |
| 5 |
| 3 |
| −1 |
| −3 |

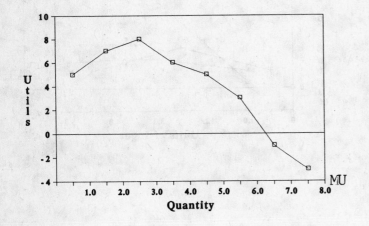

d. zero

e. slope

335

| Units | $\dfrac{MU\ Wine}{P\ Wine}$ | $\dfrac{MU\ Beer}{P\ Beer}$ | $\dfrac{MU\ Soda}{P\ Soda}$ | MU$ |
|-------|------|------|------|------|
| 1 | 10 | 20 | 1 | 14 |
| 2 | 8 | 16 | .5 | 12 |
| 3 | 5 | 12 | 0 | 10 |
| 4 | 3 | 8 | -.5 | 8 |
| 5 | 1 | 4 | -1 | 6 |

```
2 units of Wine at $2/ea.   =    $ 4
4 units of Beer at $.50 ea. =      2
                                 $ 6   Spent
                                 $ 4   Saved
                                 $10   Income
```

## Chapter 22: "The Costs of Production"    Self-test Questions
1. C; 2. B; 3. C; 4. C; 5. D; 6. C; 7. A; 8. B; 9. D; 10 D; 11. C; 12. B; 13. D; 14. B; 15. C;

### Problem 1

| Units of Variable Factor | Total Product | Average Product | Marginal Product |
|-------|------|------|------|
| 0 | 0 | - | |
| 1 | 3 | 3 | 3 |
| 2 | 8 | 4 | 5 |
| 3 | 15 | 5 | 7 |
| 4 | 20 | 5 | 5 |
| 5 | 23 | 4.6 | 3 |
| 6. | 20 | 1.3 | -3 |

b. Answer the following questions with reference to the graphs you have drawn:

(1) When marginal product is greater than average product, average product is (rising/constant/falling).

rising

(2) When marginal product is less than average product, average product is (rising/constant/falling).

falling

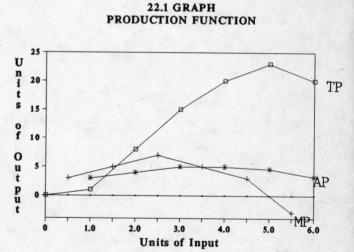

## 22.1 GRAPH
## PRODUCTION FUNCTION

## 22. GRAPH
## COST CURVES

**Problem 2**

| Output per day | FC | VC | TC | ATC | AVC | MC |
|---|---|---|---|---|---|---|
| 0 | 14 | 0 | 14 | - | - | |
| 1 | 14 | 2 | 16 | 16 | 2 | 2 |
| 2 | 14 | 4 | 18 | 9 | 2 | 2 |
| 3 | 14 | 6 | 20 | 6.67 | 2 | 2 |
| 4 | 14 | 10 | 24 | 6 | 2.5 | 4 |
| 5 | 14 | 16 | 30 | 6 | 3.2 | 6 |
| 6 | 14 | 24 | 38 | 6.33 | 4 | 8 |
| 7 | 14 | 34 | 48 | 6.86 | 4.86 | 10 |
| 8 | 14 | 46 | 60 | 7.5 | 5.76 | 12 |
| 9 | 14 | 60 | 74 | 8.22 | 6.67 | 14 |
| 10 | 14 | 76 | 90 | 9 | 7.6 | 16 |

Graph: COSTS $ (vertical axis 0 to 20) vs OUTPUT (horizontal axis 1.0 to 10.0), showing curves labeled MC, ATC, AVC.

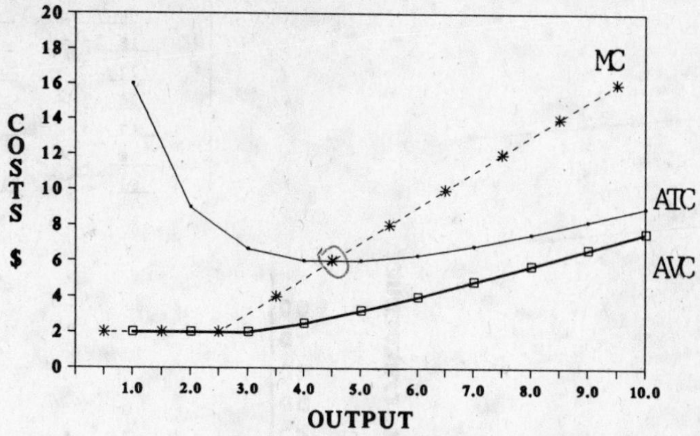

## Chapter 23: "Price and Output Determination: Pure Competition"   Self-test Questions
1. B; 2. D; 3. A; 4. C; 5. C; 6. B; 7. D; 8. D; 9. C; 10. B

**Problem 1**

Profit maximization in the short-run

**A. Case 1**

| QTY | Price | TR | VC | FC | TC | MR | MC | NR |
|---|---|---|---|---|---|---|---|---|
| 0 | $5.99 | 0 | $0 | $5 | 5 | | | $-5.00* |
| 1 | | 5.99 | 6 | | 11 | $5.99 | $6 | -5.01 |
| 2 | | 11.98 | 14 | | 19 | 5.99 | 8 | -7.02 |
| 3 | | 17.97 | 24 | | 29 | 5.99 | 10 | -11.03 |
| 4 | | 23.96 | 36 | | 41 | 5.99 | 12 | -17.04 |

**B. Case 2**

| QTY | Price | TR | VC | FC | TC | MR | MC | NR |
|---|---|---|---|---|---|---|---|---|
| 0 | $6.01 | 0 | $0 | $5 | 5 | | | -5.00 |
| 1 | | 6.01 | 6 | | 11 | 6.01 | $6 | -4.99* |
| 2 | | 12.02 | 14 | | 19 | 6.01 | 8 | -6.98 |
| 3 | | 18.03 | 24 | | 29 | 6.01 | 10 | -10.97 |
| 4 | | 24.04 | 36 | | 41 | 6.01 | 12 | -16.96 |

**C. Case 3**

| QTY | Price | TR | VC | FC | TC | MR | MC | NR |
|---|---|---|---|---|---|---|---|---|
| 0 | $10.01 | 0 | $0 | $5 | 5 | | | -5.00 |
| 1 | | 10.01 | 6 | | 11 | 10.01 | $6 | -.99 |
| 2 | | 20.02 | 14 | | 19 | 10.01 | 8 | 1.02 |
| 3 | | 30.03 | 24 | | 29 | 10.01 | 10 | 1.03* |
| 4 | | 40.04 | 36 | | 41 | 10.01 | 12 | -.96 |

337

Problem 2

| QTY | PRICE | TR | TC | ATC | MC | MR | NR | |
|-----|-------|----|----|-----|----|----|----|----|
| 0 | $9 | 0 | 1 | - | | | -1.00 | |
| 1 | | 9 | 9 | 9 | 8 | 9 | 0 | BEP |
| 2 | | 18 | 16 | 8 | 7 | 9 | 2.00 | |
| 3 | | 27 | 24 | 8 | 8 | 9 | 3.00 | |
| 4 | | 36 | 34 | 8.5 | 10 | 9 | 2.00 | |
| 5 | | 45 | 45 | 9 | 11 | 9 | 0 | BEP |
| 6 | | 54 | 58 | 9.67 | 13 | 9 | -4.00 | |
| 7 | | 63 | 75 | 10.71 | 17 | 9 | -12.00 | |

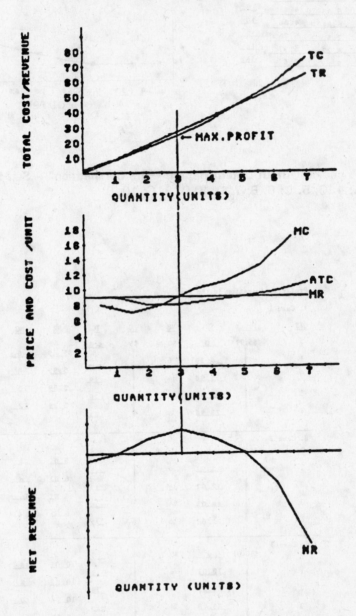

338

Problem 1

| Quantity per day | AR | TR | TC | ATC | MC | MR | NR |
|---|---|---|---|---|---|---|---|
| 0 | $12 | 0 | $20 | - | | | $-20 |
| | | | | | 4 | 11 | |
| 1 | 11 | 11 | 24 | 24 | | | -13 |
| | | | | | 3 | 9 | |
| 2 | 10 | 20 | 27 | 13.5 | | | - 7 |
| | | | | | 5 | 7 | |
| 3 | 9 | 27 | 32 | 10.67 | | | - 5 |
| | | | | | 7 | 5 | |
| 4 | 8 | 32 | 39 | 9.75 | | | - 7 |
| | | | | | 10 | 3 | |
| 5 | 7 | 35 | 49 | 9.8 | | | -14 |
| | | | | | 14 | 1 | |
| 6 | 6 | 36 | 63 | 10.8 | | | -27 |
| | | | | | 20 | -1 | |
| 7 | 5 | 35 | 83 | 11.86 | | | -48 |

See graph next page

Problem 2

| Quantity per day | AR | TR | TC | ATC | MC | MR | NR |
|---|---|---|---|---|---|---|---|
| 0 | $21 | $ 0 | $22 | $ - | | | $-22 |
| | | | | | $15 | $20 | |
| 1 | 20 | 20 | 37 | 37 | | | -17 |
| | | | | | 5 | 18 | |
| 2 | 19 | 38 | 42 | 21 | | | - 4 |
| | | | | | 3 | 16 | |
| 3 | 18 | 54 | 45 | 15 | | | 9 |
| | | | | | 2 | 14 | |
| 4 | 17 | 68 | 47 | 11.78 | | | 21 |
| | | | | | 3 | 12 | |
| 5 | 16 | 80 | 50 | 10 | | | 30 |
| | | | | | 4 | 10 | |
| 6 | 15 | 90 | 54 | 9 | | | 36 |
| | | | | | 5 | 8 | |
| 7 | 14 | 98 | 59 | 8.46 | | | 39 |
| | | | | | 6 | 6 | |
| 8 | 13 | 104 | 65 | 8.12 | | | 39 |
| | | | | | 7 | 4 | |
| 9 | 12 | 108 | 72 | 8 | | | 36 |
| | | | | | 8 | 2 | |
| 10 | 11 | 110 | 80 | .8 | | | 30 |
| | | | | | 9 | 0 | |
| 11 | 10 | 110 | 89 | 8.1 | | | 21 |
| | | | | | 10 | -2 | |
| 12 | 9 | 108 | 99 | 8.25 | | | 9 |

See graph next page

Problem #1

Copy

**TR & TC**

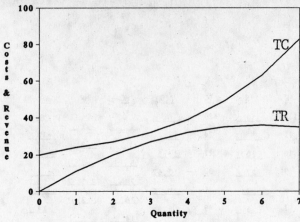

**MC, MR, & ATC**

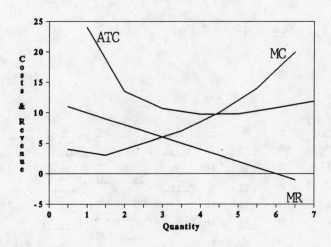

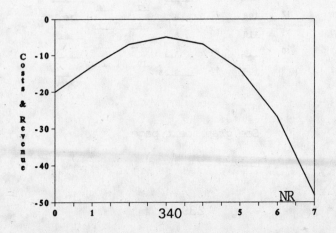

Problem #2 Copy

### TR & TC

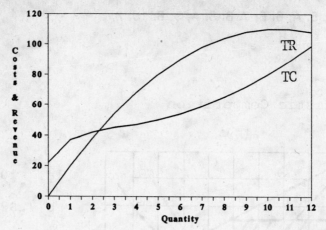

### MC, MR & ATC

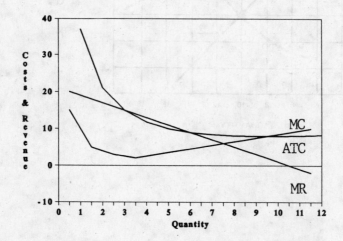

### NR

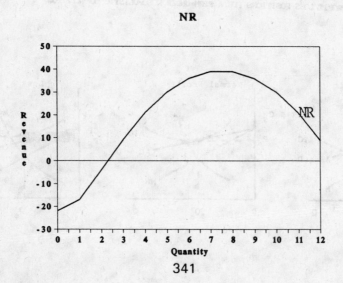

Problem 1  --Monopolistic Competition

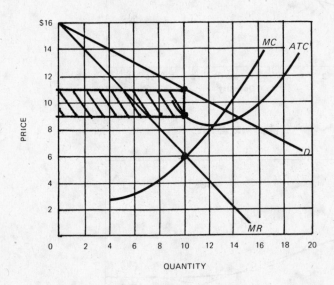

1a.   10; $11

b.   $20; Eco. profit

c.   will tend to

d.   will

Problem 2

"PROFIT/LOSS POSITIONS FOR A FIRM UNDER MONOPOLISTIC COMPETITION"

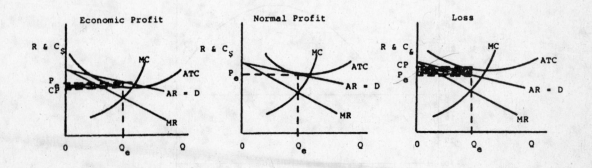

342

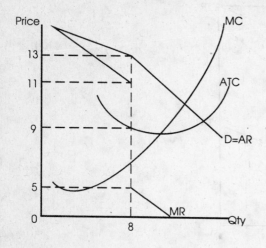

A.   8 UNITS @ $13
     Net revenue per unit = $4
     Total profit = $32

B.   Profit = $3.25/unit
     Total profit = $22.75

C.   Profit = $3.5/unit
     Total profit = $31.50

D.   No greater than $11
     reduce, increase
     No less than $5
     increase, reduce
     Oligopolists do tend

**Chapter 27: "Production and the Demand for Resources"**
     **Self-test Questions**
1. A; 2. B; 3. C; 4. C; 5. C; 6. D; 7. D; 8. D; 9. B; 10. B

Problem 1:

a.

| MP | TR | ARP | MRP |
|----|----|-----|-----|
| 14 | 34 | 34 | 28 |
| 12 | 62 | 31 | 24 |
| 10 | 86 | 28.67 | 20 |
| 7 | 106 | 26.5 | 14 |
| 5 | 120 | 24 | 10 |
|   | 130 | 21.67 | |

b.

| Units | Wage Rate | TRC | MRC |
|-------|-----------|-----|-----|
| 1 | 10 | $10 | 10 |
| 2 |  | 20 | 10 |
| 3 |  | 30 | 10 |
| 4 |  | 40 | 10 |
| 5 |  | 50 | 10 |
| 6 |  | 60 | |

c.

| Wage Rate | TRC' | MRC' |
|-----------|------|------|
| 20 | $20 | 20 |
|  | 40 | 20 |
|  | 60 | 20 |
|  | 80 | 20 |
|  | 100 | 20 |
|  | 120 | |

343

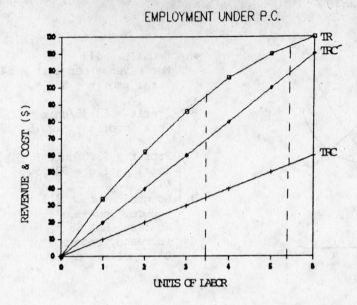

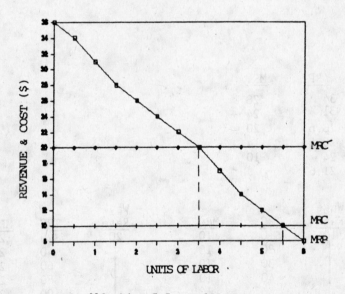

e. At $10, hire 5.5; at $20, hire 3.5

Problem 1:

a.

| TRC | MRC |
|-----|-----|
| $3.02 | |
| 6.08 | $3.06 |
| 9.18 | $3.10 |
| | |
| 900.00 | 9.02 |
| 909.02 | 9.06 |
| 918.08 | |
| | |
| 1,400.00 | 11.02 |
| 1,411.02 | 11.06 |
| 1,422.08 | |

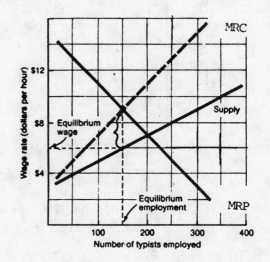

c.  $6; 150 typists
d.  $7; 200 typists

Problem 2:  Figure 32-7

| 1. | C | 4. | D |
|----|---|----|---|
| 2. | D | 5. | C |
| 3. | B | 6. | D |

Problem 3:  Figure 32-8

1.  70; $35
2.  60; $30
3.  Indeterminant
4.  $15

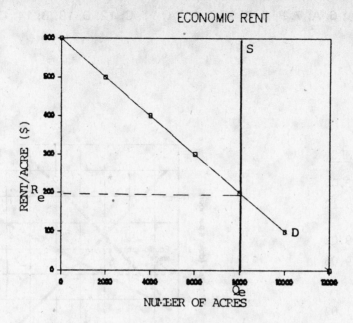

ECONOMIC RENT

a.  Rent will be $200 per acre
       $200 x 8,000 acres = $1,600,000

b.  8,000 acres are demanded at $200/acre

c.  graph see below

d.  Still 8,000 acres (tax did not effect demand or supply)

## Chapter 36: "Labor Market Issues: Unionism, Discrimination, and Immigration"
**Self-test Questions**
1. D; 2. C; 3. B; 4. B; 5. B; 6. B; 7. D; 8. A; 9. C; 10. A

See answers in the "Chapter Highlights" of this workbook.